The Role of Emotions in Social and Personality Development

History, Theory, and Research

EMOTIONS, PERSONALITY, AND PSYCHOTHERAPY

Series Editors:

Carroll E. Izard, *University of Delaware, Newark, Delaware*
and
Jerome L. Singer, *Yale University, New Haven, Connecticut*

A Continuation Order Plan is available for this series. A continuation order will bring delivery of each new volume immediately upon publication. Volumes are billed only upon actual shipment. For further information please contact the publisher.

The Role of Emotions in Social and Personality Development

History, Theory, and Research

Carol Magai

Long Island University
Brooklyn, New York

and

Susan H. McFadden

University of Wisconsin Oshkosh
Oshkosh, Wisconsin

Plenum Press • *New York and London*

Library of Congress Cataloging-in-Publication Data

Magai, Carol.
    The role of emotions in social and personality development :
history, theory, and research / Carol Magai and Susan H. McFadden.
        p.   cm. -- (Emotions, personality, and psychotherapy)
    Includes bibliographical references and index.
    ISBN 0-306-44866-1
    1. Personality and emotions.   2. Personality development.
3. Attachment behavior.   4. Emotions--Sociological aspects.
I. McFadden, Susan H.   II. Title.   III. Series.
BF698.9.E45M34   1995
152.4--dc20   94-48760
                                                           CIP

ISBN 0-306-44866-1

© 1995 Plenum Press, New York
A Division of Plenum Publishing Corporation
233 Spring Street, New York, N. Y. 10013

10 9 8 7 6 5 4 3 2 1

Printed in the United States of America

To my mother, Fred, Christopher, and the memory of my father
—CM

To my mother, father, John, Katy, and Colin
—SHM

And to the memory of our friend, Marjorie Gelfond (1948–1992)
—CM and SHM

Foreword

Studying emotions qua emotional experience has had a mixed fate in psychology. According to nineteenth-century Western philosophy, "animalistic" emotions were ill suited to the life of the civilized individual. Emotions had to be overcome by the exercise of stringent self-control. In contrast, the creation of an enlightened psychology based on an understanding of personal emotional development was a key theme in the world's first psychological novel, *Anton Reiser*, written by Karl Philipp Moritz between 1785 and 1790, drawing from autobiographical material. However, because autobiographical accounts entail "unreliable" introspection, this approach failed to stir academic psychology. Later, Wundt's sterile approach—a three-dimensional model of emotion involving activation-calming, pleasure-displeasure, and tension-relaxation— was also an inappropriate route to understanding the qualitatively rich aspects of individual emotional lives, not to mention the emotional turmoil of those seeking psychological help.

The authors describe the fascinating history of psychology's difficult entrée to people's emotional lives. In order to achieve a working model of the affective life couched in modern terms, they integrate three aspects: development, discrete emotions, and personality. Individual development has always had a special status within academic psychology, playing an equally important role in the history of nonacademic psychology of normal and abnormal personality development and clinical psychology as well. Charlotte Bühler, frequently cited among other influential scholars of our field's beginnings, was an astute commentator on the inescapable dialectic of the separability/inseparability of self and society. This division, like many others that has plagued Western culture, has been "abolished and replaced by a congenial continuum" (Sperry, 1993, p. 880). Indeed, the dualism has perished, and instead there is a new openness that taps the interwovenness of lives. Emotions are closely tied to the personal and cultural values of individuals that, as Sperry insists, "become the most critically powerful force shaping today's civilized world" (p. 879), and more knowledge about emotions may suggest answers "to current global ills and perhaps provide a key to world change" (p. 879). Understanding personal experience through a dialogue between "objective" psychology and a modern psychology of developing emotions is truly a paradigm shift, as suggested by Ainsworth a generation ago.

It is fitting that attachment theory serves as a foundation for an integrative view of emotions in personality development (Chapters 2 and 3). Most fascinating is the contrast of this modern view with the kind of research that took place under the dominant behavioristic ideology of John Watson's day (Chapter 4). An analysis of Watson's theoretical corpus as something inspired by and governed by his own distinctive emotional biases might at one time have been regarded as inappropriate in a thoroughly scholarly text, but this is no longer the case. In fact, what the authors describe as personal emotional bias is the substance at the very core of ideologies, particularly emotionally grounded ideologies. This interesting contrast is enhanced even further when the authors apply their theoretical lens to the emotional implications of life crises and life changes, and when they compare Watson's avoidant way of coping with existential crises with that of Carl Rogers's basically secure way of coping.

The authors' account of a "first wave of research" (Chapter 4) tracks the descent of a psychology of emotions into virtual oblivion. The schism between "objective" and "subjective" psychology had become too deep. A subsequent second wave of research emerged during the 1970s and 1980s, but lacked a theoretically integrated account. The authors take the discrete emotions theories of Silvan Tomkins, Paul Ekman, and Carroll Izard, and show how the now voluminous research literatures on anger and aggression (Chapter 6) and empathy and prosocial behavior (Chapter 7) can be read in a more integrative light (Chapters 8, 9, and 10), using a functionalist analysis of personality development, attachment theory, and emotions theory. The influence of Gordon Allport on today's psychology of emotions and individual development is felt as well; his personalistic psychology (strongly influenced by German thought during the first four decades of this century) has as well found a fresh reception and retains an influence that penetrates as far as the present-day five-factor models of personality with their emphasis on agreeableness, conscientiousness, emotional stability (neuroticism), surgency (or extraversion), culture, and intellect.

Have the authors accomplished all of this? Indeed, Magai and McFadden set the stage for a new approach to emotions research, as well as provide a script to forward a clearer understanding. The plot's focus is on integrative models centered around personal experience, evaluative appraisal, and orientation toward goals. The element of integration presented here is the fact that individuals use emotions to appraise ongoing experience. Persons react to events emotionally and then express or communicate the resulting feelings in a way that is organized around individual emotional biases such as anger, shame, anxiety, contempt, disgust, or some other emotion. Finally, they reflect and search for new orienting goals whenever unanticipated events create emotional imbalance. Attachment, as framed by Bowlby within the Darwinian evolutionary school of thought, provides the necessary socioemotional setting. Physical proximity (in infancy) and mental proximity (in adulthood), as well as accessibility to someone who serves as a "secure base," is each individual's foundation for opening up new horizons and for pursuing new goals worth pursuing, as well as for healthy change and improved personal coherence.

The authors provide a wealth of compelling and well-supported insights toward a working, dynamic model of emotions that will be instrumental in research, theory, and clinical practice as well when considered in the context of life change. Change and continuity have been the main dialectical issues of development. Change offers opportunities for growth but also incurs the risk of disintegration. Continuity provides security and stability, but risks boredom. Coherence, however, is the bulwark of this dialectical flux. It is essential for healthy coping with change while maintaining the person's integrity and emotional security. The central role of emotions in people's struggle to maintain a proper balance between continuity and change in highly individualized and rapidly changing societies is equally important and is given emphasis in this book. As well, the present volume affords a revealing view of the psychology's past emphasis on experimentation; learning to understand the developmental role of an individual's emotional organization as the essence of his or her personal quality of coherence all the way up to the level of biography and literature would certainly have pleased Allport, as well as Murphy and Rogers (and certainly dismayed Watson).

The book harks back to the age-old longing for an enlightened understanding of feelings in personality development. Magai and McFadden remind us that the feeling mind is the locus where much of psychology actually happens. William James's complaint about psychology as a "nasty little subject—all one cares to know lies outside" (cited in Hofstetter, 1957, p. 5), uttered more than 100 years ago, has been heard. The role of emotions in social and personality development has been decidedly put back inside—as in Moritz's *Anton Reiser*. However, at this point, after more than 200 years, the authors are able to combine scientific rigor with the humanistic enlightenment Moritz was desperately yearning for when he founded, in 1783, the first psychological journal in history, *Gnothi Sauton*, or "Journal for Experiential Science of the Mind."

KLAUS GROSSMANN
University of Regensburg

Preface

The field of social and personality development is currently enjoying an unprecedented period of growth and expansion. However, the history of its enterprise is a relatively short one. Although developmental psychology began to gather critical mass as a scientific discipline as early as the latter part of the nineteenth century, it was not until the 1930s that one could speak of a specialty area of "social developmental psychology" (Bühler, 1933). At that time the primary foci of interest were the social behaviors of children and their peers and the acquisition of what were called moral attitudes. Another separately developing field, that of personality development—which got a somewhat later start—emerged in the context of empirical tests of psychoanalytic theory concerning the origins of adult psychopathology.

We find ourselves in quite a different place today. For one thing, contemporary social developmental issues are those that largely revolve around children's understanding of interpersonal relationships and their actual social skills or behaviors with respect to social partners. Personality issues today are almost exclusively located within the context of attachment theory and research. Second, the study of social and personality development has increasingly seen the need to invoke a new mediating variable in its explanation of intra- and interpersonal behavior—that of emotion. Social, personality, and emotional development are now seen as so integrally related to one another that the term "socioemotional" has entered the psychological lexicon. Research on socioemotional development has been intense during the past few years and has accumulated a vast literature. It is thus perhaps appropriate to pause and take stock of the field's status and future prospects. It was with this purpose in mind that the current book was conceived.

We had several aims in mind when we began the project. First, we wanted to provide an up-to-date summary of research in the field as concentrated in the more well-researched domains. Second, we wanted to provide a historical context to the work, so as to place current developments within the broader framework of the field's own history and that of general developmental psychology. Third, while other texts and scholarly works on social and personality development are available, this volume highlights the pivotal role that emotions play in personality formation and social behavior. Fourth, we have attempted to treat developmental topics from both the classic age-comparative, normative-descriptive approach as well as from an individual differences approach. Finally, we analyze the adequacy of current theories of socioemotional development, assess alternate models, and propose new investigative strategies for future research.

This volume will be of particular interest to those whose own research is centered on socioemotional development; however, those in the field of personality and clinical research will find that many of the issues dealt with in this volume touch on themes that are integrally important in these disciplines. The text was written so as to be accessible to advanced undergraduates and graduate students in general developmental and seminar courses as well.

The first section of the book provides a general theoretical overview of the field and establishes the background of some of the discipline's more enduring theoretical issues. We trace the origins of developmental psychology as it emerged from the Zeitgeist of the late nineteenth century and general psychology, and examine its somewhat jagged history in relation to the larger discipline. We show how the field of socioemotional development, which appears to be fresh and original, actually is an emergent product of loosely connected strands of earlier research on children's social development and of theory and research on personality structure. In the course of tracing our history, it will become clear that certain phenomena are so compelling that we are drawn to them time and time again. Sometimes we arrive at the same conclusions, although sometimes we do not. This volume will enable the reader to gauge just how far we have or have not advanced in our understanding of fundamental processes over the past dozen decades.

Following the historical overview (Part I) we examine several aspects of socioemotional development that have been intensively researched over the past two decades. We treat issues of attachment first (Part II, Chapters 2–3) because of the centrality of attachment in early development, and because attachment phenomena have been seen as integrally related to emotional development in recent times. Chapter 2 deals with general developmental issues and describes the normative course of attachment, whereas Chapter 3 considers individual differences in attachment patterns and their relation to differential development.

Part III (Chapters 4–7) deals with the nature of expressive development— that is, facial and vocal expressions of emotion and behavioral regulation of emotion. Chapter 4 presents a critical analysis of the earliest empirical studies of emotion expression, including the meticulous observations of the baby biographers, the observational studies of Bridges and Bühler, the experimental research of Watson and Jones, as well as other well-known and less well-known studies that had a material impact on the course of emotions research during the first half of the twentieth century. Chapter 5 examines the more recent research in the field and addresses the issues that are most salient now, including the ontogeny of infant expressive behavior. In Chapters 6 and 7 we focus on research on emotion expression and regulation in older children, choosing two topics that have commanded the bulk of research attention over the past 30 years—anger and empathy. We will see that these bodies of literature provide important developmental data. However, they deal less adequately with issues of individual difference.

In the final section of the book (Part IV, Chapters 8–12), we address the role of emotion in personality functioning and deal more specifically with issues of individual difference. Here we also attempt to integrate the literatures on attachment theory and emotion expression and regulation. The chapters in this section consider not only personality and the role of emotions in personality, but the issue of personality *development*. Chapter 8 provides an overview of theory related to personality, noting that contemporary theories of personality devote surprisingly little attention to developmental issues. The remaining chapters discuss a functionalist approach to personality development that is grounded in a discrete emotions framework. Chapters 9 and 10 present the fundamentals of the theory and show how the empirical research of the past few decades—in the selected domains of research on anger/aggression and shyness/shame—can be interpreted in light of such a framework. These two chapters deal chiefly with the early ontogeny of emotion-based personality patterns, and focus on how certain behavioral propensities and biases become structuralized in personality. To provide balance, Chapter 11 takes us beyond the continuity model of development to consider the role of emotions in personality change. Finally, the Afterword provides some concluding reflections that embed the theory within a larger lifespan and contextualistic developmental framework.

Throughout the book, and to the extent possible, we include biographical information on the individuals who have shaped the history of our field. We take it as a given that the construction of theory and the conduct of research does not occur in an interpersonal vacuum, that the developmental history of an individual is not immaterial to the theories that he or she will elaborate. Although the application of a detailed psychology of knowledge analysis to the material at hand is beyond the scope of this volume, some personal biography and historical contextualization is necessary to humanize the telling of our story, and to more fully illuminate the nature of human development and the development of theories.

Acknowledgments

There are a number of people and organizations we would like to thank for their support during the various stages of writing this book. First we would like to thank Jeannette Haviland for her influential role in igniting an interest in emotion and personality in the first author that goes back to 1977 and Haviland's graduate course "Examining Emotions." We also thank the countless students who listened to our lectures and participated in our seminars on the topic of emotional development over the past 14 years and who challenged us to put our thoughts and historical analyses to paper. We thank the Deutscher Akademische Austausch Dienst for the travel grant that made it possible to go to Berlin to study archival material on German contributions to early developmental psychology, and Paul Baltes and the Max Planck Institut für Bildungsforschung for hosting the visit.

Contents

I

Introduction

Historical Background

OVERVIEW

In 1983, the Society for Research in Child Development (SRCD), the largest and oldest professional organization for developmental psychologists, celebrated the fiftieth anniversary of its founding. At the organization's convention that year, a number of symposia and discussion groups featured historical retrospectives of the field of developmental psychology. Such forays into the field's past are only now becoming more visible. One of the earliest attempts to reconstruct the opening decades of the field appeared in a 1975 SRCD Monograph (Senn, 1975). Professional handbooks, such as the authoritative *Carmichael's Handbook of Developmental Psychology*, are also now starting to show a newly awakened disciplinary self-consciousness. For example, the 1970 edition of the handbook, a two-volume, 29-chapter work, lacked a chapter devoted specifically to a historical analysis of the field; in contrast, the 1983 edition devoted an entire volume (Volume 1 of four volumes) to a critique of history, theory, and methods. In one of the chapters in that volume, "The Emergence of Developmental Psychology," Cairns (1983) remarks that it "is mildly ironic that an area that is committed to the study of the origins of behavior and consciousness should have shown so little interest in its own origins" (p. 42). That attitude is clearly changing. The present volume is designed to add a historically informed assessment of the study of *social and personality development* to that of the emerging general history of the field. As we examine this history, we begin to develop a broader perspective on the way in which the field of developmental psychology grew and matured, how it related to the other branches of psychology, and the way in which it was influenced by the larger sociopolitical and cultural context in which it was embedded. A historical assessment also helps explain why the study of emotions and personality development, as a legitimate field of inquiry, has had such an uneven record and sometimes an invisible presence.

In the present volume, it will not be possible to undertake a detailed recapitulation of the history of general psychology and the place of developmental psychology within it, or to cover the history of developmental psychology itself at very great length. The focus of the current volume is more circumscribed; as indicated, we have chosen to concentrate fairly exclusively on those aspects of theory and research that have a direct bearing on developments in the selected field of socioemotional development. However, our treatment of this area is organized so as to provide the reader with a sense of the historical ebb and flow of the discipline over the past century against the backdrop of the larger historical landscape.

BEGINNINGS

Developmental psychology's place in history with respect to the general discipline of psychology as an emerging social science has at times been trivialized or ignored. For example, as Cairns and Ornstein (1979) point out in their chapter in the edited volume *The First Century of Experimental Psychology*, an earlier volume on psychology's history—Boring's (1950) classic *History of Experimental Psychology*—did not include a single chapter on developmental science, apparently because he did not regard developmental psychology as sufficiently experimental to warrant inclusion within the ranks of its discipline. In his own professional lifetime, Boring zealously tried to eliminate from psychology any branch that had the taint of an applied perspective (O'Donnell, 1979). Boring's disdain for anything less than strict experimentalism was a more magnified version of the bias that existed during Wundt's day.

Wundt offered a tripartite division of general psychology: psychophysics, physiology, and embryology/genetics. It was clear that he regarded psychophysics and physiology as representing "real experimental psychology," with embryology and genetics (including developmental psychology) falling into second-class status (Cairns, 1983; Cairns & Ornstein, 1979). However, Wundt was not in favor of excluding nonexperimental work and even wrote a ten-volume *Völkerpsychologie* as a counterweight to the excesses of experimentalism.

Despite the mildly disdainful stance psychologists sometimes took toward developmentalists and their work, it is a point of history that developmental ideas were often critical elements within other theoretical systems and commonly provided fertile grounds for experimental research. In fact, earlier in the century, it was the rare theorist who did *not* try to come to terms with developmental issues (Baldwin, 1967). Almost every major theorist tried to accommodate the facts of child development within the context of his or her more general theories, including G. S. Hall—the founder of the first experimental psychology laboratory in the United States—J. B. Watson—the founder of modern American behaviorism—William Stern—whose personalistic theory was so important to the elaboration of Gordon Allport's theory of personality—Kurt Koffka—a founding father of Gestalt psychology—J. M. Baldwin—the cofounder of three influential psychological journals, and Alfred Binet—the developer of the IQ test, to mention just a few.

Developmental issues thus commanded the attention of the field's most eminent minds. Consequently, it may have been the *methods* of science employed by developmentalists that were regarded as less than satisfactory to researchers trained in the classic experimental method. To be sure, the early developmentalists relied on detailed observational studies and survey research rather than experiments with manipulated variables. Moreover, although much contemporary developmental research is experimental in design and nature, observational research is still a mainstay of the field. Research that explores the impact of certain naturally occurring variables on development enjoys a preferred status with developmentalists for the very reason that it does not compromise the developmental integrity of the organism that is being studied; moreover, it is often considered more ecologically valid than data afforded by laboratory-based experimental research. In recent times powerful and innovative statistical models have been developed for dealing with nonmanipulated observational data; these newer tools have allowed the field to move from the pure description of earlier studies to causal modeling. However, despite these material advances, observational research, to some minds, still does not carry the same weight as experimental research. Developmental designs (with age as one of the more important independent variables) are often referred to as "quasi-experimental." Ostensibly this is because subject age cannot be randomly assigned as can true experimental variables; but the term may also reflect earlier attitudinal biases. In comparison, one can note that the literature does not refer to experimental work conducted with children as "quasi-developmental," though in some sense this could be considered justified. In any case, it is true that developmental psychology's history has not always run on a track parallel to that of the rest of psychology. Indeed, at times it has actually courted isolation—for example, during the time of the "growth studies" and during the time it was concerned with social policy and child welfare (Cairns, 1983).

Developmental psychology began to establish itself as a scientific discipline during the nineteenth century, as did the other branches of psychology, but developmental psychology had different roots, goals, agendas, and methods from the outset. Unlike experimental psychology, which modeled itself after physics, developmental psychology was deeply influenced by philosophy on the one hand, and biology on the other. During the nineteenth century, it looked to the biological sciences for its scientific models. Its root metaphor from the very beginning was an organismic one—that is, the living, behaving, biological organism (Reese & Overton, 1970). The influence of Darwinian evolutionary theory was particularly strong during the early decades of the field.

Another factor that distinguished developmental psychology from the other branches of psychology has to do with its lack of discomfort with social activism. Developmentalists traditionally have been (and remain) more willing to openly acknowledge that their science is affected by the culture in which it is embedded (i.e., that it is not as "culture free" as science typically aspires to be), and equally, that their our science also affects the culture in return. More and more, in recent times especially, positions of advocacy are being taken by developmentalists, as witnessed by the index of papers and symposia held at national and international developmental conventions. While such a lack of separation between science and society is eschewed by the larger field, there is growing evidence that the ideal of pure science may be unattainable in developmental psychology, and perhaps not even desirable. Developmental psychology, like the other social sciences, finds itself both constrained by and informed by its subject matter, as in the classic hermeneutical circle. However, developmental psychology has been more openly responsive to the social movements of its time than other branches of psychology, trying to provide answers of substance to issues of import, such as the plight of children working in factories during the early part of the industrial revolution, and, in more recent times, the importance of "Head Start" programs, and the risks of latchkey care.

The beginning of experimental psychology has been formally designated as 1879, a time that coincides with the opening of Wilhelm Wundt's laboratory at the University of Leipzig. Cairns (1983) has recommended the year 1882 as a comparable index date for the beginning of a scientifically based developmental psychology. This is the year following the publication of Wilhelm Preyer's influential developmental text, *Die Seele des Kindes* (*The Mind of the Child*). (Though the original date of publication was 1881, it is typically referenced as 1882, a confusion caused by Preyer himself; see Murchison & Langer, 1929).

Wilhelm Thierry Preyer was born in England in 1841 but was educated in Germany. He began his life's career as an exploring scientist in Iceland, and then traveled to Bonn, where he took up the study of physiology. Later, as a professor of physiology at Jena, his work was primarily concerned with embryology. He published the important work *Specielle Physiologie des Embryo* in 1885. However, as a comparative and physiological psychologist, he also developed an avid interest in child psychology, which expanded his work on growth and development to an even broader comparative framework. Preyer was convinced that the methods and concepts of embryology could be applied advantageously to the study of behavior, and this included human behavior.

Preyer's first and most famous foray into the study of human development was *Die Seele des Kindes*. This work was an extended (two-volume, 670-page) excursion into the psyche of the developing infant; the material for the volume was based on Preyer's meticulous notes on the behavior and mental development of his son during the first three years of life. *Die Seele des Kindes* divides the basic human faculties into the senses, the will, and the intellect. Interestingly, emotions are included in the section on the senses.

Preyer was not alone in relating emotions to sensory functioning. Ribot (1903), for example, a contemporary of Preyer (and sometimes referred to as the French Wundt), held similar views, describing the earliest emotions as "organic sensations." This position appears to have been common around the turn of the century and then to have fallen into disfavor. In fact, in contemporary theory only Izard and his colleagues (Izard & Malatesta, 1987) have espoused such a view. Although it is not known whether Izard was aware of the earlier positions taken by Preyer and Ribot, he clearly articulates such a view in his differential emotions theory (see Chapter 5, this volume). Arguing by analogy, Izard draws a parallel between the sensory experience of taste and the experience of emotion in young organisms. He points out that although young infants may not be "conscious" of their sensory experiences, they do in fact discriminate tastes, and thus at some level "experience" taste. In the same way, though emotions may not be conscious, they may nevertheless be apprehended in a sensory way. Thus for both Izard and Preyer, there is a similarity between the organic sensations associated with emotional feelings and those associated with sensory impressions such as gustation.

Preyer's volume on the developing mind of the infant represents an extended example of a kind of detailed behavioral observation known as the baby biography. Although a masterwork of observational virtuosity, it was not the first of its kind. Dietrich Tiedemann's "Die Beobachtungen über die Entwicklung der Seelenfahigheiten bei Kindern" (Observations of the mental development of children) published in 1787, is regarded as the earliest of such published records (Murchison & Langer, 1929). At the publication of Preyer's 670-page opus in 1881/82, there were already at least 80 studies of this type in existence.

There was another, even earlier contribution to the philosophical/psychological foundations of developmental psychology—one that placed emphasis on the emotions as integral to human development—by Johann Nicolas Tetens, an eighteenth-century German philosopher and physicist (1736–1807). The second half of Tetens's volume *Philosophische Versuche über die menschliche Natur und ihre Entwicklung*, was devoted to issues of development, and can be considered as constituting one of the first contributions to the field. This work, however, lay in relative obscurity until more recently for various reasons, including the fact that Tetens was overshadowed by Kant in his own time, and because later founding fathers of psychology, such as Wundt, dismissed Tetens's work because he seemed to endorse the antiquated theory of faculties (Müller-Brettel & Dixon, 1990). Nevertheless, Tetens offered a number of original ideas that anticipated current understandings of human development, such as the concept of the child as an active participant in her own development, the notion of epigenesis as a cardinal developmental principle, a lifespan orientation, a focus on individual differences in development, and, important for our purposes here, the notion of the centrality of affect in development. The very lifeblood of development is feeling, Tetens maintained; it is feeling through which the outside world makes its impact on the child; it is feelings that transform the latent abilities of the child into sensations, images, thoughts, abilities, and free will (Müller-Brettel, 1993). Today we might assimilate this position to Tomkins's idea that emotions are the primary motivational system in humans (see Chapter 8, this volume).

With Tetens's writings and the work of the baby biographers we thus see that the origins of developmental psychology predate experimental psychology by over a century. We will review the works of Tiedemann, Preyer, and other baby biographers in more detail in another section. It will suffice to point out here that when developmental psychology emerged as a discipline, whether one wants to fix its beginnings in the eighteenth or nineteenth century, its primary method of analysis was detailed behavioral observation, not introspection or experimental manipulation. This, then, is a significant departure from the initial direction pursued by the other branches of psychology. It is also worth noting, in passing, that such studies addressed themselves to the whole, functioning child, not merely some restricted domain of psychological functioning, such as memory. Preyer's book, for example, as noted above, catalogued growth and development of the total domain of human experience—the senses, will, and intellect. Because Preyer focused on immediately observable behavior, he did not neglect discussion of the emotions, taking as evidence for emotional states all of vocal, facial, and bodily behavior. Tiedemann and Preyer's accounts of their children's expressive development are some of the first detailed, descriptive data on the emotions and represent a significant chapter in the history of research on the emotions. We will return to their observations later so that we may discuss the findings in greater detail.

A major shift in both the methodology and content of developmental psychology took place around the turn of the century with Alfred Binet's study of cognitive processes and the development of the test that was to evolve into the Binet-Simon intelligence scales for children. These mental assessment scales appeared to present a unique and powerful quantitative means of measuring psychological development, and eventually gave rise to the mental measurement movement that dominated psychological research on development until the 1920s. These scales also coincidentally introduced the study of individual differences, though the immediate consequence of the movement was a fundamentally age-comparative, "normative" approach to development.

Another influential figure of the times was James Mark Baldwin. Baldwin's career began auspiciously enough—with two widely acclaimed and influential texts concerning the mental development of the child published while he was still a young professor at Princeton: *Mental Development in the Child and the Race*, and *Social and Ethical Interpretation in Mental Development*. As it turned out, Baldwin's career was cut short by an unfortunate personal scandal. The influence of his theoretical contributions was also foreshortened at least during his lifetime. However, among cognitive developmentalists, there has been a revival of interest in Baldwin's work and a fresh examination of his depiction of the forces and processes behind cognitive growth.

What is less well recognized is that Baldwin's work was not limited to formulations concerning cognitive developmental processes; indeed, his analysis of cognitive growth is actually subordinate to his analysis of growth of the child as a social being. Interestingly, emotion and expressive development play an important part in his formulations. Perhaps this is not so remarkable. Baldwin was a widely read scholar, and Darwin's (1872) *The Expression of Emotions in Man and Animals* could not have escaped his attention; his work bears marks of having been influenced by this seminal piece of thinking on emotion. The unique perspective that Baldwin brought to the understanding of emotional expressive development had to do with his formulations concerning how basic species-typical emotion patterns developed within the context of social influence and thus established the rudiments of differential personality. His general theory of behavioral development revolved largely around the concept of motor imitation and the development of habits in the context of "the social enclosure of childhood." We will have more to say about Baldwin's theory of personality development in Chapter 7, which deals with the topic of empathy and its development. During the 1920s Watsonian behaviorism swept general psychology, and it was not without its influence on developmental psychology as well. Curiously, however, whereas behaviorism was a dominant force within general psychology for decades, its impact within developmental psychology was less pronounced, relatively circumscribed, and somewhat short-lived.

Developmentalists were most taken with Watson's formulations concerning innate emotions and acquired emotional responses, and this prompted another brief flirtation with the subject of personality and its development. According to Watson, individual differences in personality resulted from an interaction between early, primitive emotional reflexes on the one hand, and the individual's unique conditioning history on the other. Watson's thesis thus represents one of the first formulations about emotional development and differentiation of the personality since Baldwin. Unlike Baldwin's work, however, the impact of Watson's pronouncements was immediate and vigorous. Experimental tests of the theory soon made their way into the literature and prompted a lively debate. In the long run, however, it appeared that some of Watson's most basic assertions could not be experimentally validated.

As far as the continued influence of behaviorism is concerned, differential effects were felt in developmental psychology and general experimental psychology. Behaviorism continued to flourish in certain local temples of academe, such as the great midwestern universities. For example, Dale Harris (personal communication, March 8, 1994) remembers that Minnesota in the 1930s was known as a bastion of dustbowl empiricism (Richard Elliot's phrase); the psychology department was said to hold confirmation classes in behaviorism. But behaviorism's impact on developmental psychology was limited and rapidly waned. In contrast, within general psychology, behaviorism was seen as having a much broader range of applicability, namely as a powerful analytic tool applied to the core problem of learning. The fact that behaviorism had a greater impact on general psychology than on developmental psychology is somewhat surprising, given that the basic research on conditioning, generalization, and counterconditioning was conducted with children, and had important theoretical ramifications for developmental issues. However, developmental psychology had confronted aspects of Watsonian theory using empirical methods, only to be disillusioned by the outcome (see Chapter 4, this volume). In the wake of this disappointment, developmentalists fashioned other agendas and pursued other problems.

At the same time that disaffection with behaviorism had reached its peak (at least among academic developmentalists), major sources of research funding became available to those with an interest in child development, initially from the private sector in terms of philanthropic contributions to "child research stations" across the country and later through government funding. This new infusion of wealth and a growing public expectation that developmental science could supply needed answers to pressing social problems promoted a period of expansion in the field, the most visible result of which was the launching of an ambitious set of longitudinal studies during the late twenties and early thirties, including the well-known Berkeley and Oakland growth projects.

Because of developmental psychology's early and enduring alliance with the biological sciences, it was only natural that the first longitudinal studies should employ a maturationally guided set of formulations concerning behavioral development and that they should focus on physical and motor aspects of ontogeny. The other major focus of the early longitudinal studies was on mental development, and this was a direct consequence of the availability of mental assessment tools developed by Binet and colleagues.

The longitudinal studies of this era helped both to consolidate the field of developmental psychology and define a discipline that was unique unto itself. At the same time, they led to developmental psychology's isolation from mainstream psychology—which had taken up the question of learning in earnest. The rift between developmental and general psychology was furthered by the specialization of longitudinal studies in the methods of direct observation and measurement of unmanipulated variables. The early developmental studies were not expressly interested in aspects of social and personality development (although later secondary analyses have attempted to mine some of the structured interview protocols for such material, e.g., Caspi, Elder, & Ben, 1987). Thus, aside from a few isolated studies of expressive behaviors by people like Jersild and Holmes (1935) and Goodenough (1931), the decade of the thirties contributed relatively little to the corpus of literature on socioemotional development.

Developmental psychology returned to the general psychology fold during the 1940s and 1950s as it began to grapple with the issue of learning. It was also at this time that the field returned to questions of differential personality development, as Freudian theory, formulated earlier in the century, first began to have a material impact on the social sciences.

Psychoanalytic theory was originally introduced to the American public in 1909 during a series of lectures Freud gave at Clark University at G. Stanley Hall's invitation. Although Freud's theory found a receptive audience within some sectors of the medical establishment, and separate professional organizations grew up and sustained an increasingly large membership, it was years before the theory generated research designed to test formulations derived from it. It was not until some two to three decades after the first series of lectures that the theory would seem a fit topic for psychological research.

Two waves of research on classic, preobject relations psychoanalytic theory can be discerned. The first wave of research on the developmental aspects of the theory started appearing in the late 1930s and 1940s and was largely inspired by observations of children in institutions and clinical reports that attempted to relate child-rearing experiences of adult patients to subsequent personality development (Tomkins, 1943). A second wave of research emerged during the 1940s and 1950s from within the academic disciplines.

In 1936 a group of social scientists at Yale's Institute of Human Relations began an interdisciplinary seminar that was to continue for a decade and leave a lasting impact on the field of developmental psychology. The group, which included representatives of various disciplines, had as its goal an attempt to integrate the many findings of the various social sciences into a single theoretical framework. Members of the seminar included experimental psychologists Clark Hull and O. H. Mowrer, sociologist John Dollard, and psychologist Neal Miller, who had been trained in psychoanalytic theory. Anthropologist Bea Whiting and developmentalist Robert Sears were also participants. One of the more important consequential products to emerge from this long-running and heterogeneous seminar was the body of literature that has since been identified as social learning theory—a synthesis of Hullian drive theory and psychoanalytic instinct theory. One of the challenges of the Yale group was to cast psychoanalytic formulations such as "identification" into learning theory principles and then to test the formulations with objective, behavioral measures of the constructs. Several major studies were launched; however, the upshot of the first wave of this research was somewhat disappointing. After several years of intense research, it was concluded that little in the way of support of Freudian constructs could be found. However, social learning theory research continued to test and explore developmental issues, with notable achievements in identifying new principles of learning (Bandura & Walters, 1963), and in the specification of some of the factors involved in the establishment and maintenance of certain kinds of behavior such as aggression. Consequently, social learning theory over time became less tied to any specific theory, such as Freudian psychoanalysis, and became a more general study of the influence of childhood experience upon personality and its growth.

Social learning theory also spawned three other schools of behavioral analysis that can be discerned in contemporary research, namely models of "interactional analysis," "social-cognitive reinterpretation," and "social-environmental structure."

The interest in personality and its psychological underpinnings that emerged during the 1940s and 1950s was soon eclipsed by the great surge of cognitive research in the 1960s and 1970s. The space race and competitive tensions between the superpowers had helped to launch the so-called cognitive revolution. In general psychology, cybernetic science and the emerging availability of computers as fast-paced thinking devices played a role in the shift from questions of learning to questions of cognition and artificial intelligence, and resulted in a focus on problems of memory and information processing. In developmental psychology, the writings of Jean Piaget—the Swiss cognitive developmentalist—available since the 1920s and 1930s, but little read before the 1960s, soon came to dominate the developmental field.

We will have relatively little to say about cognitive developmental research in the current volume except as germane to the treatment of social and personality development. We will also not review the rather extensive literature on social cognition, due to limitations of space, and because summaries of this literature are widely available. It is worth noting, however, that the literature on "social cognition" in some ways served as a transition piece between Piagetian theory and the most recent expansion of research on emotions and personality development. Piaget's theory was principally concerned with the properties of cognitive development and the structure and content of children's cognitions about nonsocial objects. Social cognition was a direct outgrowth of this literature extended to the domain of social objects.

The most recent epoch in psychology's history (mid-1970s to the present) has witnessed yet another shift in emphasis, this time expressed as an intensified interest in the emotions and their impact on an array of psychological processes. This is the case in both general psychology and developmental psychology. Although it would be inaccurate to say that psychologists have entered an age we could characterize as an "emotions revolution" on the order of magnitude of the cognitive revolution of the 1960s and 1970s, it is safe to say that this is a period that is remarkable for the consensus across disciplines about the importance of the topic for understanding a range of psychological processes, the sheer amount of energy being devoted to it, and in the use of common methods and analyses.

Within general psychology investigators are confronting the issue of the relation between emotion and cognition (Zajonc, 1980); the ways in which emotions affect perception (Forgas & Bower, 1987), information processing (Bower, 1981; Bower & Mayer, 1989) and schema formation (Forgas, 1982); the way in which emotions affect social interactions (Clark, Ouellette, Powell, & Milberg, 1987); and the way they relate to personality functioning (McCrae & Costa, 1985). Within developmental psychology there has been a growing number of studies on the ontogeny of emotion expression (Izard & Malatesta, 1987), the formation of affectional relationships (Ainsworth, 1989), the relation between emotion and social information processing (Lemerise & Dodge, 1993), and the role of emotion in aggressive and coercive interactions (Olweus, 1980; Patterson, 1980) and in prosocial processes (Strayer, 1985).

Before proceeding to a coverage of the literature on socioemotional development, let us pause to reflect on the nature of events that have contributed to a resurgence of interest in the emotions in recent times. Although a definitive answer cannot be provided, it is almost certainly a product of several converging events, including (1) sociopolitical and economic changes in the larger culture, (2) shifts in the dominance of certain theoretical paradigms, and (3) technological advances.

Psychologists have typically underestimated the role played by the larger sociopolitical context in determining the critical questions and research agendas of their discipline. Even analyses of paradigm shifts in theory (Reese & Overton, 1970) are couched in terms of the limits of the theories themselves as evident in the accumulation of "anomalies" that elude the explanatory power of the dominant paradigm (Kuhn, 1962). Although flaws and inadequacies in theoretical models are obviously operative forces in the search for alternative paradigms and shifts in research focus, they cannot be the sole explanation. For example, the study of emotions has come of age in the current decade, but the "cognitive revolution" shows no sign of abating and developmental work on aspects of cognition and learning continues to flourish.

From a broader sociocultural perspective it is interesting to note that a return to a consideration of the emotions coincides with the entry of more women into the workforce and the professions. Although it would be glib and misleading to attribute our recovery of human emotions to women's efforts (research is still disproportionately a male activity, even in the field of emotions research and in developmental psychology itself), the massive influx of women into the workforce and the changes that this turn of events wrought in family and workplace structure could not have been without effect on the values and consciousness of the larger culture. It is perhaps more than a coincidence that the most intense periods of research activity on socioemotional processes, especially in terms of focus on emotions and their expression during the first three decades of this century, and then again today, coincide with the two periods during which women played a significant role in the field of developmental psychology. Hooper's (1988) content analysis of the Carmichael/Mussen series of handbooks on child development over the past sixty years reveals this. Hooper found that there was parity in male and female authorship of handbook chapters in 1931 and 1933. However, in the 1970 edition, authorship was 83% male. The ratio of male to female authorship starts to approach parity again in the 1983 edition, with 42% of the chapters authored by women and 58% authored by men. The emphasis on attachment theory and "affectional ties" within the past 15 years may also reflect changes in the composition of the discipline and preference for certain types of research problems. Concerns about latchkey children and the relationship between quality of attachment and day care are just two of the contemporary research topics that are directly traceable to changes in workforce demographics (Clarke-Stewart, 1989).

Today, the fact that researchers of both genders are challenged by and interested in the task of understanding emotions and their influence on human information processing and behavior underscores the fact that we are not dealing with an isolated demographic change, but a broader social phenomenon, which is perhaps traceable to a sociological event of an earlier vintage—that of the countercultural revolution of the late 1960s and early 1970s. A significant number, perhaps the majority, of mid-rank faculty among the U.S. professoriat, came of age during this time, and it seems unlikely that they were unaffected by the most massive social movement of their time. This was a social movement that rejected a calculating materialism and self-centeredness in favor of sentiment, social activism, and commitment to community. Although that kind of ethos and ethic seems submerged in recent times, the generation that would challenge the countercultural agenda and play out a new conservatism and retreat from humanism in its research agenda has not quite come of age within the academy.

Obviously, there were other factors at work in laying the groundwork for a revitalized interest in the emotions, and some of these were theoretical. First, is the emergence of a new American functionalism, which can be seen to cut across disciplinary boundaries (Beilen, 1983; Hooper, 1988); modified versions of functionalism are found in the areas of language, systems or field theory, emotions, information theory, and social processes. Functionalism was a dominant theoretical presence at the turn of the century. As William James used the term, it referred to a Darwinian or psychoevolutionary view that regarded mental events as adaptive acts that could be meaningfully studied in their natural biological context. The return of a functionalist perspective is probably in large measure a result of the successes of modern European ethology (see Chapter 2, this volume), with its emphasis on the social ecology of the organism and organized patterns of behavior. As biology and the psychological sciences turned back to Darwin, they also rediscovered the emotions. Although *The Origin of Species* (1859) is clearly Darwin's most revolutionary and acclaimed work, *The Expression of Emotions in Man and Animals* (1872) is a magnificent work of observation and theory itself, and has played an influential role in four contemporary theories of emotion—namely, Tomkins's (1962, 1963, 1991, 1993) affect theory, Izard's (1971, 1977, 1991), differential emotions theory, Plutchik's (1962, 1980) psychoevolutionary theory, and Ekman's (1984) neurocultural theory.

Another theoretical force that seems to have had an impact on the field at large and which may have contributed to a renewed interest in emotions and emotional processes is general systems theory and its more recent development, dynamical systems theory (Thelen, Kelso, & Fogel, 1987). Dynamical systems, whether they be weather fronts, hydroelectric forces, or biological systems have their own shifting, organizing dynamic that has both linear and nonlinear features. In psychology, it is no longer possible to treat psychological processes as separate domains of functioning, relatively free from contamination from other systems. Recent reviews of cognitive science admit that information processing is saturated through and through with affect and that cognition and emotion are indissociable processes of the same dynamic system.

A third impetus to a return to the subject matter of the emotions relates to breakthroughs in methods of study, an emerging consensus concerning the universality of basic human emotions (Ekman, Friesen, & Ellsworth, 1972; Izard, 1971), and the development of a technology that facilitated the collection and storage of emotions data, and permitted analysis of patterns of emotional expression. This technology included more sensitive polygraph recording of patterns of physiological arousal, video and audio recording of vocal and facial expressions of emotion, and the development of sophisticated microanalytic facial affect coding schemes, such as FACS and EMFACS (1978, 1987)—developed by Ekman and colleagues (Ekman & Friesen, 1978)—and MAX and AFFEX (1979, 1983)—developed by Izard and colleagues (Izard, 1979; Izard & Dougherty, 1981). These four systems permit the identification of fundamental emotions and their blends by coding anatomical changes in facial muscle patterns.

In light of the collective developments cited above, it should perhaps come as no surprise that tremendous headway in understanding the emotions, and their growth and differentiation over time, has been made in recent years. This book will take us back over the history of the field—its frustrations as well as triumphs—on up through the most recent research and theory. With a sense of the field's trajectory, we may be in a better position to envision where it is headed next.

II

Attachment

Human attachment inspires an array of emotions from the mundane to the sublime. It is only in recent times that the theme has become an acceptable focus for research endeavors. That literature has grown enormously over the past two decades and shows little sign of abating. Historically, the literature on attachment has developed along two lines—one a normative/descriptive level, the other that of individual differences. In this part we treat both issues, beginning with the course of normative development, after which we turn to individual differences and personality development.

2

The Development of Attachment

There are three conditions which often look alike
Yet differ completely, flourish in the same hedgerow
Attachment to self and to things and to persons, detachment
From self and from things and from persons
                    T. S. ELIOT, *Little Gidding*

The experience and expression of affectional relationships is a deeply human phenomenon, so much so that we rarely question its significance in our lives. If pressed to consider what we mean by affection, it is likely that we would report some of the following features: (1) affection is something that one person feels towards a specific other person, (2) which involves liking the other person, (3) having warm, positive feelings toward him or her, (3) caring for and having concern for the other, (5) and feeling upset when involuntarily separated from the other. Hence, affection has a large emotional component to it and is manifest in certain behavioral propensities—such as keeping company with the object of affection, wanting to be in close physical contact with that person, and behaving in ways so as to sustain the relationship, or recover it if it is threatened.

The phenomenon of affection is so deeply human that it is easy to overlook the fact that it is a capacity we share with other animals—specifically, those animals that are members of the order Mammalia. Among the specializations that set mammals apart from other animals is the possession of a limbic brain, the phylogenetically early core of the cerebral hemispheres. This part of the brain in particular is integrally involved in emotional responding, the tendency to form social organizations, and the tendency to invest extraordinary energy in care of the young. In fact, MacLean (1972) has suggested that the ability to develop social

17

bonds and experience emotion is unique in phylogenesis and evolved with the limbic brain.

Although we cannot assess the emotional states of animals very readily, certain behaviors that we would regard as indices of affection or positive affect seem evident. Among domestic animals, dogs seem to display almost human traits in this respect. They tend to develop preferences for a certain member of the household and seek contact with this person, often following him or her from room to room; they seem unhappy when the person departs and show apparent delight at the person's return; they also will go to considerable lengths to guard their particular human from harm.

One way of summarizing the above behaviors is to say that the animal appears to be "attached" to its human caretaker. Outside of the domestic animal–human relationship, attachment behaviors are ubiquitous in other mammalian species. Their clearest indicators are found in the parent–young relationship. Mammalian parental behavior typically consists of nursing the young, maintaining close proximity with them, and fighting valiantly if separated from them. While this kind of parental behavior is most typically manifest in females, males show signs of affection and attachment to offspring as well; in fact, in some species the male parent takes primary responsibility for rearing the young, as in the case of the cotton-eared monkey of South America.

What about attachment behavior displayed by the young mammal toward its parents? Immature mammals nurse, engage in close physical contact (nestling among rats, clinging among monkeys), show distress upon separation (ultrasonic vocalizations among mice, crying sounds among primates), and engage in behavior motivated to restore contact (crawling after, running after, or otherwise pursuing the parent).

WHENCE ATTACHMENT AND AFFECTION?

The study of attachment behavior has become a major research focus for animal and human developmentalists alike in recent times. Some of the contemporary questions about attachment have been aired before, although disguised as different constructs. For example, Freudian theory dealt with the phenomena of love, affection, and attachment by reference to the theoretical constructs of libido (sexual drive), cathexis (investment of energy in an object or person), and object relations (interpersonal relationships). In early development, the infant forms an attachment to the mother because she supplies milk and therefore reduces tension and "unpleasure." Anna Freud referred to this kind of infantile devotion to the mother as inspired by "greedy stomach love." Learning theory also was predicated on a drive reduction model of motivation, claiming that as the child ingests milk and hunger is alleviated, the association of the mother with drive reduction causes positive affect to attach to her as well. Learning theory constructs concerning attachment have all but been abandoned today, but aspects of psychoanalytic theory found their way into John Bowlby's (1969) influential work on the subject, including the notion of mental representations of attachment relationships and in notions of coping and defense. However, Bowlby's work was also affected by other intellectual currents, as described below.

Before we proceed to a discussion of attachment in humans, we first examine the early roots and larger theoretical context of contemporary attachment theory, including the influence of the biological sciences and general systems theory.

Larger Theoretical Context

The formal study of children's affective development is now well launched, and penetrating questions about process and organization are finally beginning to be asked. But, as indicated in Chapter 1, there was a time when no one would have predicted the legitimization of such a field of enquiry. What happened? Here we would like to suggest that the study of emotion, and the study of emotional development, became a going concern only after its theoretical linkage with a more well-established science was secured and a technology commensurate with a postmodern, technological science had been developed. Thus, only within the tough-minded society of science and technology could the tender-minded domain of affect be pursued in earnest. The two antecedent preconditions we refer to are the adoption of contemporary theories and metaphors from the biological sciences on the one hand, and modern instrumentation for the measurement of expressive behavior on the other. For the time being, we restrict our treatment to the contribution of theory from the biological sciences.

As indicated earlier, developmental psychology—more than any other branch of psychology—has had a history of particularly close association with the biological sciences. Consequently, it is not surprising that it has often borrowed its scientific methods and root metaphors (Kuhn, 1962; Reese & Overton, 1970) from biology. As such, its conceptualizations of the determinants of normative and differential development have shifted, in a somewhat parallel fashion, with advances in theory and research within the biological sciences best exemplified today by the influence of evolutionary theory, general systems, and ethological approaches. Ethology, in particular, provided not only a theoretical lens, but was also successful in redignifying the ancient method of behavioral observation. In addition, it provided a theoretical basis for considering affective behavior as integral to the growth and development of social relationships.

Darwin and the Biological Sciences

In the latter part of the nineteenth century and early twentieth, the biological sciences were deeply influenced by evolutionary theory. Darwin had enunciated the doctrine that the physiology and anatomy of organisms had evolved over great periods of time in the context of species diversity or variability and survival of the fittest. Structural and physiological traits that favored an organism's ability to adapt to its environment were passed on to successive generations. Over the course of evolution species evolved such that they were distinguished from one another in ways that bore a functional relationship to their particular ecological niches.

Darwin's theory excited great interest across and within scientific disciplines, but particularly so in the biological sciences and developmental psychology. In the decades that followed the publication of *The Origin of Species*, scientists began to test extrapolations from the theory; others applied the comparative method of careful detailed observation of physiological and behavioral development in different species of animals. In Germany, Ernst Haeckel (1900), much influenced by Darwinian theory, proposed that the course of evolution could be discerned in miniature in the stages of prenatal and postnatal development ("ontogeny recapitulates phylogeny"). Thus, for some time, an important area of research in embryology documented the stages of development in prenatal epigenesis. In other laboratories experiments were designed to determine the degree of ease or difficulty with which normal fetal development could be subverted. Still other biologists became interested in exploring the parameters of "instinctual" behavior; animals were experimentally challenged in various ways, by either adding or subtracting something from their environment.

Developmentalists adapted these kinds of questions and methods for their own science. Operating from the assumption that organisms are born with a set of species-specific functional structures that permit them to interact with the environment in ways that allow incorporation of stimulation and experience, and exploiting the stimulus-addition and stimulus-subtraction methodology, developmentalists and comparative psychologists explored the boundaries of developmental modifiability (Thompson & Grusec, 1970). These and other related questions were ultimately subsumed within what came to be known as the nativist-empiricist controversy, a debate around a set of issues that dominated the field for the better part of the first half of the twentieth century. Over this time, a great deal of argumentation and research activity was directed at estimating the degree to which a particular behavior or developmental outcome was innate, or within-the-organism, and how much was governed by environmental influences.

The nature versus nurture controversy assumed that the developmental process is controlled by two completely different and independent factors—genes and environment. Growing dissatisfaction with this "main effects" model of human behavior and development eventually led to alternative formulations, such as Werner's orthogenic principle (Langer, 1969), Erikson's (1963) notion of epigenesis (a concept borrowed from embryology), organismic, or active-organism, conceptualizations of human development borrowed from biology (Piaget, 1971), and transactional models (Sameroff & Chandler, 1975). The most recent trend in developmental psychology once again mirrors changes occurring in biology and related sciences.

Within the biological sciences in general, and especially within comparative biology, Darwinian theory, modernized to accommodate recent findings and conceptualizations, has had a continuing impact on developmental psychology. In addition, there has developed a great deal of interest in models that are driven by general systems theory (von Bertalanffy, 1968). General systems theory is to be distinguished from other systems approaches. In *systems approaches*, behavior is seen as transactional, that is, as the product of interacting influences rather than as the sum of separate influences. *General systems theory* incorporates the transactional view but also tries to describe the organization and properties of systems (Sameroff, 1983). Among those psychologists working most closely with biologists—namely, comparative and physiological psychologists—there has been a growing appreciation of general systems theory. Within the past 15 years these researchers have increasingly seen cause to adopt the framework in their own thinking. Since then, the ideas have diffused across other disciplinary boundaries to the point where developmental psychology seems ready to explore the meaning of these dynamic systems models for our understanding of behavioral development. At the same time, there has been a growing appreciation of the value of animal models and, in general, a return to functionalist (Darwinian) accounts of behavior and development.

One general property of systems is that they are characterized by self-correcting or self-regulatory mechanisms (Sameroff, 1983). The concept of self-regulation refers to the capacity of a system (an organ, an individual, a dyad, a society) to compensate for changing conditions in the environment by making coordinated changes in its internal variables. Recently, this concept has been applied to an understanding of attachment behavior and infant responses to separations from the mother.

General Systems Theory Applied to Attachment Behavior

It is now recognized that the human infant's response to separation from its mother resembles the pattern observed in other mammalian species. In animals as diverse as kittens, rats, monkeys, and puppies, the basic behavioral response to prolonged separation from the mother is similar, involving intense vocalization, aimless locomotion, self-grooming activity, rocking, and, less commonly, withdrawal and apathy. Not all of these behaviors appear at once; they tend to emerge gradually over time and their emergence depends on the length of separation. Nevertheless, two separate subphases can be distinguished. The first stage, immediately following separation, is called the *protest subphase* and involves agitated behavior (hyperactivity) and strong vocalizations. If the separation persists, the infant enters a *despair subphase,* which tends to involve a cessation of activity, decrease in food intake, and withdrawal. Research has disclosed that these behavioral changes are accompanied by physiological changes in a fairly predictable and system-specific fashion.

Early explanations for the pattern of separation-induced protest and despair and physiological changes were couched in terms of a cognitive/affective response to perceived loss, related in kind to the adult bereavement response. However, a series of experiments by Hofer (1987) revealed that the responses to separation are likely mediated by the interruption of a complex process of reciprocal regulation between mother and infant. Though the findings are with laboratory rats, the mechanisms are thought to be similar across mammalian species.

Laboratory rats display a pattern of response to maternal separation that is characteristic of other mammals. Following separation the pup emits high-pitched (ultrasonic) cries and shows classic protest and despair subphases. Hofer and colleagues found that the distress vocalization could be alleviated by either restoring the mother or providing a litter mate. In further experiments they determined that interaction of the mother or littermate with the pup was, per se, not necessary to produce the reduction in distress vocalization since an *anesthetized* mother or littermate sufficed; however, a warm plastic object in the shape of the mother or sibling did not.

In another series of experiments designed to isolate the particular stimuli that affected the pups' separation and reunion behavior, various sensorimotor aspects of the mother (warmth, tactile sensation, olfactory cues, milk, periodicity) were manipulated. Hofer and colleagues found that different cues regulated different aspects of the infant behavioral system. Moreover, the elimination of one would affect only the aspect of physiology or behavior with which it was linked, without affecting the others. Certain stimuli were apparently responsible for the "hyperactivity" aspect of the infant response to separation. When pups had visual access to the mother following separation (i.e. they could see the mother behind wire mesh) the hyperactivity effect was partially ameliorated. Making the pups anosmic reversed the benefit. Mechanical simulation of maternal tactile and kinesthetic stimuli also reduced or eliminated hyperactivity in the pups during maternal absence. Other manipulations were found to affect other aspects of the separation response. The emerging picture then was that various thermal, tactile, and olfactory stimulations of the mother in effect regulate various aspects of the infant's behavior and physiology, and they do so in ways that affect the pup's separation response. Normally, these *maternal regulators* act in concert to exert ongoing and long-term control over infant behavioral responsiveness. The infant needs the mother to regulate its behavioral systems; without her or her surrogate, its behavior gradually deteriorates.

However, research is also beginning to indicate that the mother has a reciprocal need for the pup. That is, *maternal regulators* have their counterpart in *infant regulators*. Research on the nursing behavior of the rat by Lincoln (1983) has provided evidence of the symbiotic relationship between the mother and her young, with both maternal and infant regulators being expressed. The mother's ability to feed her young depends upon the positive maternal ejection of milk from the mammary gland, a phenomenon that in the rat is evoked by the periodic, explosive activation of oxytocin-releasing neurons located in the hypothalamus. The activation of these neurons for 2–4 seconds releases a pulse of oxytocin from the posterior pituitary gland that, on reaching the mammary gland, promotes a transient contraction. The phenomenon repeats itself at intervals of 3–10 minutes provided that the pups remain attached to the nipples; thus, the efferent output from the brain is episodic. The sensory input, on the other hand, appears to be sustained and derives from the prolonged attachment of the young to the nipples. It has been estimated that rats suckle their young for upwards of 18 hours every day, which would seem to imply strong maternal motivation, possibly augmented by the sensory input provided by the young. Curiously, the mother has to be in a state of sleep in order to eject milk. In that respect it is interesting to note that suckling by the pups operates as a sleep-inducing signal, unlike most forms of exteroceptive or proprioceptive stimulation. Thus, the attachment of the pups to the nipples—their suckling—along with their relative behavioral inactivity, has the effect of sending the mother to sleep. That, by definition, effectively implies that the mother is never consciously aware of the key event evoked by this afferent input, that is, milk ejection. However, at milk ejection the pups, on sensing the flow of milk, nurse with increased vigor, which causes the mother to awaken. At this time she often attends to the grooming of her young, even while they are still attached to her nipples. A key component of this aspect of maternal behavior is the induction of the micturition reflex, that is, the young are induced to empty their bladders through the mother's grooming/licking behavior. The behavior of the mother and her family are thus entrained to one another's behavioral patterns, both while awake, and during periodic "rat naps," in an interdependent, reciprocal, symbiotic fashion.

Hofer has proposed that these kinds of data and similar observations help explain the infant's response to maternal separation. The behavior and physiology of the one partner is enmeshed with the behavior and physiology of the other. It would thus appear that the infant's behavioral response to separation is a consequence of the down regulation of its physiological systems in the absence of maternal regulatory mechanisms.

Although the human infant is infinitely more complex than the rat pup, it may not be unreasonable to assume that similar patterns of reciprocal regulatory control of behavioral and physiological systems are at work in the human mother–infant dyad. This is not to say that the child's response to maternal separation is mediated solely by disruption of externally regulated behavioral systems, and that "missing" the mother and the affective disturbance it generates is not a contributory factor. Indeed, the facial expression changes observed in institution-reared children separated from their mothers for a prolonged period of time appear to index the intense emotions we associate with anxiety and grief (Spitz, 1965). However, the animal data seriously challenge the idea that the protest–despair response of infants to maternal separation is solely a consequence of the infant's awareness of loss, as per earlier formulations. The data are strongly persuasive of the likelihood that much of infant behavior is dyadically bound and constrained in an enmeshed fashion by systemic factors.

Hofer has suggested that the rat pup's homeostatic system is relatively "open" and thus biologic regulation is delegated in part to the mother. One can also observe "openness" in the human infant's physiological systems. It is well known that infant state (i.e., pattern of physiological organization) is highly variable and unstable during the first two months of life, and that the growing stabilization of state owes much both to maturation of the infant's nervous system as well as to the nature, quality, and reliability of caregiver interventions (Fogel, 1982; Sander, 1969). By the end of the third month, the human infant has made major advances in the regulation of state and in the stability of circadian rhythms. However, it is conceivable that maternal presence and patterns of interaction continue to support and influence the infant's regulation of state far beyond the opening months. We have only to examine the literature on children's behavioral and hormonal responses to maternal separations (Bretherton, 1985; Spitz, 1965; Tennes, 1982; see Chapter 3, this volume). The evidence indicates that psychological mechanisms rapidly become ever more important in mediating and sustaining the human infant's behavioral organization.

The Maintenance of Regulation beyond Infancy

The animal literature has illustrated that tactile, olfactory, and kinesthetic cues are important regulators of behavior and physiology in the life of the young organism. It is likely that these proximal stimuli are important in humans as well, but we would add to the list the importance of auditory and visual stimuli. The eyes of human infants, unlike those of rat pups, are open at birth and rapidly become capable of processing complex stimuli; the infant auditory system is also rather well developed at birth and infants are responsive to a wide range of auditory stimuli, including, and apparently especially, the human voice. It is likely that these sensory cues play a particularly important role in the regulation of infant state. Beyond early infancy, we propose they become ever more important because they can serve as "long-distance" stimuli; that is, they can continue to affect the child's behavior at a far remove, a point that is important to recognize since most infants are ambulatory by 6 months with the onset of creeping and crawling. Furthermore, we propose that it is primarily the emotional dimension of these kinds of cues that is so interpersonally affecting (see Part IV).

In summary, recent research has shown that the classic features of attachment behavior in mammals can be understood within the framework of general systems theory whereby complex behavioral and physiological processes operate in the context of larger regulatory systems, in this case, the dyadic system of mother and infant. The "input" from one part of the larger system affects the operation of the constituent parts of the rest of the system. Attachment behavior is no longer regarded as something that inheres in infants, as in earlier "instinct" or "drive reduction" models, but as operating within a system of mutual regulation. We turn now to a discussion of the contribution of another theoretical orientation from the biological sciences—the ethological.

ETHOLOGY

The ethological approach represents an epistemology and a methodology that derive from an originally European brand of biology. As an epistemology, ethology seeks to understand behavior as examined through the lens of evolutionary theory and behavioral adaptation. As a methodology, it chooses to study the behavior of organisms in the context of the natural environment. As absorbed into the field of psychology, and particularly developmental psychology, it views human behavior from the broader context of the entire animal kingdom. Interestingly, its incorporation in developmental psychology in recent times reflects, in some ways, a return to the field's pre-twentieth-century roots in Darwinian evolutionary theory and the comparative psychology of Preyer. Darwin's original theory proposed that human life evolved from animal ancestry, structurally and physiologically. What ethology suggested is that certain behavioral patterns also represent evolutionary adaptations.

Ethology's Origins

The term, ethology (from the Greek *ethos*, meaning manner of behavior), as used to describe the natural history method, was apparently in use prior to modern times. However, two European zoologists—Konrad Lorenz and Niko Tinbergen—put the term on the map with their pioneering research during the 1930s, 1940s, and 1950s. Today, ethology is recognized as a distinct scientific discipline in its own right.

Konrad Lorenz, the Austrian naturalist who was trained by Karl Bühler, first used the term *Ethologie* in the title of a 1931 paper. The paper, an exemplary representation of the natural history method, contained detailed observational notes on the behavior of the jackdaw, a common European crow. The natural history method, which involved the recording and analysis of behavioral observation, was not an unusual activity at the time, but Lorenz was the first to recognize and articulate the importance of what he and other naturalists were observing—that animal behavior was characterized by multiple common forms of behaviors, that were organized into coherent chunks or sequences too complex to be construed as reflexes. These complex behavioral chains were patterned; they were variable and yet somehow reliable in their organization. The Dutch zoologist Niko Tinbergen drew further attention to these complex forms of behavior with the publication of his book *The Study of Instinct* (Tinbergen, 1951), which he designated as a "programme for ethology."

The choice of the word *instinct* was perhaps unfortunate. The term had been maligned on both sides of the Atlantic because of past association as a construct with imprecise meaning and indiscriminate application. It also had disturbing associations with the term reflex. However, Tinbergen was careful to point out the distinction between reflex behavior and the chunks of "endogenously" controlled behavior to which he was referring. A *reflex* was defined as something that occurs at all times unless habituated or centrally suppressed during the execution of other behavior; in contrast, an *instinctive behavior* was defined as something that will occur only when there is a central nervous system (CNS) readiness. Lorenz called this CNS readiness "*action specific energy.*"

There are certain concepts that are most closely identified with classic ethological theory. The "chunks" of behavior that Lorenz thought so highly significant have been termed *fixed action patterns* (FAPs). Fixed action patterns are species-specific and stereotypical in nature; they involve coordination of several muscle movements, which, when released, proceed to completion without requiring further sensory input. These complex innate behaviors—or motor patterns— have a distinctive adaptive significance and are typically associated with feeding, courtship, mating, and parenting activities. The motor patterns can range from relatively simple to relatively complex sets of behaviors and sequences of behavior. An example of a simple FAP is the "gaping" behavior of young nestlings when the parent returns to the nest with food (which can be triggered by kinesthetic cues elicited by nest movement). More complex behavioral acts are frequently seen as part of courtship ritual or mating behavior, which can involve a long string of alternating or coordinated FAPs. For example, a pair of mockingbirds was once observed in the backyard of one of the authors during early spring. The two birds alighted on the ground and performed a complex avian dance. They began by facing one another and then proceeded to enact a sequence of head-bobbing actions, advances, and retreats, all interspersed with intermittent wing and tail flourishes. (Both male and female mockingbirds have bright bands of white across their otherwise gray wings and tail, which make for striking displays.) The highly coordinated activity of the pair lasted for about 3 min, after which they flew off together into the foliage.

Parental behavior also involves quite complex FAPs at times. When the Australian brush turkey, *Alectura lathami*—a huge, ostrichlike creature that inhabits the region of the Great Dividing Range—is ready for nesting, it gathers up specialized material and constructs a tall mound within which it will bury its eggs. The parent keeps a close watch on the temperature of the mound as the material in it begins to decompose, probing it and adding and subtracting material as it decomposes so that the eggs within are incubated at precisely the right temperature. Like all FAPs, the behavior is species-specific and stereotypical; however, as indicated, it is also fairly complex and far more flexible than reflex behaviors. Although FAPs were first identified in birds, they are not restricted to avian species, but occur broadly among animals. The nut-gathering and -burying behavior of the common ground squirrel is one such example in another class of animal (Eibl-Eibesfeldt, 1951).

Fixed action patterns operate in conjunction with sign stimuli, or releasers. The presence of a *sign stimulus* elicits an FAP. It can be of a relatively simple nature, such as the red dot on a herring gull's bill, which will elicit a pecking response in chicks (causing the parent to regurgitate food), or the buteric acid emitted by mammals passing through a woods, which causes wood ticks to drop to the backs of their victims. Or it can be more complex, such as relational cues exhibited by a prospective mate. The key-in-lock association between sign stimuli and FAPs and the speed with which FAPs are activated, especially in the case of lower organisms, provide a measure of built-in functional adaptation to a variety of environmental challenges. For example, Lorenz discovered that hatchling birds, with literally no experience under their wings, react instantly at the sight of a hawk overhead by flocking for cover. In a subsequent study, using an assortment of cardboard silhouettes of hawks, Lorenz was able to identify the essential characteristics of "hawkness" (i.e., the constellation of sign stimuli) that released the young birds' extremely adaptive behavioral response.

Fixed action patterns and sign stimuli do not function alone; there are also dynamic systems features that come into play. According to Lorenz's conceptualization, action-specific energy—that is, energy specific to a drive that builds up within the nervous system—accumulates over time. The more of it that builds up, the more likely the sign stimulus will release the FAP.

There are two related concepts that appear in subsequent elaborations of the model. When a FAP appears with sudden onset and is performed in spite of the absence of any external releaser, it is referred to as *vacuum activity*. For example, a postpartum rat that has been deprived of her litter will be in such a state of readiness to retrieve her young that she will resort to carrying her hind leg or tail in substitution. Vacuum activity is said to result when there is too great an accumulation of unreleased action-specific energy. *Displacement*, which involves an enactment of a FAP in a context that is inappropriate, typically occurs under situations of stress; for example, it can occur if the situation is ambiguous for two different behaviors, especially if the behaviors are fundamentally opposite, such as the attack and withdrawal behaviors of participants in a cockfight, or the ambivalent mating and attack impulses shown by stickelbacks in the course of early courtship ritual. (For behavior in humans that is reminiscent of animal displacement activity, see the section in Chapter 3 on attachment in children and their conflicted behavior in the Strange Situation paradigm.)

The pioneering work of behavioral programming is *imprinting* (*Praegung*), first described by Lorenz in his study of greylag geese. What Lorenz observed, and other ethologists subsequently confirmed, was that the young of many species (geese, goats) will become selectively attached to a parent and follow them about shortly after birth. Lorenz originally believed that the young of certain species became permanently imprinted (attached) and that these early events had a lasting and irreversible effect on the animals' subsequent behavior—extending as far out ontogenetically as adulthood and affecting even the selection of mates.

The pioneering work of the early ethologists had a material impact on the field of biology and other related disciplines. Lorenz and Tinbergen had discerned that much complex behavior in animals consists of strings of innate motor programs and that there was a genetic involvement in the chunks of behavior; this understanding provided a major advance in perceiving how complex behavior patterns may have evolved. In 1973, Lorenz, Tinbergen, and another European ethologist, Karl von Frisch (who identified complex communication patterns among bees), shared in the Nobel prize for physiology or medicine for their ground-breaking studies in animal behavior. Amazingly, when the news broke in the United States, the three did not receive the usual kudos associated with winning the Nobel prize. Hoyle (1984) notes that "While the furor was still raging, students of animal behavior were crowding libraries trying to find out what these 'unknowns' had discovered; indeed, what was all the fuss about?" (p. 368).

The field of ethology continued to test and refine its ideas, and a number of the original constructs have undergone revision. For example, it is now recognized that certain motor programs are more variable than the classic FAP; these more variable programs are sometimes referred to as "modal action patterns" (MAPs). As for sign stimuli, although Lorenz originally hypothesized that releasers are discriminated as "schemata" or patterns, research has indicated that they consist of discrete features, which are often the optimum stimuli for well-known classes of feature detector neurons in the visual and auditory systems of higher animals. It is also recognized that some of the requirement that the sign stimulus be *specific*, actually reflected the nature of the sensory system rather than innate mechanisms in the CNS. Our understanding of imprinting phenomena has undergone considerable modification as well, in the light of extensive observational and experimental testing. For example, the doctrine of irreversibility has been revised, and it is now recognized that offspring imprint on their parents and their species separately. Finally, and most importantly, it is recognized that both innate motor programs (instincts) and learning are intimately intertwined and dependent on one another for the full expression of many complex forms of behavior (Gould, 1982).

A question for the field of developmental psychology that naturally arises is whether we can use the ethological perspective and its concepts to extend our understanding of human development. Is there any evidence that the behavior of humans is governed by some of the same kinds of innate motor programs and preadapted behavioral propensities that are found in most other animal species? What would we use as evidence? A branch of ethology, known as human ethology, has begun to address just these kinds of questions.

Human Ethology

Irenaeus Eibl-Eibesfeldt of the Max Planck Institut, Forschungsstelle Humanethologie, in Erling-Andechs, Germany, is generally considered to be the founder of human ethology, defined as the biology of human behavior. Eibl-Eibesfeldt was among the first to try to create a bridge between psychology and ethology, pointing out that many human behaviors appeared to qualify as FAPs or MAPs. Over the years he developed his argument based on data derived from comparative animal research as well as from his own extensive cross-cultural investigations. Although he is sometimes criticized for making too much of "similarities" between species, especially those involving human and lower organisms, the examples he offers are remarkably striking and bear some explanation. Eibl-Eibesfelt hypothesizes that such similarities are due in some cases to the operation of similar selective pressures that have shaped behavior during phylogenetic and cultural evolution alike, and/or, in other cases, from a shared ancestor.

The Comparative Evidence

Across animal species similarities of behavioral patterns that appear due to common selective pressures are called *analogies*; patterns that appear related to a shared animal ancestry are called *homologies*. Eibl-Eibesfeldt (1979; 1983; 1989) provides a number of interesting examples of both.

Analogies. Gift-giving and mutual feeding are practices that are common in birds and humans. For example, among flightless cormorants, both males and females play a pre-parental role in incubating eggs. When the male returns to the nest to relieve his mate, he is allowed to stay only if he brings a twig; if he approaches without a present he is attacked. Thus the twig serves an appeasing function. There are analogous culturally evolved gift-giving rituals among human cultures that seem to serve the same purpose.

Mutual feeding is also observed across species. It is common as part of the courtship ritual among many species of birds. Female herring gulls beg like nestlings and thereby avert the natural aggressiveness of males, permitting them to get fed rather than attacked. Mutual feeding can be seen among human adults during the early phases of courtship, and mouth-to-mouth feeding is also widespread as a feature of maternal behavior in many human cultures, where the practice is known as kiss-feeding. Affectionate face-to-face touching during human courtship, once colloquially referred to as "billing and cooing," also has an obvious avian counterpart.

Homologies. Eibl-Eibesfeldt has adduced many examples of homologies between human and nonhuman primates. The human smile is seen as being homologous to the silent bared-teeth display of monkeys and apes, the human laugh to their play face or relaxed open-mouth display. There are striking similarities in the greeting display of chimpanzee and human; van Lawick-Goodall (1971) has observed friendly encounters between chimpanzees in which they embrace one another and kiss. Among monkeys, phallic displays are used to establish dominance and to threaten conspecifics. Eibl-Eibesfeldt's cross-cultural research has accumulated evidence that males in preliterate culture sometimes use direct phallic displays in confrontation with enemies (e.g., the Eipo of Westirian, New Guinea) and display substitutes—phallic figurines, which are known throughout Europe, tropical Asia, New Guinea, South America, and Africa—were (and in some cultures continue to be) commonly found as guardians of edifices and fields or were worn as personal amulets.

Cross-Cultural Evidence

Eibl-Eibesfeldt's cross-cultural data come from extensive film records he and his colleagues have taken of various rapidly vanishing cultures around the world; the footage is from cultures that represent different stages of cultural evolution including hunter-gatherer, incipient agriculture, neolithic agriculture, pastoral, and rice farming. By using mirror lenses his research team has been able to film unobtrusively and obtain rich naturalistic data.

From these film records Eibl-Eibesfeldt was able to identify a striking number of nonverbal motor patterns that seem to qualify as phylogenetic adaptations. That is, they appear in widely different cultures and are found to have the same form, pattern, and signal value, and serve the same functions in the same types of contexts. For example, a particular form of greeting signal, termed the "eyebrow flash," involves a flicker of raised brows usually accompanied by a head-tilt, smile, and head-nodding. It is noticeable in situations where people reencounter one another after a period of being out of touch. The eyebrow flash signal lasts but a third of a second and happens so routinely that we are usually not consciously aware of it. However, the unconscious nature of it ceases as soon as a person whom we like stops performing it. The eyebrow flash is a friendly gesture that signals readiness for social contact. It is observed cross-culturally in greetings, in flirting, in emphasizing agreement during conversation, and in other situations expressing contact readiness. Raised brows in general are a signal of openness and approachability. It is interesting to note that females, who are generally regarded as more socially responsive than men (Maccoby & Jacklin, 1974), typically emphasize the raisedness of their brows by penciling the brows high, by plucking, and by whitening or coloring the area under the brows.

Another cross-culturally ubiquitous motor pattern is what Eibl-Eibesfeldt calls the "coyness response." A coy or shy child displays the behavior when, at the approach of a stranger, he hides behind his mother's skirt, and then from this safe vantage point alternates between gazing at the stranger and hiding or averting his head. A coy adolescent will look at a person, avert her head and lower the eyelids, and then look back from under her lids or then face the person again, only to turn away again, repeating the sequence anew. At the same time the individual may smile while simultaneously activating the antagonistic muscles involved in suppressing the smile, which results in a seductive appearance. The person may then hide the mouth behind the hand or attempt to hide behind a nearby person. (Ekman [1985] finds that the "mysterious" smile of the Mona Lisa is codable via facial action coding systems as being a coy smile—as distinct from the 18 other mixed but nondeceptive smiling patterns that have been identified). What is also interesting about the coyness pattern—from a comparative viewpoint—is that it seems to index conflicted feelings, and sometimes is accompanied by what could be regarded as "displacement" behavior. For example, the coy adolescent may perform an eyebrow flash when meeting an attractive partner, then lower her lids breaking eye contact, smile but turn away, perhaps even showing her shoulder. She may even combine the pattern with aggressive gestures such as stamping the feet or punching the other, all the while smiling. These alternating friendly/aggressive/rejecting behaviors seem to indicate that two conflicting motivational systems have been activated—one a friendly approach system, the other an avoidance system oriented towards flight and escape. Instead, the individual remains, and a form of attack behavior is released.

The regulation of eye contact between interactants also shows certain universal features cross-culturally. When two adults are engaged in conversation they do not sustain eye contact for long periods of time, but avert the gaze and otherwise break eye contact intermittently and repeatedly throughout the course of interaction. Unless, of course, the two are lovers. Among interactants who are not already romantically involved with one another, sustained eye contact by one of the parties typically is interpreted as a sign of flirtation. A particular kind of prolonged eye contact, that of staring, communicates something altogether different. Staring signals dominance behavior and can have strong aggressive overtones; one of the last things a sane person does on a subway is to stare at another individual. Its counterpart in the animal kingdom is the "threat stare," a powerful elicitor of aggressive behavior. Among humans, Tomkins (1962) has documented the universal nature of the "tabu on looking" using a rich array of cross-cultural and historical data. Interocular intimacy, as Tomkins refers to interpersonal gazing, is a highly regulated affair. One cannot get along in polite society by avoiding face-to-face contact altogether; some eye contact is necessary and desirable in order to feel in touch with the other person. However, too much looking also seems improper. When one is looked at, one feels looked into, and the privacy that one naturally guards from all but one's most intimate partners feels threatened. Being the target of another's stare is experienced as unpleasant and it generates tension between interactants. Thus, gazing patterns are well regulated in human societies, and the regulation is achieved in fairly universal fashion cross-culturally. It is apparently a behavior that is unlearned. Young infants show similar need to regulate eye contact between themselves and interactants, and they will avert their gaze or cry to effective advantage if their partner is insensitive.

Another area where innate motor programs among humans are implicated is in the expression of emotion. This literature will be discussed in detail later on and so we only mention it here in passing. Suffice it to note that the evidence for the universality of certain basic emotion expressions is quite strong; facial expressions of emotion are not only cross-culturally recognizable, they appear to be elicited under the same conditions in different cultures and to serve the same purposes. This is not to say that facial expressions of emotion, or any of the other motor patterns mentioned above—regulation of eye contact, coyness behavior, and eyebrow flash—are unmodified by culture. For example, although the eyebrow flash is found in every culture studied, its use may be more or less restricted. Polynesians are liberal in its use, displaying it readily to adults and children. The Japanese, however, display it during interaction with children and familiar adults but tend to repress it during encounters with all others. Americans show an intermediate use of the signal; it can be seen during flirtatious encounters, in greeting good friends, and as a signal emphasizing agreement during conversation. The behavior can be found even in the infant repertoire; Malatesta (1985) has observed the eyebrow flash in 3-month-olds when their mothers returned after a brief separation.

The Impact of Ethology on the Study of Child Development

Ethological concepts and methods have found their way into the field of child development—most notably in the context of research on the development of attachment relationships. The impact of ethology has also been felt in the area of emotion expression development, as described in a later section. For the present we examine how ethological theory is instantiated in contemporary attachment research. But first some background.

Within developmental psychology, three figures stand out as having made major early contributions to our understanding of human attachment relationships: Rene Spitz, the Viennese psychoanalyst, John Bowlby, the British child psychiatrist, and Mary Ainsworth, the American developmentalist.

Spitz

For most, the name of Rene Spitz is most closely associated with the work on the effects of institution rearing and the term "hospitalism." Spitz's (1946, 1965) pioneering work documented the profound deterioration of infants separated from their mothers and reared in a foundling home or hospital. Although it is now recognized that some of the effects he observed were due to an impoverished environment and lack of sensory stimulation, as well as lack of a consistent caregiver, his work was influential in alerting professionals as well as the lay public to the potentially damaging effects of institutional rearing.

Spitz had studied under Freud and thus was first and foremost a psychoanalyst; however, unlike most of his contemporaries who trained with Freud and then went on to study and treat adults, Spitz became intrigued with questions of infant development. He took his mentor quite at his word when Freud said that direct observation of infants was the only mode in which one could hope to arrive at any information about them. The usual method of psychoanalytic investigation—free association—demanded verbal facilities infants lacked. Indeed, the Latin root of the word *infant* means "unable to speak." As Spitz recognized, however, being unable to speak does not mean being unable to communicate, and he devoted over 35 years of his professional life to close observational study of infants' behavior, including their nonverbal, affective communications.

At a time during which the status of affects was at an all-time low in terms of scientific credibility (in the wake of failed emotion validation studies—see Chapter 4), and dismissed as ephemera or "humbug" (Meyer, 1933), Spitz was busy making 16-mm films of infant affective communications, in what was an early forerunner of today's complex technology of videotaping and coding affect expressions. Spitz began the film approach in 1935 as a teaching instrument. He found that he could run film at 24 frames per second and slow it down by as much as three times to illustrate points that he wanted to make; he referred to his technique as screen analysis. The archives of his film records (located at the University of Colorado, School of Medicine)—many of them collected during visits to children's institutions—document with devastating clarity the kinds of emotional traumata suffered by infants who experienced separations from their caregivers and subsequent institutional rearing.

The Contribution of John Bowlby (1907–1990)

John Bowlby was born in England in 1907, the second son of a leading London surgeon, at a time and in a milieu in which it was common for children to live apart from their parents and to be tended by a succession of nannies (Ainsworth, 1992; Goleman, 1990; Karen, 1990). These children rarely saw their parents except at teatime until they reached the age when they were sent away to boarding school. Whether or not this experience affected Bowlby's subsequent interest in neglected children and in children's responses to separation cannot be said. He was certainly affected by his early clinical experiences and by the plight of children separated from their families during the war.

Bowlby attended Cambridge where he studied natural science and psychology. His medical degree was earned at University College Medical School in London, and he was trained in psychiatry at Maudsley Hospital. He also undertook training as a psychoanalyst and became a member of the British Psychoanalytic Society, although the publication of his first book on attachment theory drew rather severe criticism from the psychoanalytic establishment, including Anna

Freud, who thought he had misinterpreted and oversimplified psychoanalytic theory.

As a practicing psychiatrist, he became interested in children's reactions to separation, an interest dating back to 1927 and his work in a home for emotionally disturbed boys (Bretherton & Waters, 1985). In 1948 he and James Robertson began what was intended to be systematic inquiry into long-term consequences of family separations in early childhood. They observed a number of children during and after short-term separations from their parents—a few weeks to a few months—during the second and third years of life and were especially impressed with the intensity and duration of the disturbance that resulted. The children not only were clearly upset during the separation itself, but seemed to have difficulty reestablishing a warm and unconflicted relationship when they were once again reunited with their families.

> We were concerned particularly with the great changes in a child's relation to his mother that are often to be seen when he returns home after a period away; on the one hand, "an intense clinging to the mother which can continue for weeks, months or years'; on the other, 'a rejection of the mother as a love object, which may be temporary or permanent." The latter state, to which we later came to refer as detachment, we held to be a result of the child's feelings for his mother having undergone repression. (Bowlby, 1969, p. xiii)

Bowlby and Robertson also observed that the effects of separation could be long-lasting, extending over a period of years and affecting subsequent personality development.

In his absorption with the problem of understanding the child's response to separation and its emotional repercussions, he sought a theoretical explanation that could encompass the range of phenomena he had observed. At the time that Bowlby began facing the problem, explanations for affectional ties were couched mainly in psychoanalytic and learning theory terms. As Bowlby pointed out, these theories did not explain the whole host of attachment-related phenomena he and others had observed, and moreover, they were contradicted by research that was emerging from several laboratories at the time. For example, Harlow's research with rhesus monkeys demonstrated that contact comfort was more important than being fed (drive reduction) in promoting the attachment of an infant to a surrogate mother. Consequently, Bowlby sought another conceptual scheme, and he eventually settled on one that incorporated elements from two different theoretical approaches.

Bowlby was trained as a psychoanalyst, but read widely and had became interested in ethological theory as it was developing on the Continent. While he accepted the psychoanalytic notion that the child's personality is forged in his or her relationship with the mother during the opening years of life, he was not convinced that the psychoanalytic explanation for the child's attachment to the caregiver was sufficient to account for the complex reactions to separation he and others had observed. To his mind, the explanation of how and why children developed a specialized attachment or bond to their parents and why they reacted to separations the way they did resided in a synthesis of the two theories.

A turning point in his thinking emerged from conversations he had with biologist Sir Julian Huxley, who talked to him about ethology and urged him to read the work of Konrad Lorenz and other ethologists. He did so and was deeply impressed; moreover, it occurred to him that some of the constructs developed by the ethologists, and indeed, some of their observations of animals in the wild, seemed to fit the human situation as well, at least in principled outline. Bowlby noted that certain behavioral patterns in human infants resembled fixed action patterns, and that the child's sometimes conflicted behavior upon reunion with a parent following separation resembled displacement activity. He also had been particularly struck by Spitz's observation that infants suffered their most marked disturbance to loss of the caregiver beginning around 6 months of life, the implication being that this was a sensitive period for the formation of attachment. It occurred to Bowlby that this bore a striking resemblance to the imprinting phenomenon described by ethologists observing avian species, and that something like imprinting might be involved in the development of human bonding.

Although the fit between animal and human models is not as good as it first promised to be, and the notion of "critical period" has been modified even within the animal literature (Gewirtz & Petrovich, 1982), Bowlby's formulations, which did much to advance the scientific study of the development of affectional ties between human infants and their caregivers, today remain a dominant theoretical force in the child developmental literature.

Attachment Theory

Attachment theory, as presented in Bowlby's (1969, 1973, 1980) three- volume work, *Attachment and Loss*, interprets social behavior from within the framework of an evolutionary perspective, and thus draws heavily on instinct theory as formulated by ethologists. It also makes use of constructs derived from systems theory, as developed by Miller, Galanter and Pribram in *Plans and the Structure of Behavior*, and by Young (1964) in *A Model of the Brain*, including notions that behavioral systems are regulated by information, feedback loops, and a behavioral form of homeostasis.

The child's tie to the caregiver is said to arise in the context of the activation of a preadapted, biologically based, goal-corrected, motivational system subserving survival. Attachment behavior is not a function of "needs" or "drives" but a result of the activation of behavioral systems. The behavioral systems, themselves products of evolution, involve autonomous propensities to act in certain ways toward objects with certain properties, and are species typical. Behavioral systems involved in attachment take the form of ensuring that the young of the species stay in contact with more mature members of the species who will provide for them and protect them until they are capable of doing so themselves. In precocial species (certain avian species and ungulates) this takes the form of following the mother immediately after birth. In other animals it takes the form of clinging to the mother, or calling after her. In humans it involves another set of behaviors, as described below, and the form of the attachment behaviors shows a developmental progression over time.

It is important to note that the attachment propensity involves the activation of behavioral systems in both parent and offspring. In humans, the parent and infant are innately predisposed to respond to one another in a preferential way. For their parts, infants are predisposed to emit certain kinds of *attachment behaviors*—namely, crying, clinging, smiling, tracking with the eyes, and babbling—which signal the need for the caregiver. In a complementary fashion, caregivers are said to be innately prepared to respond to such signals in a way that fosters the development of the attachment relationship. It is in the context of these early attachment behaviors and reciprocal interactions that the child comes to develop an attachment bond to the caregiver. At the emotional level, attachment implies "felt security"; the child discriminates the caregiver from others and prefers to be in this person's presence, especially under conditions of stress. Over time, the attachment process undergoes transformations at the behavioral and symbolic levels, as indicated below. Although both caregiver and infant are said to form attachments, the bulk of the research literature has focused on the growth and development of the child's attachment to the parent.

Stages of Infant Attachment

Bowlby identified four stages in the growth and development of the attachment relationship:

1. *Phase of undiscriminating social responsiveness* (1–2 months). At birth the infant does not discriminate among the various persons who attend him, nor does he express any preferences for one caregiver over another. However, both infant and parent possess certain innate behavioral propensities that encourage discrimination and selective responding, and thereby set the stage for the development of attachment. One elementary but important response on the part of the infant is the ability to orient to salient stimuli. The orientation response (OR), which has certain stereotypical behavioral components—head turning, pupil dilation, heart rate change, and the concentration of attention on the eliciting stimulus—is a prerequisite for the processing of information. Young infants show the orienting response, and certain sensory cues are more effective than others in eliciting it. Olfactory cues and speech sounds are among the most effective, with visual stimuli becoming important later on as visual acuity improves. These are cues that infants use to make discriminations between individuals. Bowlby originally believed that the ability to discriminate specific persons marked the transition to the second stage (2–7 months), but research indicates that infants develop the ability to discriminate their caregivers very early on. By as early as 1 week of age, infants can discriminate their mothers by the smell of their milk alone (MacFarlane, 1975) and there is also some evidence that young infants can discriminate their mothers on the basis of voice cues (Eibl-Eibesfeldt, 1983). Infants orient to speech sounds by turning and facing the speaker; even blind infants fixate on their speaking mothers (Freedman, 1964).

Though young infants rapidly develop the ability to discriminate persons, they lack the talent either to cling to their caregivers or pursue them in the way that the offspring of other species do. However, they have two other advantages operating for them—sets of features and behaviors that act as "releasers" of parenting behavior. Certain features of infant morphology are intrinsically appealing to adults; among nonhuman primates these include small stature and color of pelage. These infantile features, or "babyness" factors (referred to originally by Lorenz as the *Kindchen-schema*), signal juvenile status, and tend to facilitate nurturance on the part of adults, as well as serve to deflect aggression. In humans, the particularly appealing aspects of infant morphology consist of large head-to-body ratio, high forehead, plump cheeks, and large eyes.

The other means by which human infants encourage parents to take care of them—a sine qua non for survival—are the infant's attachment behaviors. Although the infant does not become capable of attachment proper (defined as a selective preference to be in proximity with another individual and which is accompanied by felt security) until the second half of the first year of life, any behavior that results in the parent staying close to the child is instrumental in promoting attachment and can be regarded as an attachment behavior. The most common forms of attachment behavior in the very young infant are sucking, crying, and gazing. During the second phase (2–7 months), when the social smile enters the repertoire, another powerful releaser of parental attachment comes into play. Still later, following and babbling join the attachment behavior repertoire.

2. *Phase of discriminating sociability* (2–7 months). Between the second and third month of life there are significant maturational changes taking place in the nervous system of infants that will affect their emotional repertoire, influence the organization of behavior, and affect the way in which behavioral systems are activated. In the affective domain, crying patterns become more differentiated and come to signal various motivational states. There is also a decrease in the amount of nonhunger fussiness (see Chapter 4). In addition, we see the emergence of the social smile, that is, the full-faced expressions of joy in response to social stimulation (occasional earlier smiles appear dim, not fully articulated and coordinated, and seemingly prompted by endogenous events). In terms of overall motor organization, reflexes (rooting, Moro, Darwinian) have disappeared from the repertoire, and, in general, behavior is less stereotypical, more fluid, and coordinated. Behavioral states are more stable (less labile) and patterns of circadian rhythm have become established.

All of these state and organizational changes have the effect of enhancing the infant's ability to extract meaningful data from his or her environment, including meaningful data about social partners. During this stage of the attachment process, the child moves beyond mere discrimination of individuals to the establishment of preferences. Although the pattern of preference does not yet signal that a selective attachment has taken place (a development that is attendant on further psychological and maturational changes that will occur in the second half of the first year), the child now demonstrates that she can differentiate caregiving that feels good and is responsive to her needs, and that which is less optimal. Differential patterns of preference are indexed largely by the quality of affective response—the fullness and intensity of the joy response to the appearance of different social partners, the differential degrees of babbling that are stimulated during interaction, and, when in distress, the ease or difficulty with which the adult is able to comfort the child. Ainsworth (1967) distinguished two phases of discriminating social responsiveness, the earlier one involving differential smiling, vocalization, and crying, the later one involving differential greeting and crying when the attachment figure leaves the room.

3. *Attachment: Proximity-seeking phase* (7–24 months). With the onset of locomotion and the understanding of means-ends relationships, the child is now more well equipped to form and pursue goals. Persons are recognized as familiar or unfamiliar and a rudimentary form of person permanence has been established; that is, the child has come to realize that a person who disappears from view does not cease to exist; this also implies that the person can be recalled. Decided preferences are now manifest and active contact-making and contact-avoiding behaviors come into play.

Spitz's and Bowlby's original research had indicated that strong preferential attachment to the caregiver did not take hold until the second half of the first year of life. From their observations of children who were involuntarily separated from their mothers, it became clear that definitive separations from the mother (long-term or permanent) could have a differential impact on the child, depending on whether the separation took place in the first half or the second half of the first year. If it occurred under 6 months, children responded with emotional distress and disturbed behavioral patterns, but the reactions were short-lived, diffuse, and the child readily adapted to a substitute caregiver. On the other hand, if the separation occurred after 7 months, the infant's distress was more profound and long-lasting. The initial efforts of the child were clearly directed at trying to recover the mother (Protest Stage), and its distress was not readily alleviated by a substitute caregiver. When the child was unable to recover the mother, he eventually drifted into the Despair Stage; he still showed evidence of missing the mother, but the behavior suggested increasing hopelessness. He may have cried intermittently, seemed withdrawn and inactive, and may have even appeared to have been in a state of deep mourning. After a while, the child once again began to show more interest in his surroundings, and appeared to be entering a period of recovery; in fact, he was slipping into a Detachment Phase. Although he may have accepted the ministrations of his substitute caregiver and may even have shown smiling and sociability, if his mother then returned he responded as though he had lost all interest in her.

On the basis of these observations Bowlby concluded that attachment was in place by 7 months. Most children, of course, are not exposed to such traumatic separation experiences, though their behavior is clearly organized in a way that reflects the underlying attachment. There are a number of attachment-related behaviors that are evident during this stage of the attachment process. Included are all of the attachment behaviors seen earlier in development—that is, smiling, crying, tracking with the eyes, babbling, and clinging—but now they are deployed more actively at the service of the set-goal of maintaining proximity with the caregiver, and several new behaviors—ambulation and calling—are also brought to bear. These behaviors are found embedded in behavioral patterns that foster the child's attachment goals. The patterns that are typical of this stage are (1) proximity-seeking and -maintaining behaviors (smiling, crying, following), (2), distress at separation and efforts to restore contact (crying, calling, following), (3) greeting behavior on reunion (smiling, babbling), and (4) fear of strangers (ambulation away from the unfamiliar person and retreat to the caregiver).

Behavioral systems subserving the exploratory instinct are also developing during this time and thus children do not maintain proximity to their caregivers continually. Instead, they tend to alternate between intervals of contact or proximity with the mother, and brief forays away from her to explore other people and objects. In this way they use the caregiver as a "secure base" from which to explore the world and confront novelty; they know that they may return for safety and comfort when they need to. In this sense, attachment behaviors imply "felt security," the feeling component of the more behavioral manifestation of attachment. According to the systems theory from which Bowlby is operating, behavioral systems seek homeostasis, and behavior is regulated accordingly. In normal growth and development, the natural tendency is to find the right balance between exploratory and attachment goals. Ideally the child must find ways of satisfying his curiosity without jeopardizing his feelings of security. He develops a set-goal for a comfortable balance between the two. In the context of moment-to-moment feedback from the environment and his own goal-corrected responses (alterations in quality, direction, and speed), he is able to maintain a homeostatic balance between the two systems. What the homeostatic balance will look like and the behaviors that will be deployed to achieve it, however, will vary from child to child. Bowlby and others have observed that there may be individual differences in how readily and intensely instinctual behaviors like attachment and exploration are activated, in the degree of competition between the systems, and in the manner of homeostatic regulation. There are various ways of implementing the balance between behavioral systems, a topic that is explored at greater length in Chapter 3 in our discussion of individual differences.

4. *Phase of goal-corrected partnership* (24 months and beyond). During this stage the child begins to understand and predict some of the caregiver's goals and needs, and begins to take them into account during his interactions with her. In the previous phase he accomplished his own set-goals by altering his own behavior so as to coincide with hers. For example, if he wanted to maintain proximity, he would simply follow her about and attempt to stay within range of her. Unable to perceive what his caregiver's future plans might be, he adopted an empirical strategy of accommodating to her behavior on a moment- to-moment basis. Sooner or later, however, in the course of observing her behavior and the contexts in which they occur, he begins to understand what prompts her actions and the likely courses of action she will take. In other words, he begins to acquire some insight into her character, motives, and feelings. At this point he has developed a more sophisticated view of the world and the people in it, all of which increases the flexibility of his own behavior, since he can now foresee that he can achieve different goals via a variety of strategies, and that he can do so in

cooperation with other individuals. In Bowlby's words, the child now becomes capable of "collaboration" with the parent; at the same time, when two goals are at odds, this sets the stage for the development of conflict and a pitting of one will against the other.

It is during the course of the above developments that the child begins to elaborate "internal working models" of the attachment relationship and of interpersonal relationships in general. That is, he evolves cognitive-emotional schemata about the way that his mother and other significant others may be expected to behave, the rules for his own behavior, and scenarios about how he and others may be expected to interact with one another. The internal working models, as they become elaborated, come to mediate the child's perception and interpretation of the interpersonal world, his predictions about behavior, and his formulation of goals and plans of action. These affective/cognitive schemas need not be very sophisticated to guide behavior. In fact, research on episode cognition and event schemas (Forgas, 1982; Nelson, 1981; Schank & Abelson, 1977) indicates that working models or internal representations of social interactions in both adults and children are organized in terms of a limited number of highly salient schematized routines and images that define the essence of socialized behavior. These rudimentary frames, however, apparently play a major role in guiding interpersonal behavior. There are three things that are particularly interesting about these schemas. First, they are imbued with a strong affective aspect and this aspect appears to be more important than objective episode features. Second, they tend to be focused on the *relationship* between the partners in the interaction. Third, research indicates that there is a strong individual difference component of episode cognitions and that they reflect differences in personality organization (Forgas, 1978). In young children it is assumed that these schemas and their idiosyncratic components derive from early attachment experiences (Bretherton, 1985).

Research on Attachment in Infancy

Systematic research on the attachment construct as it applied to human mother–infant relationships was initiated with Mary Ainsworth, a developmentalist who was first exposed to Bowlby's ideas in the early 1950s while she was associated with the Tavistock Clinic—a special research unit he had founded in London following World War II. Ainsworth subsequently tested Bowlby's ideas during a field study in Uganda, the results of which were published in 1967. As her work evolved she confirmed a number of Bowlby's formulations concerning normative development; however, in addition, she discovered there were interesting qualitative differences in the way in which individual children expressed their attachment needs. In Chapter 3 we review her original studies and examine contemporary research findings. In particular, we are especially concerned with evidence of different organizational patterns and the attempts of researchers to determine the contributing factors involved in differential development.

How Universal Is the Attachment Phenomenon in Humans?

If the attachment process in humans is analogous to that found in other animal species and represents a phylogenetic adaptation, as Bowlby's theory supposes, we would expect there to be relatively little cross-cultural variability— at least in terms of rudimentary processes and manifestations. According to Bowlby, the attachment process involves certain key behaviors in humans, and unfolds in an orderly species-typical sequence. As noted above, Mary Ainsworth was the first to document the attachment phenomenon in a systematic fashion. She was able to confirm the existence of the pattern in a sample of Ugandan families (Ainsworth, 1967); a subsequent study by Schaffer (1963) established that the phenomenon held for a sample of Scottish families as well. More recently, there has been an attempt to examine how the *component* features of the attachment pattern—(1) selective discrimination and attachment, (2) proximity seeking, (3) stranger fear, and (4) separation protest—express themselves cross-culturally.

Many years prior to Bowlby's work, Margaret Mead (1930) had promulgated the notion that a preferential emotional tie to one person was not universal, and that in some cultures— especially communal ones, as in Samoa—children are multiply attached, with no particular tie to the mother. However, Derek Freedman (1983), who also studied Samoa intensively, subsequently challenged this view, pointing out, in particular, instances of preferential following of the mother and separation protest.

Eibl-Eibesfeldt has examined various cultures for evidence of "preferential" or selective attachment by filming family and communal life. A preferential mother–child bond was found in all the cultures, even in the least likely. That is, even among the !ko bushmen, who are one of the most communal of nonliterate cultures, children develop selective emotional ties to their mothers. At one point he counted the number of different contacts that two babies in the group had. The children did make contact with a variety of individuals. During the total observation time, 486 and 542 minutes, respectively, an 8-month-old girl had 46 contacts with 289 persons other than her mother, and a young boy had 98 contacts with 22 persons other than his mother. Nevertheless, they spent 47–49% of their time in bodily contact with their mothers, 26–30% of the time was spent alone or asleep, and only 24% of the time was spent with other people. The children themselves showed preferential attachment to the mother, for example, retreating to her when strangers approached (Eibl-Eibesfeldt, 1983).

Universality of the other key attachment features also seems established. Super and Harkness (1982) have reviewed the literature on separation protest and stranger anxiety and have concluded that not only are these features invariably found across cultures, but they are found to occur with the same developmental progression.

Although it is now clear that the attachment urge is part of a biologically based adaptational system, is universal, and involves reciprocal behaviors between infant and caregiver, this in no way guarantees that it cannot go awry. Most biologically based systems are capable of some deflection from their normal trajectories, and this is no less true of the attachment system. Although all human children form some kind of attachment to their caregivers, the pattern it takes may vary from child to child because we are talking about instinctual behavior, which is patterned but not invariable, unlike reflexive behavior. Infants sometimes are born with congenital defects or difficult temperaments that do not make it easy for them to establish a good working attachment. Parents do not always provide the kind of behavior that optimally meshes with the child's attachment needs, because of personality defects in the parent, or because the wider culture sanctions less than sensitive treatment of children. It is clear that cultural traditions have a great deal to say about the kind of care children receive. The fact that attachment theory is one of the most active areas of research in developmental psychology today speaks to contemporary Western culture's general investment in and concern for children and their welfare. This was not so in earlier times. The work of John Boswell (1989) indicates that earlier in the millennium it was common for parents to treat their children with a level of neglect, abuse, and insensitivity that we would today find abhorrent. During late antiquity and the early Middle Ages, Roman families, even wealthy ones, apparently often disposed of their female infants, and even young sons were often abandoned or sold to infertile couples for adoption. Children were also sold for prostitution. Abandonment was common elsewhere on the Continent for centuries. Rousseau, an otherwise charitable and caring individual, reported in his *Confessions* that he sent all of his own five infants away to a foundling home, adding with some degree of defiance that he "made no secret of my action because I saw nothing wrong in it." The abandonment of children during the eighteenth century occurred on a very wide scale. Records indicate that at least one in four children in Toulouse were abandoned, and in Lyons and Paris it was approximately one in three. The abandonment of children apparently was a socially acceptable form of after-the-fact birth control. All of which is to say that although parents may naturally form attachments to their offspring and vice versa, biology does not guarantee this, and the tendency can be overridden by exigency, choice, or perversity.

Having introduced the idea of individual difference into the attachment equation, we now turn to a more formal treatment of that literature.

Differential Attachment
Origins and Sequelae

THE CONTRIBUTION OF MARY AINSWORTH

In 1989, Mary Ainsworth and John Bowlby received APA's award for Distinguished Scientific Contribution. Ainsworth's research was especially pivotal in forwarding the study of attachment. Her investigations established two themes that have become prominent in the literature: The role of maternal sensitivity in the establishment of secure attachment, and individual differences in the quality of the attachment relationship. She also introduced a laboratory procedure for the measurement of individual differences—the Strange Situation—a paradigm that has seen extensive use in developmental research.

Mary Salter Ainsworth was born in 1913 in Pennsylvania, but within four years the family had moved to Toronto due to her father's job transfer (Ainsworth, in O'Connell & Russo, 1983; Karen, 1990), a move that may have been more than a little upsetting given her age. Her life's work on the nature of security thus may have had some early roots. Later she admitted in an interview, "I was pretty insecure as a child, and I suppose I never really let it go" (Karen, 1990, p. 42). Ainsworth first discovered that she wanted to be a psychologist during her final year in high school after reading William McDougall's *Character and the Conduct of Life*, in some ways presaging her interest in patterns of personality.

She enrolled at the University of Toronto at the age of 16 and completed an honor's program in psychology, after which she wanted to stay on and do graduate work. Her family was supportive, but, the year being 1935, her father thought she should rather take up stenography for a while before marrying. Fortunately for psychology she persisted in her own plans. For her master's research she investigated the relation between attitudes and emotional response, using the galvanic skin response (GSR) as the measure of emotion. For her dissertation she came under the tuteledge of William Blatz, whose own life's work was absorbed with "security theory," which held that the individual needed to develop a secure dependency on parents during childhood and then to work out a mature dependency in relation to peers and eventually a life partner. The dissertation itself involved constructing two self-report scales to assess young adults regarding their relations with parents and peers. Following graduation, she applied for a job at Queens University in Ontario, and even though the department head wanted to hire her, the Senate of Queens University refused to appoint a woman (they went on to hire Donald Hebb). Instead, she took a position as lecturer back at Toronto.

During World War II she joined the Canadian Women's Army Corps to become an Army Examiner, spent 3 years in service, and mustered out as a major. She returned to teaching psychology, met her husband-to-be, and accompanied him to London when he went on to finish his Ph.D. On arrival, and quite adventitiously, a friend drew her attention to a notice in a London newspaper concerning a research position at the Tavistock Clinic under the direction of John Bowlby. The study involved an examination of the effect of separation from the mother in early childhood on personality development. Her background in security theory made her the perfect candidate and she was hired. She attended Bowlby's seminars and became deeply involved in the research at the clinic. Personally, she felt that Bowlby's acceptance of ethological explanations for attachment were off the mark, being convinced by drive theory accounts herself, and wrote him so after she had left London. Fortunately, he was not much swayed by her arguments, and in time, of course, she not only came around to his way of thinking, but became a leading exponent and produced some of the most compelling data in support of the theory. Some feel that it was she who put Bowlby on the map, and indeed Bowlby recounts in an interview, "Her work has been indispensable [in promoting attachment constructs]. It's difficult to know what might have happened otherwise" (Karen, 1990, p. 39).

Although Bowlby was of the opinion that very early experiences with maternal separations formed the basis of later deviancy and psychopathology (his book on *Forty-four Juvenile Thieves* pointed out the high proportion of delinquent boys who had experienced early maternal separations), he was not particularly interested in the interactions between infants and their mothers, finding children easier to study. Fortunately, Ainsworth had such an interest and her first opportunity to put some of Bowlby's ideas to empirical test came during a move to Africa. Her husband had secured an appointment at the East African Institute of Social Research in Kampala, Uganda, and although she felt the move might pose an obstacle to her own career, she accompanied him and exploited it in a way that was providential. Although she had applied for a government grant on mother–infant interaction and was turned down, the director of the East African Institute managed to find enough money for a salary for her and an interpreter.

Originally, Ainsworth thought she might study the weaning practices of Ganda mothers and its impact on children. In that culture, she had heard, mothers weaned their children by sending them to stay with their grandparents. However, upon her arrival, she discovered the practice no longer obtained and so, being a resourceful person, she decided to study attachment. She was able to enlist the cooperation of 28 mothers for the study. Somewhat to her surprise, what she observed converted her entirely to Bowlby's point of view and the value of the ethological perspective. Her findings are detailed in her book *Infancy in Uganda* (1967).

The First Study: Uganda

In her original study, Ainsworth observed Ganda infants and mothers over a period of several months as they went about their daily activities. She was able to establish that many of the attachment behaviors Bowlby had described could be noted in the behaviors of the youngsters she observed. By and large, infants appeared to form specific attachments to their caregivers and protested separation from them by crying or attempting to follow them. Moreover, the different stages of attachment-related behaviors appeared to unfold in a fairly predictable sequence. However, there were a number of exceptions to this rule, and it was this aspect of the data that most captivated Ainsworth's interest. Most importantly, she was struck by the fact that despite the general regularity of attachment behavior in terms of the timing and form of its appearance—which seemed to support ethological formulations concerning its basis in evolution and adaptation—some children's responses deviated from this pattern. Although in much of her future research Ainsworth was to focus on individual differences in maternal sensitivity as the chief factor behind differences in infants' attachment patterns, she did not rule out constitutional factors as contributors, and as we will see later, recent research sustains the idea that both maternal and infant factors contribute to differences in the quality of attachment. Interestingly enough, there is much in her book, *Infancy in Uganda*, to support the contribution of both factors. In her original study she discerned three groups according to the apparent strength and security of the baby's attachment to the mother: (1) a securely attached group consisting of 16 children, (2) an insecurely-attached group of seven children, and (3) a "nonattached" group of five children. The latter children were so designated because they did not show any of the usual patterns of attachment throughout the entire period of observation.

The designation of a group of children as nonattached was provisional and not sustained in her future work. Her later work convinced her that all children become attached, though they may vary in the level of felt security and certain children may conceal their need for their mothers. With respect to the present study and the nonattached group, there were certain features that stood out. One child, who was developmentally delayed and did not seem to discriminate her mother from others even by 15 months, was considered nonattached since theory held that discrimination is necessary for attachment. Another child (at 1 year) did not show a discrimination of her own mother from another mother who was a familiar caretaker and a member of the household. She did not cry when her mother left nor attempt to follow. Greeting responses were not observed. She liked to explore her world but did not use her mother as a secure base for exploration. Ainsworth remarked that she showed features of being "precociously independent." Another baby had perinatal complications; the mother did not or could not breast-feed her and the baby did not flourish on artificial feeding. Though a friendly baby who smiled a great deal, the smiling appeared to be undiscriminating even at 47 weeks of age. She accepted the attentions of the other wife in the household as readily as those of her own mother. Differential discriminations of her mother and father did not occur till about 40 weeks, a feat most infants accomplished in the first quarter of the first year. Finally, a set of twins demonstrated very little attachment behavior. At 23 weeks they were described as lifting their heads and vocalizing, a rather late developmental accomplishment. At 32 weeks one twin would cry when strangers were present, but the other "liked people." Neither baby cried when the mother left the room and both were described as behaving toward the mother no differently than they behaved toward others.

Because of the foregoing characteristics, this group could not be described as attached. Ainsworth felt that the root cause of the failure in attachment had to do with infant confusion over multiple caregivers, or as stemming from inadequate maternal attention. However, it is moot as to whether the lack of clear attachment behavior was caused by caregiver factors alone. One child was physically weak because of feeding difficulties; others appeared to be developmentally delayed; one did not appear so much nonattached as multiply attached (perhaps not surprising given the somewhat communal and polygynous nature of this community), and the difference in the fraternal twins can be interpreted as suggesting temperament differences.

The securely attached group showed following, approaching, active greeting, and the like. These children were judged to be securely attached largely on the basis of the criterion of infrequent crying, although they might cry if parted from their mothers or if particularly hungry.

The seven insecurely attached children were so classified largely on the basis of frequent crying. These children were relatively fussy babies. They cried when parted from their mothers, but they also cried a great deal when their mothers were present. They cried to be picked up and then cried when they were put down. Although three of the children were weak and sickly for various reasons (illness, insufficient breast milk), Ainsworth felt that maternal anxiety and some level of rejection were at the heart of the problem for all of the insecurely attached children. Four of the mothers had been separated from or deserted by their husbands. One mother had conflict with another wife in the household. Ainsworth also guessed that certain infant care practices were not conducive to the formation of secure attachment such as multiple mothering and substitute caretaking.

In an attempt to get a better idea of the variables involved in differential attachment, she generated seven maternal care factors that were potential contributors to attachment, classified each of the mothers, and used median split tests and chi-square analysis to assess significant differences among the securely attached, nonattached, and weakly attached children. The list of factors included (1) maternal warmth, (2) individual or multiple mothering, (3) demand versus scheduled feeding, (4) the adequacy of the mother's milk supply, (5) amount of care given by the mother, (6) her excellence as an informant about her infant, and (7) her attitude toward breast feeding.

Only the latter three variables were found to discriminate the groups. Contrary to Ainsworth's expectation, it did not seem to matter if the infant had multiple mothers, and yet, if the sharing of mothering duties unduly reduced the amount of care the mother gave the baby, attachment appeared to be adversely affected. Low ratings on amount of care were found only for the nonattached group. The mothers of the nonattached infants regularly left their babies for long periods and shared their mothering duties with others even when they themselves were available to give the babies care. Although this finding appears to implicate uncaring mothers, this group of children was previously described as developmentally delayed (except for one "precociously independent" child) and somewhat passive. It is generally known that more passive, so-called easy babies do not elicit the amount of care that more active and demanding infants do, as acknowledged by Bowlby himself (second edition of *Attachment and Loss*, 1982), so there may have been some confounding in these findings.

In terms of the variable "mother's excellence as an informant"; Ainsworth found that the data they had on the nonattached babies were more meager than was the case of the other children, and thus those mothers received low ratings on this variable. Implicit in a high rating is that the mother had a keen interest in her baby, was sensitively perceptive to his ways of behaving, and enjoyed talking about him. In contrast, low ratings seemed to indicate a lack of interest and lack of knowledge of the baby.

The third variable, mother's attitude toward breast-feeding, also discriminated the nonattached children from the other children. Fourteen mothers stated without qualification that they enjoyed breast-feeding. Twelve of these were mothers of securely attached infants; none were mothers of nonattached babies.

In summarizing these results it is important to note that the main differences were between the nonattached children and the others. How much of their differential attachment can be attributed to maternal behaviors and how much to constitutional differences in the infants themselves could not be discriminated. There were no major findings with respect to the insecurely or weakly attached group. This may have been due to inadequacies of measurement, or to the small sample size. A replication study was clearly called for. Ainsworth came away from this study convinced of the value of the ethological approach. She had been able to document the features of attachment behavior and to confirm some of the basic assumptions of attachment theory. She was, however, most intrigued by the individual differences she observed among infants and felt she had made some headway in understanding their origins. She believed that qualitative differences in infant-mother attachments were related to differences in the way mothers responded to the emotional signals of their infants early in life, which could stem from personality factors and the exigencies of harsh economic circumstances. At this point she viewed her findings with respect to the maternal contributory variables as preliminary—as appropriate—since her analyses had been post hoc, but her detailed and astute observations served her well and laid the groundwork for the more formal test she later conducted in Baltimore (Ainsworth et al., 1978).

The Second Study: Baltimore

In 1962 Ainsworth launched the landmark Baltimore study of mother–infant attachment. Because she believed that differences in maternal sensitivity to infant cues were at the heart of differential treatment of infants and resulted in differences in attachment, she set out to study this more systematically. In particular, she sought detailed information on the nature of early mother–infant interaction before the onset of attachment. Twenty-six Baltimore families agreed to participate in the study. Home visits for most of the children began at 3 to 4 weeks following delivery and continued at 3-week intervals to about 54 weeks. Each visit lasted about 4 hours for a total of approximately 72 hours of observation on each infant.

The mothers and infants were observed during feeding sessions and other routine caregiving. Bowlby (1969) originally defined maternal sensitivity as the caregiver's ability to read and respond appropriately to infant attachment signals, and Ainsworth believed that routine caregiving in the context of the home would be the most natural and optimal way to get a reading on sensitivity. Maternal sensitivity to infant cues was evaluated by coding and scoring variables such as the mother's attention to the infant, her timing of responses to the infant's signals, the pacing of the feeding session, the degree of en face orientation to the infant, and the way in which the feeding session was terminated.

One aspect of the study that disappointed her was the failure to observe the "secure base" phenomenon. Recall that this refers to the child's tendency to explore while in the presence of the caregiver, and consists of tentative exploration with intermittent returns to the caregiver to restore confidence. In the African study, Ganda babies displayed the secure base phenomenon. If the mother was at home, the child would roam about exploring the environment and would look back occasionally; if the mother left the room the baby would tend to cry and would cease further exploration. However, in the Baltimore study the children were more used to having their mothers come and go. Because of the lack of a secure base phenomenon, Ainsworth suspected that she would need an environment other than the home in which to assess the security of attachment and this was the impetus to the laboratory part of the study. The development of the laboratory procedure, which has come to be known as the Strange Situation, was developed in an inspirational half hour, according to Ainsworth (Karen, 1990). The basic goal at the time was to provide an environment in which the child would be tempted to explore, but which would be sufficiently strange and unfamiliar so as to elicit the secure base phenomenon. Ainsworth decided to use a laboratory at the university that she could turn into a playroom.

The Strange Situation procedure consists of a set of eight episodes—seven 3-minute episodes and one slightly longer introductory session. Collectively, these episodes constitute a graded series of increasingly stressful events that challenge the child's felt security. In the first session the child and mother meet the experimenter. In the second they are left to wait in an unfamiliar but nicely furnished playroom. During the third episode, an unfamiliar female enters the room and after an interval of time attempts to engage the child in conversation and play. In episode 4, the mother leaves the room on signal and the child is left alone with the stranger. In episode 5, the mother returns and the stranger leaves. In the sixth episode the mother leaves and the infant is alone. During the seventh episode the stranger returns, and in episode 8 the mother returns.

In the original Baltimore study, Ainsworth used the Strange Situation for the assessment of attachment when the children were 12 months old. Twenty-three of the original mother–infant dyads participated. Three major types of attachment patterns were identified: An anxious, avoidant attachment (A classification), a secure attachment (B), and an anxious, resistant attachment, later known as an ambivalent attachment (C). Subtypes were also discriminated, including a passive C2 subtype and an angry C1 subtype, A1 and A2 subtypes, and four subclassifications within the B group. A fourth major classification (D) has recently been added to the classification scheme, representing a disorganized pattern of behavior that includes elements of the A and C categories (i.e., both avoidant and ambivalent behaviors), but this type still remains to be validated against home observations during the first year.

Attachment patterns are discriminated on the basis of the child's behavior in all the episodes, but especially on how the child responds to the mother during the two reunion episodes (episodes 5 and 8). Children who are classified as *avoidantly attached* rarely show positive affect to the mother during preseparation and there is an avoidance of proximity. During the reunion the child either ignores the mother, greets her casually, or actively avoids her and turns away. If the child is picked up there is no tendency to cling, but there is also little active resistance to contact. *Securely attached* children, in contrast, appear happy when the mother is around and distressed upon separation. At reunion they stop crying if they have been crying, or show some combination of greeting behavior, joy, and relief. They actively seek comfort, and are comforted by the mother's ministrations. They are able to recover from their distress and return to play in a relatively short period of time. *Ambivalent/resistant* children display conspicuous contact-seeking behavior mixed with contact-avoiding behavior, and thus they appear ambivalent. They may cry continuously while the mother is gone and may be unable to calm down even after the mother has returned. If they show the passive pattern (C2), they tend to cry piteously and do not seem to be able to get the comfort they need even when the mother returns. The C1 children allow themselves to be picked up but then show resistance; they may hit or strike the mother and squirm angrily in her arms.

Ainsworth's goal was to relate the different attachment patterns to the maternal sensitivity ratings that were made earlier in infancy. Consistent with expectations, all the 1-year-olds whose feeding pattern reflected relatively high sensitivity on the part of the mother were found to be securely attached. Mothers whose feeding style was rated as relatively insensitive had children who showed insecure attachments (A and C); they were less likely to pick up their infants when they cried, and were less affectionate and tender. Home ratings of the mother's behavior during the fourth quarter of the first year also predicted children's attachment behavior as either secure or insecure. Mothers whose infants showed the avoidant pattern tended to be rejecting, averse to close bodily contact, and emotionally flat.

Although Bowlby (1958) referred to sensitivity as an important factor facilitating the attachment process, a detailed description of the component parts was first articulated by Ainsworth and is found in Ainsworth, Bell, and Stayton (1971). According to these authors, maternal sensitivity consists of (1) the mother's awareness of her infant's signals, (2) her ability to accurately interpret them, (3) her tendency to respond appropriately, that is with the right intervention, and (4) the promptness and contingency of her response.

There are three other maternal-difference variables thought to affect the development of attachment and which are scored on the basis of mother–infant interaction. These include the bipolar dimensions of (1) acceptance versus rejection, (2) cooperation versus interference, and (3) accessibility versus ignoring. An *accepting* mother is characterized as having an open emotional awareness of both positive and negative feelings toward her infant, and a nondefensive acceptance of these feelings within herself and of the infant's expression of positive and negative affect. The *cooperating* mother adjusts to her baby as much as she facilitates the baby's adjustment to herself; she guides rather than controls her infant's behavior. In contrast, the interfering mother seems to want to "train" her infant and to shape it to fit her own conception of the good baby. She also tends to overwhelm the baby with verbal and physical manipulations. *Accessible* mothers are emotionally available to their infants. In contrast, ignoring mothers tend to neglect them, either because they are distracted, overly self-involved, or because they do not know how to meet their baby's needs. Assessments of each of the three dimensions, plus that of sensitivity, are based on global ratings involving 9-point scales. Maternal sensitivity is highly intercorrelated with the other three dimensions.

During the 1970s Ainsworth's work began to receive more and more attention. The attachment construct and attention to children's emotional lives filled a void in a literature that had been dominated almost exclusively by cognitive models of child development. Much new research on children's affective development was initiated during the 1970s and 1980s and as a result of these investigations, there is now a considerable literature on attachment. A great deal is now known about the distribution of the various attachment types in the population at large, about the persistence of attachment styles beyond infancy, and about the way in which attachment style relates to other aspects of personality and cognitive development. At this point we turn to that literature.

DISTRIBUTION OF ATTACHMENT TYPES

How common is the avoidant attachment style? Is it a truly deviant style, or simply one of several fairly common variations on the attachment theme? What about the relative numbers of secure or ambivalent attachments? Following the original Baltimore study, Ainsworth and colleagues extended her work with further samples of subjects. The resulting research is detailed in *Patterns of*

Attachment, a Psychological Study of the Strange Situation (Ainsworth et al., 1978). In that report, the majority of a total pool of 106 children, 66%, were evaluated as securely attached, 22% were classified as avoidantly attached, and only 12% as ambivalently attached. Because the sample was modest in size and because there had been no attempt to achieve a demographically representative sample, there was a lingering question as to whether the relative distribution of attachment types found in this study was generally true of the population at large, or whether it was only locally applicable. Fortunately, in the decades since the publication of her Baltimore study, dozens of studies employing the Strange Situation assessment of children's attachment styles have been conducted in this country as well as in Germany, Great Britain, the Netherlands, China, Japan, Israel, and Sweden.

IJzendoorn & Kroonenberg (1988) reviewed all of the extant studies that met certain criteria and aggregated the data from nearly 2,000 Strange Situation assessments (from eight different countries) in several ways. Their goal was to compare different samples of attachment distributions in order to assess the degree of intersample variation. They also wanted to assess intercultural and intracultural variation across different societies. The authors found that in each sample the B classification (secure) was modal, except for one sample from the northern part of what was at that time West Germany, in which the A classification (avoidant) was modal. Table 1 presents the percentages of A, B, and C classifications for the eight countries representing 32 individual samples as well as for the entire pooled data. As indicated in the table, the overall distribution (across all 32 samples) closely approximates Ainsworth's distribution. It is also obvious that the distributions vary somewhat for certain areas of the world. Only certain differences are statistically significant, namely, that A classifications are relatively more prevalent in Western European countries and C classifications relatively more frequent in Israel and Japan. We will have more to say about cross-cultural differences later on. Suffice it to say that the overall pattern, as well as the pattern within the United States, closely matches the distributions originally found by Ainsworth.

Table 1. Distribution of Attachment Types (Percentages) across Various Samples

Samples	Attachment type (%)		
	A	B	C
Germany (FRG) (3 samples, N = 136)	35	57	8
Great Britain (1 sample, N = 72)	22	75	3
Netherlands (4 samples, N = 251)	26	67	6
Sweden (1 sample, N = 51)	22	74	4
Israel (2 sample, N = 118)	7	64	29
Japan (2 samples, N = 96)	5	68	27
China (1 sample, N = 36)	25	50	25
USA (18 samples, N = 1230)	21	65	14
Total (32 samples, N = 1990)	21	65	14

CONTINUITY OF ATTACHMENT CLASSIFICATION OVER TIME

Attachment classification is rarely assessed before 12 months. Most studies apply the Strange Situation procedure around 12 to 13 months, although it is said to be valid up until the second year, and several investigators have used it beyond the second year, sometimes with multiple assessments. How stable are the classifications derived from the Strange Situation over time? This question relates to concerns about both the test–retest reliability of the assessment instrument (the Strange Situation) and the continuity of the behavior that is being measured. If the Strange Situation is unduly sensitive to day-to-day fluctuations in children's moods or vulnerable to the effect of transitory stress or illness, such that classification status changes readily from one period of measurement to another, then the ultimate value of the procedure and the conclusions that can be drawn about the meaning of an individual child's classification status would be very much suspect. If the procedure were this vulnerable, one would have to question whether it really measured something as fundamental as an attachment relationship that had taken 12 months or more to consolidate, or whether something more variable and trivial were being measured.

Campos, Barrett, Lamb, Goldsmith, and Stenberg (1983) performed an analysis based on eight studies in which the Strange Situation procedure had been used to assess attachment on two different occasions. They found that the degree of agreement over classification status as measured at two points in time ranged from an overall of 48% to 96%, with three of the studies showing an association that was hardly different from chance, two indicating near-perfect concordance, and the other three showing a moderate degree of concordance. Taken together, this might be viewed as damaging evidence with respect to the procedure as well as the theory. However, closer inspection of how the studies cluster in terms of those that find consistency and those that do not is elucidating. In general, samples that involve largely intact, middle-class families show a high concordance between the two points of measurement, whereas those reporting low concordance usually involve samples undergoing greater environmental stress or a relatively major change in family circumstances.

In summary, it appears that in the main, attachment classifications are "relatively" stable, unless families are subjected to undue adverse circumstances. However, even those studies showing rates of concordance in the 70s and 80s fail to account for a sizable percentage of children who do not show such stability, a point to which we later return. Studies showing continuity of attachment classification over time tend to interpret such findings as evidence of the influence of what Bowlby termed "internal working models."

The Role of Internal Working Models in Stability of Attachment Classification

Bowlby (1973) introduced the concept of "working models" as a means of conceptualizing the way in which the brain receives, stores, and processes information about the environment in relation to an individual's coping ability. Young children, he believed, come to elaborate internal working models (affective/cognitive representations) of the attachment figure and of close relationships in general in the course of early development. Over time multiple working models of other significant individuals in the child's environment also come to be elaborated. These representations become further internalized and incorporated into an individual's sense of self and sense of self-in-relation. Working models then come to constitute a central component of personality, organizing thoughts, emotions, and behaviors relevant to the attachment object as well as the self. For example, the securely attached child develops a working model of relationships as rewarding, comes to trust in the availability of the person or persons to whom she is attached, comes to see the self as worthy, and is able to regulate distress in adaptive ways. In contrast, the insecure child comes to perceive close relationships as aversive and unsatisfying, and develops a concept of the self as devalued and unworthy of receiving attention and care. Once organized, working models are said to operate largely outside of conscious experience. Moreover, since new information is assimilated to existing models, these models are thought to become relatively resistant to significant change (Bretherton, 1985).

Bowlby's concept of internal working models went far beyond the kind of internal representation that was known in the psychoanalytic literature of the time. Bowlby had trained with and respected the eminent émigré psychoanalyst, Melanie Klein, the developer of psychoanalytic play therapy. But he did not take well to her theories concerning the mental life of the infant, which often portrayed the infant as holding extremely aggressive and destructive fantasies and intentions.

> I trained with the Kleinians... but I parted company with them, because I held that real-life events—the way parents treat a child—are of key importance in determining development, and Melanie Klein would have none of it. The object relations that she was talking about were entirely internal relationships [i.e., fantasy]. The notion that internal relationships reflect external relationships was totally missing from her thinking. (Karen, 1990, p. 44)

Bowlby felt that his own type of reality-grounded internal working models was more heuristically viable than the kind of idea the Kleinians were working with, and he continued to elaborate on the properties of internal models over the course of his three-volume work. With respect to the issue of the stability of attachment patterns and internal working models, although Bowlby was of the opinion that internal models functioned in relatively stable ways in the personality, he also understood that working models can undergo adjustment at significant personal junctures in development. Furthermore, as Bretherton (1985) notes, internal models of attachment figures must be revised, especially in childhood when growth and development are rapid. In large measure, modifications will take the form of developing ever more sophisticated conceptualizations of the self, social partners, and the physical world. The *working* aspect of working models can be interpreted as meaning that models are ultimately provisional. This part of the construct has received less attention in developmental research, but will be theoretically valuable when we attempt to consider some of the anomalies that have accumulated in the attachment literature. In the meantime we can begin to consider what the mental representations of attachment relationships look like and how they are played out in personality development; some of this literature is discussed within the context of studies that have looked at the emotional and cognitive sequelae of different styles of attachment as assessed in infancy.

Predictive Validity of Early Attachment Relationships and Their Developmental Sequelae

Originally Ainsworth distinguished three major attachment classifications and eight subclassifications. A review of the literature by Malatesta (1990) indicates that there is ample evidence for the utility of distinguishing between secure and insecure attachments in terms of the ability of these classifications to predict future socioemotional and cognitive developments. Collectively, the literature indicates that securely attached infants have longer attention spans and are more affectively positive during free play. They exhibit greater curiosity, more autonomous exploration, and have more flexible egos. They also show less frustration in problem-solving situations and are more enthusiastic. In interaction with peers they show greater social competence and in interaction with adults they are described as more compliant (Ainsworth et al., 1978) or obedient (Bretherton, 1990). In contrast, children who are insecurely attached are more negative with peers and less compliant with teachers. They also display less empathy toward others in distress, are more likely to misperceive cartoon stimuli as having negative intentions, and are less likely to reveal their own distressed feelings when under conditions of stress. During problem-solving tasks, they are more readily frustrated, whiny, and negativistic.

In summary, securely attached children appear to be more generally competent and more well-adjusted than children who are classified into either one of the insecure groups. Few studies have reported longitudinal data on the developmental sequelae related to the distinction between avoidant and resistant types of insecure classifications. Part of the reason for this is that the C classification is not well represented in most studies since attachment study sample sizes tend to be relatively small and the C category accounts for only 7% to 15% of the subjects (Cassidy & Berlin, 1994). Consequently, the Cs are typically combined with the As in one larger "insecure group," which is then contrasted with the secure group. Of those studies that differentiate between children classified as A versus C, or A versus D (disorganized pattern), the following differences have been noted.

In a preschool follow-up study, Sroufe (1983) found that children who had been classified as resistant on the basis of their Strange Situation behavior during the first year showed more low-level dependency with their teachers, were more impulsive, and displayed ineptness in their transactions with peers, whereas children classified as avoidant tended not to seek help from teachers when injured, disappointed, or otherwise stressed, and showed greater hostility and distance toward their peers.

In a study of 6-year-olds who had been previously classified during a Strange Situation assessment at 1 year (Main, Kaplan, & Cassidy, 1985), children were asked to draw a picture of their family and to respond to a set of pictures involving mild and severe separation scenes and to the presentation of a family photograph. Children's conversations with their parents upon reunion following a 1-hour separation were also analyzed. Family drawings by children who were rated as securely attached in infancy depicted family members as close but not clinging, often with outstretched arms. They responded to pictured separations with coherent, open responses, and well-elaborated stories. Their responses to a family photograph shown to them during separation were also responsive and open. Upon reunion with their mothers they were able to converse in a fluent manner and to discuss a wide range of topics. In contrast, children who had been classified as avoidant in infancy drew pictures of their family in which family members were more removed from one another, sometimes lacked arms, and at times appeared to be masking their emotions with false smiles. In the pictured separation, they described the children as sad but were unable to think of a solution to the children's distress. When examining a family photograph while separated from their own parents, they turned away, dropped the photograph, or handed it to the examiner. Upon reunion, their talk tended to be unelaborated and impersonal; and they sometimes asked questions of a rhetorical nature or which had yes/no answers. Children who as infants had shown a disorganized/disoriented (D) pattern, drew family pictures that had bizarre elements, including strange marks and odd items that did not fit with the theme of the rest of the picture; objects and figures were sometimes left unfinished or were blotted out. Their response to a pictured separation either was one of silence or was irrational or odd. They reacted to photographs of their own family with depressed affect or disorganization. Upon reunion their conversations were dysfluent and they tended to focus almost exclusively on relationship topics.

The above investigations had sufficient distributions of secure, avoidant, and ambivalent children to detect differences between avoidant and ambivalent behavior patterns within the same study, but these kinds of studies are in the minority. The profile of the avoidant and ambivalent child is more clearly in evidence in samples with either a higher than average proportion of avoidant children (Suess, Grossmann, & Sroufe, 1992), a higher than average proportion of ambivalent children (Miyake, Chen, & Campos, 1985; Sagi et al., 1985), or when the findings are aggregated across studies (Cassidy & Berlin, 1994).

In the Suess et al. (1992) study, children who were avoidantly (versus securely) attached to their mothers in infancy, at 5 years showed less concentrated play, less autonomous conflict resolution, a greater tendency to withdraw under conflict, lower impulse control, more of a tendency to interpret cartoon stimuli as having negative intentions, and more scapegoating; an avoidant attachment relationship to the father predicted greater negative affect during play, greater tension in interpersonal contact, and less autonomous conflict resolution.

Cassidy and Berlin's (1994) narrative review of the attachment literature, with respect to the developmental outcome of infants classified as falling into the ambivalent (C) category, indicates that in contrast to securely attached children, ambivalently attached youngsters display more fearfulness, submissiveness, and inhibition in exploration with both toys and peers.

In summary, the predictive validity of the classifications derived from the Strange Situation assessment procedure is well established for the secure versus insecure distinction, less so for A versus C or D. There has been almost no attempt to establish the predictive validity of the A1 versus A2, or C1 versus C2, nor among the several B subclassifications. As indicated, this may be partly due to restrictions imposed by sample size, but in a later section we consider the possibility, advanced by Campos et al. (1983) and Malatesta (1990), that attachment classifications may not constitute the most optimal system for summarizing individual differences in Strange Situation behavior or in identifying aspects of personality and character that will predict and explicate a greater range of behaviors. Chapters 9 and 10 develop this idea in greater detail and provide a theoretical framework that may prove fruitful. We turn now to a consideration of how infant temperament and other factors may influence children's behavior in the Strange Situation and thus their attachment classification. We also consider the differential contribution of infant and caregiver to attachment outcomes.

DIFFERENTIAL CONTRIBUTION OF CAREGIVER AND INFANT TO OBSERVED DIFFERENCES IN STRANGE SITUATION CLASSIFICATIONS

Consistent with Ainsworth's original formulations, many attachment researchers regard differences in children's attachment classifications as a function of maternal sensitivity (or insensitivity) to infant emotional signals. In this section we discuss other maternal behaviors that have been implicated in differential attachment, as well as sources of variance that derive from child characteristics.

A first question we might ask is, how well do maternal variables predict attachment classification? Recall that Ainsworth's original research revealed a relation between measures of maternal sensitivity as observed in the first few months of life, and the child's attachment patterns at 12 months. Since that time, there have been several replication studies utilizing the rating scales developed by Ainsworth, as well as other conceptually similar measures as predictors of subsequent attachment. A meta-analysis of these studies by Goldsmith and Alansky (1987) indicated that the relation between maternal sensitivity and Strange Situation behavior (secure versus insecure attachment groups) had an average effect size of .36 (which corresponds to a Pearson correlation of about .16); this is considerably lower than that found in the original Ainsworth study. The stronger effect observed in Ainsworth's study probably relates to the fact that the Ainsworth data were admittedly selected (Ainsworth et al., 1978, p. 148) with the consequent risk of confounding between the measures of maternal sensitivity and measures of children's behavior patterns. Nevertheless, the meta-analysis, based on nonconfounded studies, sustains the thesis that children's attachment patterns are significantly associated with maternal sensitivity as assessed during infancy.

Although the above findings seem to validate attachment theory claims that maternal sensitivity is a key variable in determining the quality of attachment, some authors have pointed out that since maternal sensitivity in these studies is assessed in the context of caregiving—that is, during interaction with infants—it is essentially confounded with infant characteristics, especially since the measurement is taken several weeks after birth in most instances (see, e.g., discussion by Goldberg, Perotta, Minde, & Corter [1986]). In effect, a dyad is being assessed, not just the mother; moreover, it involves the history of the dyad—which means that some amount of mutual adjustment has already taken place. If an infant is sickly or irritable, the mother's solicitations may not work very effectively and she may appear "insensitive" despite her efforts, or she may have become insensitive over time after experiencing frustration in her efforts to minister to the infant. Of course, one could argue that a sensitive mother would be able to accommodate to and successfully deal with any infant, no matter how difficult. The mother is, after all, an adult and should be able to adjust her behavior to that of the infant no matter what. However, it is conceivable that there are upper limits to this kind of accommodation and to the infant's ultimate responsiveness. In any event, it is still of interest to examine how temperament factors may constitute risk for the development of certain patterns of attachment. While there has been a good deal of research looking at the correlation between temperament variables and attachment classification, the most valid studies are those that have assessed temperament in the opening days of life.

The Role of Temperament in Quality of Attachment

Kagan (1982) has suggested that the differential behavioral patterns of children in the Strange Situation may not be purely due to differences in maternal sensitivity or other aspects of the mother–infant relationship history, but to individual differences in the infant's susceptibility to stress, the Strange Situation being one such stressor that releases the differences. He implies that the differential behaviors are not so much an emotional reaction to separation from the caregiver figure per se, but to the overall stress of the situation. Any stressful situation would serve to differentiate the groups. Babies showing the A pattern may appear undisturbed and nonchalant with respect to mother's leave-taking and return, not so much because they are not attached to their mothers or are defensively denying their attachment needs, but because they have a high threshold for stress and do not become upset easily. Children who show the C pattern may simply have a very low threshold for distress, and children with the B pattern an intermediate level of susceptibility to stress. If Kagan's argument is correct, and if one could expose children to varying levels of stress, it should be possible to make any child look like an A, B, or C child. There is little doubt that a child who classifies as A in the Strange Situation could be induced to come apart if frightening enough circumstances could be arranged, but this is not an idea that appeals to many psychologists. However, data from studies of temperament and from studies using the Strange Situation in other cultures indicate that there is more than an element of truth to the threshold argument.

Frodi and Thompson (1985) analyzed infants' patterns of crying during the Strange Situation and found that cry-onset characteristics, intensity of crying, and recovery characteristics varied along a continuum across A1, A2, B1, B2, B3, B4, C1, and C2 classifications, from the low end at A1 to the high end at C2. As such, cry characteristics of infants in the B1 and B2 subgroups were more similar to those of the avoidant infants than to those infants in the B3 and B4 groups, whose cry characteristics, in turn, were more similar to those of resistant/ambivalent (C1, C2) infants. Thus, the separation and reunion reactions split the samples into two groups that cut across the secure versus insecure group distinction. These data suggest that infants may vary in their arousal levels in the way that Kagan indicated, which may set up a susceptibility to behave in ways that suggest insecure attachment if cry characteristics are either very mild or very extreme. A subsequent study by Belsky and Rovine (1987) found significant concordance between infant–mother and infant–father Strange Situation classifications when scored in terms of A1–B2 versus B3–C2, but not when scored in terms of the traditional A, B, C distinction. Mothers of A1-B2 infants described their infants as less difficult to care for at 3 months and newborn data on these infants indicated that they had shown more autonomic stability than B3–C2 infants and were more alert and positively responsive. These authors interpret their data as indicating that temperament factors influence whether or not the child places in the A1–B2 group or in the B3–C2 group. However, in their view, temperament does not necessarily determine whether infants develop secure or insecure relationships with their parents. Infant temperament affects the manner in which security or insecurity is expressed rather than whether or not the infant develops a secure or insecure attachment. For example, an irritable child with a sensitive mother might achieve a relationship that would result in a B4 classification, whereas an irritable child with an insensitive mother might develop a relationship that would result in a C1 or C2 classification.

Goldsmith and Alansky (1987) reasoned that temperamental proneness to distress should be related to contact resistance in the Strange Situation, which is the major defining feature of the ambivalent form of insecure attachment. Consequently, they examined the relation between this variable and subsequent classification as ambivalent (C) versus secure (B). Eighteen studies relevant to the temperament/attachment issue were identified and subjected to meta-analysis. The data indicated that distress proneness predicted resistant behavior in the Strange Situation with a small significant effect ($r = .16$). This is equivalent to the correlational effect size for maternal contribution to attachment style, as assessed in the same meta-analysis.

A study by Grossmann, Grossmann, Spangler, Suess, and Unzner (1985) found a relation between another temperament variable during the neonatal period—ability to orient to facial and vocal stimuli—and was able to link this to differential attachment, specifically, to avoidant (A) attachment. In this investigation, which was the first cross-cultural replication attempt of the original Ainsworth study, 49 north German families participated from earliest infancy. The study took advantage of the low level of maternal sedation during delivery and the longer hospital stay (about 9 days) of German mothers, to administer Brazelton's Neonatal Behavioral Assessment Scale (NBAS) on three separate occasions. A factor analysis of the NBAS measure yielded two main factors,

Orienting Ability (attention to visual and auditory stimuli) and Irritability. The first factor was found to discriminate securely attached infants from avoidantly attached infants to a significant degree, and the item that was the single best predictor was Orienting to Face. Infants who were poor orientors during the neonatal period were more likely to show the avoidant attachment pattern at 12 months. Maternal sensitivity ratings made during home visits at 2 and 6 months also predicted attachment security. However, newborn orientation scores were not related to maternal sensitivity ratings and the two measures made independent and equivalent contributions to attachment security. Thus, once again, both maternal and infant variables were found to contribute to the quality of attachment, in this case to the avoidant style. The Irritation factor was not significantly related to attachment style. From other research one would expect it to be related to the C classification. C classifications were relatively rare in this sample and thus the association could have been attenuated.

The Grossmann et al. (1985) study also provided data that indicate that certain temperament traits may be more resistant to the effects of attentive caregiving than others. Some of the mothers in a selected subsample received an experimental treatment during the lying-in period. In terms of contact with their infants while they were in the hospital, mothers received early, extended contact, both early and extended contact, or routine contact. It was therefore possible to evaluate the extent to which increased contact by the mother affected infant irritability or orientation during the first 9 days of life. Mother–infant dyads who had early, extended, or early/extended contact had greater scores in four of the five items making up the orientation factor than infants in the routine care condition. Only two of the irritability items showed an effect of the mother's contact condition and even these did not indicate a consistent and interpretable pattern. As such, the data appeared to indicate that infant orientation is susceptible to improvement with mothering in the first few days of life, whereas irritability may be more resistant to effects of the mother.

In summary, both maternal sensitivity ratings and infant temperament variables have been found to be significant predictors of infant attachment at 1 year. The Goldsmith and Alansky (1987) meta-analysis, which was based on a large number of studies, found that the effect sizes associated with maternal sensitivity and with infant distress proneness, while significant, were not very great, which is somewhat disappointing, since psychologists obviously would like to account for a large percentage of the variance in children's personality development. Nevertheless, these two factors are obviously at play in the formation of differential personality, as predicted by theory. Although attachment researchers have tended to place greater emphasis on the role of maternal variables, Bowlby's view, as informed by Waddington's theory of epigenesis (described in Volume 2 of *Attachment and Loss* in the chapter "Pathways for the Growth of Personality"), was that personality is a product of the constant interaction between genetic and environmental influences. Contemporary research thus seems to support this understanding of development.

The fact that maternal sensitivity ratings and infant temperament ratings account for a relatively small amount of the variance in children's attachment classification status suggests that other influences are at work. Moreover, as the Grossmanns point out (Grossmann & Grossmann, 1990; Grossmann et al., 1985) the attachment construct encompasses far more behavior than is likely captured by a single standardized assessment procedure, in this case the Strange Situation. We turn now to a consideration of maternal personality variables beyond sensitivity that are thought to contribute to the quality of the child's attachment.

Maternal Personality Characteristics Associated with Differential Attachment Classifications

What other factors besides the infant variables of distress proneness and poor orienting and the maternal variables of sensitivity might be involved in differential attachment? A good number of studies have examined maternal personality variables as assessed by observations of behavior and through personality tests. Behavioral assessments of maternal personality are frequently made in the context of early mother–infant interaction, or concurrently with child attachment ratings, and thus are confounded with child variables. Consequently, it is difficult to ascertain the causal connection between these factors, if any. For example, as indicated earlier, mothers of avoidantly attached infants were found to be less emotionally expressive than the mothers of securely attached infants and to engage in less close bodily contact, as observed several weeks prior to the infant attachment assessment. However, infants later classed as avoidant tend to be less emotionally labile than infants later classified as secure (Thompson & Lamb, 1984). Thus both A babies and their mothers may be constitutionally less disposed toward physical contact and to less overt expressivity—that is, they may share a genetic trait. Or it could be that A babies who are congenitally phlegmatic reward their mothers less often with bright smiles and animated vocalization than their more active counterparts, and thus cause their mothers to relate to them in a more subdued manner. Alternatively, it may be that affectively "cold" mothers cause their infants to avoid them and to control their emotional displays. Any one of these patterns could account for the above observation. Unfortunately, the data at hand do not allow us to chose among such alternatives. Consequently, the literature on maternal personality variables and infant attachment patterns should be read with this in mind.

As assessed largely in home settings, mothers of avoidant infants have been described as having more of an aversion to physical contact, as being angrier, as handling their infants more roughly, and as being more restricted in emotional expressivity than mothers of secure infants (Main & Weston, 1981; Thompson & Lamb, 1984;). In laboratory face-to-face play sessions, mothers of infants who develop avoidant attachment relationships tend to be intrusive and overstimulating (Belsky, Rovine, & Taylor, 1984; Isabella & Belsky, 1991; Malatesta et al., 1989). Less is known about the characteristics of mothers whose children display the ambivalent or resistant pattern, but Ainsworth and co-workers have characterized such mothers as being inconsistently responsive during the first year and as showing low maternal involvement. In a series of studies, Belsky and colleagues (Belsky et al., 1984; Isabella, Belsky, & von Eye, 1989; Isabella & Belsky,

1991) investigated patterns of early mother–infant interaction. Behavior was videorecorded and later subjected to microanalytic coding. The researchers found that in dyads that would eventually be classified as avoidant, interactions at 1 month were more dysynchronous than expected, and at all three ages (1, 3, 9 months) mothers tended to vocalize to their infants considerably more frequently than expected, almost irrespective of what the baby was doing. In dyads that would eventually be classified as resistant, the mothers and infants at 1 and 3 months showed higher levels of dysynchrony than expected. There were relatively few mutual and reciprocal behavioral exchanges. Mothers tended to try to interact with their infants when the infants were disengaged, but also tended not to respond when the infants themselves initiated interaction. They were also less responsive to infant distress at 3 and 9 months and were less responsive to positive vocalizations at 9 months than the mothers of B group infants. In summary, then, mothers of secure children were more consistent and contingently responsive than the other two groups. Mothers of avoidant infants were more intrusive and less responsive to the infants' own overtures, and mothers of resistant infants were generally less involved and more inconsistent.

The patterns noted above with respect to both maternal and infant behaviors were observed in unselected samples of subjects, that is, in nonclinical samples. It is important to note that they describe individual differences within the normal range. When we turn to clinical samples, the picture that emerges is much more disturbing. Two of the most extensively studied populations thought to be at risk for problematic attachment relationships are children exposed to abuse and neglect, and those of parents with clinical depression, as discussed below. In general, the percentage of insecure attachments is quite high in both populations, and many are characterized by the D attachment pattern. The D attachment style has been variously described as featuring a mixed pattern of avoidant and resistant behaviors during the reunion phase of the Strange Situation, and involving disorganized and odd behavior. The several attachment styles will be discussed within the larger framework of the socioemotional and cognitive deficits displayed by these children.

ATTACHMENT PATTERNS OF INFANTS EXPOSED TO MALTREATMENT

There have been several studies of abused and neglected infants. Four are highlighted here. Egeland and Sroufe (1981) compared the attachment outcomes of 31 maltreated and 31 nonmaltreated children as assessed at 12 and 18 months. Neglected infants ($N = 24$) were found to be disproportionately represented in the resistant group at 12 months (50%); by 18 months there was a significant shift, with considerable movement toward the A group classification (avoidant attachment). Case histories of mothers of C group babies indicated that a number were heavy drug users, one was schizophrenic, and all appeared to be experiencing chaotic lives and lacked contact with their families. In the same study there were seven abused and abused/neglected children. None of these children showed the C pattern at either 12 or 18 months; all showed either the A or B pattern.

Lyons-Ruth, Connell, Zoll, and Stahl (1987) also examined the attachment patterns of maltreated infants (abused and neglected). They found that infants of maltreating mothers were more avoidant of their mothers than nonmaltreated infants. When observed earlier in the home, maltreating mothers were rated as higher than nonmaltreating mothers on covert hostility and on interfering behaviors toward the infants.

Lamb, Gaensbauer, Malkin, and Schultz (1985) replicated the finding that maltreated children were significantly more avoidantly attached than comparison groups of children. They also found that maltreated infants demonstrated muted or flattened affect regardless of their attachment status.

Finally, a large longitudinal study by Cicchetti and colleagues (summarized in Cicchetti, 1990; Cicchetti & Rizley, 1981; Schneider-Rosen, Braunwald, Carlson, & Cicchetti, 1985) supplies even more information about the consequences of abuse not only for the development of attachment but also for its impact on other aspects of socioemotional and cognitive functioning. In the larger study, from which several of the individual analyses were drawn, there were 200 abused and 200 nonabused children, with several waves of data collection over a 7-year period. Both groups of subjects came from low socioeconomic status backgrounds.

Children were seen for attachment assessment at 12, 18, and 24 months of age in the Strange Situation. The majority of maltreated children were insecurely attached at each of the ages. When the children were originally assessed they were classified according to the traditional A, B, and C categories. A good proportion of the insecure attachments were of the A pattern, and there was also considerable instability in attachment classifications over time with many of those who were securely attached at 12 months shifting to insecurely attached; there were also more shifts from the C to the A category. Since the initial classifications, Main and colleagues (1985) have described a D category indexing more disturbed and disorganized behavior. Cicchetti and colleagues reanalyzed their tapes using the new 4-way classification system and found that approximately 80% of the maltreated infants fell into the disorganized/disoriented category.

Cicchetti's group assessed the cognitive competence of the study children in several ways. They found, as had other investigators, that securely attached infants score higher on the Bayley test—a measure of developmental maturity. The investigators also assessed the ability of the infants to recognize themselves, using the visual self-recognition test, which involves smudging the child's nose with rouge without her knowledge and then exposing her to a mirror (the children who recognize themselves in the mirror tend to touch their nose, whereas those without self-recognition do not). Disregarding maltreatment status, securely attached infants showed evidence of earlier self-recognition. There was no difference between the maltreated and nonmaltreated infants in terms of the age at which self-recognition was achieved. However, there were clear differences in the affective response to self-recognition. Whereas 78% of the non-maltreated children showed positive affect to their rouge-altered faces, 80% of the maltreated children showed negative or neutral reactions. The authors suggest that these findings indicate that maltreated youngsters try to mask their feelings and/or experience themselves primarily in negative ways, again revealing an impaired self-image.

Language function was assessed at 24 and 30 months in two different laboratory situations, a 30-minute free play session, and 15 minutes of language free play designed to elicit symbolic play and communication. In terms of quality of attachment and language skills, insecurely (versus securely) attached children had smaller MLUs (mean length of utterances), made fewer internal state comments (feelings, physical sensations), and referred less often to themselves; most of these were the maltreated children. Cicchetti (personal communication) also reports that the affective displays of maltreated children are flatter (as noted by Lamb et al., 1985). Thus it appears that maltreated children may mute their affectivity in several ways. They may need to blunt awareness of their feelings, especially negative ones, as a defensive adaptation. Alternatively, they may simply have not had sufficient tuition in the discrimination of and use of negative affect terms. Cicchetti speculates that maltreated children receive parental disapproval for the expression of affect, and perhaps particular types of affect, and thus adopt an overcontrolled style that meshes with parental demands.

CHILDREN OF DEPRESSED PARENTS

Radke-Yarrow, Cummings, Kuczynski, and Chapman (1985) examined patterns of attachment in 2- and 3-year-old children from families with well and depressed parents. They found a higher proportion of A, C, or A/C attachment patterns in families where mothers had a form of major depression (unipolar or bipolar) than they found in families with well mothers or mothers with minor depression. Behavior rated as A/C included moderate to high avoidance and moderate to high resistance during the reunion, and most children also displayed either affectlessness or depressed affect, and/or odd or atypical body postures and movements. The greatest number of insecure attachments occurred in the group with bipolar mothers, and this was the group with the highest number of A/C attachment patterns. In families with a depressed mother, depression in the father did not increase the likelihood of insecure attachment with the mother. However, if a mother was separated from her husband and had a major depression, the risk of insecure mother–child attachment was significantly increased.

In summary, the existence of an emotionally harsh environment brought on by maltreatment or parental depression significantly increases the likelihood not only that children will develop an insecure attachment with their parents, but that the quality of the attachment will be especially disturbed.

ECOLOGICAL VALIDITY OF THE STRANGE SITUATION

In the assessment of attachment, and of overall socioemotional functioning, the Strange Situation is one of the most frequently used measures in the United

States, where it was first developed. Within the last few years, reservations have been articulated concerning the ecological validity of this measure as applied in settings outside the United States and as the sole means of evaluating a child's socioemotional functioning. Concerns have been most notably expressed in the context of cross-cultural research and in studies of the impact of day care on children's emotional development. We turn now to a consideration of these studies.

Cross-Cultural Studies of Attachment

IJzendoorn & Kroonenberg's (1988) meta-analysis of cross-cultural studies of attachment found that the A classification was relatively more prevalent in Western European countries and the C classification was relatively more frequent in Israel and Japan, though the importance of this finding is somewhat moot, since the same review found that the magnitude of intracultural variation among samples was greater than that of the amount of intercultural variation. Nevertheless, the intercultural differences are provocative and raise the question of whether certain cultures foster more ambivalent and avoidant attachments in children, or whether the patterns displayed relate less to insecurity than to cultural ideals of behavior, and thus the larger adaptive context. Studies from the three countries that seem to have the most discrepant distributional patterns are discussed.

Germany

Grossmann and colleagues were among the first to test the applicability of the Strange Situation for use in another culture. In their original study (Grossmann, Grossmann, Huber, & Wartner, 1981; Grossmann et al., 1985), 49 families from the area of Bielefeld (north Germany) participated in a replication of Ainsworth's Baltimore study. Mother–infant interactions were observed during home visits when the infants were 2, 6, and 10 months of age. Quality of attachment to the mother and to the father was assessed via the Strange Situation procedure at 12 and 18 months, respectively. They observed the same kinds of behavioral patterns described by Ainsworth and colleagues, but, quite unexpectedly, found a different distribution of attachment types. In the Baltimore sample, the majority of infants were found to be securely attached. In contrast, two-thirds of the Bielefeld children appeared to be insecurely attached whether as assessed with their mothers or fathers. In particular, a disproportionate number of children (about half the sample) were classified as avoidantly attached, that is, as showing the A1 and A2 types of attachment pattern. These children failed to display relief, joy, and happiness in response to the parent's return following separations. The clearest avoiders (A1s) seemed to demonstrate remarkable self-control. Their facial expressions tended to be calm and sober, although their voices sometimes indicated less than perfect equanimity. Their facial expressions were described as serious, rather than poker-faced.

The finding of a greater proportion of avoidant attachment patterns raised a problem for the interpretation of Grossmann et al.'s data. Theoretically, these children would be considered insecurely attached and thus at risk for later socioemotional development. There was a further problem for attachment theory, since attachment behavior was seen as having evolved at the service of promoting survival. The anomaly, as noted by Grossmann et al. (1981), was "what does it mean when 41% of our children do not exhibit the evolutionarily adaptive behavior vis-à-vis at least one parent?" (p. 179). In their original paper they hypothesized that the higher proportion of avoidant attachments might have arisen as a product of greater emphasis on independence training in the geographic region from which the sample had been recruited. They also entertained the idea that the avoidant behavior might not be ultimately maladaptive, especially if it is tailored to fit with cultural expectations of controlled emotionality and self-sufficiency.

A second sample, drawn from a south German population (Regensburg), found a distribution of attachment types similar to that obtained by Ainsworth and colleagues, thus the overrepresentation of avoidant infants was limited to the north German sample and was possibly related to greater emphasis on independence training in that area. An analysis of the home observations of the Bielefeld group appeared to sustain this interpretation. Grossmann et al. found that mothers of securely attached infants were significantly more sensitive than mothers of insecurely attached infants at 2 and 6 months but not at 10 months of age. This finding was interpreted as meaning that by 10 months these German mothers as a whole were shifting their child-rearing strategies so as to prepare their children for the greater independence that would be demanded of them by the larger culture. In an analysis of tape recordings during the home observations, Grossmann, Friedl, and Grossmann (1987) identified three maternal conversational patterns: tender (expressions of quiet pleasure, few directives, little impatience or tension), sober (slow tempo of speech, fewer and shorter utterances, long reaction time), and lighthearted (fast tempo, frequent and sometimes extreme variability in loudness and pitch, dramatic inflections). The more overwhelming and controlling lighthearted style was more characteristic of the mothers of children later classified as A and C, whereas B children tended to have mothers who displayed the more mellow tender style.

Follow-up studies of the two German samples permitted the researchers to evaluate whether the avoidant attachment pattern was indexing precocious independence and lack of separation distress, rather than anxious attachment. The idea was not supported. A close inspection of the Strange Situation tapes indicated that it was not the case that avoidant infants were less distressed than their secure counterparts during the procedure; instead, they appeared to be controlling their affective display. Indeed, the more that infants with an avoidant attachment were impaired in their mood and play behavior by the two separations, the less they communicated directly to the parent. As a result, there was less comforting by the parent that could have relieved the infant's distress. It is important to note that avoidant and nonavoidant children signaled their affect about the same amount during the nonstressful episodes of the Strange Situation; it was only under conditions of stress that there was a breakdown in communication between avoidant youngsters and their parents. According to Darwin, affective behaviors evolved over time for their adaptive signaling value. In the north German sample the adaptational value of the negative signals seems to have been temporarily subverted, since the children avoided communicating with those individuals who would normally be most capable of relieving their suffering. But what about later development? Were the avoidant youngsters, especially the Bielefeld children, being prepared for greater adaptational success in the long run? Would they do better as they moved out of the home and into the wider world where stress was placed on autonomy and independence? To answer this question a follow-up investigation was undertaken.

When the Regensburg sample of children were 5 years old the quality of their play and interactions with peers was assessed. Securely attached children played with more concentration and higher quality than avoidantly attached children, and although severe behavior problems were rare in this nonclinical, normal, population, the child who had more than a minor problem tended to be insecurely attached. In addition, securely attached children received more positive and more favorable ratings by teachers on measures of ego-control and ego-resiliency (Grossmann & Grossmann, 1991).

In summary, the studies of Grossmann and colleagues indicated that the Strange Situation could be applied in at least one other cultural context and that attachment patterns were meaningfully related to the child's ability to communicate distress both in early infancy and later on. As mentioned in a previous section, patterns of attachment were found to be related to variables of both infant temperament (orienting ability) and maternal sensitivity. The somewhat higher proportion of avoidant attachments in the Bielefeld sample appeared to be attributable to cultural demands for early independence training in at least that particular geographic region. Culture can affect the proportion of ambivalent attachments as well, as seen in the Israeli and Japanese studies.

Israel

A study by Sagi and colleagues (1985) tested a logical inference derived from attachment theory. The theory specifies that infants form discriminating attachments to their caregivers based on the consistency and sensitivity of caregiving. In Israel, rearing experiences associated with life in a kibbutz might conceivably alter the nature of mother–infant bonding. Kibbutzim infants reside in central children's houses that are tended by *metaplot* (nurse caregivers). Thus infants live with and are reared by caregivers other than their mothers, though they do see their parents during daily and weekend visits. Kibbutzim rearing might pose the risk of deleterious effects for a variety of reasons. First, the nurses might not be as invested in the emotional well-being of their charges since they are not related to the infant, and since they had not chosen this particular job out of interest, but had been assigned. Reduced responsiveness could create conditions for insecurity. The infant might also experience confusion in part because of multiple mothering. In addition, the child might experience inconsistency from the mother herself, since her behavior might differ between the day visits in the public sphere of the children's house and the more private visits at the parent's home.

Eighty-six families participated in the study. Infants ranging in age from 11 to 14 months were observed in the Strange Situation three times—once with the mother, once with the father, and once with the *metapelet*. The distribution of attachment types differed from the American norms. There were somewhat fewer Bs (56%), fewer As (8%), and more Cs (33%) than are commonly observed in the United States. The authors questioned whether these figures truly reflect an increase in the number of insecure attachments. In the first place, contrary to the experience of researchers in other countries, a large proportion of the sessions (32%) had to be terminated prematurely because of severe distress on the part of the infants. In a post hoc analysis of the data on "terminators" versus "completers," Sagi et al. found that completers showed the same amount of distress as in the American norms. Most of the terminators were classified as C2 because their extreme distress had resulted in passivity and inability to gain comfort from the adult when he or she returned. They also noted that there was significant intra-individual consistency in the need to terminate the procedure early, irrespective of whether the infant had been tested with the mother, father, or *metapelet*. The authors suggest that the classification of some infants in the Strange Situation may have reflected infant characteristics of reactivity or fearfulness. However, in a sample of city-reared Israeli infants from comparable backgrounds who were enrolled in full-time day care, there were still more Cs than As. Only one child was classified as avoidant (3%), 27 infants (81%) fell in the B group, and 5 infants (16%) in group C. Note that the proportion of secure versus insecure attachments in the city sample corresponded with American norms. Still, both samples have more Cs than As, which is the reverse of the pattern found in U.S. samples, and the kibbutz sample had even more Cs than the city-reared infants. Collectively, these findings suggest that both factors—being Israeli, and having a kibbutz rearing experience—have independent effects on quality of attachment. The authors speculate that the effects are due to some aspect of Israeli rearing practices, and/or a cultural difference in temperament or emotionality. The authors also draw into question the validity of the Strange Situation procedure for assessing security of attachment in this particular culture. In their view it is not clear that the infants classified as ambivalently attached (C) are really insecurely attached; rather, the Strange Situation may be an inappropriate assessment tool for this population. More needs to be known about how Israeli infants appraise the strange laboratory situation against the backdrop of their prior experiences. The investigators found that the subgroup of infants whose sessions had to be terminated prematurely were often rendered distraught by the entrance of the stranger in episode 3. Given a usual degree of stranger anxiety, once they were distressed neither the departure of the stranger nor the return of the attachment figures was successful in calming the infants. Despite the attractiveness of these potential explanations, one still has to contend with the anomaly that most of the Israeli infants did display secure attachments; thus the "Israeli" experience is not uniform in its effects on infants.

Japan

A study by Takahashi (1986) also found an unusual distribution of attachment types. In this investigation a total of 60 Japanese mother–infant dyads from intact families living in an urban area were observed. The mothers were full-time primary caregivers who rarely left their infants with anyone else. Findings revealed a comparable proportion of secure attachments (B) and insecure attachments (A and C combined) with respect to Ainsworth's sample. However, unlike the U.S. sample, Japanese infants in the insecure group were all classified as Cs. Fifty-seven percent of the infants who would have been regarded as securely attached moved in the direction of an anxious/ambivalent attachment pattern in episodes 6–8 of the Strange Situation (episode 6 is the one in which the infant is left alone). Japanese infants also received higher scores on the proximity/contact-seeking scale and lower scores on avoidance. The mothers had greater difficulty in soothing their infants largely because their children exhibited a stronger and more prolonged reaction to the Strange Situation (i.e., 91% cried throughout episode 6).

Takahashi proposes that the greater number of Cs in the Japanese sample may be explained by differences in the early experiences of Japanese infants and perhaps also by culture-bound aspects of the Strange Situation procedure. Japanese infants are almost constantly with their mothers and are almost never left with other individuals. Thus, the introduction of strangers and the experience of being alone may have created a stress that was too strong for Japanese infants. The very absence of any A attachment patterns in the sample suggests that infants could not afford to display avoidant behavior. In another study in which infants were tested in their homes, half of the children who had classified as C in the laboratory version Strange Situation procedure shifted to a B classification in the home.

In summary, the use of the Strange Situation procedure in other cultures has revealed somewhat different proportions of the three types of attachment classification. This has raised the issue of the procedure's ecological validity in cultures outside of the one in which it was developed. The meaning of strange environments, strangers, separations from and reunions with mothers may have quite different emotional significance for infants depending on the experiences they have had earlier in life in the context of their own culture. However, the fact that infants classified as insecurely attached in the Grossmann studies showed less well adjusted behavior in later follow-up studies suggests that, at least in the German culture, A and C classifications do reflect insecure attachments. The same cannot be said for the Japanese and Israeli children because the appropriate follow-up studies have not yet been conducted.

The issue of the ecological validity of the Strange Situation emerges again in the context of the impact of day care on children's socioemotional development. Many American mothers send their young children to day-care centers while they work, an increasingly common trend. Thus many U.S. children experience non-maternal care in communal settings much like Israeli kibbutz-reared children. What are the consequences?

Effects of Day Care on Children's Emotional Development as Assessed by the Strange Situation

Child-rearing issues are particularly vulnerable to politicization, especially in times of rapid social change. When women entered the workforce in massive numbers during the 1970s and 1980s, more and more children required alternatives to home care. This was true for infants as well; by the end of the 1980s half the infants in the United States had employed mothers—twice the proportion that prevailed in 1970.

Concern was raised that day care might result in emotional insecurity, and the issue received much attention in the popular press. What light does developmental research have to shed on the issue? A number of investigators have attempted to assess the impact of maternal employment on child development, and attachment security has been one of the main variables under consideration. The findings have been mixed, which is not surprising given the degree of controversy on the subject. A recent review of the literature by Alison Clarke-Stewart (1989) makes it clear that the controversy is still active, although some trends in the data are apparent. We summarize her findings here because they are based on one of the most comprehensive examinations of the literature, because they seem to indicate that the issue of how children fare under day care is complex, and because they once again raise the issue of the ecological validity of the Strange Situation.

In tabulating the distribution of attachment classifications from studies providing data on the employment status of mothers, Clarke-Stewart (1989) found that differences are typically not significant in individual studies, but that when studies are combined an effect emerges: a greater proportion of infants of full-time working mothers show insecure attachments (36% versus 29%). However, as Clarke-Stewart points out, the question of whether these differences mean that infants of working mothers are more at risk for emotional disturbance—because they will interpret their mothers' absence as rejection—is moot. In the first place, there is no way of knowing whether the Strange Situation is ecologically valid with infants whose mothers work since the procedure depends on creating a situation in which infants feel moderately stressed and thus seek proximity; the Strange Situation may be less stressful to infants of working mothers because these infants are more used to the mothers' comings and goings. Secondly, when the infants of working mothers are assessed in a range of situations and with a variety of partners, using other measures of security, self-confidence, and emotional adjustment, children who were in day care as infants do as well as children who did not have day care. In addition, children of working mothers who were coded as insecure in the Strange Situation have been found to do better than children of nonworking mothers on a variety of other tasks. They have also been found to be more aggressive with their peers and less compliant with adults, but as Clark-Stewart points out, this appears not to index maladjustment so much as independence.

In summary, day care appears to influence the pattern of behavior displayed by infants during the Strange Situation assessment, although the differences are not great, and the meaning of the differential behavior is not entirely clear. When considering other measures of social and intellectual functioning, the children do not look particularly maladjusted, if at all. This is not to say that day care never has adverse effects on children. The literature is consistent in showing that children clearly suffer when day-care experience is bad, just as they suffer from bad care from their parents. However, when day care is of high quality, the children appear to do well socially, emotionally, and cognitively.

ATTACHMENT RESEARCH BEYOND INFANCY AND EARLY CHILDHOOD

Bowlby's concept of internal working models suggests that attachment models will be carried forward in time even into adulthood and that, as such, these internal working models of relationships formed in childhood may continue to affect the nature of attachment relationships adults have with their parents, and might also color other significant interpersonal relationships.

One of the first studies to explore this question occurred in the context of Main, Kaplan, and Cassidy's (1985) sixth-year follow-up of children seen as infants in their longitudinal study of attachment. The results of tests with the children were reported in an earlier section. In the same study, the investigators also conducted in-depth interviews with the mothers of these children. The interview, developed by George, Kaplan, and Main (1984), has come to be known as the Adult Attachment Interview. In administering the interview, interviewers follow a set of guidelines and a semistructured format in which they attempt to elicit material concerning the adults' thoughts and feelings about their own childhood attachment experiences. Among other things, subjects are asked to generate adjectives to describe the relationship they had with their mother and with their father, and to recollect experiences that illustrate the adjectives chosen.

Four types of attachment style were discriminated: Parents labelled *secure* were those who were able to describe their attachment relationships in a fluent, coherent manner and were able to articulate both positive and negative aspects of their early experiences and to integrate the two in expression and feeling. These individuals clearly valued attachments and attachment-related experiences, felt they were influential, but could be relatively independent and objective in evaluating particular experiences or relationships. Memories were mainly positive but not exclusively so; when negative experiences were recalled, the individual was able to integrate them into a broader picture of the relationship.

A second type of attachment, termed *dismissive* or avoidant, was discerned in parents who generally had difficulty recalling their childhoods. In cases where subjects could retrieve early memories, they tended to describe parents who were unaffectionate or rejecting. There were also frequently discrepancies between the subjects' global statements about their parents and specific events—that is, they might portray the mother as "great, fine, a good mother" but go on to describe incidents that revealed a rejecting or neglectful parent.

A third group of parents were described as being *preoccupied* or enmeshed in attitudes toward attachment. They seemed to have access to early experiences but had a difficult time integrating the experiences into a coherent overall picture. They recounted negative aspects of their relationships with parents but still endeavored to please them. Their own children tended to be ambivalently attached.

A fourth group, who tended to be the parents of children classified as disorganized/disoriented, had experienced the death of an attachment figure before maturity and were still dealing with issues of loss and mourning.

The attachment assessments of the parents were made independent of knowledge of the attachment status of their children. Interestingly, there was significant concordance between the classifications of parents and infants; the preoccupied parental style was equated with the resistant/ambivalent infant style, and the dismissive adult style was equated with the avoidant infant style. In the case of mothers, the relation to infant security of attachment was significant at the .001 level, for fathers, at the .05 level. These data would seem to suggest that parents socialize their children with respect to issues of nurturance, dependency, and attachment in the manner in which they themselves have been reared, so that working models of relationships are transmitted from one generation to the next. Although it might seem a less likely source of influence, one also needs to consider the impact of similar temperaments within families. Given what we know about the relation between infant temperament and attachment style, it is certainly possible that shared temperament characteristics, transmitted genetically, could account for at least some of the similarity in attachment styles between generations within the same family.

In the Grossmann and Grossmann series of replication studies with two German samples (Grossmann & Grossmann, 1990; 1991), a correspondence between attachment styles of infants and recollected attachment relationships of the children's mothers with their own mothers was also found. In that study four patterns of maternal attachment representation were found, two "autonomous" patterns associated with secure attachments in children ("positive" and "reflexive") and two patterns associated with having insecurely attached children ("defensive" and "repressive").

One anomaly stands out in both the Main et al. (1985) and Grossmann and Grossmann (1990, 1991) studies, and that has to do with the fact that mothers of securely attached infants ("secure" or "autonomous" mothers) had mixed attachment histories. Some mothers of securely attached infants described their own attachment histories as involving sensitive, nurturing parents; however, others related unhappy childhoods involving rejection or other trauma. These parents, despite having negative experiences in childhood, were able to overcome the negative effects and develop a mature, well-integrated internal understanding that did not involve the defensiveness or enmeshment shown by parents in the other subtypes. The Grossmanns (1991) report that their "reflexive" autonomous mothers developed a post-hoc understanding of their attachment-related experiences which was deep enough to achieve the necessary mental integration of their emotions. They developed an openness for reality and for their own children's expressions of their emotional needs because they did not have to avoid negative emotions and the reality represented by them. (pp. 7–8)

Similarly, Main et al. (1985) indicate that "parents of secure as well as insecure infants sometimes reported histories of rejection or traumatic experiences, including early loss of attachment figures" (p. 97).

The crux of the question raised by these observations is how to account for the differential development. That is, some individuals experienced rejection and apparently went on to grow up in healthy, nondefensive ways, whereas others exposed to rejection developed defensive coping mechanisms and internal working models of attachment that lacked coherency, as well as acted out a less than optimal style of relating to their own children. A similarly puzzling finding was noted in the early Berkeley growth study (Block & Haan, 1971), which tracked the development of the original study participants into late adulthood. This study showed that some of the individuals who had had very unfortunate childhoods and rather unattractive personalities developed into some of the more creative, healthy, and satisfied individuals in later life. Further research will need to address why and how these departures from expected developmental trajectories occurred. Bowlby had indicated that working models are permeable to new experiences and that the internal models from earlier experience can be modified so as to accommodate a new understanding of the world and of relationships. What we still do not know, however, is what these new experiences might be, and that remains a subject for future research.

OTHER RESEARCH ON ATTACHMENT RELATIONSHIPS IN ADULT LIFE

Some of the most recent research on attachment is focused on analysis of patterns of affect regulation in adulthood, and on delineating the features of close interpersonal relationships, including romantic relationships. A study by Kobak and Sceery (1988) assessed attachment relationships in a group of college freshman using the Adult Attachment Interview, self-reports of personality, and outside ratings by two individuals acquainted with the subject. As in the work of Main and colleagues (Main et al., 1985), the authors discriminated three different types of internal working models of attachment in these young adult subjects. Dismissive individuals endorsed the attitude that attachment relationships were not very important or worth pursuing. Secure individuals valued attachment relationships, and preoccupied individuals were still troubled by and immersed in dealing with issues of attachment to parents. The investigators found that secure subjects were seen by acquaintances as more socially competent, charming, cheerful, and likable than the other two types of individuals. The dismissive or avoidant students were low on ego-resilience, were rated higher on defensiveness and hostility by peers, and reported more distant relationships with others. The preoccupied students were viewed as less ego-resilient and more anxious by peers and reported high levels of personal distress, but viewed their family as more supportive than the dismissive group. One of the more important aspects of this study concerns the finding that individuals who are dismissive of attachment relationships are characterized by greater defensiveness and greater anger affect. The dismissive adult appears to be the counterpart of the avoidant infant who does not seem to need the mother under conditions of stress and who has been described as "covertly hostile." The preoccupied adult, who is still enmeshed in issues of attachment/individuation with parents, and is particularly anxious, seems to be the counterpart of the ambivalent infant who is distressed by separation from the parent but who is also not assuaged by his or her return.

Other studies have attempted to investigate how attachment styles might correspond with relatedness in other spheres of social functioning, in particular, in adult romantic relationships. For example, Hazen and Shaver (1987) conceptualized adult love relationships as forms of attachment and examined the continuity between the quality of adult love relationships and qualities of early attachment. Key aspects of the descriptors of the three attachment styles were translated into terms appropriate to adult romantic love. Subjects, who were individuals who had responded to a survey published in a local newspaper, were asked to classify themselves into one of the three categories. The secure style was characterized as one in which individuals felt at ease in getting close to others, felt comfortable depending on others as well as having others depend on them, and did not worry about being abandoned or about someone getting too close to them. The avoidant style was characterized as one in which the individual felt uncomfortable being close to others, found it difficult to trust others completely and depend on them, and felt nervous when anyone got too close, often experiencing partners as wanting greater intimacy than the individual felt comfortable with. The anxious/ambivalent style was characterized as one in which individuals were reluctant to get close to others, worried that their partners did not really love them and might not want to stay with them, wanted to merge completely with the other person, and found that this desire sometimes scared people away.

Subjects endorsed the above descriptions of themselves in relation to their most important love experiences in a distribution of types closely resembling the relative prevalence of attachment types found in studies of infants. Moreover, the three kinds of adults differed significantly in the ways they experienced romantic love in a fashion that was predictable from attachment theory. Specifically, adults of the secure type had happier relationships with their partners, were more likely to consider their partners as their best friends, to experience complete trust in the other, and were less likely to fear closeness than either of the two insecure types; they emphasized being able to accept and support their partner despite the partner's faults. Adults who were avoidant, described their love relationships as involving more fear of intimacy, emotional highs and lows, and jealousy; anxious/ambivalent adults were characterized as being more obsessively preoccupied with their lover, having fallen in love at first sight, as desiring reciprocation and union, and as experiencing more extreme sexual attraction and jealousy than either of the other two types. The study also provided data on the length of relationships for the three groups. The average length of the secure group was 10 years, versus not quite 5 years for the anxious/ambivalent subjects and 6 years for the avoidant subjects.

The research also indicated that adult attachment styles were related in a meaningful way to perceived relationships subjects recalled having with their parents and the parents' relationship with each other. In general, secure subjects reported warmer relationships with both parents and between their two parents. Avoidant subjects described their mothers as cold and rejecting.

A replication study with additional items tapping mental models of attachment relationships was conducted with a non-self-selected sample of undergraduates. The distribution of attachment types was essentially the same as that in the larger community sample. In general, the undergraduates were less jaded about romantic love than the community sample, possibly because of their more limited experiences. However, the three types differed with respect to two items. Item 6 ("It's easy to fall in love. I feel myself beginning to fall in love often") was endorsed by 32% of the anxious group, 15% of the secure, and none of the avoidant subjects. The item "It's rare to find someone you can really fall in love with" was endorsed by 80% of the avoidant, 55% of the secure, and 41% of the anxious/ambivalent subjects. In terms of attachment history, discriminant function analysis indicated anxious/ambivalent subjects differed from the other two groups in perceiving their fathers as less caring, confident, humorous, warm, and respectful, and more cold, and their mothers as less understanding; the parental relationship also differed in that it was described as less good-humored. A second function, which separated avoidant from secure subjects indicated that the avoidant subjects saw their parents as more critical, rejecting, and disinterested than the secure subjects. This study also tested subjects on their degree of experienced loneliness; anxious/ambivalent subjects were found to be higher on both state and trait loneliness than either of the other two groups; avoidant subjects admitted being distant from others but did not report feeling lonely.

Feeney and Noller (1990) administered questionnaire measures of attachment style, attachment history, beliefs about relationships, self-esteem, and love style to a large sample of undergraduates. They found that avoidant subjects were most likely to report childhood separations from their mothers and to be characterized as lacking in trust in others. Anxious ambivalent subjects were less likely than avoidant individuals to see their father as supportive. The researchers also found that attachment style was strongly related to self-esteem, with self-esteem highest in secure subjects and lowest in ambivalent subjects.

Most recently, Milkulincer, Florian, and Tolmacz (1990) evaluated the relation between adult attachment styles and the way that fear of personal death is experienced. Fear of death was chosen as an arena in which to assess the impact of attachment on affect regulation because fear of death is a universal fear and it involves the ultimate separation from loved ones. A sample of undergraduates were classified into secure, anxious, and avoidant attachment types on the basis of two instruments that rated how individuals felt in close relationships. Subjects also filled out a self-report questionnaire concerning their attachment history and answered questions about their reactions to separation in close relationships. Fear of death was assessed on the basis of responses to four Thematic Apperception Test (TAT) cards. The experimenters hypothesized that due to the nature of different coping styles for dealing with distress, ambivalent persons who are hypervigilant of occasions for distress would evidence a stronger fear of death at both the conscious and below-conscious level of awareness in comparison with securely and avoidantly attached individuals. Avoidant individuals who route negative emotions from consciousness should show stronger fear of death, but mainly at a low level of awareness.

Results indicated that avoidant subjects perceived their mothers in less positive terms than the other two groups; both avoidant and ambivalent subjects perceived their fathers in less positive terms than did secure subjects. In terms of reactions to separations, ambivalent subjects were found to be more hypervigilant to separation and suffered from stronger distress related to the severing of affective bonds than did secure subjects.

In terms of their reasons for fear of death, ambivalent individuals were more likely to fear loss of social identity, and avoidant individuals were more likely to fear death on account of its unknown nature. Both avoidant and ambivalent subjects scored higher on the anxiety and centrality of death scales than did secure subjects. When the projective tests were evaluated for themes of death anxiety, the ambivalent subjects evidenced a stronger overt fear of death than the other two groups. Avoidant subjects did not show stronger overt fear of death than the secure subjects, but they did evidence stronger fear of death at a low level of awareness. Finally, the study confirmed the expectation that subjects' overt reactions to death were related to their overt reactions to separation in close relationships.

A study by Birigen (1990) assessed the relation between maternal recollections of parental acceptance, personality characteristics (self esteem, covert and overt anxiety), and present mother–child interactions. The investigator found a significant association between recalled parental acceptance and maternal sensitivity, dyadic physical avoidance, and dyadic harmony, with greater acceptance being associated with greater sensitivity and dyadic harmony, and less physical avoidance. Two measures of anxiety, covert and overt, intercorrelated with various measures in different ways. Individuals scoring high on overt anxiety tended to report physical symptoms that were visible to others but which were not particularly reflective of concern with how others viewed or judged them, that is, trembling or perspiring when thinking of an imminent challenge. High scores on covert anxiety had to do with mainly psychological symptoms concerning self-presentation, that is, concerns about whether people were interested in what they were saying, criticism from others, and so forth. The study found that ratings of self-esteem and overt anxiety were not significantly correlated with any of the mother–child interactive variables; however, covert anxiety was positively correlated with dyadic physical avoidance, and negatively correlated with maternal sensitivity and dyadic harmony. In addition, those who perceived familial rejection scored higher on covert anxiety, though not overt anxiety or self-esteem.

In summarizing the above studies we note that the findings are generally consistent with predictions from attachment theory. According to Bowlby's (1973) original formulations, avoidant individuals modulate negative affect by restricting the acknowledgment of distress and adopting "compulsive self-reliance." From Bowlby's account, and as confirmed by studies such as the above, avoidant individuals are those likely to emphasize autonomy and self-reliance, deny the importance of attachment relationships, keep their distance from attachment figures, and inhibit their display of negative emotions. Thus defended, the avoidant individual does not have to contend with the threat of rejection from others on a conscious level.

Bowlby (1973) also described the anxious/ambivalent adult as one who tends to galvanize negative feelings by attending to distress and potential distress in a hypervigilant fashion; these individuals should experience high levels of conscious anxiety and distress. As a result there can be excessive worry about being rejected or abandoned, which would lead to dependent relationships that are ineffective in reducing anxiety. Again, the recent literature on adult attachment seems to confirm Bowlby's formulations.

SUMMARY OF ATTACHMENT RESEARCH AND COMMENTARY

In the two decades of research following Ainsworth's seminal studies, a number of investigations have replicated the relationship between ratings of maternal sensitivity in early infancy and attachment patterns at 12 months. There is also growing recognition among researchers today that maternal sensitivity is not the only factor involved in differential attachment patterns. Among other factors that have been implicated are innate constitutional differences in infants, differential amount of experience with separations and with novel environments, differential cultural emphasis on interpersonal dependence and independence, and factors such as environmental stress and family instability.

Attachment theory has provided an extraordinarily fruitful approach to the study of human development and it has established itself as a domain of critical research as well. Moreover, its message has begun to penetrate public awareness in a way that Freudian theory began to do in the 1940s and 1950s. With this comes the attendant risk that results will be overinterpreted and imbued with greater significance than may be warranted. The very designation of children who fall outside the B category as "insecurely" attached carries the connotation that not only is there something imperfect about them but they are also at risk for pathology. Parents have expressed concern about the meaning of these designations and have begun to ask psychologists to test their children in the Strange Situation (Karen, 1990) to see if they achieve the right (attachment) grade—one of the rare instances in our culture where a B is more highly prized than an A. Parents as well as others who would make use of the findings from attachment research need to note that while the literature has been consistent in demonstrating that children who are rated as securely attached to their mothers in early infancy show a profile of being more generally competent and more well-adjusted than their insecure counterparts, the differences in nonclinical samples are not great, and it is not even clear that effects are related to attachment experiences alone.

It is also true that though patterns of behavior encompassed by the B designation represent the ideal as viewed by current attachment researchers, as well as by current Western mental health criteria, these criteria need to be seen in a relativistic light. It is a point of history that mental health criteria are responsive to the received wisdom and even the fashions of the day, can be limited in historical perspective, and can even unwittingly perpetuate prejudice. For example, Broverman, Clarkson, Rosenkrantz, and Vogel's (1970) study of mental health criteria applied to men and women demonstrated that men and women are held to different standards, and the very criteria that are considered unhealthy in men and people "in general," are seen as sex-role appropriate in women.

Will the behavioral pattern exemplified by B children become the ultimate in child-rearing aspirations? The question begs examination. An example from our field's recent past may be germane. Relatively late in life, Erik Erikson began to question some of the earlier ideas he had advanced in his lifespan model of psychosexual development. In particular, he began to question the wisdom of assuming that the healthy older adult faced with the late-life task of resolving the issue between integrity versus despair would optimally resolve it in favor of integrity. In earlier versions of that model, integrity was valorized. Integrity was defined as involving a process of coming to accept, in old age, one's life as being the only life that one could have lived, and to find contentment in it even if it was not perfect. Later in his writings Erikson came to question that notion as his theory became more politically and contextually sensitive. For example, he reasoned that despair rather than integrity may be the appropriate and "mature" response in old age in the case of a person who had tolerated or even practiced fascism during earlier adulthood.

In the same way, we need to examine our implicit assumptions concerning whether "B" children are "healthy" in every way; and whether or not certain behaviors that we esteem in childhood may not make for the very best kind of adult citizens. Will children who are "compliant" and obedient in response to adult goals and admonitions in childhood (an emblem of the behavior of the modal "B" child) also be those who are less inclined to challenge authority in adulthood? This may seem an odd question to raise until one reflects on the very fact that the average (i.e., modal) American is in fact relatively compliant, and moreover, that the compliant personality is not always the most endearing of personalities. Recall that in Stanley Milgram's (1963) classic conformity experiment, the vast majority of subjects willingly administered what they believed were high-voltage electric shocks to other "subjects" in an adjacent room, even when they could see and hear them writhing in apparent pain.

One unintended consequence of the three-way classification system is that not only will some children be seen as having realized the ideal, but those who fall outside the range may get tracked as being maladjusted. A teacher who spots a child who, engrossed in play, is not overjoyed when her parents come to pick her up at the end of a school day might conclude that he has identified an avoidantly attached child. The self-fulfilling prophesy is a well-known psychological phenomenon. Unfortunately, the A and C classification patterns are not simply viewed as variants, whose broader and long-term significance are not yet fully understood, but as laden with clinical implications. An uninitiated reader can come away from the current literature with the sense that the A or C child is a thoroughly compromised and blighted individual with poor future prospects. This may in fact be true of some children, but the A and C categories hide a wide range of behavior patterns and coping strategies, and they derive from a diverse range of experiences related to caregiving, culture, and temperament. Moreover, the long-range follow-up studies that would validate pathological sequelae, and justify the concern raised about the well-being of "insecurely attached" children, have not yet been published. The "anomaly" of the rejected child who grows up to be a healthy adult who nurtures secure children has already been mentioned in relation to the studies of Main et al. and Grossmann et al.

The valorization of B children and pathologization of non-B children is troubling in its own right, but also masks another issue related to individual difference. What do we know about the relations between A and C behaviors and children's ability to cope with the adverse circumstances that may have given rise to these behaviors? Might not these very circumstances (whether they be due to difficulties of temperament or parental dereliction) be the same ones that move individuals to works of outstanding creativity or to acts of great statesmanship? For example, as a child, Winston Churchill was raised under what we might today regard as quite neglectful conditions (Storr, 1988). But, as the British would say, he somehow seems to have muddled through. One could think of countless other examples. This is not to recommend adversity in child-rearing as a means of building character (although many early Greek writers advocated this, and certainly many cultures outside of our own feature rites of passage that subject their young initiates to conditions so severe and grueling that some do not live). It is simply to note that there is much more that goes into development than we currently understand, and cultures have much to say about how attachment needs can and should be expressed.

Bowlby himself, and much of his upper-class British cohort, experienced what contemporary attachment researchers might regard as neglect during childhood. And yet many also seem to have led satisfactory if not enviable lives. Obviously, the yardstick we use today for assessing what is optimal in child-rearing practices and what is ideal in behavioral characteristics is very different than it was 50 years ago (see further discussion and examples in Chapter 4), and may be different in another 50 years from now. Much of what qualifies as "sensitive" caregiving (pacing of and termination of feeding dictated by infant rather than parent, etc.) would have, in an earlier era, been regarded as "permissive" parenting, and greatly frowned upon. The point is that child-rearing trends are without doubt always responsive to larger cultural and historical contexts. Nevertheless,

Bowlby would (and did) argue that whatever the original "cause" of a particular pattern of attachment, the emotional consequences for the individuals concerned would be the same.

FUTURE DIRECTIONS

All of the major attachment theoreticians and researchers acknowledge that advances in theory will likely accrue from cross-fertilization with other theoretical approaches. Attachment theory itself is a hybrid that opportunistically drew from theoretical enterprises that at first seemed quite discrepant from if not hostile to one another: ethology, psychoanalysis, systems theory. As Ainsworth and Bowlby (1991) reflect, in an historical account of their partnership and the course of attachment research over the past quarter century, attachment theory

> is an open-ended theory and, we hope, open enough to be able to comprehend new findings that result from other approaches. From its outset it has been eclectic, drawing on a number of scientific disciplines, including developmental, cognitive, social, and personality psychology, systems theory, and various branches of biological science, including genetics. Although, at present, attachment theory leaves open many questions, both theoretical and practical, we are confident that attachment theorists will continue to be alert to new developments, in these and other areas, that will help to provide answers to problems still outstanding. (p. 340)

Currently, two emerging areas of cross-fertilization look particularly promising. One approach seeks to further our understanding of working models and their ramifications by drawing on concepts concerning representation from cognitive science and from object relations theory (Bretherton, 1990). A second approach attempts to understand different styles of attachment behavior from the vantage point of emotional strategies and emotion regulation (Cassidy & Kobak, 1988; Cassidy & Berlin, 1994). In Part IV of this volume these approaches are addressed in the context of a discrete emotions, functionalist analysis of personality development. We also show how the communicational aspects of emotion that Grossmann and colleagues emphasize in treating attachment theory, and the feeling/motivational aspects that Bowlby emphasized, are subsumable in a model of human motivation that addresses both attachment and nonattachment spheres of functioning.

III

Emotion Expression and Its Socialization

The history of research on emotion expression is rich and extensive. Unlike the study of attachment, which spans approximately three decades, research on emotion expression goes back as far as the field of developmental psychology itself, aside from a temporary lull during the decades of the 1950s, 1960s, and early 1970s. We will refer to the pre-1950s era as the first wave of emotions research, and that beginning in the late 1970s as the second wave. This is a somewhat rough cutting point since there were certainly a number of scholars who persisted in their own research on emotion during the "middle years"; however, these investigators found it extraordinarily difficult to get funding or to publish during this era.

The present section opens with an historical overview of the past century, tracing the course of attitudes towards, and conceptualizations about, emotions and their expression. We note how the study of emotion within psychology itself has undergone transformation in the brief 100 years of its existence. We then take up an examination of some of the earliest studies of emotion, especially those regarded as classic. Descriptions of the studies are accompanied by theoretical and historical contextualization, along with biographies of key figures. A critique is also offered of these studies. As we will see, many of the conclusions of the early studies were pivotal in producing a general disillusion with the study of emotion. This led directly to the stasis of the middle years.

Subsequent chapters in the section are organized in the following way: Chapter 5 provides an overview of the key issues of the second wave of research on expressive behavior, as well as details on one of the most actively researched areas, that of infant expressive behavior. Chapters 6 and 7 take up two other areas concerning children's expression of anger/aggression and empathy. Although the emphasis is on current research, the chapters show how contemporary research is indebted to earlier understanding of these constructs. The two chapters also suggest reasons for the intensity of research in these two domains of child development, alluding to the Western world's growing concern with the socialization of children's anger, aggression, and empathy.

4

The First Wave of Research

Behaviorism and Psychoanalysis

Reason is, and ought only to be, the slave of the passions, and can
never pretend to any other office that to serve and obey them
DAVID HUME, *A Treatise of Human Nature*

HISTORICAL OVERVIEW: TAMING THE HUMAN PASSIONS

Hume's wry comment on the subjugation of reason by passion was not really a
recommendation, but rather a suggestion that this is the way the real world works,
nevermind the Western world's age-old preoccupation with treating emotion and
cognition as adversarial and regarding emotion as something to be mastered and
overcome. Such attitudes toward emotion are found everywhere in Western
culture, from poetry to philosophy. For example, in the poem "East Coker," T. S.
Eliot expresses his contempt for "undisciplined squads of emotion."

The notion that emotions need to be tamed, controlled, restrained, or educated, goes back to antiquity, at least within the Western world. Philosophical
discussions of the mind, as well as early medical treatises, took distinctly different
stances toward the emotions versus the intellect. The intellectual faculties of
mind—understanding, memory, reason, and the like—were generally extolled;
the emotions were either ignored or treated as an impediment to intellectual
processes, and especially, as forces of human ruination. As early as pre-Aristote-
lian thought, metaphors of the time reflected the fear that when emotions were
unleashed they would wreck havoc. "It is more necessary to extinguish wanton-
ness than a conflagration" (Heraclitis, 505 B.C., cited in Ruckmick, 1936, p. 30).

Although many of the ancient Greeks and Romans had argued for restraint
and control in dealing with the affective aspect of life, the real rallying cry came

from the Stoics. The emotions, or "passions," were regarded by the Stoics as commotions arising from unbridled, irrational, contrary-to-nature impulses. Stoic philosophers maintained that emotions, especially the "turbulent passions" such as anger, fear, and hate, affected judgment disastrously and interfered with the pursuit of the good life; thus every effort had to be made to eradicate them.

The second-century Greek physician Galen, operating within the Stoical tradition, described the passions as "diseases of the soul." His treatise, "On the passions and errors of the soul" (Galen, 1963), describes how the disease of emotion interfered with the daily conduct of life and how it might be cured. In Galen's view, emotions had to be tamed; man's ultimate goal should be to strive for stoical apathy. This could be accomplished through appropriate training. Children as well as adults were exhorted to follow a basic program that would allow them to master their emotions. For example, Galen recommended that observers or tutors be employed to follow the child about and draw attention to emotional outbursts as they occurred so that the individual could become more self-aware and thereby exercise the rule of reason and intellectual control. If the emotions had not been mastered by adulthood, additional training and self-discipline were called for. This could involve a lengthy and arduous program. Galen speaks of improvements in the second year, with expectations of continued improvements in the third, fourth, and fifth years.

As an aside, some of Galen's descriptions of ancient Greek behavior suggest that all of the emphasis on controlling the emotions in Western philosophy and popular culture over the centuries may have had some effect. By Galen's account, Greek men and women of the second century could be quite violent. Biting was a common accompaniment of the expression of anger. "Therefore, do not consider him a wise man who only stands acquitted of this very thing, namely, kicking, biting, and stabbing those nearby" (Galen, 1963, p. 43). Galen's own mother "was so very prone to anger that sometimes she bit her handmaids . . ." (p. 57). "Whenever a man becomes violently angry over little things and bites and kicks his servants, you are sure that this man is in a state of passion" (p. 30). Given the banality of such barbaric behavior in early Greek times, one wonders whether there has not been some historical progress in the management of emotion (although see Chapter 6, this volume).

By the medieval period, emotions were still seen as perversions of reason, or at least in hostile opposition to rational process. Thomas Aquinas, for example, complained that emotions disturbed pure thought. In the seventeenth century, Descartes reified the distinction between thought and emotions in his dualistic split between body and mind. It was clear that he prized the faculties of reason above those of the emotions. In *Traité de l'homme* (1662) he attempted to explain human passions by their causes; he also tried to show the way in which the mind might come to a perfect mastery of them. Once again, emotions were seen as contaminants of thought and as requiring intervention for their eradication.

In modern times, the study of the mind, especially that aspect dealing with emotion, became primarily the province of the psychologist, but distrust of the emotions, and the conviction that emotion interferes with the clarity and purity of mind, persisted. Carl Lange, in the *Principles of Psychology*, eagerly anticipated the day when, through "the results of education and the intellectual life, we may achieve Kant's ideal of man as a creature of pure intelligence for whom all of the emotions, if he is still subject to them, will be looked upon as mental troubles little worthy of him" ("Conclusions").

With the advent of twentieth-century psychology, Cartesian theory took a new twist. The emotions, earlier subsumable under the "body" half of the equation, came under threat of disappearing altogether within the deep convolutions of the cerebral cortex. Emotions were co-opted by a corporeal mind, at least in the context of one dominant (physiological) position. In his book *The Psychology of the Emotions*, the French psychologist Ribot, writing in 1903, could already distinguish between two radically distinct positions in the field with respect to the emotions, which he referred to as the *intellectualist* and the *physiological*.

The physiological thesis was a direct descendant of Cartesian views and found representation in the writings of William James and Carl Lange. States of feeling were held to be primitive and autonomous, connected with biological conditions, and not reducible to intellectual functions. On this thesis, the very primitive nature of feelings also meant that they were plunged deep into the individual psyche, rendered opaque and in some ways ultimately unfathomable. They were embedded in ancient needs and instincts; as such, consciousness could only deliver up a part of their secrets. This aspect of the thesis, of course, was exploited by Freud.

The contrasting intellectualist thesis arose originally from the Herbartian school, which maintained that every state of feeling existed only through its reciprocal relation of representation. The intellectualist thesis contended that emotions or feelings were merely secondary processes derived from modes of knowledge, and that they only existed through these higher functions. If one suppressed intellectual activity, all feeling would disappear. In this view, emotions possess only a "borrowed life, that of a parasite" (Ribot, 1903, p. vii).

Lev Vygotsky, the Soviet psychologist, was of a different mind altogether. Lecturing during the early 1930s, he argued that both positions fail to address a very significant aspect of the question of emotions, and that concerns the **development** of emotional life. To Vygotsky's mind, emotions were neither epiphenomena of consciousness—"gypsies of the mind"—nor simple animal sensations (Vygotsky, in Rieber & Carton, 1987). Going quite against the grain of the times, he maintained that emotions in human and animal were not directly comparable and that human emotions were not merely atrophied versions of animal instincts, but a rich and significant component of personality and mental life, on an equal plane with other mental processes.

Vygotsky also rejected the notion that the course of emotional development in childhood was merely one of suppression and curtailment. Instead, he saw emotional development as a process involving the transformation of emotion from an external to an internal role in mental life. He proposed that Karl Bühler's model of the development of pleasure from *Endlust* (pleasure at goal accomplishment), through *Functionslust* (pleasure in activity itself), to *Vorlust* (the pleasure of anticipation) might serve as a more general model for the emotions, incorporating principles of instinct, association and habit, and interiorization or centralization.

Vygotsky's conceptualizations of emotion were original and provocative. Had he lived longer (he died an early and untimely death in 1934) and had his lecture notes on the emotions been more widely available (an English version was not published until 1987 [Rieber and Carton, eds.]), the history of psychology in the present century might have been a different one. As it was, history took another path altogether. Indeed, during the 1920s and 1930s behavioristic views and analyses of the emotions were predominant. Although the issue of transformation was taken into consideration in accounts of human development, this understanding of transformation was informed and ultimately constrained by the behaviorist agenda. John Watson, the father of behaviorism, proposed that a set of innate emotions became modified by learning over the course of development and that personality was thereby a product of successive conditioning experiences. His work was consequential for a number of researchers who followed him.

Somewhat later, during the late 1920s and early 1930s, Katharine Bridges undertook an observational study of the emotional behaviors of infants and young children and was led in the course of her work to formulate a second formal model of emotional development in infancy and early childhood (Bridges, 1931, 1932). In contrast to Watson's view that there were certain innate fundamental emotions, Bridges proposed that emotions were originally undifferentiated and that changes in emotional expression over time occurred as a function of both maturation and the cumulative impact of social conditioning.

Watson's formulations concerning the conditioning of emotions and Bridges's genetic model of emotional development constituted two of the earliest models of emotion socialization to be found in the psychological literature. Of course Galen had proposed a program of developmental training around emotion management in the first millennium, but Watson's and Bridges's behavioral models were more sophisticated. Emotion socialization was not seen as being limited to teaching children not to bite their elders and elders not to bite their servants, but as a process embedded in the larger context of personality development and informed by an understanding of developmental dynamics.

In the main, the influence of Watson's and Bridges's work was short-lived and the study of emotions and their development was relinquished for the time being. Psychology pursued other agendas, as noted earlier. When psychology rediscovered the emotions during the late 1970s and early 1980s, so many changes had taken place in the subject matter of the broader field that a fresh perspective was brought to the scene. This work is discussed in Chapter 5. For now, we turn to a more detailed examination of developmental models of emotion as they emerged during the first half of this century.

EARLIEST STUDIES OF INFANT EMOTION

As indicated previously, Western culture has held rather jaundiced views concerning the nature and character of emotion. Psychology inherited some of this same attitude, and thus approached its subject matter with ambivalence if not outright disdain. A particularly colorful example of the latter is found in a 1933 *Psychological Review* article by Max Meyer of the University of Missouri, entitled "That Whale among the Fishes—The Theory of Emotions." In this article he likens a theory of the emotions to a whale—a beast that has a twofold distinction among the fishes: When first observed from a distance it looms large and impressive among them. On closer inspection we find that it is not even a fish.

Of course, this was Meyer's way of saying that the emotions were not a fit subject for psychology. He blamed William James for having inflicted the topic on the field, a topic that more rightfully belonged to poetry or philosophy, not psychology, or so he believed. Psychology, he maintained, needed to rid itself of some of the "humbug" it had acquired during its infancy just as the other, more well-established sciences had done in the course of their development. Just as physiology had rid itself of the theory of the four humors, physics the four elements, and chemistry the substance of phlogiston, psychology would have to eliminate its own humbug— the theory of the emotions. Meyer concluded his piece with the prediction that emotion would be a dead issue by the 1950s; emotion would go the way of the "will"—a concept that had already been rooted out of psychology at the time he was writing. "In 1950 American psychologists will smile at both these terms as curiosities of the past" (Meyer, 1933, p. 300).

A scan of the literature of the 1950s indicates that that decade was indeed one of hard times for the field, since, thanks to the ascendancy of activation theory, emotion was no longer regarded as a phenomenologically meaningful construct, being reduced to a point or a set of points on a continuum of arousal. The topic of emotion receded in importance and did not find a home for itself in psychology until the second wave, or modern era.

In 1946, the second edition of the *Handbook of Child Psychology* included a chapter by Jersild that provides a retrospective of the research on emotional development that took place during the field's first wave. One of the most consuming issues, apparently, revolved around the identification of "primary emotions." Although taxonomy has been regarded by at least one writer as the lowest form of philosophy, this has never rendered psychologists reticent, as judged by Jirsild's review as well as others'. Anyone who has ever written anything on the emotions seems to have gravitated to the question. In the first few decades of psychology's history this penchant amounted to a rather popular parlor game, with many of the field's leading psychologists offering their own lists of primary or fundamental emotions. William James, in surveying a literature consumed with this question seems to have been singular in dismissing the pastime as "tedious" and implying that the task of differentiating the emotions was about at interesting and worthy as counting "the shapes of the rocks on a New Hampshire farm" (James, 1983/1890, p. 1064).

Despite this, the activity was a common one during James's time and well into the twentieth century, with many long and short lists generated. William McDougall, the British psychologist, proposed one of the longer lists—a set of instinctual emotions or sentiments, all of which were framed so as to emphasize the evolutionary basis of human emotions, and which thus anticipates Plutchik's

(1980) psychoevolutionary theory (see Chapter 5, this volume). McDougall identified the following seven as primary: flight-fear (i.e., the behavior of *flight* and the sentiment of *fear*), repulsion-disgust, curiosity-wonder, pugnacity-anger, self-abasement (or subjection-negative self-feeling), self-assertion (or self-display-elation), and parental instinct-tender emotion.

J. B. Watson proposed one of the shorter lists of emotion as observed in infants (Watson & Morgan, 1917): fear, rage, and love. Hollingsworth (1928) thought Watson's list rather short and so added "gloom" as a fourth category; but she was most perturbed by what she saw as an adultomorphic error in Watson's approach in labeling the primary emotions. With respect to the latter she suggested that the appropriate infant analogues of fear, rage, and love should be "startle," "resistance," and "content." Thus Hollingsworth was suggesting that infants did not possess genuine emotions as adults understand them, but mere rudimentary precursors devoid of affective sentience.

Another issue identified by Jersild (1946) as having been of particular concern to developmental psychologists during psychology's early history had to do with the identification of the earliest emotions, and the related issue of whether emotions were innate or learned. Developmental research in this area probably began with a basic prejudice inherited from the larger culture. It seems to have been a common and long-standing practice to assume that young infants were mindless and affectless. Dietrich Tiedemann, a professor of Greek and philosophy at Marburg University, writing in 1787, alluded to a common assumption that infancy was "a stage of stupor." In 1903, the philosopher/psychologist Sully likewise described the young infant as "dim and mindless."

Given the prevailing bias among philosophers and psychologists at large against attributing affect to young infants, research on expressive behavior might never have gotten underway earlier this century had it not been for the advent of behaviorism in American psychology. Ironically, and somewhat later, behaviorism would also inspire a rejection of the study of emotion and other "mentalistic" events. In the early days, however, behaviorism inspired two kinds of research that provided data on infant expressive behavior: experimental studies designed to define the necessary and sufficient elicitors of innate emotions and the means of conditioning them, and "genetic" or growth studies involving systematic observation of emotions over time. We will examine the research that occurred in direct response to this movement as well as consider another source of information on infant expressive behavior, that of the baby biography. Although baby biographies were not written expressly for the purpose of detailing infants' emotional displays, these behaviors are acutely salient to even the most casual observer, and the detailed behavioral descriptions contained within the baby biographies offer a unique source of information on expressive behavior that has not heretofore been examined in this light.

In reviewing the literature on expressive behavior that accumulated during the earliest history of developmental psychology, we thus will be examining three kinds of developmental research on the emotions; chronologically, they are (1) the earliest observational studies of individual children, (2) the earliest experimental studies of infant emotion, and (3) the earliest genetic studies of emotional development.

Earliest Observational Studies of Individual Children: The Baby Biographies

Baby biographies provide us with some of the earliest records of detailed, systematic observations of infant emotional expressions; written and published from the 1780s to the 1930s they span an impressive period of time. They typically consisted of records kept by parents, many of whom tended to be academicians with a philosophical (Tiedemann), biological (Darwin, Preyer), or psychological bent (Piaget, Baldwin). Dietrich Tiedemann's 1878 account of his infant son's development is generally regarded as the earliest of such published records (Murchison & Langer, 1929); however, the golden age of the baby biography coincided with the opening decades of scientific psychology, that is, the turn-of-the-century decades, when parent-psychologists turned their analytic minds and trained observational skills to their own offspring. Even Wundt, the arch-experimentalist who had expressed so many reservations about the scientific potential of developmental psychology, collected extensive observational data on his two oldest children during the late 1870s.

The advantages of using baby biographies to explore issues of emotional development are obvious, as are the liabilities and limitations. On the one hand, when conducted by meticulous observers, baby biographies provide rich behavioral detail. On the other hand, there is the risk of observer bias, a risk that is never entirely obviated in psychological research, but perhaps is an even greater problem in the case of parents observing their own children. There is also the risk of nonrepresentativeness of single biographies—as well illustrated by Dietrich Tiedemann's description of the behavior of his infant son. When little Tiedemann's development is compared with that of other infants, it becomes obvious that he is quite precocious. Fortunately, the very presence of multiple records of infant expressive development, as undertaken by different baby biographers, provides us with a built-in check on interobserver reliability.

The following analysis of the baby biography data was undertaken by the first author and a graduate student, Marie Doorey. We were particularly interested in determining whether the longitudinal narratives of the diaries contained enough information to judge the timetable of the emergence of the primary emotions. Dennis's 1936 bibliography of baby biographies, which covers the period from the eighteenth century up to 1933, was used as a primary reference for identifying relevant sources. The bibliography lists 39 studies; of these, only English-language or English-translation studies were considered for further analysis. Two additional studies were unavailable to us and two others were nonlongitudinal. The remaining 26 studies were carefully examined for information concerning (1) the first appearance of any fundamental emotional expressions, (2) their eliciting circumstances, and (3) the criteria used to infer emotions. The diaries were searched for mention of seven specific emotions: interest, joy, surprise, sadness, anger, disgust, and fear, and the motive state of pain. These particular emotions were selected on the basis of research indicating that even untrained observers can reliably identify facial expressions of these emotions in infants as judged against objective criteria (Izard, Huebner, Risser, McGinnes, & Dougherty, 1980).

Four of the baby biographies were particularly meticulous from a methodological point of view, and were the most consistently informative with respect to the full range of emotions. These were the records of Darwin, Preyer, Shinn, and Lowden; their data are summarized in Table 2. The remainder of the baby biographies provided only incomplete or fragmentary data, or mentioned emotions but did not identify the criteria the biographer was using to make his or her inferences. Nevertheless, certain aspects of selected data sets were credible enough for inclusion in the table, as noted.

There are several things that are noteworthy about the data in Table 2. First, when we examine the criteria used to infer the existence of a particular emotion, we note a remarkable degree of consistency across biographers. Thus, biographers are basically focusing on the same aspects of behavior when they make attributions about specific emotions. Interestingly, many of the facial criteria used to infer emotions are the same ones that are the basis for contemporary facial affect coding schemes (e.g., Izard's 1979 Maximally Discriminative Facial Movement Coding System).

Second, there is wide variability across infants in terms of when infants are first seen displaying clear signs of the various discrete emotions. For example, interest is first observed anywhere from 1 to 8 weeks; the onset of anger is first observed anywhere from 1 to 44 weeks.

Although the variability in onset times for the various emotions may seem to cast doubt on either the accuracy of the observations or the clarity of the phenomena, the fact that there is a high degree of consistency in criteria across studies in judging the presence of particular kinds of emotion, as noted above, suggests that the largest source of variance is the infants themselves rather than their observers.

There are a number of reasons to place confidence in the above assumption. In the first place, considerable interindividual variability in onset times for other developmental domains is fairly well established. In terms of Gesell's norms for motor development, babies accomplish the following behaviors in a somewhat predictable order: lifting the head, sitting up, crawling, standing, and walking. However, not all infants achieve these milestones at the same time, nor do they always go through all of the stages. Some infants skip crawling and go directly from sitting to standing. In terms of language development, some infants go from one-word utterances to short sentences, whereas other infants go through an intermediate pivot-open grammar stage. Most infants begin speaking toward the end of the first year. Some particularly precocious infants begin speaking as early as the first 6 months, whereas late bloomers, like Virginia Woolf, do not start until the third year.

It is also possible that differential onsets may reflect the presence or absence of different kinds of elicitors in the environment. Some elicitors that may be well represented in one family's home may be absent in another's. It is germane to note

Table 2. Emergence of Eight Discrete Emotion Expressions: Their Onsets and Associated Elicitors as Adduced from Baby Biographies

Emotion	First noted[a]	Eliciting condition	Criteria
Interest	7 w (Darwin)	Bright colored tassel	Fixed eyes, quieting
	1 w (Preyer)	Ordinary daylight, brilliant, brightly shining objects	Eyes wide open, forehead wrinkled
	4 w (Shinn)	Faces	Effortful staring
	2 w (Lowden)	Father's face	Looking intently
	5 w (Moore)	Father calling infant	Looking attentively
	8 w (Rasmussen)	Sound of harmonica	Slight attentiveness
Joy	6 w (Darwin)	Sight of mother	Eyes brightened, smile
	4 w (Preyer)	Sight of mother	Smile, new sounds
	5 w (Shinn)	Father's face	Social smile
	8 w (Lowden)	Father's smile	Smile
	1 w (Tiedemann)	Internal	Smile during sleep
	4 w (Tiedemann)	External	Smile in response to talking or mimicry
	1 w (Major)	Taste of saffron tea	Face assumed a more pleasant expression than before
	2 w (Willard)	Black door being shut in a white wall	Smile
	4 w (Major)	Playful shaking of infant hand and arm	Broad smiles
	1 w (Dearborn)	Tickled on cheek/chin	Dim smiles
	8 w (Dearborn)	Animated face and voice	Social smiles
	1 w (Fenton)		"Reflex smiles"
	8 w (Fenton)	Singing	First "true smiles"
	4 w (Rasmussen)	When the curtain was drawn from her cradle	Smile
Surprise	19 w (Darwin)	Father's voice when standing behind infant in front of mirror	None given
	44 w (Preyer)	Nearby stranger	Mouth and eyes wide open, immobility
	7 w (Shinn)	Her own first crowing sound	"Ludicrous astonishment"; jaw fell, brows raised
	5 w (Lowden)	Red ball swung before infant	Hands & feet active, eyes wide open & fixed on ball
	22 w (Tiedemann)	Saw something new and delightful	Exclamation "ach!"
	16 w (Moore)	Novel events	Protrusion of the lips, wide open eyes, forward inclination of body, reaching of hands, accelerated respiration
	5 w (McLeish)	Yellow colored sheet	Eyebrows drawn up, mouth pursed into small "o", protruding lips
	3 w (Dearborn)	Gentle slap on cheek; bottle within seeing distance	Eyes and mouth wide open

(continued)

Table 2. (*Continued*)

Emotion	First noted[a]	Eliciting condition	Criteria
	12 w (Fenton)	When being propped up for the first time	Blank, wide-eyed expression
	27 w (Rasmussen)	Sound of dog barking	Stopped feeding, opened eyes wide and gazed at ceiling
Sadness	26 w (Darwin)	Nurse's fake weeping	Corners of mouth well-depressed
	23 w (Preyer)	Addressed in harsh tone	Stared at person, corners of mouth drawn down, plaintive cry, naso-labial corrugation
	8 w (Shinn)	Desired contact	Silent, looking soberly about, fretting
	6 w (Lowden)	Brother hit him	Tears
Anger	28 w (Darwin)	Could not reach an object that had slipped out of reach	Quality of cry, blood rush to the face & scalp
	16 w (Preyer)	(None given)	Screaming, squarish mouth
	44 w (Shinn)	Being dressed an extra time	Tone of crying
	1 w (Lowden)	Being unable to put fingers back in mouth	Reddening of face & head, repeated tries
	30 w (Moore)	Being annoyed	Frowning
	7 w (Tiedemann)	If not responded to immediately	Angry screams
Distress/ Pain	1 w (Darwin)	Unidentified; occurred before a crying fit	Frown, skin around eyes wrinkled
	newborn (Preyer)	Middle of upper tongue was touched on surface	Eyes shut tight, nostrils and corners of mouth raised
	4 w (Shinn)	Seemed connected to faint sensations of discomfort	Violent grimacing
	22 hr (Lowden)	Vinegar on tongue	Muscles of face contorted, eyes firmly shut, lips puckered
Disgust	1 w (Preyer)	Salted food	Shudder, shut eyes distorted face
	6 w (Shinn)	Reaction to water following sugar	Same face Preyer reports to new tastes
	5 w (Tiedemann)	Administration of medicine	"Obvious repulsion"
Fear	9 w (Darwin)	Loud sneeze	Started violently, looked frightened, then cried
	9 w (Preyer)	Abrupt approach to face	Quick shutting of eyes, throwing up of arms
	5 w (Shinn)	(None given, baby had been half asleep)	Started violently, cried loudly, pulled up lip, had disturbed face for 5 minutes
	6 w (Lowden)	Strange faces of father	Sound of crying
	> 6 m (Willard)	Stranger	(Not given)
	9 m (Champneys)	Unusual sound	Wide eyes, crying

[a] w = week (days rounded up or down to nearest week)

that almost all contemporary emotions researchers date the emergence of the fear response as the second half of the first year of life. Nevertheless, Gaensbauer and Harmon (1982) report observing fear much earlier in an infant who was physically abused by its parents. A child may also be inadvertently exposed to a very frightening event. Such examples illustrate that certain emotions may be "in the repertoire" in the sense of being functionally available, but may *typically* not be observed due to the absence of precipitating circumstances.

A third reason to trust the data on emotional expression derives from the fact that the observations in general were particularly astute. Many of the baby biographies contain notes on developmental phenomena that are only now being reported and validated by psychologists in large-scale empirical studies of children. Tiedemann's 1787 account is particularly instructive. His observations included the finding that young infants prefer to look at moving rather than stationary targets (Tiedemann, 1787, p. 206; Kagan & Lewis, 1965), that they show evidence of intermodal mapping (Tiedemann, 1787, p. 209; Meltzoff, 1981), that there are two different types of smiles developmentally (Tiedemann, 1787; Emde, Gaensbauer, & Harmon, 1976), that intelligence first manifests itself as action, that is, is sensorimotor (Tiedemann, 1787, p. 210; Piaget, 1932/1952), that infants have a contagious response to facial and vocal emotional sounds and that this is a forerunner of sympathy (Tiedemann, 1787, p. 211; Sagi & Hoffman, 1976), and so on. Similar examples could be cited from other baby biographies.

However, returning to the issue of variability, it is also important to point out that Tiedemann's child was a precocious infant. He displayed contingency learning at day 13, laughed at 1 month, performed motor mimicry at 1 month, and deployed crying instrumentally by $1\frac{3}{4}$ months. Thus, the use of a single case, no matter how well documented, runs the risk of overestimating or underestimating the abilities of children at different developmental stages.

It is possible that much of the interinfant variability in onset times for the emergence of discrete emotions has less to do with precocity per se than it does with temperamental differences. Haviland (1976) observed and video recorded the facial expressions of her fraternal twins and noted quite distinct differences between the children in their facial expressions as early as the opening days of life. She also noted that the expressions of her own children differed strikingly from the expressions of Zinacanteco Indian children from Chiapas, Mexico. Whereas the most common brow positions for her children were relaxed or slightly raised, the Indian children never showed these configurations and, instead, weak frowns were extremely common.

Moving to another point with reference to Table 2, we note that despite the variability of onset times within affect categories, it also seems evident that across studies certain emotions appear earlier in development than others. The tabulated data indicate that distress/pain is the first expressive behavior to be identified, appearing during the newborn period. Disgust (mean age = 4 weeks) and joy are seen next (mean age = 3.6 weeks when including internal, "dim," and reflex smiles, 5.1 weeks when excluding them). Fear is the next to be seen (mean = 7.3 weeks). The emotions of sadness and surprise appear to mature somewhat later, being seen at a mean age of 16 weeks. Anger appears to be seen on the average at a later age than any of the other emotions, with a mean of 21 weeks. By these data, all the fundamental emotions are in the expressive repertoire within the first $4\frac{1}{2}$ months of life. In Chapter 5 we will see that contemporary emotions theorists think that some emotions, namely fear, surprise, and sadness, are not present until quite a bit later than this. However, few systematic studies of the development of emotion expression from the earliest days have been conducted. We turn now to a discussion of the place of emotions research in the context of the dawn of experimental psychology.

Earliest "Scientific" Studies of Emotion

The work of John Broadus Watson and his student Mary Cover Jones set the stage for much of the research on emotional development that occurred during the decades of the 1920s and 1930s. This is not to slight the influence of William James's theory which inspired considerable research culminating in what became known as the James-Lange/Cannon-Bard debate, a debate that all but consumed experimental psychology during the same time period. However, the latter work was nondevelopmental, being concerned instead with fundamental questions concerning the physiology of emotion and the role of visceral feedback in emotional experience. James's theory also failed to generate research on expressive behavior (the somatic aspect of emotion), despite the fact that James's feedback theory, which was being so vigorously attacked, originally indicated that both somatic and visceral aspects were responsible for the subjective experience of emotion. Thus, it was largely owing to the behavioristic movement that psychology became involved in research on expressive behavior and developmental issues. Before that research is examined it would be helpful to take a look at Watson's background and Zeitgeist in order to understand why he was such a galvanizing force in American psychology.

Watson and Behaviorism

Watson and his behavioristic psychology had a profound and enduring impact on the course of psychology in this century. By the mid-1920s, behaviorism had swept America. It was regarded as a particularly American phenomenon. Karl Bühler's 1926 work, *Die Krise der Psychologie*, linked what the author described as psychology's crisis to the Tower of Babel created by the different schools of psychology. He was referring to the three rival schools that dominated the scene at the time: (1) the old tradition of introspection and phenomenology, (2) the newer German product, gestalt psychology, and (3) behaviorism. The three schools did indeed have a different working vocabulary and epistemology even if they did not really constitute totally different languages. Still the metaphor was apt, and behaviorism, the newest school, seemed the strangest tongue of all, especially to the European ear. Much of the credit for behaviorism's eventual success goes to Watson. It was he who originated the term, and he who italicized it at every opportunity so as to distinguish it from other schools of psychology.

Behaviorism found a warm reception among Americans for several reasons. According to Gardner Murphy (Senn, 1975), Watson's own personality was a not inconsiderable force. Watson was a hard-driving, ambitious, and, by some accounts, charismatic individual. He lectured fairly extensively, had stage presence, and a forceful style of delivery. He was also outspoken and opinionated and given to flamboyant and highly quotable statements (Buckley, 1989; Watson, 1936). These personality characteristics gave him a distinct visibility—one that he exploited to his advantage and to the advantage of promoting the new "scientific" psychology as it developed in America. In Murphy's analysis, another important factor was the nature and character of Watson's research. The conditioning of fear in little Albert and in what he called the psychopathological dog coincided with shell shock problems of the first world war and fit popular conceptions of psychopathology that were emerging from the war experience.

A third factor accounting for the popularity of behaviorism, according to David Elkind (Senn, 1975) related to the concordance between the behavioristic epistemology and the American social ethic which stressed pragmatism, individualism, and self-reliance; all of the latter principles went comfortably hand in hand with the strict environmentalism that Watson was advancing. Thus Watson's stance was in a sense thoroughly American and totally assimilable to contemporary local ideals.

Before we proceed to his theory, we include an extended biographical note on Watson's life. The treatment of biography is more detailed here than in earlier sections not only for the historical contextualization, but also because it provides a particularly good example of the interpenetration of personality and the construction of knowledge. Aspects of Watson's biography suggest an attachment history and attachment style, as well as indicate specific emotion biases in his personality. In Chapters 9 and 10 we discuss how a person's emotional organization (attachment style and emotion biases) impact on information processing and the elaboration of behavior and thought. Thus we will have opportunity to return to Watson's biography as a particularly apt illustration of the principle.

Biography of Watson (1878–1958)

Watson, the man, and behaviorism, the theory, are inextricably bound up with one another as we will see from a somewhat extended biographical sketch. As a youngster, Watson was shy and aloof. He grew up in an isolated, rural South Carolina community, the son of a devout Baptist mother and a hard-drinking father who had an explosive temper and who was often absent from home for months at a time. John's mother had named him after a prominent Southern Baptist minister and hoped that her son would grow up to be evangelically inclined. In some ways Watson did enact an evangelical mission in adult life, but his devotion was to behaviorism, not religion. For Watson's mother, however, the church was the center of her existence and she raised her children in strict accordance with its teachings, all the while struggling to manage a growing family and a not very prosperous farm largely on her own. Watson as a boy learned to keep busy and not dwell on his problems; he became self-reliant at an early age and learned to avoid his father, whose unpredictable absences and violent temper left the family in desperate economic straits and certainly placed them under considerable emotional strain.

Thus, as a youngster, Watson was buffeted between the strictures of religious fundamentalism, with emphasis on order, control, responsibility, hard work, and discipline on the one hand, and the tempestuous emotionality and irresponsible behavior of his father on the other. These dual influences would prefigure his own struggle to control his emotions and moderate his impulsivity, an effort at which he was not entirely successful. In any case, it was no accident that he would develop a philosophy and behavioristic principles that would be applied to the goal of the ultimate subjugation of the emotions. His early life had been a source of great personal distress, but he preferred not to introspect or dwell on this. Watson displayed little overt emotional response when his mother died not long after he graduated from college; he seldom spoke of his father as an adult and on the rare occasion that he did, it was with resentment. Later in life, when his father sought forgiveness and reconciliation, Watson turned his back.

John was 12 when his mother sold the farm, picked up the family, and moved to the larger city of Greenville. Watson felt awkward and socially inept being thrown in with a new and more sophisticated crowd. He became the target of classroom jokes; responding with belligerence, he was often drawn into fights. Later he attended the local Baptist college, Furman University. There he put himself through school by working as an assistant in the chemistry laboratory. He was regarded as unsocial and one professor remembered him as "bright, but more interested in ideas and theories than . . . people" (Buckley, 1989, p. 11). He did not have a particularly distinguished academic career, graduating 14th in a class of 22. Upon graduation he went on to become a principal of Batesburg Institute, a small private academy near Columbia. He disliked the tedium of teaching rudimentary-level courses and maintaining order in the classroom. When his mother became gravely ill and then died, he decided to cut his ties with South Carolina and strike off for better prospects. He realized that he needed further professional training to advance himself. He chose the University of Chicago and left South Carolina in the fall of 1900. At the time, psychology was considered a bright and promising field, though not yet distinct from philosophy. Chicago was viewed as being at the cutting edge of various new educational and philosophical programs, including the new American functionalism that was sweeping the country and which was the immediate predecessor of behaviorism.

At Chicago Watson worked under James Rowland Angell (who eventually went on to become president of Yale) and H. H. Donaldson, the comparative psychologist. Watson's own course of studies was focused on experimental and comparative work and his dissertation involved investigating the relation between behavior and the growth of the nervous system in the white rat. The white rat, incidentally, ubiquitous as it is now, was only first introduced into laboratory research in 1892 by the Swiss-born neuropathologist Adolf Meyer; by the turn of the century, Chicago was the only psychological laboratory to employ the animal in experiments.

Angell had some degree of ambition for the field and began to agitate for a separate department of psychology; in 1904 a department of psychology was organized and Angell became chairman. Among Angell's goals for the newly independent science were to sever its ties with philosophy and to form a closer alliance with the biological sciences. Watson became a vocal advocate for this position both personally and in his work. His graduate thesis received a flattering review in *The Nation* and was commended in several journals. Angell saw particular promise in Watson and managed to get his protégé an appointment as his assistant.

Watson's teaching assignment included instructing introductory psychology, and it was in one of these classes that he encountered his future wife, Mary Ickes. The marriage was an ill-fated one from the very beginning. Watson did not have a wholly positive view of marriage to begin with and it became even less positive over time. He also was ambivalent about parenthood, though he seemed charmed enough at the birth of his first child, a daughter, commenting that a baby could be "more fun to the square inch than all the frogs and rats in creation " (Buckley, 1989, p. 52). Watson was not particularly affectionate with his children; his daughter could recall only one instance of physical affection—when he departed for Europe during World War I—and then he simply kissed her on the forehead. As we will see, his bias against physical displays of affection and his antisentimental attitude toward children became a prescription for parents at large, as promulgated in his book, *The Psychological Care of the Infant and Child* (1928).

Watson's marriage suffered from financial as well as emotional strain, and was placed under further strain when an affair with an old flame was discovered by his wife's brother, who brought the scandal to the attention not only of Watson's wife but of the administration of the university. Watson would have been dismissed on the spot but the matter was smoothed over through the intervention of Angell. Still, the event was not without repercussions.

While at Chicago Watson's reputation as entrepreneur of the new brand of scientific psychology grew and by 1908 he had distinguished himself far beyond his peers. Nevertheless, he did not advance in rank or salary, and began to look elsewhere, eventually accepting a position at Johns Hopkins University. On leaving Chicago he reflected that as a comparative psychologist he had already solidly grounded himself in the study of animal behavior and was now ready to "get busy on the human side" (Buckley, 1989, p. 58).

The department at Johns Hopkins was headed by James Mark Baldwin, a prominent and influential psychologist who had raised the department's budget to the fifth largest in the University. However, within a year his fortunes were reversed in the midst of a personal scandal and he was forced to resign; he eventually left the country.

Baldwin's misfortune was Watson's personal gain; he quickly slipped into the role of running the department and by the age of 31 he had become the head of a department at a major research institution. With hard work and a somewhat messianic sense of himself and his goals for a scientific psychology, he actively promoted his agenda not only at Hopkins but also from his pulpit as the editor of the *Psychological Review*, and as cofounder, with Robert Yerkes, of the *Journal of Animal Behavior*. However, even as he was extending the frontiers of his influence in animal research, he foresaw that he had to cross over to research on humans if he was to carve out a unique niche for psychology.

At midcareer Watson was recognized as one of America's leading researchers in comparative psychology and thus was singularly well placed to forward his scientific agenda. The observed continuities between human and animal behavior suggested to him that some of the same principles of behavior he had been discovering in lower animals might apply equally to human behavior and that principles of behavior might be reduced to the same objectively measured noncognitive dimensions. Over the course of the next 10 to 12 years he proceeded to organize a program of research designed to forward this understanding of behavior.

From 1913 to 1917 Watson began developing his behavioristic framework and marketing it for public consumption. In 1913 he delivered a series of lectures at Columbia University that sent shock waves throughout the psychological community. He billed himself as "the behaviorist" and defined the behavioristic mission as a "purely objective experimental branch of natural science," with its "theoretical goal" being nothing less than the "prediction and control of behavior" (Buckley, 1989, p. 74). It was this emphasis on prediction and control of behavior that set behaviorism apart from structuralism, functionalism, and the rest of psychology.

Watson wanted no competitors and took aim at his rivals. Both Freudian psychoanalysis and introspectionism came under his fire. He regarded psychoanalysis as a somewhat occult enterprise, and berated its reliance on untestable hypothetical constructs and mystical notions such as the "unconscious." Many of Freud's observations, he felt, could be rendered in more behavioral terms. For example, affection could be restated as an "organic sensory response," and transference as "stimulus generalization." Introspectionism, which was more deeply entrenched in American psychology, had to be more forcibly rooted out. In a letter to Robert Yerkes, Watson wrote that he had been experimenting with conditioning in humans and was elated to find that "it works so beautifully in place of introspection that . . . it deserves to be driven home; we can work on the human being as we can on animals and from the same point of view" (cited in Buckley, 1989, p. 86).

In 1914 at the age of 36, Watson became the youngest nominee for president of the American Psychological Association (APA) in the history of this body, and he was elected over many other senior psychologists. Such a remarkable achievement is probably attributable to the fact that Watson had given expression to the hopes of a majority of his colleagues that psychology would one day enter the ranks of the other sciences on an equal footing. But Watson not only verbalized the hopes, he also offered a program, that of behaviorism, for achieving the new promised land. As such, it should come as no surprise that he was hailed as a "second Moses."

Watson made certain basic assumptions about human personality and its origins, namely, that there are a limited number of innate emotions and reflexes at birth and that everything else arises from conditioning based on environmental forces. The two mechanisms of conditioning and learning, he felt, could explain the means by which emotions and behavior were elaborated in development, with personality emerging from an increasingly complex organization of behavior.

With this theoretical framework, it is not surprising that he chose to work with infants. The rationale seemed persuasive. In order to "understand man, one must begin with the history of the behavior" (cited in Cairns, 1983). At Hopkins Watson engineered an alliance with Adolph Meyer, a major figure in the development of American psychiatry and the head of a clinic and psychology laboratory at the Johns Hopkins Medical School. Through Meyer, Watson gained access to the clinic, where he hoped to set up a laboratory to carry out his investigation of the conditioning of emotions; he was excited by the prospect that he would be next door to the obstetrical ward where he would have access to about 40 babies a month for observation and, he hoped, experimentation to implement Pavlovian and Bechterewian conditions. The attraction for Meyer in having Watson set up a laboratory in his clinic resided in the inherent promise of articulating a model of psychopathology that would reveal the social and biological factors involved in personality development. However, Meyer soon became disillusioned, being particularly put off by the mechanistic flavor of behaviorism as it was developed by Watson. He felt that Watson had merely turned structuralism upside down, "substituting a mechanistic model of simple reflexes and perpetuating a dualism on the side of body that was no better than the structuralists' preoccupation with mind" (cited in Buckley, 1989, p. 90).

Despite Meyer's growing reservations, Watson was able to launch his studies on emotion and conditioning during this time. At the base of the research agenda was what would later be regarded as a preoccupation with methods designed to control emotional reactions, which Watson saw as an overarching social goal. What he had in mind was an ambitious agenda that involved nothing less than the social reconstruction of American culture. Emotions were immensely powerful, volatile, and potentially dangerous. Though once useful to mankind, we were "no longer living in a frontier society," where, "strong expressions of emotion were needed in the struggle for existence" (cited in Buckley, 1989, p. 119). If the energy of emotions could be harnessed, tamed, and channeled in socially constructive ways, they could be made to serve modern man, and assist in reaching ever higher levels of individual achievement.

When seen within the context of a longer historical perspective, the above views are not out of step with the dominant Western philosophic tradition, though Watson may have expressed one of the more extreme versions of it. However, Watson went well beyond the early Greeks and Romans and his own contemporaries in his preoccupation with the control of emotions. He was ultimately successful in proving that emotion could be harnessed (conditioned) and he used this impressive demonstration as a springboard to propose social engineering agendas and child training strategies that were more radical than even those advocated by Galen, the second-century Stoic.

Watson's preoccupation with control of the emotions was conceivably a reflection of his own lifelong struggle with containing his own emotional impulses. At some level he may have had a premonition that his emotions would overcome his better judgment, for it was only a few years later that a personal scandal would force him to leave academia.

Prelude to the Conditioning Research of Watson: Description of the Emotions and Their Elicitors

Watson had advanced the theory that the conditioned reflex could be used as a means of controlling emotional responses. With access to infants from Meyer's hospital clinic he had an opportunity to put his theory to the test and he approached the task vigorously and programmatically. The first efforts involved identifying the basic reflexive apparatus of the young infant, including its innate emotions. In behavioristic language, he sought to describe both the responses (i.e., the emotional reactions) as well as the "stimuli," or elicitors, that provoked them. The subsequent effort would involve an experimental demonstration of the conditioning of an emotion.

Innate Emotional Responses

In 1917 Watson and Morgan published the results of their studies of the emotional repertoire of young infants. Three basic emotional responses were discriminated: fear, rage, and love. Watson's account of this research is interesting from a number of standpoints. It is worthwhile examining the original research because it was primarily this work that provoked a series of studies designed to confirm or refute his basic assertions. A review of Watson's study is also instructive since it helps explain why the effects he reported were so difficult to replicate. The reporting style left much to be desired in terms of today's standards. In the original 1917 paper, as well as other summary reports, few details are provided in terms of subject characteristics (number, their ages, whether the mother had received anesthesia during delivery, etc.), specific procedures, data on the proportion of infants who did and did not reach criteria for various responses, and so forth. For example, in the 1917 report, the section devoted to a description of the subjects merely states that the experimenters' procedures involved "observing a large number of infants, especially during the first months of life . . ." (Watson & Morgan, 1917, p. 165). The authors' description of elicitors and responses is somewhat better, but again, no data are presented on the distribution of infants who did and did not display the responses in question and to what degree. Let us examine each of the three emotions investigated.

Fear. Sachs (1893) was one of the first investigators to call attention to the fact that intense auditory stimuli evoked gross muscular responses in infants and that these responses were appropriately labeled fear. However, it was Watson who designated these responses as constituting a class of primary emotion. (Watson's proposal that fear dated from the moment of birth was not unheard of in his day; Rank [1929] had already proposed that fear was a response to birth trauma, and

Sadger [1941] proposed that anxiety might apply to the embryo, and even to spermatozoa and ova.)

The *unconditioned stimulus* for fear involved loud sounds such as the striking of a steel bar with a hammer, loss of bodily support, "especially when the body is not set to compensate for it" (Watson, 1926, p. 338), or shaking or jarring:

> It can best be observed in newborns just when they are falling asleep. If dropped then, or if the blanket upon which they lie is suddenly jerked, pulling the infant along with it, the response invariably occurs. (p. 338)

In addition, the fear response could be elicited when the child had just fallen to sleep or was just ready to awaken . . . . [with] a sudden push or a slight shake . . . (Watson & Morgan, 1917, p. 166). Thus, the three innate elicitors of the primary emotion of fear were loud noises, shaking or jarring, or loss of support.

The unconditioned response for fear was said to have the following classic features: "Checking of breathing, jump or start of whole body, crying, often defecation and urination (and many others not worked out experimentally). Probably the largest group of fear reactions are visceral" (Watson, 1926, p. 340).

Rage. The *unconditioned stimulus.* The innate eliciting conditions for rage were said to involve

> hampering of bodily movements, ... This can be observed from the moment of birth but more easily observed in infants 10 to 15 days of age. When the head is held lightly between the hands; when the arms are pressed to the sides; and when the legs are held tightly together, rage behavior begins. (Watson, 1926, p. 339)

The *unconditioned response* for rage includes:

> The unlearned behavior elements in rage behavior have never been completely catalogued. Some of the elements, however, are easily observed, such as the stiffening of the whole body, the free slashing movements of hands, arms and legs [otherwise referred to as "defensive responses"], and the holding of the breath. There is no crying at first, then the mouth is opened to the fullest extent and the breath is held until the face appears blue. These states can be brought on without the pressure in any case being severe enough to produce the slightest injury to the child. The experiments are discontinued the moment the slightest blueness appears in the skin. (Watson, 1924, p. 339)

Love. Watson apparently felt a bit more squeamish about the laboratory induction of "love" in infants. He reported the following features of the *unconditioned stimulus*:

> The study of this emotion in the infant is beset with a great many difficulties on the conventional side. Our observations consequently have been incidental rather than directly experimental. The stimulus to love responses apparently is stroking of the skin, tickling, gentle rocking, patting. The responses are especially easy to bring out by the stimulation of what, for lack of a better term, we may call the erogenous zones. (Watson, 1924, p. 339)

As for the *unconditioned response*, Watson noted the following:

The response varies—if the infant is crying, crying ceases, a smile may begin, attempts at gurgling, cooing, and finally, in slightly older children, the extension of the arms which we should class as the forerunner of clasping in the narrowed sex act in coitus. The smile and the laugh which Freud connects with the release of repression (we are not denying in the case of adults that this may not be true) we should thus class as original reaction tendencies intimately connected from infancy with the stimulation of the erogenous zones. By original nature the child is not *polymorphous perverse*, nor addicted to playing with urine, fecal matter or (originally) even with the anus or sex organs. Habits (conditioned reflexes) are rapidly set up in connection with these objects at a *very* early age and they may when not looked after sadly warp the child. (Watson & Morgan, 1917, p. 167)

The unconditioned emotional responses Watson and Morgan reported were viewed as elemental and primitive, but Watson believed that they were the building blocks for personality development. It was at this time that he began to formulate the theory of emotional conditioning, which he viewed within the context of habit formation and which directly gave rise to the fear conditioning experiment with the child known as little Albert. In the Watson and Morgan (1917) paper he noted, "so far no one has tried explicitly to introduce the illuminating concept of habit formation into the realm of emotions" (p. 168). He then acknowledged that Freud had used the concept *Übertragung* (transference), but derided this as a mystification of what was really simply only habit. Moreover, Freud's notion of transference appeared to be limited to the sphere of sexual emotion whereby the patient's attachment to parents was reenacted with the analyst. Watson proposed that "transference" encompassed a much broader phenomenon. He saw it as a generalized response tendency organized around an emotion, and it could involve any emotion. Freud had talked about transference with respect to the "love-reaction."

> But there is no reason to suppose that the same thing does not occur in the other emotions. Rage likewise is capable of being attached now to one object, now to another in an ever widening series—i.e., given an original situation which will arouse rage . . . and you will have transfers wherever the conditions are at hand for the arousal of conditioned reflexes. An individual hampers my use of my arms and legs, constrains me, holds me badly when dressing me, etc. [original conditions for arousing rage]—shortly the mere sight of that individual arouses the rage components. Finally an entire stranger whose behavior is even slightly similar to that of the first individual may set off the responses. (Watson and Morgan, 1917, p. 169)

Obviously, Watson was already beginning to formulate the notion of "generalization," and indeed he was to see the phenomenon *in vivo* as he undertook the experimental conditioning of little Albert. In this case he sought to condition fear.

EARLIEST EXPERIMENTAL STUDIES OF EMOTION

Watson and the Conditioning of Fear

The conditioning of little Albert is possibly one of the most well-known experiments in the history of psychology (Watson & Rayner, 1920). In brief,

Watson and his graduate student Rosalie Rayner took as their subject a plump, phlegmatic, 11-month-old infant with no prior history of fears as their subject. By pairing a loud sound (a hammer striking an iron bar) with the presentation of a white rat, the boy acquired a fear not only of the rat, but of other objects as well; moreover, the fear appeared to be resistant to extinction. As Watson put it, "guts can learn" (Watson, 1928). Although Watson had some reservations about having produced a fear in a child who had previously had none, he did not attempt to apply his behavioristic skills to the eradication of the fear. Moreover, much to his discredit, he was never really concerned about the subsequent fate of Albert, and even joked that if Albert developed a fear of fur coats later in life, a psychiatrist would probably attribute it to a sexual neurosis.

Watson's Career Comes to an End

Watson's association with Rayner extended beyond their experimental collaboration and they were soon the subject of scandal. There was a very public divorce and Watson was asked to resign his academic post. He moved to New York where he was taken in by a friend, and eventually got a job at the J. Walter Thompson Company, an advertising firm. For a man of his accomplishment, fame, and sense of self-importance, it must have been a painful experience to find himself starting at the bottom rung of a new career at the age of 42, though in his autobiography (Watson, 1936) he gives no indication of this. For a while he was commissioned to study the rubber boot market along the Mississippi River; later he was sent out to sell Yuban Coffee to retailers and wholesalers. Eventually, he worked his way through all the departments of media, research, and copy. He applied himself with his usual hard work and stoicism and was made vice president of the company 4 years later. In the midst of this experience he was to later claim, "I began to learn that it can be just as thrilling to watch the growth of a sales curve of a new product as to watch the learning curve of animals or men" (Watson, 1936).

Watson's only remaining academic ties were in the form of occasional teaching at the New School for Social Research and a lecture series at Clark University. However, he continued to seek publication outlets for his behavioristic views and it is perhaps during this stage of his life and work that he had his most significant impact on American culture, consciousness, and child rearing. The more isolated he became from academia and the colleagueship of other scientists, the more extreme Watson's pronouncements on human development became, and the more he turned to the popular press to communicate his ideas. From 1922 on, he wrote popular articles for various magazines, and in 1928 he published *Psychological Care of the Infant and Child*. As his ideas about child rearing were diffused through the popular media, an era of behavioristic childrearing in American was launched.

Watson's main pitch was that child-rearing practices could be made more efficacious by removing all of the needless sentimentality with which it was currently infused. He had decided that the expression of affection was infantaliz-ing and robbed children of the ability to become autonomous. Since Americans prized individualism and autonomy, and Watson was touting early autonomy in his prescriptions for rearing independent children, the book became a bestseller. Parents were impressed with the apparent scientific authority with which he presented his views, although his writings included virtually no empirical documentation outside of references to some of his early works on the conditioning of emotions.

The following excerpts from *Psychological Care of the Infant and Child* (1928) illustrate quite forcefully Watson's views on emotions, and can be seen as unwittingly reflecting on his own emotionally brutal childhood. They also are a glimpse into the mind of an American public during the immediate postwar years, a mind and spirit that would readily embrace prescriptions we would today find cold, if not peculiar.

> The fact that our children are always crying and always whining shows the unhappy, unwholesome state they are in. Their digestion is interfered with and probably their whole glandular system is deranged. (p. 81)

> There is a sensible way of treating children. Treat them as though they were young adults. Dress them, bathe them with care and circumspection. Let your behavior always be objective and kindly firm. Never hug and kiss them, never let them sit in your lap. If you must, kiss them once on the forehead when they say good night. Shake hands with them in the morning. Give them a pat on the head if they have made an extraordinary good job of a difficult task. Try it out. In a week's time you will find how easy it is to be perfectly objective with your child and at the same time kindly. You will be utterly ashamed of the mawkish, sentimental way you have been handling it. (pp. 81–82)

> I sometimes wish that we could live in a community of homes where each home is supplied with a well-trained nurse so that we could have the babies fed and bathed each week by a different nurse. (p. 83)

> If you haven't a nurse and cannot leave the child, put it out in the backyard a large part of the day. Build a fence around the yard so that you are sure no harm can come to it. Do this from the time it is born. When the child can crawl, give it a sandpile and be sure to dig some small holes in the yard so it has to crawl in and out of them. Let it learn to overcome difficulties almost from the moment of birth. The child should learn to conquer difficulties away from your watchful eye. (p. 84)

> Modern training calls always for an orderly life. Usually from 1 year of age to 3 pediatricians specify that orange juice shall be given when the child wakes up in the morning. Children who sleep properly awaken on a schedule. The waking time can easily be set for 6:30. The orange juice should then be given regularly at that hour every morning, the child put on the toilet for the relief of the bladder (only). Put the child back to bed and allow it to sit up in bed and play quietly alone with one or two chosen toys. It should be taken up at 7 o'clock, sponged lightly, dressed and given its breakfast at 7:30; then allowed to romp until 8, then put upon the toilet for 20 minutes or less (until the bowel movement is complete). The infant from 8 months of age onward should have a special toilet seat into which he can be safely strapped. *The child should be left in the bathroom without toys and with the door closed.* Under no circumstances should the door be left open or the mother or nurse stay with the child. This is a rule which seems to be almost universally broken. When broken it leads to dawdling, loud conversation, in general to unsocial and dependent behavior. (pp. 121–122)

Watson was ambivalent about the publication of this book.

> [It] . . . was another book I feel sorry about—not because of its sketchy form, but because I did not know enough to write the book I wanted to write. I feel that I had a right to publish this, sketchy as it is, since I planned never to go back into academic work. (Watson, 1936, p. 280)

It is hard to gauge the full impact of Watson's child-rearing advice. Many parents certainly accepted it and adopted it in practice. An example follows: Watson had preached early behavioral control and conditioning. Some of the earliest predilections of infants especially came under his scrutiny. Thumb sucking, he warned, would give rise to "introversion, dependent individuals, and possibly confirmed masturbators" (Buckley, 1989, p. 152). Myrtle McGrew recalls how influential behaviorism was during the 1920s. She was a student at Teachers College at the time, and as part of a course assignment she had to do a home study of an infant. She chose the daughter of the educational progressive, Lawrence Frank, since she was acquainted with his wife and knew that the couple, living in Greenwich Village, was interested in all that was new and avant garde.

> I'll never forget how funny it was because, if you'll remember, in those days behaviorism rigidities of management was in vogue, and, together with a pediatrician's antiseptic attitudes, thumbsucking was very bad. So when I walked into the baby's bedroom . . . the first thing I saw were these braces on the thumb and those lip-tongue depressors on the elbow so that the baby couldn't get her thumb to her mouth; and she was blissfully sucking away on her big toe. (Senn, 1975, p. 28)

As Watson was rising in the advertising hierarchy and moonlighting articles on child care, the impact of his early observational and experimental work continued to yield experimental reverberations. The conditioning of fear in little Albert led, through the subsequent work of Mary Cover Jones, to the development of the first behavioral therapeutic intervention and reversal of a conditioned fear; this work thus anticipated the later behavior modification movement. His thesis concerning early innate affects also led directly to a whole series of experimental studies designed to confirm or refute his formulations. We turn to these sequelae now.

Mary Cover Jones and the Development of Counterconditioning

Recognition of Mary Cover Jones's role in the history of developmental psychology is typically limited to reciting her most famous case—the counterconditioning of the little boy Peter. However, her impact was considerable. In 1968 she was awarded developmental psychology's prestigious G. Stanley Hall Award in recognition of her "widely cited experiments on the development and elimination of children's fears and for her pioneering research on their emotional social development" (SRCD newsletter, 1983). She published over 70 articles, among them studies of the effects of early and late maturation and investigations into personality antecedents of drinking problems, became president of APA's Division 7 (developmental), and was a central participant in the California growth studies.

Biography of Jones (b. 1896)

Mary Cover was born in 1896 in Johnstown, Pennsylvania, the middle child in a family of three and the oldest girl; although her parents had little education beyond high school, she was encouraged, especially by her father, in her own academic pursuits. Her female relatives were all recalled as particularly nurturing (Jones, 1983). She attended Vassar as an undergraduate and was one of the few Vassar graduates in her cohort to go on to advanced study; she entered Columbia University in 1919. At the time, she was still undecided about a career but was initially attracted to economics. Though she had already heard about the work of John Watson from a Vassar classmate—Rosalie Rayner—before the latter went to Johns Hopkins to become his laboratory assistant, it wasn't until later that she was to hear more of his work and think seriously about a career in psychology. She was at Columbia in New York during a presentation by Watson, and as he was describing the research with little Albert, she began to contemplate what it might be like to try to eliminate rather than induce fears. Later she was to have an opportunity to develop such a plan when the right convergence of events and financial support came about.

During the first few decades of the twentieth century, research was supported by private foundations rather than through the federal government. One of the foundations that supported developmental research and had a material impact on the field was the Laura Spellman Rockefeller Memorial Foundation. This foundation established the first child research station in Iowa in 1917, and during the next two decades it funded the establishment of several other centers of developmental research and helped launch the important longitudinal growth studies of the 1920s and 1930s. Among other grants, the Laura Spellman Rockefeller Foundation had given Teachers College of Columbia University $15,000 to continue the infant work that John Watson had begun at Johns Hopkins. In fact, it picked Watson himself to supervise experiments on preschool children at the college's Manhattan Day Nursery, because the foundation's overseers admired Watson's unsentimental, scientific way of studying human conduct. In his role as adviser to the foundation, Watson suggested experiments on the conditioning of fears in children and other tests concerning the stimuli that called forth emotional reactions, and picked Mary Cover Jones, a friend of his wife, Rosalie, to undertake the research. Jones was not interested in continuing the work of conditioning fears because of her strong ethical reservations. Instead, she pursued her earlier idea of eradicating an already established fear. As it turns out, a neighbor's child provided the opportunity.

> Harold [her husband] and I had a snake and some white rats and when the children were playing we took them in to see what the children would do with them. Peter was afraid of them. He was the most afraid and so we took him. . . . his mother had an approach which tended to frighten him. He wanted to go out when I was there visiting with her, and she said, "Don't go out, Peter, somebody might get you." (Jones, 1983, pp. 56–57)

Jones treated the child using deconditioning principles and was successful in eliminating his fear. Ironically, the study, which later became a classic, was originally dismissed as unacceptable for a dissertation because there were not enough cases, although she did get her Ph.D. in 1926. It was during her years at Columbia that she met her husband-to-be, Harold Jones. They had a mutual impact on one another's careers, she turning him toward developmental psychology at a time that few men considered it a masculine enough field, and he influencing her to abandon a career in psychotherapy in favor of continuing her experimental work. Their mutual respect for one another as peers and colleagues was foreshadowed in an early meeting. Mary had met Harold in a history class at the New School taught by one of its founders, James Harvey Robinson, while they were both psychology graduate students at Columbia. He walked her home afterward and recalls his remark on first seeing her library. "I never thought I'd meet a girl who would have books like that." In turn, she responded, "I'm glad to have met a man who let me put my own nickel in the subway turnstile" (Logan, 1980, p. 136). Mary Cover Jones left New York when her husband was offered a job at the University of California, Berkeley. In 1927, Berkeley was one of the principle sites established by the Laura Spellman Rockefeller Memorial Foundation for the new studies on child development. Mary became deeply involved in these seminal longitudinal studies, and her most well-known postbehaviorism era work involved her studies of the problems of early and late maturation in adolescents, and personality antecedents of problem drinkers. She had little to do with the behavioristic movement after her move to California, though her name continued to be associated with Watson's. Indeed, though she had applauded Watson's scientific objectivity in his observational studies of infants, and clearly liked him as a person (Jones, 1983), she was appalled by the child-rearing advice pieces that appeared in the 1920s and 1930s and was decidedly opposed to following his advice when it came to rearing her own children.

> Some people have been surprised at this. I know that when one of my girls was in school and was misbehaving, the principal told me that one of the mothers saw her doing something she didn't approve of and she said: "What can you expect? That child has been conditioned and unconditioned since birth." This was because she knew that I had worked with Watson, but I have always tried to steer clear of too much association with the school and to raise my children more naturally. (Senn, 1975, p.28)

Harold E. Jones and Psychophysiological Experiments in Emotion Conditioning

Mary Cover Jones's husband and colleague, Harold E. Jones, also made a significant contribution to the study of emotional development. Raised in New Brunswick, New Jersey, he attended Auburn College as an undergraduate and received his Ph.D. from Columbia. In California, he became director of research at the Institute of Child Welfare, and later served as its director. The institute was one of the centers founded by the Laura Spellman Rockefeller Foundation during the 1920s. In addition to his role as director of research at the institute, Harold continued to publish studies that explored aspects of Watson's work. Watson had maintained that the effects of physiological conditioning were long-lived—guts could learn and they had good memories. Subsequent work by Jones challenged this.

Jones's work on emotion began as a collaboration with David Wechsler (1928) while Jones was still at Columbia (Wechsler & Jones, 1928). Their research challenged the notion that people vary merely along a dimension of general emotionality, though this aspect of their research did not receive much attention at the time. Specifically, what Wechsler and Jones found was that a person's reaction to one type of emotional stimulus could be quite different from that person's response to other types of stimuli. They employed the galvanic skin response (GSR) to measure emotional responding, since this was regarded at the time as the most "delicate, reliable, and quantitatively accurate method at present known for detecting and measuring emotional changes" (Smith, 1922, cited in Jones & Wechsler, 1928, p. 607). Adult subjects were exposed to a series of stimuli that were thought to provoke different emotional responses, including the sound of a Klaxon, word and picture association tasks involving emotionally charged material, aggression of the experimenter, ("E approached S unexpectedly and grasped his nose between thumb and forefinger" [p. 602]), and administration of shock. Responses to the shock stimuli were not analyzed because the electric shocks "were hard to control and in sensitive Ss [subjects] often produced deflections beyond the edge of the paper . . ." (p. 603). The researchers found that intraindividual correlations within categories of emotional stimuli were high, and between different classes of stimuli low; this was taken as some of the first physiological evidence of emotion specificity.

Jones's most enduring contribution to the field of emotions research is considered to be his discovery of the reciprocal relation between external expression of emotion and internal physiological responding, which he related to the socialization of emotion as well as to innate temperamental differences.

Reacting against the "conditioned emotion" canon that had taken hold of psychology in the wake of Watson's experimental work with Albert—that is, the assumption that all emotional idiosyncrasies were the result of conditioning in early childhood—Jones began some of his own investigations with infants. In one study (Jones, 1930b) he tested whether or not "internal" emotional responses, as well as outer behaviors that Watson had studied, could be conditioned. He found, among other things, that they could. The internal responses were tested using the GSR response. The sound of a bell and an electrotactile stimulus (mild shock) served as unconditioned stimuli and these were paired with neutral stimuli, in this case a tapping sound or the flash of an electric bulb. Jones notes that care was taken not to use too intense a level of shock; however, that was almost beside the point because it was believed at the time that infants did not register pain in the same way adults did (Jones, 1930a).

Three infants ranging in age from 3 to 9 months were the subjects. Jones successfully established conditioned GSR responses in the infants with 6 to 14 pairings of unconditioned and neutral stimuli. He found that the conditioned responses (GSRs) could be maintained by intermittent reinforcement, and that they underwent extinction usually after four or five unreinforced stimulations. Spontaneous recovery was also observed, but by and large the conditioned response disappeared by 2 months. This study was important in demonstrating that conditioned emotional responses decayed over time in infants. This, of course, created problems for the theory that adult emotional problems stemmed from early and intransigent conditioning experiences, though Jones was cautious in interpreting his results and recommended further research involving a greater variety of test conditions applied during different developmental stages. For the time being, however, others took his findings as a serious challenge to Watson's claim about the long-term stability of the conditioned emotional response.

Jones also found that in general infants had a weaker electrodermal response than older children and adults and that overt expressive activity in infants, such as crying, was accompanied by even less of an internal response. Over the course of his subsequent research with older children and adults, Jones observed that subjects who showed little overt emotional reactivity to stimuli tended to have the more pronounced GSR reactions and those who had weak GSR responses tended to have strong overt responses (Jones, 1935). He thus formally distinguished two general modes of dealing with emotional stimuli, an internalizing mode involving low overt expressivity but high electrodermal responding, and an externalizing mode involving high overt expressivity but low electrodermal responding. A few subjects showed a third, "generalizing" pattern in which they tended to respond with a total discharge of both overt and internal activity, and a few other subjects showed a mixed pattern. It was Jones's theory that in the course of learning to control their emotions, children shifted their emotional reactivity from an external to an internal pattern of responding. Not all children were successful at the displacement. Jones thought that the externalizing pattern was more infantile and the internalizing more mature. This opinion was consistent with the then dominant behavioristic attitude that favored the inhibition of emotion and its ultimate control. Although Jones was able to recognize and characterize the different patterns of emotional responding, work on the origins of individual differences would await both detailed observational studies on the growth of children's emotions (see later section) as well as theories that would deal with the differential socialization of emotion. Before we turn to this work, we will discuss the second major series of studies inspired by Watson's original work, in this case, the experimental tests of innate emotions in infants.

Experimental Tests of Watson's Claim of Innate Emotions

During the 1920s, Mandell and Irene Sherman conducted a series of studies that seriously challenged Watson's assertion that there were three innate, differentiated emotions in young infants.

The First Challenge

The Shermans (Sherman, 1927a,b, 1928; Sherman & Sherman, 1925) undertook to determine whether people's ability to differentiate emotional expressions in infants was based on the discreteness of the emotional response or on knowledge of the eliciting situation. In a series of experiments they exposed young infants to a variety of experimental procedures designed to produce fear, hunger, pain, and anger. The specific eliciting conditions were sudden dropping, delay of feeding, pricking the infant's face with a needle, and restraint of the head and face. The infants' behaviors were either observed directly by judges or were filmed for later presentation. Depending on the study, judges were medical students, graduate students, undergraduates, and/or student nurses.

Under one condition the observers saw a silent film in which the infants' responses were shown but not the elicitors; another group saw both the elicitors and the responses; a third group saw the responses paired with stimulus conditions that were different from the ones that aroused them (transposition condition); a fourth group of judges were exposed to a "live presentation," where the infant's face and voice could be observed, but the actual stimulation of the infants took place out of sight; in a fifth condition, also involving a live presentation, judges heard only the infants' cries, but once again did not see the eliciting circumstances. The experimenters' expectation was that if the emotional expressions were differentiated, subjects would show good interjudge agreement in their emotional attributions; however, if the expressions were unclear or undifferentiated, the subjects would tend to disagree.

The results indicated that judges did fairly well when they could observe the eliciting circumstances, but they did very poorly if trying to judge the expressions on the basis of observing the babies or hearing their cries alone, and they did poorly under the transposition condition. The Shermans concluded that a young infant's emotional expressions varied only along the dimension of intensity, since his or her condition could be ascertained only if observers are aware of the context. In light of these results, they proposed that the very first responses of infants to sensory stimuli are undifferentiated, becoming more specific only with maturation. Major reviews of emotions studies in 1946 and 1954 came to the same conclusion and rather consistently interpreted the Shermans' results as indicating that early infant affect is undifferentiated (e.g., Jersild, 1946; Pratt, 1946).

However, on closer inspection, there are reasons for questioning the data and the conclusions. In the first place, the finding of poor interjudge reliability with respect to observations of the expressive behavior from film is not particularly surprising given the quality of film during the 1920s. Even today, investigators who code infant facial expressions from videotape have difficulty unless the filming is done with high resolution cameras fitted with zoom lenses.

In the case of the live presentations there were three problems. First, subjects did not see the infants' immediate emotional responses to the stimuli since they were initially hidden from view so as to obscure the eliciting conditions. It is quite possible that many of the emotional responses were fleeting, and thus undetectable by the time the infant was brought around from behind the screen. A startle response to sudden dropping, for example, would probably not still be visible by the time the child was moved to the front of the screen. Second, the reports do not contain information on where the judges—who observed in groups—stood with reference to the babies, or how the infants were presented. Were the observers close enough to observe subtle muscle movement changes that discriminate different emotions? Did the experimenter present the child in his or her arms so that only a side view of the face was possible, or was the infant suspended in front of the audience? The reports do not speak to these issues.

A third problem, this time in the case of the cry judgments, was that certain manipulations may have masked precisely those cry cues that are most diagnostic of differential emotion states; moreover, observers were on occasion unwittingly given misleading information. An example follows:

> For the first reaction an infant whose feeding period was delayed for from fifteen to thirty minutes was placed behind the screen. It was sometimes necessary to wait several minutes until the infant began to cry, but the observers were led to believe that this delay was due to a delay in applying the stimulus. In order that the crying of an infant as a result of hunger might be comparable to the crying following the application of the other stimuli, the infants were removed from the room after about ten seconds unless the cry subsided in a shorter time. First, the duration of the crying as a result of hunger was universally greater than as a result of the other stimuli employed. Second, all observers tended to designate hunger as the cause when the crying was rather prolonged. Third, since the observers were told that each infant would be stimulated only once, they would question the reason for the frequent intervals of quiet during the "reaction period" which is almost always observed in hungry infants. (Sherman, 1927, p. 336)

Thus, not only were the subjects led to believe that they would hear a cry in response to a stimulus of sudden onset (which is contrary to the conditions for hunger), the most essential identifying features of the hunger cry—slow onset and slow decay (Wolff, 1966)—were removed. Under these conditions a correct identification of the cry would have been remarkable.

We also might question how the infant was placed behind the screen and how it was handled while the experimenters were waiting for the hunger cry. Was the infant held somewhat roughly or placed in an uncomfortable position so as to encourage it to initiate its hunger cry as the audience listened and waited? The hunger cry is not a cry that is elicitable on demand. Another factor not described in the study was the condition of the infants who were required to respond to the stimuli. Were all infants in an equally alert, responsive state? In the first set of studies the infants were 3–6 days old, and in the last, "below twelve days of age." Today it is well known that maternal anesthesia can affect the responsiveness of an infant for a number of days after birth; there is no mention of whether the mothers' births were assisted with anesthesia or not, though it is quite likely that they were. It is also well known that infants have few periods of true alertness during the neonatal period and that even infants who look awake (i.e., have their eyes open) can be in deep REM sleep. If the infants were not uniformly in an optimal state, crying would not have been as vigorous, and the weakness of their responses could have made discrimination between emotions more difficult.

In summary, given the conditions described above and the paucity of details on the subjects and procedures, it is difficult to judge whether an appropriate test of the differentiation thesis was in fact conducted in these studies. Watson's own response to the Sherman studies (Watson, 1930) was to dismiss the results as attributable to the fact that the observers were not trained in infant observation. Nevertheless, to many who had originally accepted Watson's assertions, this study constituted a serious challenge to the thesis of innate differentiated affects and galvanized further research on early infant affect.

Of the three emotions that Watson claimed were innate, the bulk of studies tried to elicit the anger response, although some tested fear. As Taylor (1934) pointed out, none of the studies constituted deliberate replications, although in some studies the conditions appeared to be approximated in some form.

Experimental Study of the Fear Response

Probably the biggest obstacle to the research on infant fear resided in definitional problems. Watson had indicated that shaking or jarring could release the innate fear reaction. However, Moro (1918) had described this as the appropriate stimulus for the reflex clasping response. Moreover, later writers determined the response could be elicited by a variety of stimuli, including intense auditory stimulation (which Watson had also listed as a response to fear). Thus, on any given occasion of a sudden stimulus it was unclear whether a fear or Moro response was being elicited. The status of the startle response was also drawn into question since this was a component of the adult fear response but not reducible to it.

Despite these problems Irwin (1932b) attempted to replicate Watson's fear response in infants under the age of 1 month. Twenty-four infants were subjected to sudden dropping, which consisted of suspending the infant above the experimenter's head and dropping a distance of 2 feet. The author reported that in only 2 out of 85 trials did the infants show crying, one of the primary behavioral criteria Watson had mentioned as indexing fear to loss of support. Moreover, in 12% of the trials no overt responses at all could be detected. Questions concerning infant state at testing, as in other studies of infant affect during that era, were not addressed.

A later study by Landis and Hunt (1939) found that the startle response could be elicited in infants with a sudden or intense stimulus applied to any sense modality, but especially as a reaction to sudden, sharp noises. This was detected by using high-speed motion picture photography, a feature that probably greatly enhanced the ability to detect the desired effect. However, even Landis and Hunt did not regard the elicited startles as representing a true fear response, preferring to call them "pre-emotional."

Experimental Study of the Rage Response

Sherman and Sherman (1925), in one of their initial forays into the study of infant emotion, used a form of "restraint of movement" to test Watson's claims. The specific procedure involved the experimenter applying pressure with his or her finger to the chin of the neonate. The authors report finding no coordinated defensive movements (a criteria of the rage response) during the first 24 hours after birth, although defensive movements could be observed by the fifth day. As such, the innateness of the reaction could not be fully substantiated. Once again, however, no details on the state of the newborns were given in the report.

In another study, Pratt, Nelson, and Sun (1930) used arm restraint as one of the stimuli for rage in 2- to 3-week-old infants. Unaccountably, they also used blockage of breathing as a stimulus (Watson himself had not recommended this as a stimulus to rage). In the latter procedure the infants' nostrils were compressed to prevent breathing for periods ranging from 5 to 15 seconds. By the experimenters' account, defensive reactions were not elicited. In the case of arm restraint (pinning the infant's arms to its sides) 58% of the infants quieted or went to sleep, 26% were active for a short time, 16% all the time, and 3% at first passive and later active; again, defensive reactions were not apparent.

Dennis (1942) was concerned that failure to replicate Watson's findings may have been due to the fact that investigators did not employ as intense and prolonged stimulation as Watson had used. In his own study he found that negative reactions indeed did not occur in response to mild restraint of movement, but that more intense and prolonged stimulation, including rough restraint of movement, produced crying and restlessness. Since the restraint procedures were harsh, it is not clear that anger was elicited; pain may have been more likely.

One of the most careful attempts to replicate Watson's study was conducted by Taylor (1934); as such, it is reported in some detail, especially since it was widely cited in the literature of the time. Taylor studied 40 infants ranging in age from 1 to 12 days. No mention was made of whether mothers were exposed to anesthesia, but the investigator does report that all infants were judged as normal and healthy by the medical staff. There were two conditions for rage: arm restraint, which involved pinning the infant's arms to the sides for 20 seconds, and nose restraint, which involved holding the infant's nose "firmly" between the experimenter's thumb and index finger for 10 seconds. ("Enough pressure was applied to the pinch to close the nostrils and to prevent inhalation through the nose; but care was taken not to bruise the cartilage in the nasal cavity or the external skin surface of the nose" [Taylor, 1934, p. 71]). There were also two conditions for fear, one involving sudden dropping and the other a loud noise. The infants were tested directly following a feeding and received the following order of stimuli: arm restraint, nose restraint, drop, and loud noise. Behavioral responses were noted and frequency counts tabulated. The following categories were scored: arm, leg, trunk, head, facial, vocal, respiratory, and sucking responses. Facial responses included grimacing, eye blinking, eye opening and closing, and mouth opening and closing. Vocal movements included crying, sneezing, hiccoughing, "and so forth."

The results indicated that judges had great difficulty in identifying clear differential responses with respect to the four different stimuli. They concluded that any condition produces any and all responses. The authors also compared their responses to those reported by Watson as typical of certain conditions, namely, crying, screaming, body stiffening, arm slashing, flex-extension of the legs and breath holding to the rage stimuli; and gasp, grasp, eye blink, pucker, crying, arm clutching, and leg extension to the fear stimuli. They found that there were no responses that occurred frequently enough to be called typical. For example, the most frequent response during arm restraint was a stiffening of the body, but only 15 infants (38%) made this response. In the sudden dropping condition the most typical response was a rapid upward extension of the arms followed by clutching. However, once again, this response was made by only 18 (45%) of the infants.

Using a more liberal approach, the authors found that 55% of the infants in the drop condition and 30% of the infants in the noise condition gave at least one response conforming to Watson's criteria; under the rage condition 32% during arm restraint and 32% under nose restraint showed a least one of the behavioral criteria. However, instead of treating these findings as support for Watson, they interpreted the data as showing that the behaviors Watson claimed as typical in response to certain emotional stimuli were, in fact, atypical. However, in another section the authors indicate that 18% of the infants failed to show any observable response to the drop stimulus and 28% failed to show any response to the noise stimulus. It is the latter observations that are particularly informative, because they suggest that infant state may have interfered with evocation of the emotional responses. Recalling that testing was conducted immediately after a feeding, which we now know induces sleep in young infants, it is perhaps not surprising that the responses they were looking for were not more typical. Many of the infants were probably in light sleep, making it less likely that they would show pronounced behavioral responding to the stimuli.

Summary

As indicated above, most of the attempts to put Watson's claims concerning innate differentiated emotions to the test failed to support his contentions. As we have seen however, many of the studies were seriously flawed. During the 1920s and 1930s investigators were generally ignorant of the effects of infant state on tests of behavioral responding, and thus weak or null results were attributed to a competence deficit rather than performance failure in infants. However, these studies and several others to be discussed shortly were extremely influential in altering the course of history with respect to the study of emotion. As a result of the general failure of the above experimental studies to support Watson's assertions about innate and differentiated emotional responses, not only did his statements about early infant affect fall into disrepute, but the field at large began to conclude that infant affect was undifferentiated. Moreover, there was a general falling away from notions of emotion specificity, which probably laid the groundwork for the activation or arousal theories of emotion of the 1950s.

We turn now to examine other influential studies that challenged the notion of emotion specificity. The first two studies, by Kathryn Bridges, perpetuated and extended the notion that infants are born with undifferentiated emotions that only evolve over time. The second set of studies, by Carney Landis, challenged the notion that even adult affect is characterized by different emotions.

LARGE-SCALE OBSERVATIONAL STUDIES OF INFANTS' AND CHILDREN'S EXPRESSIVE BEHAVIOR

Charlotte Bühler, one of the key figures in German developmental psychology, was actually the first to conduct a large observational study of infant behavior. However, since the work was originally published in German, it was not widely available to American scholars. Instead, Kathryn Bridges's study of infants became the reference point for textbooks that cite early work on infant affect and hence we begin with her work; we present Bühler's work later. Before we turn to this literature, a brief biographic sketch is presented.

Contribution of Kathryn Bridges

Kathryn Banham Bridges

Kathryn Banham was raised in Sheffield, England, the daughter of a physician (Bridges, 1983). It was James's *Principles of Psychology* (1890), which she first encountered in high school, that helped crystalize her interest in psychology as a career. Her family's economic circumstances during and around the first world war did not permit her to attend Cambridge or Oxford, as she would have liked, so she enrolled at the University of Manchester. She received a B.Sc. in psychology and physiology and then spent a postgraduate year in a teacher-training course in education. When her family's economic standing improved she was able to take a year of graduate study at Cambridge, where her thesis was concerned with experimental studies of mental conflict and its impact on memory, conscious experience, and emotional reactions. Though her examiners were satisfied with her thesis, she was denied a masters from Cambridge because although women were admitted to all classes, and could sit for examinations, they were not granted university degrees, a rule that held till as late as 1948.

She applied for research fellowships abroad and was instead offered a position as lecturer in experimental psychology and social psychology in the School of Social Work at the University of Toronto. It was during her tenure there that she both taught social work students and completed her own masters degree in psychology, the latter so as to obtain the paper credentials denied her at Cambridge. Later she was appointed research psychologist for the Canadian National Committee for Mental Hygiene, where she worked with the man whom she later married. When the McGill University Nursery School was opened for child study a year later, she was asked to carry on research in this setting. It was here and at two foundling hospitals in Montreal that she conducted the research that formed the foundation for her book, *The Social and Emotional Development of the Preschool Child*. That book was published in 1931 and was submitted for her doctoral thesis in 1934. In the interim she enrolled as a doctoral candidate at the University of Montreal. The program for the doctorate in philosophy and psychology included a requirement to take a tutorial course on Thomasian philosophy. Because the instructor was a priest of that order and because it was unusual at that time for a woman to be admitted to a monastery, her tutorials took place in a confessional booth.

She was awarded her degree "avec distinction" and had the additional distinction of being the first woman to obtain a D. Phil. at the University of Montreal. In subsequent years she worked in Iowa and New Jersey, supervising psychological services in institutions for delinquent or mentally retarded children. She also went on to become associate professor of psychology at Duke

University, where she was one of the first two women faculty members in the Department of Psychology. She retired from teaching in 1967, although she continued to do psychological evaluations of infants at a rehabilitation project in North Carolina.

Bridges is best known for her theory of emotional differentiation in infancy and early childhood, though she also proposed a lifespan model of emotional development somewhat later in her own career (Banham, 1951). Her various research studies and her theoretical perspectives are detailed below.

Bridges's Study of Infants

Bridges observed 62 infants in the Montreal Foundling and Baby Home for 4 months and was led to conclude that "the infant does not start life with 3 fully matured pattern reactions, such as have been mentioned by behaviorists and named fear, rage and love" (Bridges, 1932, p. 325). She assumed that early infant affect was undifferentiated for two reasons. The first is that she was apparently unable to discern differential patterns of emotion, at least in younger infants. The second reason stemmed from her observation that there did not appear to be any stimulus–response specificity between elicitors and emotional responses. Since the differentiation view is still advanced today (e.g., Sroufe, 1979) usually with reference to Bridges's original work as the supporting reference, the data on which it rests should be examined critically.

The most problematic aspect of this study are her statements concerning earliest infant affect. First, even though she had rejected the presence of Watson's three emotions at birth, she herself did not observe any newborns; the youngest subject in her study was "2–3 weeks old." She attempted to deflect potential criticism by asserting that the expressions were not present at that time and argues that if the three emotions were present at birth, they would be observable at 2–3 weeks and 1–2 months, but she found that they were not. This is no guarantee however, because as we now know, many infant behaviors that are present early in life disappear after a short time, only to reappear later on. For example, a newborn baby can walk on a flat surface with an adult's support via the placing reflex; 8 weeks later he has lost the ability (Thelen, 1985). Two-week-olds can reach out toward, touch, and sometimes even grasp objects, but then this type of eye–hand coordination disappears until the infant is about 5 months old (Bower, 1979). A 1-year-old does not realize a piece of clay weighs the same whether it is shaped as a ball or a sausage, but at 18 months, according to experiments by Bower (1979), he does; at 2 years he does not. Field, Woodson, Greenberg, and Cohen (1982) found imitation of emotional expressions in neonates, as have others (see review by Malatesta & Izard, 1984), but the response seems to disappear and then to reemerge about 4 to 6 months later.

Another problem with the Bridges study is in the lack of detail in the presentation of data. She speaks in generalities and trends rather than in terms of numbers of infants who showed or failed to show specific responses to specific stimuli on what number of trials. As evidence of lack of differentiation in early infancy she relates

. . . presentation of certain strong stimuli [caused the infants to] become agitated, their arm and hand muscles tensed, their breath quickened, and their legs made jerky kicking movements. Their eyes opened, the upper lid arched, and they gazed into the distance. The stimuli capable of producing this response were various: bright sun directly in the infant's eyes, sudden picking up and putting down on the bed, pulling the child's arm through his dress sleeve, holding the arms tight to the sides, rapping the baby's knuckles, pressing the bottle nipple into the child's mouth, and the noisy clatter of a small tin basin thrown on to a metal table whence it fell to the radiator and the floor. (Bridges, 1932, p. 325)

The implication was that the emotional responses were diffuse and the stimuli eliciting them broad. However, the behavioral description was not as detailed as we would today demand. One thing that a contemporary emotions researcher would note immediately is the lack of reference, in the above description, to the infants' mouth configuration. In contemporary coding systems (see Chapter 5, this volume), anger is distinguished by a tense open mouth, fear by a backward retraction of the lips, sadness by a horseshoe mouth, and so on. The lack of attention to this level of detail is unfortunate because it is just such details that enable emotions researchers as well as parents to differentiate their infants' emotional expressions.

The external validity of her results is also brought into critical question by the very nature of the population she chose to study—infants in a foundling home. The apathetic quality of the infants' responses suggest that they may have been suffering the effects of "hospitalism," a condition of deterioration described by Spitz in his studies of institution-reared children. Certain anomalies in Bridges's report call attention to this and indicate that it may have been a factor in the failure to elicit differentiated affects. Bridges (1932) indicated, for example, that loud sound startled only four of the 1- to 2-month-old babies, while six others lay practically undisturbed. She also recorded that "light pinching of the arm left the 3- or 4-week old baby unmoved" (p. 326). In light of what we know about infant sensitivity to loud noise and pain, these results are hard to reconcile with an assumption that this is a basically normal sample of infants. Bridges also notes a great deal of rocking among the subjects, and we know from Spitz's work that this is characteristic of institution-reared infants.

In summary, Bridges's observations of infant affect were based on an atypical sample of institution-reared infants; moreover, there were no actual observations of very early infant expressions, and the level of reporting leaves much to be desired. All in all this study does not provide very convincing evidence that early infant affect is undifferentiated. However, this was the position she advanced and in a subsequent work she elaborated a genetic or developmental theory of emotions in part based on it.

Bridges's Observational Study of the Growth and Differentiation of Emotion in the Preschool Child

Bridges's work on the preschool-age child (Bridges, 1931) was inspired by the appearance of a wide variety of scales for mental development in the preschool years; these had been concerned chiefly with the development of more and more discriminating and skillful behaviors with respect to inanimate objects and non-social situations. At the time that she was writing there were no standardized tests for social and emotional development, nor was there theoretical consensus on what constituted "emotional development," although three general models could be discerned at the time. The first model viewed emotional reactions as inherited, unchanging, and primitive; learning to control emotional behavior was the order of the day. This view thus emphasized the response side of the stimulus–response equation—and development consisted of learning to suppress the response. In the second model, emotional reactions remained essentially the same throughout the lifetime of the individual. They were aroused by different objects or situations in the course of development and development per se consisted of transferring original patterns of emotional reaction to more and more complex and socially approved situations. Here the responses remained the same; it was the stimuli to which they became attached that became more complex. In the third model, emotional responses became associated progressively with a series of different situations, and the nature of the response also changed. Bridges noted that little empirical research substantiate any of these models. Her study was to be the remedy.

The subjects for her study were 50 youngsters at the McGill University Nursery School; she observed them almost daily for a period of 3 years. The children were from middle- to upper-middle-class homes and their parents were English-speaking Canadians. She began with a subgroup of 20 children in order to develop a working coding scheme for the larger sample. Two groups were observed, a group of $2\frac{1}{2}$- to $3\frac{1}{2}$-year-olds and a group of $3\frac{1}{2}$- to 5-year-olds. She made daily observations, recording all socioemotional behavior without regard to any a priori selectivity, and kept the observations strictly behavioral. From the data at hand she created categories of behavior and ranked them according to developmental "maturity," which was based on noting which behaviors were more often exhibited by the older children and less so by the younger ones. The scale was subsequently revised according to an item analysis. In the end, she was mainly led to revise the emotion items, making them increasingly more specific. For example, she was forced to reclassify items that were originally counted under the "feelings" category into the more specific behaviors of "tears," "fear," "anger," and the like; she also found a need to subdivide the category of "excitement," eventually differentiating between delighted excitement and distressed excite-ment, the former associated with affection, the latter with enuresis. The successive alterations in her coding scheme allowed her to make fine-grained analyses of developmental change in several basic emotion expressions. The revised scale was subsequently applied to the rest of the children for the remainder of the study.

Summary of Results and Formulation of the Genetic Theory of the Emotions

Of all the results produced in this study, Bridges is best known for her specification of an ontogenetic model of emotional development. The Genetic Theory of the Emotions, as she called it, was the first developmental theory of emotions which entailed observation of a large number of children. (Although G. Stanley Hall before her had collected volumes of data on the emotions in the course of his survey studies, he was never able to systematize the findings or extract a theory.)

Bridges criticized the prevailing preoccupation with visceral aspects of emotional responses that had emerged in the course of the James-Lange/Cannon-Bard debate. She felt the emphasis on visceral responses was misplaced and that an analysis of the emotions should more appropriately be focused on the total personality. She also concluded, on the basis of her own observations, that there were no distinctly patterned visceral reactions corresponding to the different emotions, because flushing, quick breathing, perspiration, and the like, could be observed in such disparate emotions as fear, anger, and delighted excitement, either in infants or older children.

The genetic theory maintained that excitement, the original undifferentiated emotion present at birth, becomes differentiated and associated with certain situations and certain motor responses to form the separate emotions of later life (see Figure 1). For example, general excitement differentiates perhaps within a matter of hours or days into two general types of emotion: The first expression, distress, involves unsatisfying experience and, Bridges thought probably corresponded to what Watson was calling fear and rage; the second, delight, indexed by the infant's cooing or cessation of crying, probably corresponded to what Watson was calling love. The differentiation of emotion takes place only gradually, so that at different ages different emotions are distinguishable. There was no designation for sadness; this is because Bridges felt that this emotion is not prominent until adolescence, an assumption that was shared by many developmentalists and clinicians and which has been relinquished only recently.

As far as the forces responsible for the gradual differentiation of the emotions go, Bridges suggested that both maturation and socialization played a role. Under the influence of these forces, development consisted of three changes: (1) a decreasing frequency of intense emotional responses, (2) a progressive transfer of responses to a series of stimuli determined by experience and social approval, and (3) a gradual change in the nature of the overt responses in accord with social dictates.

The above constitutes the first formal developmental theory of emotions ontogenesis. It had a distinctly behavioristic cast to it, as one would expect from research emanating from this era in psychology's history. As we see later on, contemporary models of emotional development for the most part abandon stimulus–response conceptualizations of emotional developments, and yet Bridges's model continues to be influential for at least some theoretical positions (e.g., Sroufe, 1979).

Bridges's/Banham's Lifespan Model of Development

Later in her life, Bridges (née Banham) proposed a genetic theory of emotions that encompassed the entire lifespan (Banham, 1951). This extended version of her earlier model was based on several sources, including her own research on

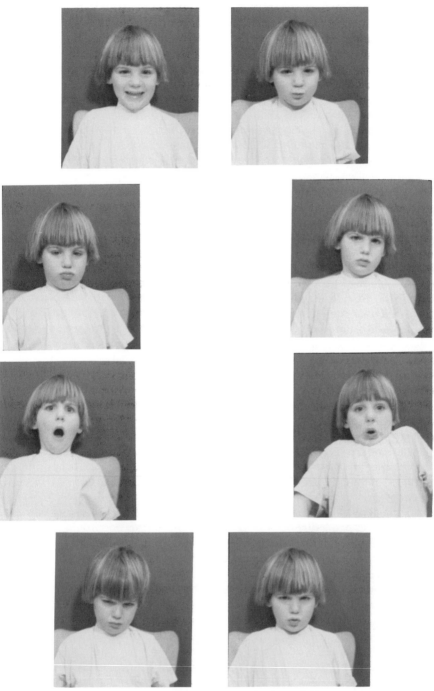

Figure 1. Emotions in the preschool-age child.

infancy and the preschool child, G. Stanley Hall's first textbook on aging—*Senescence, the Last Half of Life* (Hall, 1922)—various studies of aging that were published in the 1940s, as well as her own extrapolations from this literature as it might be reflected in changes in emotionality over the lifespan. As such it constituted the first lifespan model of emotional development. Although others had written about (though not researched) concepts such as "emotional maturity" (Jersild, 1946), no other author before her had attempted such an integrated, life-developmental view of emotions. Charlotte Bühler had initiated lifespan studies of human development during the same time (Bühler, 1933), using a biographical approach. However, hers was a theory of "self" development, and focused on external events and activities, inner experiences, and physical and mental productions. This "self" theory did not emphasize, and indeed rather neglected, the distinctly social and emotional aspects of individual development. Other authors of the era were inclined to make sweeping statements about socioemotional behavior during maturity and aging, but the claims seemed to be based on folklore and stereotype rather than on scientific research. For example, the respected educator Lawrence Frank (1954), who had so advanced the cause of the child study movement during the 1920s and 1930s, relaxed his usual high standards when it came to portraying the socioemotional life of older people. He asserted that many older persons are "unhappy, often pessimistic and resentful" (Frank, 1954, p. 18). In his view, they lacked flexibility, were frequently rigid and constricted in their responses to people and situations, tended to feel isolated, and were unable to relate themselves or find any fulfillment in life. He portrayed the period following retirement as a "period of convalescence" and in place of research, offered adages such as the notion that "nothing ages a woman more rapidly than having a retired husband in the house" (p. 19). He asserted that apathy and withdrawal of interests characterized the affective lives of older people.

Aspects of Banham's model fall prey to some of the same stereotypes, and there is a regrettable absence of firsthand research on emotions in the elderly. Instead, many of the late-life aspects of the model appear to be offered on the basis of extrapolation from other literatures on motor and cognitive behavior, and on informal observation. There is no evidence from Banham's biography that she had any more than casual contact with elderly individuals, though as a practicing clinician, she may have indeed seen cases involving older people.

In brief, the theory envisions an infancy and early childhood characterized by global, random, and undifferentiated affect, differentiation and integration in late childhood and adolescence, emotional sensitivity, control, and maximum differentiation of response and aesthetic feeling during "maturity," a gradual consolidation and some disintegration in later adult life, and finally rigid, constricted affectivity in old age, featuring a reduction in intensity and in variety of emotional experiences. As such, this theory constitutes a "horticultural" model of emotional development, with growth, maturity, and decay as successive products. Banham was, however, not as pessimistic as to the meaning of the changes in emotionality with age as some of her contemporaries who saw only increasing neuroticism as the predicted consequence of aging. She felt that the reduced affective sensitivity and lability of old age might actually be helpful in personal adjustment, since the older person would be less likely to become agitated and upset. Inspection of her model provides further details of the theory. The emotions of anxiety and fear become reduced in old age to worry. Anger becomes mere irritability. Sadness and grief are not represented in the early years on her chart (except, perhaps as undifferentiated distress), but appear in old age. Within the positive emotions, joy is transformed into mystical ecstasy, affection into benevolence, and sexual love devolves to gustatory sensuousness.

The model that Bridges proposed, despite what we would now regard as largely insupportable assertions about old age (Malatesta, 1981), might have served heuristic value in stimulating research had it been paid much attention. As it was, by the date of its publication, emotions research had fallen into decline due to further assaults on the notion of discrete emotions. Bridges's observational study of infant emotion certainly played a role in this, and few people challenged her findings. What was overlooked at the time was the work of Charlotte Bühler in Vienna. Her work showed quite a different picture of the emergence of affective expressions in young infants, and it is to this work that we now turn.

The Infant Research of Charlotte Bühler

In the early decades of the century, Charlotte Bühler was regarded as one of the leading developmental researchers in the German-speaking world, though her name did not become familiar to Americans until the 1960s with the birth of the humanistic psychology movement and her several books on this topic. Bühler, like her counterpart in the United States, G. Stanley Hall, was an entrepreneur of the "new psychology" that was emerging in the first two decades of this century (cf. Cairns, 1983). With the help of co-workers such as Hildegard Hetzer, Bühler established new beachheads in infant, child, adolescent, and lifespan psychology in Germany, just as Hall had done in America. Her first publication, resulting from her graduate work, was on children's fantasy, and thus opened a new area of developmental research (Bühler, 1918). One of her most highly regarded early works was *Das Inventar der Verhaltensweisen im 1. Lebensjahr* (Bühler & Hetzer, 1927), which became available in English translation (*The First Year of Life*) as early as 1930. In this work, she described the normative stages of development during the first year as based on the observations that she and Hetzer made on a large cross-sectional sample of infants. Moreover, she and Hetzer advanced the state of developmental psychology—which in the early part of the century was largely that of IQ testing and baby biography—to that of systematic behavioral observation of more representative samples of children. The study also included descriptions of the emergence and development of facial and vocal expressions of emotion; she and Hetzer thus anticipated the work of Kathryn Bridges by several years. Before we turn to this work, and the experimental work on infants' understanding of emotional expressions and reactions to unfamiliar expressions (Bühler & Hetzer, 1927; Bühler & Hetzer, 1928), we provide a brief biographical sketch (Bürmann & Herwartz-Emden, 1993; Rollett, 1984).

Biography of Bühler (1893–1974)

Charlotte Bühler (née Malachowski) was born December 20, 1893, in the Charlottenburg section of Berlin to wealthy, cultured parents of Jewish-Polish extraction. Her father was a successful civil engineer and architect, and her mother was a highly educated woman whose own career plans had been frustrated by the circumstance of gender, but who pursued various studies on her own. While Charlotte's relationship with her parents was by her own account "not close," she and her younger brother were exposed to a richly cultured and intellectually stimulating environment at home and during their various sojourns abroad.

Her undergraduate education took place at Freiburg and Berlin. She at first thought she might study medicine, but vacillated between the social and natural sciences until finally settling on psychology as her major. In Berlin she studied with Karl Stumpf, who soon invited her to do her dissertation with him and offered her a position as his assistant. However, Stumpf urged her to do a study on the perception of feelings, and Charlotte's earliest interests revolved around her experiments in the area of cognition.

Stumpf referred her to Oswald Külpe in Münich, who on Stumpf's recommendation quickly took her on and even provided her with an experimental laboratory. Külpe died unexpectedly a year later, and his position was taken over by Karl Bühler, one of the leading scientists of the time. Charlotte was an impressive student; Bühler, an impressive intellect; they quickly developed an attraction for one another and were married in 1916. She completed her dissertation work in 1918 and became the youngest and the first female, *Privatdozent* (English equivalent, Ph.D.) in the land of Saxony; her *Habilitation*—an independent piece of scholarship beyond the dissertation which is necessary to qualify for a position as a professor—was a psychological analysis of the creative process: *Discovery and Invention in Literature and Art*. In the time since matriculating in her dissertation studies and the production of her Habilitation, she also had the first two of her four children.

The Bühlers soon moved when Karl received an offer from the University of Vienna. During the 16 years they were in Vienna, they established themselves as an epicenter of educational and developmental research. The Rockefeller Foundation, which had funded a number of child research institutes in the United States, provided generous support to the Bühlers, and allowed them to establish the Psychological Institute of Vienna, which became one of Europe's most important centers of psychological research during that era. A number of students from that time went on to illustrious careers of their own, including Paul Lazarsfeld, Else Frenkel, Egon Brunswick, Hildegard Hetzer, and Lotte Schenk-Danziger. Réné Spitz and Sigmund Freud were contemporaries who also had bases in Vienna at the time, and Spitz apparently spent time at the Psychological Institute, which would have provided him with the keen observational skills he would apply in his own work.

With the annexation of Austria by Hitler in 1938, Charlotte Bühler fled to England. Her husband (who was Catholic) was imprisoned—apparently due to his liberal social and educational ideologies and because he appeared to be philosemitic in both his professional and private life. Fortunately, through his wife's efforts and with the help of Norwegian friends, he was eventually freed and fled to Norway for a time. The family finally immigrated to the United States in 1940. While they had good financial resources thanks to Charlotte's family, they still had to find a means to get reestablished in the academic world, and a means of earning a living. Charlotte found a position at St. Catherine's College, and he at St. Thomas's College, both in St. Paul, Minnesota. Eventually they moved to California, where Karl served as clinical assistant professor of psychiatry in the medical department of the University of Southern California, and also worked as a counselor at the Cedars of Lebanon Hospital. Charlotte obtained a position as a clinical psychologist at a clinic in Los Angeles in 1945, and from that point on worked primarily in the realm of clinical psychology.

In Germany and Austria, Karl had been the preeminent scholar of the pair; though Charlotte was a strong figure in her own right, she must have stood somewhat in his shadow. In America, Charlotte's stature in the psychological community increased, while Karl had to struggle to maintain his reputation. In many respects Karl did not fare as well, and his sporadic bouts of depression gave testimony to how keenly he felt his reduction in stature. Charlotte Bühler became one of the leading forces in the new humanistic movement that began to take shape in the 1950s, and her later work on goals reflects this orientation (Bühler, 1961; Bühler & Massarik, 1969). Her conviction that human development is a lifespan issue—initiated originally with her work on biographies back in Vienna and continued in the context of clinical psychology and humanistic studies—was also instrumental in the founding of a lifespan framework for developmentalists. Despite the disjunction of her life caused by her emigration and resettlement, she produced nearly 200 publications, including over a dozen books, a formidable accomplishment. She spent the last years of her life in Stuttgart, near her son, and died in 1974.

Bühler's Studies of Expressive Development during the First Year of Life

At the time that Bühler and Hetzer (1927, 1928; Bühler et al., 1928) undertook their study of the behavioral development of infants, the only other laboratory-based observations of infants (i.e., studies beyond the baby biographies) were contained in investigations by Bechterew and Gesell. Gesell had produced a description of around-the-clock observations of a 2-month-old and a 6-month-old child; Bechterew observed two newborns for nine days on a 24-h basis. Bühler and Hetzer's study encompassed daily observations on a total of 69 infants who ranged in age from 1 month to 12 months.

Of these infants, 40% came from private homes and 60% were from institutions. The latter were somewhat atypical of institution-reared children in that they spent only 3 weeks at the Reception House for Children in Vienna (Kinderübernahmsstelle), where the observations were made during quarantine while in transit to foster placement or placement at another institution. This means that the children would likely not be suffering hospitalism effects (as appears to have been the case for some of the children in Bridges's sample). However, the separation from parents was in all likelihood quite stressful for them, and we can imagine that some of their behavior would reflect the distress of separation. Thus, for our purposes in looking at the expressive behavior of these infants, the findings are somewhat compromised since the observations on normal children were mixed with those of children undergoing separation. Nevertheless, the data at least indicate the expressive capabilities of infants under stressful conditions (as in Gaensbauer & Harmon's 1982 report on an abused child). This constitutes a somewhat more extreme condition than the stress of the Strange Situation procedure used in contemporary developmental work, but it yielded data that are probably more representative than those obtained by Kathryn Bridges.

In the Bühler and Hetzer study, infants were observed around the clock; five to seven children were observed at each age interval, with the exception that only four infants were observed during the first month of life. Here we examine the findings with respect to emotional expressions and reactions. From Bühler's point of view, expressive behaviors (face, voice, gestures) represented both the feeling state and intentional behaviors. Table 3 summarizes Bühler and Hetzer's descriptions of when each emotional behavior was found to enter the repertoire of the infant and the expressive behaviors that were used to infer them.

Table 3. Developmental Timetable of the Emotions

Month (first observed)	Emotion inferred	Evidence
0–1	Startle	Convulsive movements, frowning, arms and legs drawn up, eyes shut tight, feet clenched
	Active displeasure	Restless, aimless excited movements with or without sounds, grimacing of face
1–2	Active displeasure	Tears, frowns, tight shutting of eyes
	Displeased astonishment	Eyes forcefully opened, mouth open, eyebrows drawn up, forehead taught, arms lifted
	State of pleasure	Eyes gleaming, corners of mouth drawn up
2–3	Active displeasure	Lips pressed together, head thrown back, body reared, eyes opened and shut
	Displeased astonishment	Fingers spread, arms stretched out
	State of comfort	Accompanying lalling sounds, some lusty movements
	Functionslust (pleasure at doing)	Corners of mouth drawn up, eyes gleaming during movement and experimenting
3–4		
4–5		
5–6	Joy	Lively moving of arms and legs, eyes gleaming, corners of mouth drawn up, joy sounds, mouth wide open
6–7	Joy	Laughter
7–8	Quiet ill humor (sadness?)	Eyes gleamless, corners of mouth drop
8–9	Depression	Soft crying
	Fear	Loud crying; movement of flight and defense

A comparison of the age norms described by Bühler and Hetzer with those of Bridges (Geppert & Heckhausen, 1990) indicates that Bridges saw *fear* in her sample earlier than did Bühler and Hetzer (6 versus 8 months), which may have been a function of the difference in their samples, with neglected/abandoned children (Bridges's sample) showing fear earlier, as in the case of the developmentally advanced fear shown by a maltreated child described by Gaensbauer and Harmon (1982). Also noteworthy is the description of surprise (displeased astonishment) within the first trimester of life, apparently not observed in Bridges's sample, but observed in studies by Izard using anatomically based facial affect coding systems (see Table 5 in Geppert & Heckhausen, 1990). Bridges and Bühler and Hetzer note the onset of pleasure/joy at 2–3 months in agreement with Izard (Geppert & Heckhausen, 1990). Bridges dates the onset of anger at 3–4 months, although Bühler and Hetzer note its presence as early as the first month. The other noteworthy finding in Bühler and Hetzer's study is that they observed sadness as early as the seventh month; Bridges thought sadness did not emerge until adolescence. Darwin (1872) observed sadness as early as 6 months, and recent microanalytic work (Izard & Malatesta, 1987) shows that the expressive components of sadness can be observed even earlier, though they are quite fleeting in nature.

All in all, Bühler and Hetzer's observations of infant affect do not appear to have been unduly contaminated by the inclusion of children temporarily separated from their parents; if anything, it appears to have made possible the observation of early depressive reactions among the range of expressive behaviors recorded.

Bühler's next studies on expressive behavior were experimental in nature. The first study (Bühler, Hetzer, & Mabel, 1928), which involved the presentation of unfamiliar facial and vocal stimuli to infants, tested William Stern's (1927) notion that fear of the unfamiliar had a more complicated explanation than that unfamiliarity per se was disturbing. Based on the observation of his own children and of those of others, Stern hypothesized that infant wariness of strange and unfamiliar objects had more to do with the *conjunction* of strange and familiar than with the unusualness of the unfamiliar stimulus itself.

Similarly, Bühler et al. (1928) had observed that children of a certain age will begin to react with wariness and fear when exposed to unfamiliar persons, things, and noises. Paradoxically, however, some of the same stimuli can provoke interest, curiosity, and positive reactions. In a cleverly designed study, Bühler et al. directly addressed the question of whether the fear reaction to familiar stimuli occurred as a function of the unusualness of the stimuli themselves, or the juxtaposition of strange and unfamiliar, as when an parent donned a mask in the presence of the child.

The subjects for their study were infants in three age groups: $2\frac{1}{2}$ to $4\frac{1}{2}$ months of age, $4\frac{1}{2}$ to $6\frac{1}{2}$ months, and $6\frac{1}{2}$ to $8\frac{1}{2}$ months. Two types of stimuli, presented for 30 seconds duration, were employed: Auditory stimuli in the form of a natural tone of voice, a falsetto, or a deep voice, and visual stimuli in the form of animal masks. The stimuli were presented both to the infant alone and in the presence of an experimenter with whom the infant was familiar, and they were presented in several different orders. There were 5 to 12 subjects in each of eight experimental conditions.

The main dependent measures were emotional reactions to the stimuli. Negative expressions included startle, negative astonishment, active distress, and quiet displeasure. Positive reactions included expressions of pleasure, positive astonishment, and joy. The criteria for coding into each of these categories were provided in the text of the article (Bühler et al., 1928) and generally conform to criteria used in contemporary coding schemes. For example, the criteria for "negative astonishment" were signs of eye-widening, brow raising, opening of the mouth, tension in the forehead, and sounds of displeasure. A first general level of analysis revealed that affective reactions to familiar stimuli occurred at a rate of 30% or less; affective reactions to unfamiliar or strange stimuli occurred at a rate of 50% or higher. Thus, the unfamiliar stimuli did have greater power to trigger affective reactions. A second general finding was that negative reactions were given more frequently than positive ones to unfamiliar stimuli in all three age groups, but especially in the youngest age group (43% versus 31% and 26%, respectively, in the two older groups). In contrasting strange stimuli on their own versus in conjunction with familiar sights (experimenter speaking in a strange tone, experimenter donning an animal mask), the results clearly indicated that discrepancy was the more powerful elicitor of negative reactions in infants—negative affective reactions occurred at almost twice the rate for this condition than for the former.

Next, a comparison of the effects of presenting the unfamiliar stimuli first, followed by the familiar stimulus, versus familiar stimulus first, produced an effect quite in contrast to the preceding results. While the previous observations indicated that the youngest (versus middle and oldest) subjects were most disturbed by unfamiliar stimuli, this experiment showed that all age groups emitted negative reactions about equally in response to the unfamiliar followed by familiar, but there was a dramatic increase in negative reactions over age to the condition where the familiar was replaced by an unfamiliar stimulus (familiar adult dons a strange mask). Finally, when the researchers broke their data down even further and compared the effects of the various orders of strange and familiar presentations (strange after familiar, familiar after familiar, familiar after strange) they found that there was an increase in negative reactions across time in each of the three conditions.

Taken as a whole, these various results indicated that distress to the strange and unfamiliar over time is a function of an infant's increasing apprehension of the *change* of an object from one state to another. Thus, the effects were due not so much to the observation of a static contrast effect, but to the observation of an object apparently undergoing transformation.

Bühler et al.'s investigation—uninfluenced by the work of Piaget—was the first experimental study of its kind to assess the affective impact of discrepancy. It documented, as Hebb was later to show with nonhuman primates (1946, 1949), that human infants react to discrepancy, and to the violation of expectancy, with distress. More importantly, the research indicates that it is more than mere discrepancy that produces distress, at least in humans, and provides evidence of an early form of object constancy in infants; it is apparently the violation of a constancy concept that is so distressing. The study also had far-reaching implications for a developmental model of the relation between affect and cognition. Unfortunately, this work apparently had little impact on American research of the time.

In the second experimental study, Bühler and Hetzer (1928) examined infants' responses to simulated expressions of emotion as encoded in face, voice, or gesture. This particular study is packed with acute observations on the nature of infant affectivity, many of which predate by decades the findings of more recent research. The procedure in their study consisted of having an experimenter present expressive stimuli (in vivo)—with exposures of 30 seconds; another served as observer and recorder of behavior. Bühler and Hetzer chose to study children in the age range of 3 to 12 months (10 at each monthly interval) because earlier work had suggested that though 2-month-olds reacted to both positive and negative expressions of emotion presented to them, they did not appear to discriminate between them.

The first experimental manipulation involved presenting the infant with an angry or friendly face (without accompanying sound or gesture) and observing the child's positive versus negative emotional reaction (coded in the same way as in the previous study). The data indicate that there was a heightened period of discriminating sensitivity between the fifth and seventh months. For example, in response to the presentation of an angry facial expression, at 3 months 90% showed a positive reaction, 10% a negative reaction. At 4 months 50% showed positive reactions, 50% negative. Between 5 and 7 months 100% of the infants showed a negative response. By 8 months 25% showed a positive response, 75% negative; the proportions of positive and negative reactions reversed themselves by 11 months, when 75% were positive, and 25% negative.

Bühler and Hetzer hypothesized that the difference between the 3-month-olds' predominantly positive responses and the 5-month-olds' predominantly negative responses had to do with the overwhelmingly positive attraction of the human face as well as the 3-month-olds' tendency to focus only on the eye region. By 4 months this was already beginning to change. Eighty percent of the infants showed an initial positive response to the negative facial expression, but then many of them suddenly frowned or broke into intense crying. These observations suggested to Bühler and Hetzer that 4-month-olds were beginning to do more active scanning of the entire face, and as they did so, they apprehended the angry gestalt, which then triggered a negative reaction.

Bühler and Hetzer regarded the negative reactions of the 5- to 7-month- olds (and many 4-month-olds) as a contagion response, which they dubbed *reflektorische Übertragung*—reflective transference or contagion (Bühler & Hetzer, 1928, p. 54). Whereas 80% of the 5-month-olds mimicked the friendly face and 80% mimicked the angry face, by 11 months, only 25% of the infants reflected a positive face to a positive stimulus and 25% a negative face to a negative expression. Because in the older infant—beginning at about 8 months—there was greater variance in the response, this appeared to mark a certain degree of release from the contagion phenomenon. Many of the 8-month-old infants began to react negatively, only to switch suddenly to laughter, as though freed from the grip of contagion by their comprehension that the situation had the character of a game. Thus the older infant appeared to react to the emotional expression of others with both a feeling component and an understanding component. These are important observations. They parallel in a number of ways certain tenets of Hoffman's (1982a) theory of empathic development, which is based on more contemporary research. As such, this study is one of the first to document the existence of what Hoffman termed "sympathetic distress," an early precursor of empathy (Hoffman, 1982a).

A similar experiment was conducted with tone of voice, this time presenting a friendly versus scolding voice, while keeping the face neutral. The results were similar to that found with facial expressions with the exception that the negative reactions to the negative vocal stimuli began somewhat later in development and persisted over a longer developmental period.

A third experiment used enticing versus threatening gestures, again, unaccompanied with any other affective signs (facial or vocal expressions). The data indicate that by 8 months the majority of the infants discriminated the gestures, which led Bühler and Hetzer to conclude that the eighth month heralded a new level of understanding about the social world—the intentionality of others.

A final experiment involved the study of contagious crying, or *Mitschreien*, which anticipates Sagi and Hoffman's classic 1976 work on the topic by over 40 years (see Chapter 7, this volume). Bühler and Hetzer had already observed that infants as young as a day old would begin crying in the presence of another crying infant. They decided to examine whether the phenomenon was merely that of a shock reaction to an acute auditory stimulus, or whether it was a social phenomenon akin to empathic distress. The procedure involved bringing an infant who was already crying into proximity with a quietly resting infant. Eighty-four percent of the newborn infants began crying after exposure to the crying infant. The stimulus infants cried for varying lengths of time, which allowed Bühler and Hetzer to assess the impact of short versus long exposures to crying. It was observed that the older the infant, the shorter the duration of cry exposure needed before the child cried. In the first 3 days of life it took an average of 170 seconds before the other infant began to cry, from 4 to 7 days, 94 seconds, and from 8 to 14 days only 88 seconds.

While in 43% of the cases both infants would continue to cry, a more common pattern was a pattern of "exchange crying." That is, as child A began to cry, this was followed by crying in child B. When child A quieted, child B quieted, at which point child A would begin to cry again, and so on. Such exchanges of newborn crying could be observed for up to 10 runs at a time. By the second month such reactions had fallen off. Data on the course of contagious crying over time indicated that 84% showed the response in the first 2 weeks of life, 60% at 1 month, 32% at 2 months, and only 24% in the 3- to 12-month period. Bühler and Hetzer attempted to determine whether it was the acoustic properties of the cry or the sight of the crying infant that triggered the contagious response by interposing a shield on some trials. The shielded condition had no discernable effect in the case of the newborn, but by the second month there was a differential reaction.

Sixty-eight percent of the infants failed to react when the shield was absent, whereas 90% failed to react when the shield was present. Thus it appeared that the effect of crying on the newborn and 1- to 2-month-old infant was a function of the acoustic properties of the stimulus, whereas from 2 months on there was a social enhancement.

The above finding with respect to the contagion of emotion in response to auditory stimuli was in contrast to the effect of negative facial expressions, which first became effective in producing distress at 4 months. The authors concluded that during the first 2 months of life, exposure to expressive behaviors exerts its effect on infants primarily as sensory stimulus; from 2 to 8 months the impact is more a result of its social significance; from 8 months the effect is conjoined by a dawning mental awareness.

Taken as a whole, this body of research on infant emotional responsivity constitutes one of the most important contributions to the psychology of infant development and to the area of social and emotional development during the first wave of emotions research. The research was an exemplary model of developmental research—systematic, well executed, and reported in sufficient detail that it could serve as a springboard for replications or further research. Unfortunately, Bühler did not continue her research in this area because she became interested in other developmental matters, namely, adolescent development. As such she did not continue to promote this line of research and the studies are little cited today in either German or American accounts of the contribution of early scholars to our understanding of emotional development. The fact that Bühler's experimental research on infant affect was never translated into English was in large part responsible for the neglect of this work. German-language publications started to decline after World War I as a percentage of all Western psychology and sociology publications—from 52% of the field in 1910 to 23% in 1920; today they constitute only 3.6%. In contrast, English-language publication went from 32% in 1910 to 59% in 1930 and today command the bulk of the literature (89%) (Müller-Brettel, 1993).

Because Bühler's publications on infant affect went largely unnoticed by American researchers, Bridges's idea that emotion is undifferentiated in infancy went unchallenged. Bridges did assert that emotions differentiate during childhood, but several investigators took exception to this and instead argued that emotion is undifferentiated even in older children and adults. One of the more influential of these studies was an investigation by Carney Landis. The research appeared to show, in a fairly dramatic way, that emotions lacked distinctive, differential properties even in adult subjects. However, as with analysis of other early studies, again we will see that there was reason to question this interpretation.

THE DEMISE OF DISCRETE EMOTIONS

Like many of his contemporaries, Carney Landis, of the University of Minnesota, was interested in the question of whether or not emotion expressions were discrete and differentiated, as claimed by Watson and Darwin before him (Landis, 1924, 1929). Landis studied infants and adults, but his study of adults was the more influential. The study is most frequently cited as evidence against discrete emotions; ironically enough, in light of today's advanced understanding of emotion, the very same data can be reinterpreted as support for discrete emotions theory, as we will see.

Twenty-five individuals—12 adult women, 12 adult men, and one young boy—served as Landis's subjects. With the exception of the young boy, all of the subjects were apparently well known to the experimenter. The 12 men were directly connected to the Department of Psychology in various capacities while Landis was an undergraduate majoring in sociology.

The subject was brought into the laboratory, seated at a table, and outfitted with apparatus designed to measure respiration and blood pressure—a sphygmomanometer arm band, bracelet stethoscope, and Somner pneumograph. At either side of the subject stood a 1,000 W lamp in a diffusing reflector and a screen for photographic background stood behind. Subjects were put through a variety of procedures designed to elicit emotion, and several photographs of their expressions were taken by the experimenter—Landis—at each step. The elicitors were introduced innocuously enough but built up to quite noxious conditions. There were 16 eliciting situations:

1. Listening to popular music.
2. Listening to technical music.
3. Readings from the Bible.
4. Telling lies.
5. Smelling ammonia.
6. Firecracker going off under the subject's chair.
7. Relating an embarrassing experience and having it read back.
8. Being shown color photos of morbid skin diseases.
9. Doing complicated mental multiplication.
10. Viewing pornographic pictures.
11. Viewing nude art poses.
12. Reading several pornographic case histories.
13. Being made to reach into a pail of water that unbeknownst to the subject contained live frogs, then after reacting to the frogs being made to feel the frogs again and receiving electric shock.
14. Being shocked during trials of mental multiplication. ("The shocks were of the make and break variety and were varied from a just noticeable intensity to a strength which caused the subject to jump from the chair" [Landis, 1924, p. 46].)
15. Being made to decapitate a white rat. (The table in front of the subject was covered with a cloth. A flat tray and a butcher's knife were placed on the cloth. A live white rat was then given to the subject. He was instructed to "hold this rat with your left hand and then cut off its head with the knife." [In another account of the study the author reveals that the knife provided was deliberately a blunt one.] The author states that

"this situation was tried with 21 [out of the 25] subjects. Fifteen subjects followed instructions after more or less urging. In 5 cases where the subjects could not be persuaded to follow directions the experimenter cut off the rat's head while the subject looked on. In 2 cases the decapitation for various reasons was not performed" Landis, 1924, p. 459].)

   16. A "relief" condition when it was explained that the experiment was over.

The experimenter evaluated the resulting behavioral responses to establish whether there were distinctive facial or behavioral patterns that were associated with the different eliciting conditions. He performed several levels of analysis, which consisted of (1) looking for patterns in the muscle groups of the facial expressions, (2) asking subjects to report what they had felt during the various conditions, (3) recording how subjects looked and behaved during presentation of the stimuli, and (4) later (in a report published in Landis and Hunt, 1939) having judges try to decipher the underlying feeling state of the subjects for each of the photographs. Landis claimed that the subjects' facial expressions were unsystematically related to (1) the induction conditions, (2) self-reports, or (3) to other observers' judgments of their affective state.

In fact, this study provides compelling evidence in favor of the discrete, differentiated emotions position. Despite the variety of stimulus-eliciting conditions that were scheduled, it appears that the real induction for these subjects was overwhelmingly that of embarrassment. The subjects, who knew the experimenter and were known by him, were required to do very self-revealing and potentially embarrassing things. And they were well aware of being under intense scrutiny since they were wired to several kinds of monitoring apparatus and their expressions were being repeatedly photographed. All of this would tend to make anyone acutely self-conscious, suggesting that embarrassment was the chief emotional by-product.

One key feature of shame or embarrassment is that of wanting to hide or disappear (see Malatesta-Magai & Dorval, 1992). In terms of expressive behavior, embarrassment is indexed by two emblematic features: self-conscious smiling and averted head and gaze. One can reexamine Landis's data with this in mind. Inspection of the photographs published by Landis shows that in about half the pictures the subject's head was averted to the side or down. In the remainder of the photographs, the bulk of faces are characterized by various degrees of smiling. In addition, Landis's report of the bodily reactions following presentation of the stimuli indicates that 8 of the 16 eliciting conditions were accompanied by blushing in a large proportion of subjects. Finally, judges, who did not know the conditions under which the study had been conducted, attributed joy more than any other single emotion to the various phonographs. This is in all likelihood attributable to the high frequency of embarrassed smiling.

In light of the above and contrary to Landis's conclusion, these data provide an interesting affirmation of the position that affect is differentiated, although they appear to confirm the case for essentially one emotion—that of embarrassment. There was an additional interesting aspect of the Landis study. Despite the surfeit of embarrassment that was evidently provoked, some of the other "noise" in the data apparently was contributed by stylistic habits or what more recent writers have referred to as emotion traits, emotion biases, or emotion organizations (see Chapter 5, this volume). This was apparently a salient phenomenon since Landis mentions it in three specific places; it probably also contributed to his conclusion that emotion was erratic and idiosyncratic rather than patterned. Based on his tabulation of muscle group movements for individual subjects across the range of conditions, Landis (1924) was led to comment:

> It was found that all individuals tend to use certain muscles, muscle groups or expressions in the majority of their expressive reactions, to the exclusion of other muscle groups. There are marked individual variations in the expressive patterns so produced. (p. 497)

Moreover, Landis detected two types of expressive bias. It was obvious from the data that

> certain individuals favor certain muscle patterns and neglect the use of others, as for instance, subject U who throws his head back, wrinkles his forehead and opens his mouth but never shows the vertical wrinkles between the eyebrows indicative of corrugator contraction. (p. 478)

Landis also noted that

> The absence of usage of certain muscles for certain individuals is a more frequent occurrence than the predominance of the reaction of other muscles. That is, there is a distinct tendency toward non-reaction of certain muscle patterns for most individuals. (p. 478)

This observation did not receive much attention at the time. Researchers would not rediscover this phenomenon and related aspects of expressivity for another 30–40 years. Landis's study was one of the last nails in the coffin of the theory of discrete, differentiated affect, at least for the time being, and at least within experimental circles. However, while experimental psychology abandoned the study of emotion during the ensuing decades, psychoanalytically inclined investigators continued to be interested in emotions. At this point we turn to a discussion of psychoanalytic conceptualizations of affect and the pioneering research of Spitz.

PSYCHOANALYSIS AND EMOTION

Freud

From an early date, Freud was acutely aware of the pivotal role that emotion played in neurosis. However, he was more concerned with drives and their derivatives than in affect qua affect and his writings reflected this. In brief, humans were seen as being governed by a variety of inborn drives that produced unpleasant tensions. What all drives had in common were a *source* (instinct, deprivational state), an *impetus* (strength of excitatory potential), an *aim* (to satisfy the need that had been aroused), and an *object* (substance or state of affairs that would reduce the need). Because drive tension was unpleasant, humans were motivated to reduce their drives by whatever means they could. Freud's views on emotion were inextricably bound up with his notions concerning drive, though his ideas concerning both drives and affects changed over time with successive reformulations of psychoanalytic theory.

Rapaport (1968) discerns three distinct phases in Freud's conceptualization of affect. In his earliest writings, affect was equated with psychic energy, which was derived from drives. As such, affect and energy were indistinguishable from one another conceptually. Affect was seen as exogenous somatic discharge, representing the dissipation of excess energy from too great an influx of stimulation. For example, pain associated with unsatisfied drive states such as hunger would result in an infant's kicking, thrashing, and crying.

In the next stage of his writings Freud began to distinguish between affect and energy, although affect was still viewed as a drive derivative and tied to drive dynamically. There were two representatives of drives: affect and ideas. When danger was perceived or when direct gratification of sexual or aggressive drives needed to be inhibited, internal visceral or glandular discharge resulted. Thus, Freud was saying that affect is what happens when drive is not discharged—thus, affect was a spill-over phenomenon.

In the last 20 years of Freud's writings, we see a shift from preoccupation with drive processes to increasing concern with ego processes and as a result, Freud's ideas about affect undergo substantial revision. The ego, as the executive aspect of the personality, was governed by the reality principle. Its function was to delay and control instinctual discharge and it had an arsenal of mechanisms at its disposal, including secondary thought process and unconscious mechanisms of defense. With the introduction of the ego as the conscious aspect of the self, Freud could deal with affect as a conscious, perceptual experience. The ego required sensors for the detection of imminent anxiety, since anxiety was particularly noxious and it was the *feeling* of anxiety that acted as a signal, mobilizing the ego's adaptive and defensive behavior. In this conceptualization then, affect, as inner "structure," could be reproduced as signal by the ego without affect discharge (the motor or glandular component) actually having to take place.

In summarizing Freud's treatment of affect two points need to be made. First, his theory of affect, if we can call it that, is essentially a one-affect theory. It is primarily a theory of anxiety. Freud did not address himself to a description of other emotions, although he did acknowledge that not every "unpleasure" could be called anxiety, given that there are other feelings, such as tension, pain, or grieving. Second, Freud did not treat affects in an expressly developmental context. Though he saw affect as undergoing a transformation as it became "harnessed" by "ego cathexes," he was not particularly interested in its developmental aspects. Instead, he bid those who might be interested in developmental issues to study infants in vivo. René Spitz was one colleague who took him at his word, as mentioned earlier. At this point we turn to Spitz's theories concerning infant affect. Unlike others in his psychoanalytic circle, Spitz was particularly well situated to comment on the developmental aspects of affect, since he had firsthand experience in observing infants.

Spitz on the Development and Organization of Affect

Although the next two decades would witness a virtual disappearance of affect from theoretical discourse and experimental research, Spitz's work presaged attachment theory as well as organizational models of affect that arose during the second wave of emotions research, while at the same time incorporating drive reduction and behavioristic conceptualizations of learning. As such, his theory is a transition piece between the first and second waves. In terms of the psychoanalytic movement, he was also one of the first among his analytic cohort to deemphasize drives in favor of affective relations between individuals. Emotions would be conceived as signals to others as well as to the self, and emotions would be seen as organizing forces in the development of ego rather than vice versa.

Spitz's Genetic Field Theory

Spitz's theory provided the first analytic model of emotions ontogenesis. It went well beyond Bridges's genetic theory in that it did more than describe changes in affect expression, it hypothesized dynamic mechanisms of change. While Bridges implicated maturation and social conditioning as processes in ontogenesis, she never elaborated on the latter. In contrast, Spitz specified and elaborated upon mechanisms and processes, and moved in the direction of a true emotion socialization model that tried to account for differential development.

In overview, Spitz's model began with the fundamentals of classical conditioning of emotion; however, his emphasis was on the fact that conditioning occurred within the context of "object relations," or the affective relationship between mother and infant. Affect was transformed over time as ego processes evolved and after the conditioning (and association) processes established certain links in consciousness.

According to Spitz, rudimentary emotion existed before the development of object relations but it was diffuse and nonspecific. This was because during the first 3 months of life the sensory mode of functioning was "coenesthetic." That is, it was not localized, not discrete, but extensive. There was only a general reception of sensory information. On the motor side, emotion expression was also diffuse, unspecific, and undirected. Needs were communicated via reflexive signals such as crying. The neonate was described as having prototype, or precursor, emotions, which were excitation and quiescence. Excitation in the neonate consisted preponderantly of negative affect, which Spitz called unpleasure, and which was associated with an increase of tension. Pleasure, which involved a decrease of tension, was relatively rare. Spitz felt that unpleasure was preponderant in the young infant for two reasons. First, pleasure, or positive manifestations, were relatively inconspicuous compared to those of negative affect—gentle softening of the baby's face after feeding, or its tendency to mold itself contentedly into the mother's arms were less obvious behaviors than behavior such as loud crying accompanied by thrashing and other gross motor movements. Moreover, any movements that looked like pleasure, such as smiling, did not seem linked to the right precipitating conditions. For example, the infant might show signs of a smile, but in circumstances that were accompanied by mounting tension.

According to Spitz, the child's personality, and the differentiation of emotion, emerged only in the course of extensive interactional experience with the mother, who would "shape and mold the developing personality of the child" (Spitz, 1965, p. 126). In the context of this dyadic relationship (Freud referred to this duality as a "mass of two") the mother and child participated in interchanges involving reciprocal and circular influence. The mother practiced a "near-clairvoyant" or "quasi-telepathic" manner of responding to the infant's needs; maternal empathy was matched by the baby's perception of the mother's moods. This mood information was communicated by nonverbal, nondirected, expressive signals and was received by the infant in a diffuse and undifferentiated manner.

During the next 3 months, two events of significance occurred: (1) emotional responses were progressively integrated with their facial and other behavioral expressions, and (2) they served as communicative links with the surround. By the third month the child had already mastered the capacity to turn to the surround and to signal its needs. Spitz conceptualized the cue to behavior as coming from outside during earliest development (touch to the cheek, aversive stimulus), but during the stage of what Karl Bühler referred to as "the appeal," this was reversed; the child cried to signal that she was hungry. Because these events recurred repetitively, a link in memory was forged. Thus, the two parts of the infant's experience, hunger crying and the subsequent feeling of gratification, became linked in consciousness.

In the third quarter of the first year, a definitive link between felt emotion as a signal for the ego, and the expression of emotion as a communication to the surround, was established. At that point the child not only expressed what he felt, he also communicated his wishes.

The process of organizing the random activity and establishing links occurred within the context of the emerging object relationship; the unfolding of the individual child's object relations paralleled closely the ontogenesis of the expression of emotions. In fact, Spitz found that when infants were deprived of normal object relations, emotional ontogeny went awry, as he documented in his study of institution-reared infants.

Spitz's extensive first-hand observations of infants led him to propose what he termed a genetic field theory. The basic tenets of the theory revolved around the concept of psychic organizers, which were viewed as pacemakers for different developmental axes. They represented critical nodal points in psychological development. In early ontogenesis there were three psychic organizers whose respective indicators were smiling, 8-months anxiety, and negativism (negative head-shaking and use of the word "no").

The first organizer, the smile, indicated that the child had acquired the capacity to distinguish and experience positive emotion and was a reflection of the fact that the infant experienced its relationship with its caregiver emotionally.

The smile, as expressive behavior, was of particular interest to Spitz, and he devoted a monograph to the ontogeny of its development. Through a series of experiments, he demonstrated that the smile was at first given to physical stimuli devoid of psychological meaning, and only gradually became linked in consciousness with "emotion-producing experience." Spitz assumed that there was no initial connection between experience and behavior. It was only through the process of conditioning, the dawning of consciousness and emergence of the ego, and the establishment of object relations, that the smile would come to have true socioemotional significance.

According to Spitz, the ego, which was responsible for conscious experience, came into being, in rudimentary form, around the third month. But this did not mean that expressive behavior was linked to affect in a conscious, felt manner. Instead specific facial expressions, as expressions of emotion, became meaningful only as a result of a linkage that took place when a particular facial expression became linked with a specific experience, a coordination that was "comparable to that which takes place in the conditioned reflex." Several steps were involved in the case of the smiling response.

Spitz regarded the action of "turning towards" as the precursor to positive affect or pleasure because of its survival value; the head-turning response brought the baby's mouth into contact with the mother's breast, and the rooting response insured that the infant responded reliably to the nipple when it touched the oral mucosa. The second step occurred a week or so later, when the infant produced a *Flaschenerkennungsreaktion*, or food-recognition response, as for example, when the bib was placed beneath the child's chin. The touch of the bib became associated with hunger gratification and began to take on positive signal value. The tactile stimulus of the bib was next replaced by a visual conditioned stimulus when the infant saw someone approach him just prior to feeding. Finally, the caregiving figure became endowed with significance in her own right, independent of drive state, and the child smiled at the sight of the caregiver.

The second organizer, 8-months anxiety, involved an appeal for help and involved intentional behavior. The appearance of the anxiety response indicated that the caregiver was now established not only in the cognitive sector, but also, and primarily, in the affective sector. The mother had become a special person from whom the child did not want to be separated.

The mechanisms thought to underlie the process of linkage were as follows. The emotion of anxiety, or felt anxiety, assumed a centripetally directed function; it became a danger signal, mobilizing the pleasure–unpleasure agency. At the same time the emotion expression became effective in a centrifugal direction. The feeling as it headed centrifugally, became channeled into the efferent nervous system and set into motion the range of elements that figured into its expressive aspects. These expressions served as a communication to the surround, to the libidinal object. They were perceived by the object as a sign of helplessness or as a signal for help.

Eight-months anxiety was regarded by Spitz as "anxiety proper." There were two earlier stages leading up to it. The first stage involved that of "physiological tension states." The second stage was reached when the reaction of fear was provoked by a percept that was associated with a previously experienced instance of unpleasure. It consisted of a "flight" response occasioned by the child's reexperience of a percept that had an unpleasure cathexis. In contrast, 8-months anxiety at the third stage involved a response to a percept that in itself had never before been associated with unpleasure, that is, the sight of a stranger.

The reader may wonder why the child would show anxiety to this previously neutral stimulus. According to Spitz, it was because over the course of the preceding months the child had come to respond to the absence of the mother with unpleasure. What he reacted to when confronted with a stranger was the recognition that this was not his mother; in a sense, his mother had left him, a thought that provoked anxiety. Thus, the response was really a response tied to a cognitive event as well as the maturation of an emotional response. The 8-month anxiety is the proof that, to the child, everyone "is a stranger, with the exception of the unique object; that is to say, the child has found THE partner with whom he can form object relations in the true sense of the term" (Spitz, 1965, p. 162).

The third psychic organizer, reflected in negativism, closely followed the development of locomotion, which was associated with increasing experiences of autonomy and increasing prohibitions on behavior. During this time, there occurred a shift in the nature of the relationship between mother and child with the child's onset of ambulation. Earlier exchanges between mother and child centered around infantile passivity and maternal solicitations and supportive actions. When the child achieved independent locomotion all this was altered and the exchanges were now more to be characterized as centering around bursts of infantile activity and maternal prohibitions, reproaches, and by stern commands accompanied by a loudly sounded "No!" Saying this word, the mother shook her head, while preventing the child from doing that which he wanted. Eventually the word "no" and negative head-shaking came to symbolize the concept of negation, which was then invoked by the child himself as an assertion of autonomy.

In the wake of the third psychic organizer of negativism, and the development of autonomy, followed by language, there emerged an achievement with far-reaching consequences. With the acquisition of the gesture of negativism, action was replaced by messages, and distance communication was inaugurated. This amounted to the first abstraction formed by the child and it represented the beginning of verbal communication. But, one might ask, what about the child's other early single word utterances? Spitz suggested that words like "Mama" and "Dada" were global words representing a variety of wishes and needs of the child ranging from mother, to food, to I am bored, to I am happy. In contrast, the negative head-shake and the word "no" represented a concept— that of negation.

In summary, Spitz emphasized that emotional development and object relations went hand in hand. His own research on institution-reared children provided confirmation that disturbances in object relations would lead to deflections in the normal course of emotional development. He found, for example, that the first psychic organizer, smiling, was delayed in children who did not have a consistent caregiver, and that the second psychic organizer, 8-months, or stranger, anxiety, either appeared prematurely in development or consisted of an apathetic response to all social partners. His reports received attention from clinicians and some research psychologists, and certainly his observations had an impact on Bowlby and his formulation of attachment theory. Unfortunately, psychology had begun to turn its attention away from topics expressly concerned with emotion, and Spitz's more theoretical work did not get the attention it deserved, especially outside of psychoanalytic circles. There were a number of reasons for the decline in emotions research over the next two decades.

THE MIDDLE YEARS: THE GRADUAL DISAPPEARANCE OF EMOTIONS RESEARCH

An examination of the successive editions of a widely used psychology textbook provides a perspective on what happened to emotions research during the 1950s, 1960s, and early 1970s. Floyd Ruch's text, *Psychology and Life*, published by Scott, Foresman, is one of the longest enduring texts in the field. Ruch published the first edition in 1937 and it apparently assumed a life of its own. After Ruch's death, Philip Zimbardo took over and has recently published the twelfth edition of this text.

In the first edition, which is subtitled *A Study of the Thinking, Feeling, and Doing of People*, Ruch devoted one chapter to a general introduction to the subject of emotions in which he discussed emotional expressions, the adaptive function of the emotions, and the biological outcomes of intense emotions. Because he believed that the best way to avoid what we today commonly call "stress" and its deleterious effects upon health was to avoid intense emotion, Ruch advised that college students learn to control their affects. Taking an evolutionary approach, Ruch (1937) argued, like many of his contemporaries, that modern civilization had made "cave-man emotions" (p. 228) maladaptive. In order to explain how one might eliminate or attenuate these emotions, he devoted another chapter to the development of affect. He did not mean development in a maturational sense, but as a consequence of training.

Much of the chapter on emotional development consists of a description of Watson's work on the elicitation of rage, fear, and love and on the conditioning of these emotions. Ruch elaborated upon Watson's "little Albert" study and then related how in ordinary life, conditioned emotions are lost. Ruch also depicted some studies in which conditioned responses did not obtain and he included some work that was critical of Watson. He maintained, however, that although Watson's work was flawed, it was still of fundamental importance because it demonstrated how learning techniques could be employed at the service of emotional control.

In the second edition of this text (Ruch, 1941), a significant change occurred in how emotion was portrayed. Still carrying the same subtitle, the text took on a new organizational structure. No longer was there a chapter on emotional development. Keeping essentially the same content, that chapter was retitled "Control of Emotions." Here, Ruch added a section on emotional control in the adult, offering suggestions on how to learn to show a "poker face" in order to conceal emotions. By adding this emphasis, Ruch began to move away from the focus on children that had been evident in the first edition of the text.

Interestingly, in the fourth edition (Ruch, 1953), Ruch added a lifespan perspective to the now solitary chapter on emotion. Far more attention was devoted to various theoretical positions on emotion. In the subsection on emotional development, Watson's work continued to be given several pages, although now a lengthy description of Bridges's theory of emotion differentiation was added. Also, Ruch included in this section an extended discussion of socialization and personality development.

Little change occurred in the fifth and sixth editions, published in 1958 and 1963, though the field was beginning to turn away from emotions (texts tend to lag about 5 years behind events in the field since time is necessary to fully grasp trends that are developing.) In the seventh edition, the chapter on emotion, which Ruch consistently organized as the second chapter in the text, was replaced with "The Biological Bases of Behavior," reflecting neurophysiological research and the emergence of activation theories of behavior; emotion was now treated as a physiological event. The developmental chapter moved to third place.

In the eighth edition, published in 1971, Philip Zimbardo acted for the first time as coauthor. A number of interesting changes occurred, including—most notably for our purposes—the disappearance of the chapter on emotion. Treatment of emotion was now relegated to a minor role under the section "The Cognitive Control of Behavior." In addition, the long-enduring section on emotional development disappeared entirely, leaving behind a discussion of emotion perception and the relation between emotions and health.

There were a number of reasons for the gradual disappearance of emotion as a central construct from the psychological literature. Multiple attempts at replication had failed to support some of Watson's most basic claims—for example, those having to do with innate discrete emotions. As such, there developed a general disillusion with what behaviorism had to offer the field of developmental psychology. Landis's work and that of others seemed to indicate that the very construct of differential emotions was a chimera. The sense that emotion was fuzzy and undifferentiated was further forwarded by the arrival of activation and arousal theories of human behavior, including the work of Lindsley, Malmo, and Duffy. Though these authors proposed general models of behavior as distilled from neurophysiological research (e.g., Moruzzi and Magoun's discovery of the brain stem reticular activating system), the concepts were applied to emotion as well. Duffy (1941, 1962), for example, asserted that behavior varies along two dimensions, direction and intensity. Emotion was merely a point or set of points toward the high end of behavioral arousal; thus, emotion could vary only in intensity, there being no allowance for different kinds of emotional experience. Emotions did not recover from these various blows until the late 1970s, the time that heralded the second wave of emotions research.

5

The Second Wave of Research
Functionalist and Cognitivist Approaches

> All clowns are masked and all personae
> Flow from choices; sad and gay, wise,
> Moody and humorous are chosen faces
> DELMORE SCHWARTZ, *The Repetitive Heart*

In reviewing the research of the first half of the century, we observed that most investigators tended to view emotional development as a process of relatively straightforward conditioning. Since that time, conditioning models have all but fallen by the wayside. Although various writers do not deny that development is affected by learning contingencies, the most distinctive change in our conceptualizations about emotional development during this century has been the emergence of various "organizational" models of development. Attachment theory is one such model, as already described in Chapters 2 and 3. Another important organizational model is that of differential emotions theory, which deals with the expression and socialization of emotion, and which will be treated within this chapter. In organizational models the emphasis is on the functional and adaptive qualities of emotions and the central role they play in the regulation of individual and interpersonal behavior. Emotions are no longer regarded as "stimuli" or "responses" but as central, organizing features of personality and behavior. Hence, the study of emotion is back where Lev Vygotsky had the early vision to see that it ought to be.

Vygotsky had anticipated three of the current trends in developmental research on the emotions: the socialization of emotion, its progressive "interiorization," and the relation between emotion and the rest of personality. Research on emotional socialization looks at how emotion expressions undergo change with time and examines the forces that are involved in promoting more "mature" expressions. Although this body of research still belabors the old issue of expressive control, as in the days of Galen and the Stoics, emotion socialization is seen as including the child's acquisition of skill in using emotion in social communication and learning to transfer overt expressive behavior into the internal world of elaborated representation (the interiorization process). The third aspect, the role of emotions in personality formation, is also beginning to gain a foothold in contemporary developmental research. Several writers have proposed that affect tends to become structuralized within the personality in the form of ideo-affective organizations, emotional-cognitive structures, or emotion biases, and thus plays an important role in differential personality development.

In addition to an ideological shift, we will see that the new wave of emotions research is accompanied by a more sanguine attitude towards emotions and their place in human experience. Emotions are no longer seen as the source of all human misery and in need of vigorous subjugation. In growth and maturation, emotions are not so much tamed as *developed*. The reason for the change in this stance is not immediately apparent. In part it may reflect the rather dramatic changes in the economic conditions of daily life that have occurred during the twentieth century. Many sources of human suffering that afflicted the life of the individual in earlier times have been reduced or eliminated. Indeed, the normative affective experiences of life in Western culture are more positive than negative, at least as judged by self-report. Large-scale, time-sampling surveys of mood in this country, as well as in Europe, indicate that the average individual experiences more positive than negative emotions on a moment to moment basis (Diener & Larsen, 1993).

In the next few chapters we pursue questions of emotion expression development, both in terms of general developmental issues related to the emotions (Chapter 5), as well as in terms of particular emotions (Chapters 6 and 7). The broader issue of how emotions are elaborated in differential personality development is deferred until Part IV.

DAWN OF THE SECOND WAVE

As late as the mid-1970s, research on affective development had only scratched the surface. A number of researchers included emotional phenomena as dependent variables in the study of cognitive development, but they were hardly studied in their own right. Jeannette Haviland, speaking at a meeting of the Society for Research in Child Development in 1975, could still remark upon with little fear of contradiction—"how little we know about affect itself—its forms, its origins, its development, its biological meaning and its culturally bound interpretations."

Indeed, developmental research on the emotions had all but come to a standstill since the 1950s. However, starting about 1970, a small cadre of investigators (e.g., Izard, Haviland, Saarni, Sroufe, Lewis, Campos, Emde, Zahn-Waxler) began exploring aspects of affective development. Because these individuals did research in other areas as well (mainly cognitive and social development) and thus kept a reputable foothold in their fields, their work on affect could go forward, despite the fact that there was little collegial support. The work on affect, of course, fell outside mainstream psychology, and thus there was great difficulty getting an audience for the new evidence that was accumulating concerning affective processes. Nevertheless, these individuals pursued their research on emotion, while the rest of developmental psychology concentrated on issues of cognition, learning, perception, and attention.

It is now generally acknowledged that a new consciousness with respect to the emotions began to dawn in developmental psychology toward the end of the 1970s. By 1981, papers on affect were beginning to find a hearing at local and international conferences. By 1983, such papers were not merely relegated to this or that symposium as space permitted, but formed a recognizable subject matter, and one could find whole symposia organized around affective issues. Two books are generally credited with having piqued the interest of the larger field and of having inspired the new groundswell of studies on affective development that came of age during the 1980s. One was Carroll Izard's, *Human Emotions* (1977); the other was an edited volume by Michael Lewis and Leonard Rosenblum entitled *The Development of Affect* (1978). Izard's work placed the study of emotion within a historical context and emphasized its essential relation to the life sciences and to other branches of psychology. It also introduced some of Izard's own research and his attempt to parse the important developmental issues involved in affect expression and regulation, as subsumed within his "differential emotions theory." The Lewis and Rosenblum book introduced to the larger developmental audience what would become some of the more important issues of the day, including the relation between facial expression and affect development and the relation between affect and cognition.

In the present chapter we examine these issues as well as the empirical research that speaks to them. A good deal of the most recent work on development and emotion is centered on the period of infancy, perhaps because this is where some of the more interesting controversies are located. The work on older children tends to focus on children's ability to recognize different emotions, to understand the meaning of various emotion concepts, and their awareness of the display rules of the culture. There is much less research on emotional development in adolescence, and lifespan approaches to the study of emotion are not well represented.

Before we consider these theoretical models, it will be helpful to orient to some of the key issues.

KEY DEVELOPMENTAL ISSUES

Emotional Development in Infancy

There are four key issues in developmental research on infant emotion. Two relate to debates that were most central during the 1920s and 1930s, and which were presumably settled: (1) whether there are innate emotions, and (2) whether infant emotion is discrete or differentiated. Here the focus is on overt behavior. Two newer issues have also surfaced, namely, (3) whether infants have feelings (i.e., internal states), and (4) whether there is a correspondence between surface behavior (e.g., facial expressions) and internal experience. The latter two questions indicate that at least some researchers have overcome their reluctance to address hidden mental events. Questions concerning feelings and other internal events could not be entertained during the behavioristic era. It was only with the cognitive revolution of the modern era that mental states, including feelings, could once again be approached.

For anyone who has ever observed young infants, questions concerning whether or not infants have emotions may seem odd. Indeed, if anything, infants appear to be even more emotional than older children and adults if one judges by the way they behave. Their tears, their frowns, their smiles, their grimaces, all appear to reveal an intense internal emotional life. The skeptic, however, points out that these are only surface behaviors, and we have no way of verifying internal states in infants because they cannot tell us how they feel. As we will see, behavioral scientists have resorted to various strategies in order to deduce an answer to the question of infant feeling. Parents, of course, are not skeptics. They respond as though they assumed a fundamental coherence between expressive behavior and state. They soothe the crying infant, assist the frustrated child, engage in games with the smiling infant. This is because the uninhibited expression of affect is fundamentally motivating, infant affect perhaps especially so. We respond automatically to a scream, a cry of anguish, a look of distress, immediately, and often without conscious reflection. Infant affect is particularly overt and unmodulated and thus is especially compelling in that respect. Parents, for their part, not only respond to infant affect, but respond in a way that is differentiated and contingent on the quality of inferred affect. Thus their behavior belies an epistemology that is congruent with the theses of one theoretical model to be discussed shortly—differential emotions theory.

Attempts by psychologists to settle the various issues above have followed some of the same strategies pursued in Watson's time. Since one cannot verify internal state in infants, much contemporary research has settled on questions of overt behavior. Do infants have different types of emotional expression? Can we discriminate differences, or are their facial expressions, like their internal states, a "blooming, buzzing, confusion?" More important, do the various expressions have meaning? That is, do they relate to what is going on in other aspects of the environment, or are their facial behaviors random, end-organ twitches, devoid of affective meaning? Various writers have taken a theoretical stance on these issues, and we review them shortly.

Emotional Development beyond Infancy

The key issues in research during the childhood years tend to center on how children learn to regulate their emotions. Much of the research is still largely descriptive and age comparative; however, there is greater attempt to understand some of the dynamic principles that mediate development, such as contagion, emotion regulation, language, and knowledge of display rules and other social conventions. Research on adolescence still tests the old idea that puberty is a period of *Sturm und Drang*, a temporary aberration in development, even a catastrophe (Silman, 1991). As far as adulthood goes, stasis and decline models are giving way to interest in developmental transformation. Research on all of these issues will be presented in the remaining chapters of this volume. First, however, we examine how the issues are treated within contemporary theories of emotional development.

DEVELOPMENTAL THEORIES OF EMOTION

The Darwinian Lead

Around the turn of the century, a Russian scientist by the name of N. N. Kohts raised a chimpanzee from birth to about age 4 and recorded the natural history of its development. Several years later she had her own child, a son, on whom she kept similarly copious natural history notes and photographs. In her book (written in Russian and unavailable in the United States; see a photograph from the series in Ruckmick, 1936) she juxtaposes the photographs of ape and child such that the similarities in various kinds of emotional expressions are particularly striking. Kohts was clearly following the ethological tradition of the European naturalists, and particularly the evolutionary tradition of Darwin, who had stressed the phylogenetic continuity of, and evolutionary basis of, human and nonhuman primate expressions of emotion.

Today, few would dispute the thesis that human emotions are biologically based and part of our phylogenetic heritage. However, there tends to be considerable debate on the degree to which various aspects of emotional functioning are hardwired or are the product of culture and cognition. Broadly speaking, two kinds of models can be discerned, those that take a more nativist stance and stress the functional or adaptive properties of emotion, and those that can be identified with a cognitivist/constructionist position, and which emphasize the role of cognitive appraisal and mental elaboration in emotional experience. (These two types of models appear to be historically continuous with the two traditions identified by Ribot earlier in the century—the physiological and the intellectualist.)

Models that have a functionalist orientation tend to stress that emotions are part of a common mammalian heritage, are geared to environmental adaptation, are goal-relevant, and are associated with different behavioral tendencies. In contrast, theoretical approaches that have a constructivist orientation tend to ignore or deemphasize the innate aspects of emotion in favor of focusing on emotions as "social constructions" (Harre, 1986). Among modern theories, Izard's differential emotions theory (Izard, 1971, 1977; Izard & Malatesta, 1987) and Campos and Barret's goal-organizational theory (Campos et al., 1983; Campos & Barrett, 1984) are the most closely identified with the functionalist position, whereas the work of Kagan (Kagan, 1978, 1982; Kagan, Kearsley, & Zelazo, 1971), Lewis and Michalson (1983), and Sroufe (1979) falls more within the constructivist

tradition. It should be noted that the distinction we draw here between functionalist and constructivist positions is one of heuristic contrasts rather than of sharp
dichotomy. Cognitivists do not deny the neurophysiological underpinnings of
emotion, nor do functionalists ignore the role that cognition plays in the mental
elaboration of emotional experience. Instead, the differences in theoretical positions have more to do with the degree of emphasis authors place on preadapted
propensities and cognitive elaboration, especially in early development, and in
their research focus.

Functionalist Theories

In this section we lead with the work of Carroll Izard and include a short
biographical sketch. His work is singled out for an extended exposition because
of the critical impact his writings have had on developmental research on emotion.
It was Izard (1971), along with Ekman and colleagues (Ekman, Sorenson, &
Friesen 1969), who, through his cross-cultural research on the recognition of
different emotion expressions, first challenged the notion that emotions were
undifferentiated, and validated the existence of universally recognizable expressions. Izard was also the first of the modern emotions theorists to articulate an
explicitly developmental theory of emotions (although Tomkins's theory has
many developmental aspects and implications). Izard also developed the first
facial affect coding system for infants. He has been the recipient of numerous and
continuing grants to study emotional development, and he is distinguished as
well by the sheer volume of his publications—four original theoretical works, nine
edited volumes, and over 100 journal articles and book chapters.

Carroll E. Izard (b. 1923)

Our biographical note begins autobiographically. One of the authors (C.M.)
recalls the first time she met Izard back in the fall of 1979. She was just starting
out in her own career, and there were few people doing research on emotions. She
decided to travel to Mecca, which at that time was located at the University of
Delaware where Izard held the Unidel Chair in Psychology. As it happened, she
motored down to Delaware with Jeannette Haviland. Looking back, she recalls
that her most salient memory from that visit was listening to Haviland and Izard,
two of the most seasoned researchers in the field, swapping stories over lunch—
about how difficult it was to get funding, to get published, how insulting editors
could be, how uncomprehending most psychologists were about the work, and
on and on. She was not cheered. This was only 15 years ago, which may illustrate
better than anything else how radically the Zeitgeist has changed. In 1991, she
interviewed Izard for an oral history archive of eminent emotions researchers.
The following biographical material is distilled from that interview.

Carroll Izard was born in 1923, the youngest of six children. He grew up on
a farm in Mississippi and recalls a youth characterized by a happy sense of
freedom and independence. The farm was a working truck farm and its day-to-
day operation was labor intensive, so that the children were routinely conscripted

into service. However, because Carroll was the youngest, and was kept home to help his mother with household chores, he typically finished by late morning and then was free to go horseback riding over the woodlands, pastures, and creeks.

Carroll's father was recalled as being very fond of children, and as being openly affectionate. When a nephew was born, Carroll thought that his father had abandoned him for the nephew, but then found that this was to be the case every time a new nephew, niece, or grandchild was born. His mother was recalled as being a prolific reader, who shared poetry with her son and who impressed him with the quotation: "Do noble deeds, my son. Don't dream them all day long." Apparently, he was somewhat of a dreamer in his early youth, but his mother's admonition evidently worked, since today Izard is every bit an empiricist.

His mother became very ill with asthma and emphysema when Carroll was about 10, and there were times that he thought she might die; this disturbed and frightened him, and the confrontation with issues of life and death may have in some part contributed to his subsequent interest in matters metaphysical. Izard envisioned a religious career for himself early on. His parents were members of a conservative Southern Baptist church and Carroll did church work during summers as a youth. He also attended a Southern Baptist college—Mississippi College—for his initial education. However, his religious and philosophical beliefs evolved into a more liberal orientation than that of his parents over time, and he ultimately went on to study at Yale Divinity School.

Izard's time at Yale Divinity School was an emotionally tumultuous one because its liberal and historical-critical orientation raised issues that challenged the received wisdom of his more conservative upbringing. However, even at Mississippi College he had intimations that he was heading down a more independent path than his parents had. He recalls writing an essay that upset his classmates and some professors because it was theologically and philosophically out of the mainstream, being entitled "The Whole of Man is the Soul of Man." Thus, he was already on his way to criticizing establishment views, though Yale hastened the process. Given his youth—he was 16 when he entered college and 19 when he entered divinity school—and the steady dismantling of his long-held views and values under the fire of the rigorous intellectual training he received at Yale, it is little wonder that he recalls this time in his life as intense and troubling. However, it not only generated a period of disequilibrium in his life, it also laid the groundwork for a new direction, for he would eventually leave theology for psychology. The thorough grounding in philosophy, science, hypothetico-deductive reasoning and critical analysis, as well as a chance encounter with Dr. Chester Bliss (a student of Sir Ronald Fisher's—the inventor of small sample statistics) over dinner one evening at the divinity school, all affected his subsequent path. It was through Bliss that Izard was first exposed to a person totally dedicated to scientific research and writing. Talking with Bliss also reinforced his decision to work with Hartshorne and May, whose work on children's moral behavior is now considered classic (Hartshorne & May, 1928; Hartshorne, May, & Maller, 1929; Hartshorne, May, & Suttleworth, 1930). Having found Hartshorne, he told him quite simply, "I want to major with you." Hartshorne sent Izard down to the Yale University Institute for Human Relations. With Hartshorne and May as his advisors, and as a graduate student in divinity school, he was able to enroll in graduate seminars in psychology without having majored in the subject. Among these seminars was one taught by John Dollard, at a time during which "everyone except Frank Beach" (the sex researcher) was attempting to integrate psychoanalysis, learning theory, and social anthropology. This was, of course, the beginning of social learning theory. In Dollard's seminar Izard was challenged to explain everything on the basis of drive, cue, response, and reward.

Izard later enrolled in the clinical psychology graduate program at Syracuse; he was still animated by humanitarian interests, though eventually found that clinical work could not hold him. The program at Syracuse was eclectic rather than psychodynamic, and strongly influenced by the work of Carl Rogers. While he felt comfortable in the clinical program because of its humanistic orientation, he found himself drawn more to the scientific aspects of psychology than the applied. Nevertheless, he finished his training, including a clinical internship, and went on to qualify as a Diplomate of the American Board of Examiners in Professional Psychology. He did not remain with clinical psychology because, as he explained,

I think I saw its limitations. And one of the limitations was the fact that obviously psychotherapy had to be about people's emotions in one way or another. No matter what you call your form of treatment, it had to be about emotions and the way emotions are invested and channelled and harnessed and regulated or not regulated. And the time I was trying to practice psychotherapy—in the late fifties—there just was no scientific base whatsoever for talking to people about emotions.

Even Carl Rogers, who was one of the first to apply research methods to the analysis of the psychotherapy process, did not seem able to capture the essentials as far as Izard was concerned. Izard felt that there was still something missing.

One of his major techniques was reflection of feeling, but this was typically done simply by showing the person that you understood what he said or she said. It did not really come to grips with the emotions being experienced and how it motivated the behaviors being discussed, and the influence it might have had on how a person was perceiving the world, or what it had done to a relationship

Izard went on to take up emotions in all their complexity as his life's work. He first articulated his differential emotions theory in 1971, but its seeds go back as far as his first forays into research on the emotions of crippled children, as portrayed in their TAT cards (Izard, 1950), and his first funded research from the Office of Naval Research in 1959.

Differential Emotions Theory

We begin with a word about where Izard's theory is located with reference to other kinds of emotion theory. Broadly speaking, affect theories can be classified as to whether they are "dimensional" or "typological" models. Dimensional models focus on quantitative aspects of emotion such as degree of arousal, activation, or hedonic tone, whereas typological models are concerned with the more qualitative aspects of emotion, that is, the functional, phenomenological, and physiognomic differences among different types of emotion such as joy, fear, and anger. Dimensional models, which date back to Spencer (1890) and Wundt (1905), were prevalent during the heyday of activation theory as represented by the work of Duffy (1941, 1962) and of Woodworth and Schlosberg (1954). These in turn relate back to the "mass action" model of emotion promulgated during the 1920s and 1930s by Cannon and by new discoveries concerning the reticular activating system. More recently, investigators have examined the dimensional aspects of children's and adults' conceptions of emotions (see Diener & Larsen, 1993, for a review); however, typological models are dominant today. Still, it is important to mention that the dimensional and typological approaches are not mutually exclusive. In fact, most contemporary typological approaches are concerned with the degree of arousal (intensity) and activity as well as with the particular type of emotion (anger, joy, sadness) that is elicited. Izard's theory falls within the typological category of emotion models, which are also sometimes called discrete emotions models. Thus, it shares colleagueship with other contemporary models of emotions, especially those of Plutchik (1980), Ekman (1984), and Tomkins (1962, 1963, 1991). However, among this group, Izard's work is the most developmentally oriented and most informed by contemporary developmental research.

Aspects of differential emotions theory were articulated in 1971 with the publication of *The Face of Emotion* (Izard, 1971) in the context of chronicling the history of the study of emotion over the past century. Differential emotions theory, as it was here tentatively articulated, drew important inspiration from Darwin (1872), James (1890), and Tomkins (1962, 1963), as well as from contemporary research on the psychology of the emotions. The theory has been elaborated over the years as new research findings have accumulated (Izard, 1972; Izard, 1977; Izard & Malatesta, 1987; Malatesta & Izard, 1984; Malatesta-Magai & Izard, 1991). The following presents a summary of the theory as it is currently formulated. For a more extended discussion see Izard and Malatesta (1987) and Izard (1991).

Differential emotions theory derives its name from the concept of a set of primary emotions that are discrete and differentiated and that have distinct phenomenological, motivational, and signal properties. As originally formulated, differential emotions theory highlighted the role of facial expressions as both sources of affective feedback to the self (the Jamesian aspect or theory) and signals of behavioral propensity and communications to the social surround (the Darwinian component).

According to Izard, the neural mechanisms for the experience and expression of emotion are innate and are stored in subcortical regions of the brain. The development of individual emotions is primarily a function of maturation and, secondarily, that of learning and experience. Neural programs control the patterning of facial expressions as well as other aspects of striate musculature that are involved in emotion expression.

Facial expressions are thought to play a particularly important role in the functioning of the emotion system, although the theory notes that patterned feedback from affective vocalizations and from muscular and kinesthetic movements in the rest of the body also contributes to the experience and expression of differentiated emotion. Indeed, the bulk of contemporary research has focused on the face, and there are a number of reasons for this. First, it was facial expressions of emotion, in the context of cross-cultural research, that first broke ground in gaining acceptance for the notion that different emotions could be discriminated by subjects—even by subjects who came from cultures that differed from the one in which the photographs were posed. This research helped to overcome the considerable bias against the notion of discrete, differentiated affects created by studies like those of the Shermans and of Landis, and helped to reestablish the primacy of facial expressions. Another reason the face has enjoyed so much attention is because it is the focus of interpersonal communication. This is so self-evident that when Haviland presented a talk on nonverbal communication several years ago in New York City, and emphasized the role of the face in affective communication as illustrated with slides of infant's facial expressions of emotion, a *Village Voice* article on the talk was accompanied by a cartoon of parents exchanging photographs of their offspring that featured appendages and rear ends instead of faces. In terms of sheer amount of information concerning differentiated emotional states, the face appears to supply more information than the voice or other bodily cues. Finally, the phenomenon owes something to the fact that there are relatively sophisticated coding systems for facial affect, whereas no widely available, well-validated systems for vocal or bodily affect expressions presently exist.

Differential emotions theory specifies 11 primary emotions: joy, interest, surprise, anger, sadness, fear, guilt, shyness, shame, disgust, and contempt (Izard, 1991). In earlier versions of the theory shame and shyness were treated as part of the same superordinate class, but they are now viewed as separate. Cross-cultural evidence for prototypical facial expressions of joy, anger, sadness, fear, disgust, and contempt has been adduced by Izard (1971) and Ekman and colleagues (Ekman, Sorenson, & Friesen, 1969). Izard (1971) has found cross-cultural support for the interest expression, and Eibl-Eibesfeldt (1983) has found additional evidence for the universality of shyness.

Although it might be desirable from the point of view of parsimony, symmetry, and general elegance to find distinctive facial expressions for all of the primary emotions, the theory does not demand it, nor are the data available at the present time to support it. In the first place, there are no cross-cultural data on a distinctive facial patterning for guilt. Second, in the case of shyness, the cross-cultural evidence supporting its universality seems to rest more on eye, head, and body position for its identification than on distinctive facial patterning. Third, the evidence for a distinct fear expression is somewhat mixed. Although the expression as posed by actors is readily and reliably identified by decoders, the expression is rarely encountered in daily life, and rarely seen in infants when they are placed in conditions that can reasonably be expected to prompt fear and anxiety (Campos et al., 1983; Lewis, Brooks, & Haviland, 1978; Malatesta et al., 1989). Tomkins (1963) described fear as an emotion that is particularly "physiologically toxic," and noted that young infants have only the most primitive means of protecting themselves against such toxicity. Malatesta et al. (1989) have suggested that there may be some early built-in protective measures that guard the young infant against prolonged exposure to toxic levels of affect, and that the experience of fear may be truncated very early before it crosses the threshold to full expression; thus, one might only see very weak or mild forms of fear.

Although some of the primary emotions may not have a distinct facial patterning, there does appear to be a distinct somatic patterning associated with each, as well as a distinct phenomenology, and a distinct motivational or behavioral disposition. Izard (Izard, 1977; Izard & Malatesta, 1987) has emphasized that emotional expressive behavior has two signal functions related to motivation. Emotion expressions provide feedback to the self that is used for self-evaluation and self-regulation; they also provide information to social partners—signaling dispositional tendencies and response probabilities. Malatesta and Wilson (1988) have spelled out what the functional significance of each of the original 10 emotions specified by Izard appear to be, both within the self system and within the interpersonal system; the functions relate to adaptational goals.

As indicated in Table 4, fear, which is elicited under conditions of perceived danger, operates within the self system to identify threat, which then promotes flight or attack; within the interpersonal system it signals submission, and often serves to ward off attack. Contempt, to take another primary emotion, is elicited by perception of superiority. Within the self system, it organizes and sustains awareness of social position and dominance. Within the interpersonal system it signals dominance to others and reinforces social structure. And so on with other primary emotions, as indicated in Table 4.

The foregoing emphasis on distinctiveness has led some writers to expect stimulus-response specificity in the relation between eliciting circumstances and response patterns, at least in the case of infants; assumptions are also made about how infants should interpret various kinds of stimuli. As Haviland (1975) illustrated, earlier researchers assumed that if one wanted to observe fear, he would think of a fearful stimulus and thrust it at the infant. If the infant did not appear to be afraid or was not repeatedly afraid, the psychologist concluded that the infant was not afraid *yet* or that the appearance of fear was not a valid measure of fearfulness. He concluded that fear was not an infant response.

This degree of elicitor and response specificity is explicitly denied by differential emotions theory (Izard & Malatesta, 1987; Malatesta-Magai & Izard, 1991), which stresses that emotions are best conceived of as instinct-like behaviors (patterned and organized but flexible) rather than reflex-like behaviors, a distinction that has been emphasized in the ethological literature. As such, there should be a band of elicitors that can provoke a particular response (although one expects that the band of elicitors will form some kind of identifiable "family" of provocations); moreover, because emotions are flexible response patterns and not reflexes, and because any particular adaptational demand may be met by alternative emotional strategies, we cannot expect there to be a one-to-one correspondence between a particular eliciting event and a particular emotional response—instead, there may multiple emotional reactions.

Emotion Expression Undergoes Change with Development

According to differential emotions theory, in early development there is a fundamental coherence or integrity between expressive behaviors (as indexed by facial, bodily, and vocal indicators) and feeling states; as children mature, they

Table 4. Signal Properties of Emotions: Adaptive Functions

Emotion	Elicitor	Function within the self-system	Function within the interpersonal system
Anger	Frustration of goal	Effects removal of barriers or sources of frustration toward goals	Warning of possible impending attack, aggression
Sadness	Loss of valued object; lack of efficacy	At low levels promotes empathy; at higher levels serves to immobilize the individual (possibly forestalling the occasion of further trauma)	Elicits nurturance empathy, succorance
Fear	Perception of danger	Identifies threat; promotes flight or attack	Signals submission; wards off attack
Contempt	Perception of superiority	Organizes and sustains awareness of social position and dominance	Signals dominance to others
Shame/ shyness	The perception that the self is the focus of intense scrutiny	Produces behavior that protects the self against further violations of privacy	Signals need for privacy
Guilt	Recognition that one has done wrong and the feeling that escape is not possible	Promotes attempts at reparation	Produces submissive postures that reduce likelihood of attack
Disgust	Perception of noxious substances/indi-viduals	Repels noxious substances/individuals	Signals individual's lack of receptivity
Interest/ excitement	Novelty; discrepancy; expectancy	Opens the sensory systems	Signals receptivity for information intake
Joy	Familiarity; pleasurable stimulation	Signal to self to continue the present activities	Promotes social bonding through contagion of good feeling
Surprise	Perception of novelty; violation of expectancy	Serves "channel clearing" function (Tomkins, 1982) to ready organism for new experience	Demonstrates naivete of organism, protecting it from attack

Source: Malatesta & Wilson, 1988.

acquire the means to regulate their expressive behavior and to substitute verbal descriptions and mental representations for overt expressions of affect. It is the first assumption that has generated the greatest controversy; thus we pause to examine the thesis further.

The assumption of original coherence has been termed the "innate tie" hypothesis by Camras (1988). The theory assumes that when the features that are usually identified as signaling certain emotional states in adults and older children are displayed by infants, they are linked with corresponding internal emotional states. Stated in simple terms, it means that when an infant looks angry, he feels angry. Support for this assertion is difficult to come by since infants lack the means to provide verbal confirmation of their internal states. However, Izard and colleagues (Izard & Malatesta, 1987; Malatesta, 1985; Malatesta-Magai & Izard, 1991) have argued that there is more reason to assume an original coherence between state and behavior than to assume lack of coherence. The first argument is based on consideration of the nervous system of young organisms. Carmichael's (1970) law of anticipatory function in prenatal neurogenesis indicates that many structures (and, assumably, links between structures and systems) that are required for adaptive responding in the mature organism are functional prior to the time they must actually be called into use. The usefulness of a preadapted emotion system is obvious. As indicated above, caregivers rely on affective signals to guide their caretaking behavior. Emotion-expressive behaviors prompt attention to the infant's needs for relief from distress and discomfort, affective contact, and social stimulation.

Another reason for assuming concordance between expressive behavior and feeling states is that infants display facial behaviors that bear a striking resemblance to the facial expressions of adults during emotional experiences (Izard, 1978; Malatesta & Haviland, 1982). In addition, infant facial and vocal behaviors vary as a function of the appropriateness of caregiver ministrations. Interpretations of state by caregivers based on "emotional" behaviors (Emde, 1980a,b) are typically reinforced by subsequent infant behaviors. A baby's "frustrated" crying will cease when a barrier to his goals has been removed by the caregiver. A baby's "happy" cooing will be repeatedly instigated by certain interactive games. And so forth. If expressive behavior were random and unrelated to state, these kinds of coherencies would not obtain.

Differential emotions theory proposes that there is both continuity and change in the fundamental quality of emotional experience during the course of development. As indicated above, the subjective quality derives from feedback from the facial musculature as well as from other motor-expressive behavior. Patterns of emotion expression—in terms of their gross configurational aspects— remain true to form from infancy to old age, although there may be changes in the intensity of the expression and in the degree to which all aspects of the pattern come into play. Since the patterning is preserved, differential emotions theory argues that the basic core experience of emotion remains the same throughout development. What changes is the degree of cognitive elaboration that is attached to the underlying affect. For example, frustration of goals appears to generate anger in both infants and adults, at least as judged by their expressive behavior.

Because the basic patterning of the expressive feedback is the same, the infant and adult will both experience anger (rather than some other emotion or no emotion), according to the theory. However, the theory also recognizes that it is unlikely that baby and adult will experience their anger in the same way. The infant experiences anger as a primitive organic sensation, whereas the adult will appraise and interpret any particular instance of anger from an historical and interpersonal framework.

Another change that occurs in the affective system with maturation concerns the original elicitors of affects. The physical aspects of objects, such as their color, brightness, sharpness, suddenness, unpleasant odor or taste, and particular kinds of visual gestalts seem to be the primary triggers for emotional reactions in the young infant. With later development the infant responds to the more psychological properties of persons and objects. For example, smiling and laughter can be elicited in young infants by a bulls-eye pattern, an inanimate object suddenly moving into their visual field, and by tactile stimulation (Spitz, 1965; Sroufe & Wunsch, 1972; Wolff, 1966). Later, the child responds to the familiar face of a parent with a smile. Depth cues and looming objects inspire what looks like fear in young infants (Campos & Stenberg, 1981; Cicchetti & Hesse, 1983); it is only later in development that similar reactions occur in response to the approach of someone whom the child recognizes as a stranger. Disgusting foods are rejected by young infants, "yucky" ideas by older children. From these observations it is apparent that early emotional responding is preprogrammed and "released" much in the fashion associated with other classes of instinctual behavior. Emotional responding becomes elaborated in development through the usual sources of learning, though there may also be other principles—specific to the emotion system—that control the course of development. We will have occasion to explore these issues further in another section.

Emotional Development beyond Infancy

Although certain aspects of emotion expression are innate and universal, namely, their physiognomic patterning and responsiveness to certain specific classes of threats and goals, there is also much that is variable. The actual circumstances under which emotions are expressed, and the degree to which they are modulated or not, is largely controlled by learning experiences that are particular to individual families and cultures. Such "display rules" dictate who can show what emotion to whom, under what circumstances, and with what degree of intensity (Ekman & Friesen, 1975). In the United States, expressions of anger are tolerated and even encouraged, especially in male children (Brody & Hall, 1993); this may help explain why rates of crime and aggression are particularly high in this culture. Americans also place a high value on competition and on winning. As such, there are numerous occasions for the experience of failure; however, we are not very comfortable acknowledging shame, and it is not a highly visible affect in this culture. In contrast, shame plays a prominent role in the interpersonal affairs of the Japanese.

According to Izard, the child's growing ability to regulate emotion is mediated by advances in cognition and language, and is assisted by the socialization practices of parents. As such, the theory places equal emphasis on self-tuition or learning through observation, as well as direct tuition by parents and other social agents. In general outline, the child is seen as learning to curtail the overt expression of emotion to a greater (neutralization) or lesser (dampening) extent, while also learning to substitute memory and images, and to rely on language to express feelings. Other modulatory measures include amplifying emotional displays when it is desirable to seem emotional (e.g., during the expression of gratitude), or substituting one expression for another (as in masking contempt with a smile).

As a developmental model, differential emotions theory is largely silent on the period of adolescence, although there have been some recent attempts to treat the topic of adult development and aging (Izard & Malatesta, 1987; Malatesta & Izard, 1984). In general, the theory proposes that the specific feelings associated with specific emotions remain the same over the life course, but that expressive patterns become more blended, fragmented, and miniaturized. The identity of feeling experience remains intact because the basic patterning remains the same and because adults have long-term memories; certain elicitors become associated with certain emotional experiences, and they can be re-created even without the full motor-expressive patterns. The theory also indicates that personality traits involving emotions, what Izard terms affective-cognitive structures, will show some degree of continuity, although this aspect of the theory is not well elaborated.

In summary, Izard's theory is most fully articulated with respect to the period of infancy and childhood and less so with respect to later development. This is true of other models we review here as well. In any case, Izard's position is clear regarding the four early childhood questions that have been debated with particular vigor during the past two decades. From Izard's point of view, infants are innately endowed with differentiated emotional expressions that correspond to their internal states; thus, expressive behavior can be used as a gauge of emotional development. Emotional development proceeds as a function of maturation and cognitive elaboration. Other authors, especially those in the cognitive/constructivist tradition, take a different position with respect to these issues. However, before we turn to these theorists, we examine two other functionalist positions.

The Goal-Organizational Theory of Campos and Barrett

In two of their papers, Campos and Barrett (1984; Campos et al. 1983) have proposed a functionalist theory of the emotions that attempts to address developmental issues and that has much in common with Izard's theory. This model, described here as goal-organizational theory, resembles Izard's approach in that it views emotion as a noncodified, prewired communication system that mediates crucial aspects of social and interpersonal behavior, primarily through its expressive-communicative aspects.

Like differential emotions theory, goal-organizational theory is a discrete emotions model that eschews the notion of emotions as reflexes with predictable stimulus–response configurations; instead, it views each basic emotion as constituting a family of closely related emotions. Each emotional family is linked to a specific goal outcome and is associated with a particular kind of "appreciation" or appraisal relative to outcome.

In terms of development, certain features of the emotion system are said to be in place at birth. Evidence indicates, according to these authors, that there are a number of fundamental emotions (not just their precursors) in the repertoire earlier than some theorists (e.g., see "Sroufe," below) would admit. In fact, they suggest that the emotional life of the newborn and very young infant might include members of all the basic emotions.

Certain aspects of the emotion system undergo change with development, whereas other aspects remain invariant over the lifespan. According to Campos and Barrett, the invariant aspects of an emotion include its basic goal, the type of appreciation associated with it, the type of action tendency it typically involves, and the basic feeling tone. In the case of anger, for example, goals have been frustrated. For an infant, this may mean frustration of the ability to move the arm, whereas for an older child it may involve frustration of the ability to solve a math problem. In both cases, what is invariant is the appreciation that one's desires have been blocked. As a general principle, early emotions are typically evoked by concrete goals of a biological nature. With maturation, social and symbolic goals are added to the repertoire, though they by no means replace the earlier types of goals.

Development beyond infancy is seen as a result of cognitive maturation and the pressures of socialization; however, in this theory the contribution of cognition is not paramount, as it is for cognitive/constructivist models. Critical developments in cognitive capacities influence emotions to be sure; however, cognition alone does not dictate the child's appreciation of the significance of events for her wellbeing. Cognitive advancement provides the scaffolding for a new appreciation of the relevance of events to goals, making complex emotions such as shame, guilt, envy, pride, and depression possible. At the same time, socialization also contributes to emotions ontogenesis. Socialization factors include parental input (tuition in the acquisition of coping responses) as well as child-initiated contributions such as "social referencing," which involves the child's active seeking of emotion information from others during periods of uncertainty.

The relation between expressive behavior and feeling states is also said to undergo change with development. In general, Campos and Barrett are skeptical about reliance on facial expressions for making inferences about underlying feelings. In early development, they say, expressive behavior is poorly coordinated owing to neurological immaturity, and often represents "overflow" or "noise" mixed with signal. Thus, expressive behavior is seen as nonspecific grimacing and a poor indicator of infant emotional state. Following this initial period of random discharge and overflow, expressions become more closely linked with emotional state. However, the behavior then undergoes disconnection once again as children learn personal and cultural display rules for masking their emotions. By the time of adulthood, "few emotions are expressed completely freely" (Campos & Barrett, 1984, p. 251).

Finally, there is said to be developmental change in receptivity to the emotional expressions. In earliest infancy (birth to about 6 weeks) there is minimal attention to internal details of visual gestalts so that infants cannot differentiate emotional expressions of social partners. At the second level (6 weeks to about 4 or 5 months) comes the ability to discriminate facial expressions that specify emotional states, without necessarily appreciating the emotional meaning of such expressions. The third level is defined by "emotional resonance" (4–9 months of age); that is, the infant responds to the quality of emotion displayed by a social partner with a corresponding positive or negative expression. A fourth stage, beginning about 8 or 9 months, involves communication between infant and another about an event outside of the dyadic interaction. Further changes accompany the understanding of emotions in later childhood, including an appreciation of the possibility for simultaneous feelings.

In summary the theory emphasizes that the core appraisals and motivating features associated with each emotion remain constant from birth to old age. What changes with development is the individual's responsivity to the emotional cues of others and the ability to control emotional displays. These abilities improve through childhood and, one assumes, reach asymptote during adulthood. The theory is silent on whether or not one can expect further elaboration or decline in these domains in adulthood. Indeed, there is no explicit attention to the period of adolescence or to adulthood and old age.

In comparing this theory with Izard's we see that there are many apparent commonalities. Both assume a set of fundamental emotions that are important in social commerce and in intrapsychic functioning. However, Campos and Barrett specify five basic emotions: joy, anger, sadness, fear, and interest, whereas Izard's latest writings specify eleven: joy, anger, sadness, fear, interest, surprise, disgust, contempt, shame, shyness, and guilt. Campos and Barrett regard shame, guilt, envy, and depression as examples of "more complex" emotions, which they define as patterns of two or more particular emotions that are relevant to certain socialized goals.

All of the other assumptions of the theory are similar to those proposed by Izard with the one exception that Campos and Barrett believe that there is an initial period in infancy during which facial expressions of emotion do not relate to underlying states in a reliable way. They do not specify how long the disjunction between expressive behavior and state lasts or indicate how these two aspects of emotion get coordinated later in development, a problem inherent in Lewis' model (see below) as well. Although Izard and Campos and Barrett maintain that emotions constitute communicative signals that are pivotal in social development, an examination of Campos and Barrett's chart shows that their focus is much more on the appraisal process and the self's goals; in contrast, Izard and colleagues (Izard, 1977; Izard & Malatesta, 1987; Malatesta & Izard, 1984) have consistently emphasized that emotions motivate and organize behavior in both the self and social partners. Additionally, Campos and Barrett are more skeptical about the "truthfulness" of facial and other emotional display behaviors. Given the above, we infer that their position on the four interrelated infancy questions raised above would be that infants have emotions, but that we cannot know what these are with any degree of certainty because of the unreliable link between "emotional behavior" and internal states.

A third functionalist model is found within the psychoanalytic literature, as best represented by the writings of Robert Emde.

A Psychodynamic/Functionalist Model

As Emde (1980a,b) notes, within the psychoanalytic literature there has been a turning away from the mechanistic stimulus–response models of emotion associated with Freud's earliest formulations toward elaboration of models that are closer in spirit to the more organizational approach found in his later writings. Within the psychoanalytic literature Emde detects several emergent trends involving views of affects that include the following assumptions:

1. Affects are good guides for understanding motivation and ego states.
2. In addition to the role they play within the sphere of intrapsychic conflict, affects are also autonomous ego structures that have functional or adaptive properties.
3. They constitute a continuous aspects of experience, rather than merely serving as intermittent disruptions.
4. Affects are vital to social relations.
5. They function as signals to the self, that is, provide information at the service of defensive as well as nondefensive motivation.
6. There is increasing emphasis on discrete affects as distinctly different states and behaviors.

Emde's own empirical work with infants (Emde, Gaensbauer, & Harmon, 1976), which involved testing some of the above formulations, has resulted in an elaboration of the theory. This work has shown that there are basic organizational shifts in development that coincide with those proposed originally by Spitz's genetic field theory; that is, there are major shifts in biobehavioral organization during the first year of life that are integrally associated with changes in affective function. These organizational shifts, it is believed, may represent special developmental nodes; in such cases, biobehavioral components have matured and become sensitized to the point that social learning can have a unique organizing impact on experience.

Emde subscribes to the view that affect has both a dimensional aspect (quality of hedonic tone, activation, and an internal–external orientation) and a discrete aspect. Both represent biologically meaningful messages. In terms of development, he proposes that discrete expressions are not present at birth but appear in the repertoire according to an epigenetic sequence. However, in his view, affects are biologically given, preadapted propensities, and endowed a priori with signal value; their signal value is not simply a consequence of socialization. Moreover, they function as social signals before they become psychological signals (signals to the self or ego). Their development is, of course, tied to social experiences, but it is not a one-way street in which the child's drives are tamed by social agents. Rather, affective development proceeds within a context of mutual communication and responsiveness; affects are regulated in an interpersonal, transactional context.

In summary, the psychoanalytic view of affect appears to be evolving toward a functionalist, discrete emotions position, though it is not thoroughly consonant with Izard's views or even Campos and Barrett's. Infant affect unfolds according to a biological timetable, and then the particulars of an individual's development and the refinement of the affect system occur in a mutually influential context of signal exchange. Theoretically, facial expressions are considered an important if not essential part of the signal repertoire, but there is little theoretical attention to the issue of expression/state concordance or separability. This theory also has little to say about development of the affective system beyond early childhood.

We turn now to the models that emanate from a cognitive/constructivist orientation. What these models have in common is a de-emphasis on that which is prewired or precodified and greater concern with the role that the cognitive apparatus plays in the differentiation of the emotions and in how cognitions interpenetrate and govern emotions and their expression.

The Cognitive/Constructivist Position

For authors whose work falls within the cognitive/constructivist camp (Sroufe, Lewis, Kagan), emotions are not so much given as they are "constructed" in development; the child appraises and tries to make sense of her world and learns when and how emotions are appropriate and how to express them. As such, this set of models is potentially more open to the exploration and interpretation of individual differences in emotional development, since there seems to be less that is "guaranteed" by biology. Though much of the theorizing remains centered on ideas concerning how age-graded changes in cognitive processes impact on emotional development, some of the research inspired by these models is currently focused on issues of individual difference. For example, Kagen most recently has been exploring how temperamental predispositions in children affect a whole array of behavioral tendencies and their performance on a range of cognitive tasks. Lewis is interested in how mothers' uses of different kinds of emotional vocabulary shape children's consciousness of emotions, as well as their tendency to behave in emotionally distinct ways. Sroufe is interested in the mental life of the child as a result of different attachment histories. Before this research is discussed, we review their various theoretical positions.

Sroufe

Sroufe's model of socioemotional development is based on a synthesis of Kathryn Bridges's differentiation position, Spitz's genetic field theory, Bowlby's attachment theory, and Piaget's cognitive stage theory.

According to Sroufe, there is an orderly and gradual unfolding of the fundamental emotions from precursor states. This notion derives directly from Bridges's (1931) principle of differentiation, which states that specific affects evolve from early, global states of distress or nondistress. While Bridges indicates the order in which individual emotions differentiate, the reader will recall that she is less clear about the specific timing of their emergence. Sroufe's model is designed to improve on this aspect. Differentiation of the emotions, according to Sroufe, occurs in the context of the major developmental reorganizations specified by Spitz that occur around the three psychic pacemakers of smiling, 8-months anxiety, and negative head-shaking. Sroufe adds a fourth psychic organizer that involves further differentiation of the self concept. This is indexed by the 3-year-old's capacity for symbolic play, role-taking, and the beginnings of identification, all of which are marked by a major affective change.

Sroufe takes the notion of four major psychological reorganizations and incorporates them into an eight-stage model of affective developments centered on these milestones. In the first stage of development there is a passive stimulus barrier that renders the infant relatively invulnerable to external stimulation. The second stage involves a turning toward the environment and coincides with the beginning of coordination of attention, motor activity, smiling, and cooing. This period produces the roots of interest as well as positive affect. During stage 3, (3–6 months) the social smile introduces the period of positive affect proper. The stage involves "awareness and anticipation," thus allowing for frustration and the negative emotions of rage and wariness. The fourth stage, around 7–9 months, is a period marked by social games, active participation, engagement, and mastery. It is also a period in which the infant first becomes aware of his own emotions, thereby giving rise to the affects of joy, fear, anger, and surprise. Stage 5 coincides with the period of stranger fear, and a generally subdued affective tone, attendant on the establishment of attachment to the caregiver, who becomes a source of security. During this time emotion expression becomes greatly differentiated and refined; by the end of this period, there is evidence of graded feelings, ambivalence, and moods. During stage 6 (12–18 months), a phase of self-assertiveness and exploration ushers in a period of mastery. Stage 7 involves the formation of self-concept, which gradually leads to identification, which is stage 8.

The Role of Cognition in Affective Development. Although Sroufe (1979) maintains that "affective life is the meaning and motivational system that cognition serves" (p. 462), it is clear that cognition—an all-important factor in his developmental scheme—is central to the growth, elaboration, and differentiation of the emotions. In fact, Sroufe differentiates between "true" emotions and their precursors. True emotions do not emerge until a basic differentiation between the "self" and the object world has been made—around the third month, when the ego begins to emerge. Thus, genuine emotion in his system requires the emergence of elementary forms of cognitive activity that promote "consciousness." Sroufe does allow that infants can communicate distress and views "turning toward" as the prototype of later positive emotions. However, early distress, turning toward, and quiescence cannot be counted as emotions, because the cognitive superstructures are not yet evolved; thus, what may appear to be "emotional" behavior is actually undifferentiated arousal. Only with maturation in the cognitive domain—involving an experience of the self that is different from the social surround—will true emotions come into existence.

> Only with recognition is there pleasure and disappointment; only with some development of causality, object permanence, intentionality, and meaning are there joy, anger, and fear; only with self-awareness is there shame. Also, distinctions among affects and their pre-cursors call upon cognitive achievements—for example, fear, as reflected in more immediate distress upon a second exposure to a stranger, has been referred to as a categorical reaction, dependent upon assimilation to a negative scheme. (Sroufe, 1979, p. 491.)

Although Sroufe's emphasis is clearly the influence of cognitive development on emotions ontogenesis, he does acknowledge that there are reciprocal effects. For example, he notes that affective reactions can alter the salience of incoming information and hence the child's evaluation of events. This is because the infant evaluates its feelings as part of the total event that is being apprehended. Evaluations are subjective in nature rather than of purely of cognitive interpretations.

As far as the relation between facial expressions of emotion and felt affect during infancy goes, Sroufe takes a middle ground between Izard, who thinks the face is isomorphic with feeling, and Campos and Barrett, who believe that early facial behavior is random and unconnected to state. Sroufe rejects the isomorphism position, because he believes that the infant may be capable of experiencing an affective state prior to or in the absence of facial expressions of emotion. Still, the face is an important locus of communication about affect and may help to amplify and sharpen affective experience, especially later in development.

In summarizing Sroufe's position on the key issues of early development, we may say that he subscribes to the position that affect is innate but undifferentiated in earliest infancy and that there is no inherent link between expressive behavior and state.

Affective Development beyond Infancy

In a more recent publication Sroufe has elaborated on the nature of socioemotional development beyond infancy (Sroufe, Schork, Motti, Lawroski, & LaFreniere, 1984). The behavioral expression of emotion (face, voice, whole body) is integral in the development and elaboration of social competence. Affect expressions play a role in initiating social interchanges and in responding to the social bids of others. Expressions of affect supply meaning; they provide social cues that allow social partners to interpret one another's behavior. Signals help clarify what the initiating or responding child intends, and allow her to signal how she interprets the partner's behavior. In addition, the pacing, turn-taking, and termination of interchanges are guided by affective expressions. In the end, the socially competent child should be capable of expressing the full range of emotions clearly and appropriately, though the well-adapted child will modulate her emotions so as to de-emphasize disappointment and upset, and to amplify those affects that sustain positive social interaction. Hence, affective development is not simply a matter of stoical control of the emotions, but a more temperate modulation and selective deployment.

Sroufe has not specifically dealt with issues of emotional development beyond the preschool years. However, since he views personality development as integrally related to the outcome of the attachment process, patterns of affect modulation and expressivity will largely depend on the quality of attachment and internal working models of attachment relationships.

Kagan

Kagan defines emotions as "affect states" that can be "characterized as classes of coherence among the nature of the interpreted incentive, quality of the resulting feeling state, and cognitive and behavioral sequelae" (Kagan, 1978, p. 263). In this system, elicitors of emotion are "incentive events." The incentives are hypothesized to be universal and to be linked with changes in state and with sets of cognitions. The cognitive thrust of Kagan's orientation toward emotion is obvious from his descriptions of several classes of incentive events. One class of incentives is caused by external events that are "discrepant" and cause alerting, attention, and sometimes inhibition; Kagan acknowledges that the foregoing would correspond to what others call surprise, fear, and interest reactions but thinks these terms are not very helpful. A second class of external events includes those involving loss or absence of a target object toward which the child has established behavioral dispositions. Another class involves an agent's interrupting a person's ongoing response routine. Kagan (1978) suggests that Bowlby's observations could be reframed by stating: "During the period 7 through 30 months of age, the infant is made uncertain/anxious/fearful by the incentive event of parental departure in an unfamiliar context" (p. 267). Similarly, in later development, between the ages of 4 and 8 when nightmares are common, Kagan states that

> one might infer that a major incentive for the nightmares was violation of standards on hostility to parents, obedience, sex play, masturbation, honesty, and stealing, since this is time when these standards are being socialized in a serious way by the American family. (p. 267)

Emotional feelings are said to result from changes in baseline feeling tone or normal feeling state. Differences in the quality of the change in feeling state are responsible for the distinction among affects, along with differentiated cognitions and incentive conditions. What the individual distinguishes are changes in the salience, duration, and rise-time of affective stimulation, and changes in the physiological activity of the heart, chest, stomach, and other sites. What others would call fear, for example, is the result of an "unassimilated discrepant event" leading to a salient change in state that has certain characteristics. This two-factor theory of emotion reverses the order of events held to account for emotion in Schachter and Singer's (1962) theory of emotion, which was based on the study of adults. In Kagan's theory, cognitive appraisal occurs first and then the physiological change takes place, whereas in Schachter and Singer's model, physiological change occurs and the individual tries to interpret it based on a cognitive analysis of the observables at hand.

During early infancy, the infant is not capable of differentiated affect because he has no language ability and cannot interpret and label his discrepant feelings (Kagan, 1971). The infant can experience changes in sensations, but usually exhibits only states of generalized excitement. "He cries, laughs, or thrashes to external events or internal sensations directly, not as a consequence of interpretation" (Kagan, 1971, p. 52). Specific affect states emerge ontogenetically as cognitive capacity grows, so that there is a developmental progression from the basic to the more subtly shaded affect states. An important mechanism that facilitates the development of states of infant excitement into the more differentiated affects of the older child, is the labeling of the child's emotions by caregivers and others. The child then learns to apply certain terms to certain contexts. Therefore, the qualitative differences between emotions and the appropriateness of them are governed "as much by the person's labeling of his feelings according to the context as by the raw feelings themselves" (Kagan, 1971, p. 53).

To summarize Kagan's position with respect to the key infancy questions, though affect may be part of our biological heritage, true emotion is dependent on cognitive maturation. Young babies do not have differentiated affects. To Kagan, the existence or nonexistence of facial expressions is almost irrelevant. He clearly rejects the idea that emotions are dependent on changes in facial expressions, though he does not deny that afferent feedback to the central nervous system via facial expressions might subsequently influence feeling states. Taking aim at positions such as Izard's, he suggests that

> the decision to call those states the basic emotions, and to imply that a feeling of emptiness in a hotel bedroom 1,000 miles from home on Christmas Eve is not a primary emotion because there is no necessary facial change, has the flavor of theoretical imperialism. (Kagan 1978, p. 260)

Development beyond Infancy. From Kagan's point of view, it is important to emphasize that an *incentive* is not the objective stimulus, but the person's interpretation. Since interpretation depends on cognitive development, which undergoes change with age, emotional development will show a corresponding change. Emotions in later childhood, as in infancy, are a product of incentive events accompanied by evaluations of the individual's ability to assimilate, understand, and contend with the event instrumentally, along with the resulting state change. If the event is not readily assimilable, or if the individual's appraisal leaves him with the sense that he is unprepared to cope, the reaction may be fear. If it is readily assimilable and if the individual knows what to do, confidence, anger, or boredom may be the resultant reactions. And so forth.

Kagan suggests that affect becomes less labile with age. He reasons that adult affectivity will be less labile than that of a child not because the physiology of the young child is more easily disturbed, but because children's beliefs are more readily changed. As the individual matures, her beliefs consolidate and become more resistant to change. As beliefs become crystallized, emotion becomes less episodic, and moods, as enduring emotional states, are more characteristic. In this view, "there are few dour children or terrified adults" (Kagan, 1978, p. 269).

Lewis and Michalson

For Lewis and Michalson (1983) the emotional response system has several component parts. An emotion elicitor is an event or stimulus that triggers an organism's receptor. An emotional receptor is a locus or pathway in the central nervous system that mediates changes in the organism's physiology or cognitive state. An emotional state is a patterned change in somatic and/or neural activity that accompanies the activation of an emotional receptor. An emotional expression is a change in the face, body, voice, and activity level that accompanies an emotional state. Finally, emotional experience is conscious or unconscious mental activity, including perception, interpretation, and evaluation of one's emotional state or expression. The emotion process is set into motion by internal or external elicitors that activate receptors. Once activated the receptors produce emotional states, and states in turn generate emotional expressions.

Emotion in Infancy and Childhood

According to Lewis and Michalson, a sense of self is necessary for true emotion, hence the distinction between emotional states and emotional experiences. Young infants can have emotional states, but not true emotions, which are equated with cognized experiences (whether conscious or unconscious); accordingly, "not until infants can distinguish between self and other are they capable of deriving emotional experiences from their states" (Lewis and Michalson, 1983, p. 217).

Lewis and Michalson assume that the connection between expressive behavior and internal states and experiences is not prewired. Instead, they propose a three stage process in the development of emotional expressions. During the first stage, in earliest infancy, there is no innate coordination of states and the behaviors that would ordinarily index them. Although one may see facial expressions that resemble certain emotional expressions of adults, this does not necessarily imply that infants experience emotion. Instead, Lewis and Michalson propose that the infant's internal states, which are undifferentiated for the most part, are unrelated to differential facial configurations. Any patterned facial activity one may observe in young infants is instead a "start-up or rehearsal mechanism," unrelated to underlying states.

During a second stage, the child is exposed to socialization influences that act to bring about the coordination between states and behaviors; Lewis and Michalson allow that there may also be biological factors promoting the linkage of states and expressions. In any case, during the second stage, various patterns of facial expressions will more accurately index the states with which they are usually associated. Voluntary dissociation between the two at this point is unlikely because children have not matured sufficiently to allow them to disengage the two by an act of effort. In the third stage, voluntary control of facial expressions becomes possible, experienced emotion can be concealed, and emotion can be enacted voluntarily without concomitant feeling states.

It should be apparent from the above that socialization experiences play a critical role in emotions ontogenesis in Lewis and Michalson's model. They do not accept the position of an original coherence between state and behavior; instead, children first have to learn how to coordinate their states, experiences, and behavior, and then how to exercise them independently of one another, and at will. Emotional states become emotional experiences in the course of socialization experiences as social agents label and interpret expressive behavior; self-mediation also plays a role through the processes of social referencing and observational learning. The learning process itself entails the acquisition of five rules: (1) How to express emotion, (2) when to express it, (3) how to label emotions, (4) how to manage them, and (5) how to interpret them.

In this view, because so much of emotions ontogenesis is learned rather than hardwired, and because learning is context dependent, the child's social experiences are largely responsible for how she develops emotionally. Lewis and Michalson place an especially great emphasis on the labeling and attribution of emotion by significant others as the primary learning vehicles. This opens the door wide for tremendous individual variation, including the learning of deviant and maladaptive patterns of expression. Errors in the social transmission of culturally agreed-upon convention concerning the rules of emotion, due to idiosyncrasies in early primary relationships, has potential for generating psychopathology in the child.

In summary, Lewis and Michalson's model of affective development is one that de-emphasizes the biologically hardwired aspects of the emotion system in favor of cognition and learning. Emotions per se are not differentiated at birth; rather, there are undifferentiated internal states. Facial expressions are meaningless as indicators of emotional states until later in development, and then they are reliable indicators only for a short period of time—until display rules are learned and culturally dictated patterns of masking and dissimulation are absorbed. Lewis and Michalson have little to say about later development, and hence their's is a theory only of early development.

Summary

In summarizing the foregoing contemporary theories of emotional development we note that most address the earliest stages of development and generally neglect later development. At one end of the continuum are theories that emphasize the prewired nature of emotional feeling and expression, and at the other, the social construction of emotion. One set of theories allows for more commonality across individuals, the other for more variance. Interestingly, the latter theorists have not exploited their position for an articulated model of differential personality development. Instead, individual personality development is elaborated within the context of a discrete emotions, functionalist analysis (about which we will have more to say later; see Chapters 9–11).

With reference to the issue of infant affect during the opening months of life, most theorists, with the exception of Izard and Malatesta-Magai, deny or are noncommittal on the question of infant feelings. In the next section, as well as in Chapters 6 and 7, we review the empirical literature emanating from the second wave of emotions research. Researchers, for the most part, have sidestepped the question of infant sentience, and instead have focused on simply reporting observable behavior.

Infant Expressive Behavior: The Observables

According to Bridges's (1932) early study, discriminable affect expressions are not in evidence until several weeks after birth, but, as discussed in Chapter 4, her research was handicapped by, among other things, limitations in technology. Here we consider whether there are data from more recent studies of infant affect since the advent of videotape and discrete emotion coding systems that can shed light on the issue.

Ample evidence indicates that there are at least two discrete expressions present at birth—disgust and interest (Izard & Malatesta, 1987). The interest expression is indexed by eye opening, orienting, attention, and visual fixation (Langsdorf, Izard, Rayias, & Hembree, 1983), behaviors that are every bit in evidence in the opening days of life. Steiner (1973) was able to elicit disgust in neonates in response to bitter taste, and Fox and Davidson (1984) identified facial expressions of interest and disgust (using the MAX facial coding system of Izard) in 2- to 3-day-old newborns in response to sucrose and citric acid solutions. The joy expression, at least as a social smile, enters the expressive repertoire at about 2 months (see Sroufe, 1979, for a review), although endogenous smiles have been observed as early as the opening days of life. There is much controversy about the remainder of the emotions. While the issue of what emotion expressions are in the infant repertoire at birth and soon thereafter would seem an easy matter to settle given the present state of technology, the mechanics of measurement and the difficulties of interpretation make the issue complex. In the first place, infant expressive behavior is extremely labile and expressions are fleeting. Slowing a videotape to tenths of a second to capture these phenomena often introduces ambiguity of its own because of the unclarity of the visual image so produced. In addition, discrimination of expressive behavior is normally based on pattern recognition of moving gestalts, not frozen frames or abnormally slowed images; looking at a facial expression changing imperceptibly over the course of several seconds can have a surreal quality to it. In any case, the very lack of stability of infant expressions in real time can create the perception that expressions are random, chaotic, unorganized, and unpatterned. There have been few studies of infant expression in early infancy because of these problems, and because facial coding is so labor intensive—1 min of film often taking 2–10 hours to code.

One particular area of controversy concerns whether or not there are discriminably different expressions of pain, sadness, and anger in early development, and especially whether anger and pain are discriminably different. Camras (1991), for example, notes that in the AFFEX coding system (Izard, Hembree, Daugherty, & Spizzirri, 1983) "anger" and "pain" configurations are morphologically indistinguishable from one another save that the eyes are open for anger and closed for pain. Camras also notes that the AFFEX-specified anger configuration is the most common discrete negative facial expression in studies presenting various negative elicitors to infants: DPT inoculation, arm restraint, cookie removal, separation from the mother, contingency interruption, and mother's facial and vocal expressions of sadness. Such apparent lack of differentiated responding would seem to challenge the differential emotions hypothesis of Izard. Hiatt, Campos, and Emde (1979) have argued that the sine qua non of discrete emotion status should be the ability to demonstrate affect-specific linkages, that is, different expressions under different eliciting conditions. By this criterion, the discrete status of anger and pain is not met, at least in terms of currently available literature. However, one may argue that the Hiatt et al. criterion is not one that is universally accepted. Such a criterion fails to take into account the flexibility of the affect system (one can become angry and sad in any number of situations, and there are also individual differences in the elicibility of these affects), and certain other principles of the affect system. In the first place, most of the situations listed above in which anger has been seen to occur are situations that are readily identified as anger elicitors—those involving frustration of goals (arm restraint, cookie removal, contingency interruption). The other situations may at first blush seem more problematic. One might expect to see pain, not anger, as the predominant response to DPT inoculation and sadness, not anger, to separation from mother and to maternal expressions of sadness. However, pain has been described as one of the classic elicitors of anger (Tomkins, 1991), and affect theory also notes that sadness and anger are responsive to different gradients of stimulation. Sadness rapidly degrades into anger if distress is prolonged, and with reduction in the intensity of stimulation anger may fade to sadness (Tomkins, 1962, 1963). Interestingly, Camras's data on her own infant's expressions (sampled during the fourth through ninth weeks of age) indicate that pain, anger, and sadness patterns were frequently seen together in a single episode of crying. This can be taken as evidence for Bridges's position that infant affect is global and undifferentiated, or as support for Tomkins's assertions. With respect to the latter, it is important to note that the expressions were not randomly distributed throughout the crying bout but were differentially associated with the waxing and waning of crying; sadness expressions tended to occur during the waning phase. What is also noteworthy about Camras's research is that at the time of recording—1–2 months of age—all of the following AFFEX-coded expressions were in evidence: pain, anger, sadness, disgust, surprise, and joy.

    Clearly, more work remains to be done. There has not yet been a systematic mapping of the range, intensity, duration, and frequency of the various infant emotion expressions and their context from birth onwards with an N greater than one. The interested reader is referred to the literature for more discussion of these and other issues related to early infant affect (Camras, 1991; Camras, Malatesta, & Izard, 1991; Malatesta-Magai & Izard, 1991). One thing is clear, however. The differentiation theory of Bridges with respect to early development is not substantiated by contemporary research using microanalytic coding systems. Bridges maintained that a generalized excitement was the only emotion expression observable up until about 3 weeks of age, when generalized distress began to differentiate. Disgust and delight were thought not to be observable until 3 months, fear until 6 months, anger even later, and sadness not until adolescence. Instead, contemporary research indicates disgust and interest at birth, and discernible anger, sadness, and pain by 1 to 2 months.

The data on infant expressive behavior beyond the first 2 months of life are fuller and more complete. Two longitudinal studies, one from the laboratory of Carroll Izard, the other from the laboratory of Carol Malatesta-Magai, provide some of the most detailed MAX- and AFFEX-coded data on infant and child expressive behavior over the first few years of life using relatively large samples of children. Importantly, both studies also examine the relation between expressive behavior and attachment style, thus providing some of the first bridges between these two very extensive and almost independent literatures.

ONTOGENY OF EMOTIONAL EXPRESSION

The Delaware Project

Izard and colleagues (Izard, Haynes, Chisholm & Baak, 1991; Izard et al., in preparation) sampled the behavior of 114 white, middle-class mother-infant dyads periodically between the ages of 2.5 months to 5 years of age. One analysis (Izard et al., in preparation) tested a tenet of differential emotions theory with respect to whether emotions emerge as discrete expressions or whether they differentiate over time (cf. Bridges, 1932; Sroufe, 1979). Izard and colleagues' data on the first few months of life indicate that emotion expressions emerge in early infancy without precursors and remain morphologically stable between 2.5 and 9.0 months of age. In another study (Izard et al., 1991), the analysis related infant expressive behavior and attachment at 13 months to maternal personality and expressive behavior sampled when the infants were 2.5 months of age. Maternal personality was measured by (1) the Jackson's Personality Research Form E (PRF), (2) a questionnaire that asks mothers to rate the extent to which they typically hide or express emotions in the presence of their infants, and (3) an empathy scale. Attachment behavior was assessed using the Strange Situation procedure at 13 months and an "insecurity score" (from less insecure to more insecure) was derived from ratings of selected interactive behaviors. At 2.5 months the conditions for sampling facial expressive behavior were normal face-to-face play (unrestricted interaction), contingent play (mother responds only when infant initiates interaction), and still face (mother presents still, immobile face and resists engagement). At 9 months the condition was normal face-to-face play and a negative interaction in which the mother expressed sadness and anger facially and vocally. The sessions were coded with MAX and AFFEX.

The correlation between maternal personality scores assessed when the infants were 2.5 months of age and children's attachment scores were in the expected direction. Mothers of more secure children reported experiencing less negative emotion and more positive emotion, were more open in the expression of negative emotion around their children, and were more sociable, nurturant, and empathic. Children with higher insecurity scores had mothers who experienced more negative affect but were less open in their expression of negative emotion around their infants, had a greater need for autonomy, and felt more insecure and helpless. Unexpectedly, these mothers also reported expressing more positive emotion around their infants in daily life. Izard et al. interpret the latter phenomenon as being related to defensiveness and suggest that the experience of negative affect and its masking by positive affect may send mixed messages to children that could affect their development. Work by Tesman (1992) from the first author's laboratory confirms this. Mothers who displayed discrepant messages (negative emotion in face or voice combined with positive emotion in the other channel) during their child's early development were more likely to have insecurely attached children at 22 months.

Returning to the Izard et al. (1991) study, in terms of infant emotionality, the higher the infants' insecurity scores, the higher their rate of expressing sadness and anger, and the more they cried, demanded attention, and showed distress in mildly stressful or frustrating conditions. In summary, these data indicate that maternal emotions and expressive behaviors are deeply implicated in the process that underlies the formation of infant attachment and infant expressive behavior. Research from the laboratory of Malatesta-Magai extends the work on individual differences in expressive development and links it to maternal socialization of affect; it also examines the relation between maternal affect and infant attachment.

The New York Project

In their longitudinal study of expressive development, Malatesta-Magai and colleagues (Malatesta, 1990; Malatesta, Grigoryev, Lamb, Albin, & Culver, 1986; Malatesta & Lamb, 1987; Malatesta, Culver, Tesman & Shepard, 1989; Lemerise, Shepard, and Malatesta, 1986; Malatesta-Magai, Leak, Tesman, Shepard, Culver, & Smaggia, 1994) tracked the expressive behaviors of a cohort of infants and mothers recruited in 1982 over 5 years and 6 waves of data collection. Here we describe the findings with respect to the first five waves of data; we defer a discussion of the findings of the last wave (Jones, 1990; Tesman, 1992) to Chapter 10.

In the first three waves of data collection, Malatesta et al. (1989) found a linear increase in positive affect, especially interest and joy between $2\frac{1}{2}$ to 7 months of age, and a corresponding decrease in negative affect in the context of a play, separation, and reunion paradigm. In this study as well as in a previous cross-sectional study (Malatesta & Haviland, 1982) the researchers found that mothers engaged in behaviors that could easily be construed as attempts to moderate the emotional expressions of their infants. Mothers restricted their modeled expressions to the more socially positive signals—interest and joy—and their expressive

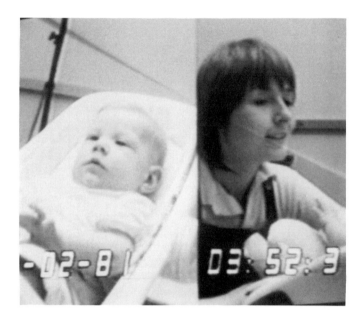

Figure 2. Mother and infant in face-to-face play.

behaviors were nonrandom and contingent on the ongoing emotional-expressive behavior of the infant. More interesting, high rates of maternal modelling of joy and interest were associated with gains in infant joy and interest expressions between $2\frac{1}{2}$ to $7\frac{1}{2}$ months of age. In terms of maternal response to specific emotions, there was an increase in contingent responding to infant interest expressions and a decrease in contingent responding to infant pain expressions over the three waves of measurement.

Superimposed on these more general patterns were differences as a function of maternal contingency patterns and infant birth status. Note here that contingency was a measure of the rate at which mothers followed infant emotion-expression changes with changes of their own; at the upper range, we are probably speaking of contingency that is inflated by a high activity level, and, from the infant's point of view, likely experienced as overstimulation. Indeed, the data in this study indicate that while moderate contingency levels predicted increases in infant positive emotion and overt expressivity for the broad middle range of infants, infants exposed to the upper range of contingency decreased their frequency of smiling over time and were more likely to drop out of the study.

In terms of birth status effects, preterm infants showed difficulty in sustaining eye contact with their mothers and showed more negative affect than full terms especially at 5 months. Correspondingly, mothers of preterm infants showed more interest expressions toward their infants, which was interpreted as indexing greater vigilance due to infant fragility and developmental delay. These mothers also showed different patterns of responses to anger and sadness. Whereas mothers of full term infants showed a pronounced pattern to match their infant's expressions for all expressions but pain, mothers of preterm infants showed more dissimilar responses. They failed to match sadness and showed a significant ignoring response to their infants' anger expressions. The authors suggest that maternal response to these affects in preterm infants is altered because of the preterm infant's greater irritability, vulnerability, and difficulty sustaining eye contact. Ignoring anger expressions may be the mothers' ultimate coping strategy in dealing with protracted infant irritability. Avoiding displays of sadness as a means of stemming affect contagion and escalation of sadness may also be rooted in an awareness of infant vulnerability.

The infants and their mothers were seen again during the second year of life for a face-to-face play session and for the assessment of attachment in the context of the Strange Situation procedure. Children who showed a decline over the three earlier waves in their apparent level of enjoyment during face-to-face play (i.e., less smiling) where more likely to be rated as insecurely attached at 22 months; this pattern was also linked to extremely high rates of maternal contingency.

One of the more interesting findings was the emergence and increasing appearance of two new configurations of facial expression as the children moved into the second year of life. One expression involved biting the lower lip (code 88) and the other consisted of a tight compression of the lips (code 67). The authors suggest that these new expressions were related to the regulation of negative affect. Both expressions tended to be restricted to the reunion (versus play) sessions, where more negative emotion was seen. Code 88 appeared to be used in the management of anxiety, and code 67, which was positively correlated with anger, appeared to be used to contain and regulate anger expression.

Once again the patterns observed above for the overall sample were moderated by individual difference variables. Girls expressed greater anger than boys when reunited with their mothers following the second separation of the strange situation procedure. The authors speculate that this may be due to differential socialization of boys and girls, with girls being encouraged to remain physically and emotionally closer, thereby setting up differential expectations with respect to separations. Girls may tolerate separations less well because of this and consequently be more openly resentful. In terms of maternal affect, mothers smiled more and showed greater overall expressivity toward daughters than sons, which may explain reports of girls' greater sociability and the tendency of girls and women to deploy frequent smiling in social interchange (Bugenthal, Love, & Gianetto, 1971).

Differences in the emotional expressions for preterm and full-term infants were most apparent during the separation phase of the study. The full-term children communicated their distress and reestablished positive communication with their mothers more readily than preterm infants. In the play session, as well, full-term infants and their mothers appeared to experience more positive emotion in one another's presence and showed more reciprocal eye contact.

In a subsequent wave of data collection (at $3\frac{1}{2}$ years of age), the children were seen for a play session with their mothers as well as for a peer play session. The videotapes of the sessions were coded for facial expressions and tonal quality of utterance. The behavior of the mothers and infants was examined for changes in expressive behavior between the second and third years of life; only the play sessions were compared because there was no comparable separation–reunion session at 3 years. Mothers showed an increase in total facial expressivity in the third year; however, children's rates remained about the same in terms of total expressivity, though there was an increase in interest expressions and a decrease in the display of surprise. In terms of the vocal expression of affect, children's total verbal/vocal expressivity showed an increase. It is interesting to note that the decrease in surprise facial expressions was accompanied by an increase in surprise in the voice; there was also an increase in interest expressions in both face and voice.

Once again, the pattern for preterms departed from that found with fullterm children. Preterm females expressed the highest rate of facial sadness and total negative affect. During the play session with their mothers, preterms were less vocally expressive than full-terms and showed less interest and less total positive affect. They were also less vocally expressive than full-terms during the peer play session.

In terms of attachment classification, insecurely attached children displayed more lip biting in both the mother–child session and in the peer play sessions, which suggests greater interpersonal anxiety. For their parts, mothers of insecurely attached children vocalized at lower rates and their affective communications in face and voice also differed in a number of ways from the patterns found with mothers of securely attached infants.

The data on preterms and on insecurely attached children can be interpreted as reflecting a greater affective disharmony between these children and their mothers, a disharmony that was already evident at age 2 and which was apparently carried forward in time to the third year. The differences in expressive behavior associated with attachment patterns most likely reflect the impact of differential rearing experiences related to maternal emotional dispositions, whereas the differences associated with birth status appear to be linked to prematurity itself and the impact it has on maternal behavior. These data then highlight the fact that though expressive behavior may be prewired as part of our biological heritage, maternal personality patterns (mediated by expressive behavior), as well as constitutional anomalies and developmental delay, affect the subsequent course of development and influence development in idiosyncratic ways. We will have more to say about this in a later section.

The analyses comparing children's expressive data in years 2 and 3 indicated that certain common assumptions about emotions ontogenesis need to be reconsidered, especially the thesis that there is a general decline in emotional expressivity with age. Various theorists, including Bridges, have assumed that emotion gets muted as part of the maturational process. In fact, Malatesta-Magai and colleagues found that children remained affectively fluent in the facial channel between the second and third years, and even augmented their expressivity using the vocal channel. The data on mothers shows that they decreased their facial expressivity but increased their vocal emotional expressivity—commensurate with the greater verbal dialogue that is possible with older children. Taken collectively, these findings suggest that as they develop, individuals gain flexibility in how they may express their emotions.

In summary, the emergence of discrete emotion coding systems and microanalytic analyses within recent years has allowed us to reexamine old issues concerning early emotional development and to move to a more sophisticated level of understanding about emotions ontogenesis. Bridges appears to have been in error about global versus discrete affect in early infancy. However, in some sense, she was correct in assuming that the emotion system becomes more differentiated, if by that we mean the capacity for more discriminating and situationally sensitive deployment of emotions. The ability to express emotion facially, vocally, and linguistically, to shift between channels, and both to amplify and dampen emotional expressivity is a largely positive gain for the child and consistent with greater overall adaptation.

There are far fewer data on expressive behavior beyond the period of infancy and the preschool years, especially with respect to fine-grained analyses involving microanalytic coding. Instead, the bulk of literature on children's emotional development during the second wave of this century's research on emotion is based on questionnaire data and behavioral observation. The literature is noteworthy for the sheer volume of work on two selected areas of socioemotional development—those of anger/aggression and empathy. The next two chapters consider these literatures in detail. Although the two chapters concentrate on research since the 1950s, the data are embedded in a historical framework showing that these foci are linked to larger social concerns of Western culture that have a considerable heritage.

6

Anger and Aggression

I was angry with my friend:
I told my wrath, my wrath did end.
I was angry with my foe:
I told it not, my wrath did grow
WILLIAM BLAKE, *A Poison Tree*

In this chapter we examine in greater detail how psychologists have approached the study of emotion expression development. As noted in Chapter 5, the bulk of recent research on emotion expression has largely been conducted with infants. There is little in the way of work exploring how the emotions repertoire unfolds over time beyond infancy. Instead, the paradigm that has dominated the field for most of the century is the single-emotion approach. Examples are Goodenough's (1931) monograph on the development of anger, and Jersild and Holmes's (1935) monograph on the development of fear. A more recent example is Kagan and colleagues' (Kagan, Snidman, & Arcus, 1992) study of "behaviorally inhibited" or shy/anxious children.

The tendency to concentrate on one emotion to the exclusion of others has its origin in certain conditions related to theory and technology. In the first place, especially in recent times, a more comprehensive approach is rendered almost impossible because of the expense and time required to use fine-grained microanalytic coding strategies. A second reason relates to the lack of an overarching theory of emotional development and of human motivation and personality—a problem that existed until fairly recently. Finally, it may be the case that certain emotions compel our attention in ways that others do not. An emotion may be compelling because it is very salient or because it is closely associated with behaviors that are problematic in the culture at large. Developmental research on emotions in Western culture has tended to concentrate on issues of anger and empathy, especially that of anger. In fact, there has been more research on anger than on any other single emotion in the developmental literature. As a culture we appear to be particularly sensitized to anger. For example, in a cross-cultural study of emotion recognition, Izard (1972) found that among the negative emotions Americans had least trouble recognizing anger.

We may also be a particularly aggressive people (see e.g., Lore & Schultz, 1993). In the developmental literature, both anger and aggression are key foci and the association between the two constructs is particularly strong; sometimes the terms are used almost interchangeably. The association is understandable, for although aggression is not a necessary outcome of anger, nor is anger a necessary condition for aggressive behavior, it is anger more than any other emotion that provokes aggression, and aggression follows anger versus some other emotion most commonly. As such, it appears that the great surfeit of literature on the emotion of anger at the expense of other emotions may be due to anger's association with aggression and the need to understand the ways in which it may be modulated. Here, the body of literature on anger will be explored for its paradigmatic utility. Perhaps by focusing on one emotion, as a prototype of primary emotions, we will be able to discover general principles concerning emotion socialization and differential personality development. We turn now to the actual research on anger and aggression.

OVERVIEW

There have been several distinct historical periods, as well as a number of recurring themes, throughout the literature on anger/aggression. Through the mid-1930s, developmental psychologists conducted several observational studies of the emotions of children in various settings. When behaviorism and its anti-developmental biases rose to dominate psychological theory and research at midcentury, these kinds of studies disappeared from the literature. The logical positivism undergirding the philosophy of psychological science at the time also dictated adherence to methodologies that promoted control of as many variables as possible. As we have noted, both emotion and the developmental study of children slipped out of favor during this time. The few studies that examined anger did so only peripherally, as the key concern was aggression. During the mid-1970s, when the grip of behaviorism on psychological theory and research had been loosened by the "cognitive revolution," more studies began to appear that examined socioemotional development. Also, as we have already noted, technological advances in recording emotion expression had by that time encouraged studies of infant emotion. Through the 1980s, numerous studies of anger in infants and children were published, not all of which dealt specifically with aggressive behavior as had been the case during the middle of the century. What the next decades will bring can only be surmised, although some speculations will be offered at the end of this chapter.

Several themes ebb and flow through this research literature, sometimes taking a central role in authors' consideration of anger and sometimes receding to the background. For example, in the early literature, much effort was expended on identifying the "age of onset" of anger in infants; the issue is still alive today (Cicchetti & Sroufe, 1978). Early researchers were also interested in facial expressions and what today would be called "contextual" determinants of anger. The biological and social triggers of emotion continue to be studied today although with different technologies and guiding theories. Interest in the modification and control of anger and associated behaviors continues as well. While some research on anger conducted in the first third of the twentieth century recognized the need to understand emotion within the framework of the developing self system, this theme has become most clearly articulated in recent years.

Other themes that have become more apparent in recent research include interest in the influence of emotions ontogenesis on personality development. In addition, although some early researchers, most notably Sherman (1927a,b), studied the way adults recognize emotion expression in infants, contemporary psychologists are conducting studies on the signal function of affect in order to understand how children recognize emotion expression in one another and in adults.

Our chronological review of the literature on the development of anger will permit us to observe these themes more clearly. We divide research conducted in the twentieth century into three periods. The first period extends from the beginning of the century until 1939, when Dollard et al. published their book on frustration and aggression. The middle period includes the years from 1940 until roughly the middle of the 1970s. During this time two theoretical worldviews—behaviorism and psychoanalysis—most strongly influenced thinking about anger and aggression. As we have noted, this was a time when aggression was studied far more than anger. (Historians would remind us that this period included three wars.) The mid to late 1970s marked a time when research on emotion expression in infants expanded due to technological advances. Systems approaches came into favor and individual differences were examined, particularly those associated with the study of "dysfunctional" families in the 1980s. Viewed collectively, this research leads us to draw several conclusions about what we now know about anger development and what future researchers might yet discover.

EARLY WRITINGS ON ANGER DEVELOPMENT

The observations of children's anger made by Darwin (1882) and Preyer (1890) laid the foundation for writers in the early twentieth century. The first observational study of emotion in children to be published in this century was conducted by D. R. Major (1906), who taught at Indiana University and, appropriately for his time, wrote introductory textbooks on both psychology and on philosophy. Major, like others in the "baby biography" tradition, conducted detailed observations of his son, "R," from birth through 3 years of age. Major declared that he could not be certain about when anger appears in children and noted that individual differences influenced this. However, he did believe that "the anger expressing apparatus is almost ready to function at birth, that the baby comes into the world prepared to act *as if angry* in the event proper influences of his environment reach him" (Major, 1906, pp. 117–118). Those influences included frustration, as when Major's son cried angrily at 17 days when he failed to locate his mother's breast. Three months later, the baby appeared to be angered when an object was removed from his hand. At age 8 months, Major's son reacted angrily to having water substituted for milk in his bottle. Modern researchers would point to this example as one of the conjunction of cognitive and emotional development because the child had presumably developed an expectation of milk. The infant recognized he had received a poor substitute, and he responded in a way guaranteed to attract the attention of caregivers. By the 12th month, R had developed the motor coordination necessary for a new form of anger expression. Now angry cries were accompanied by "striking up and down with the arms" (p. 120). Major continued to make careful observations of his son's mental growth for the next 2 years and he concluded that the situations that provoked anger did not change much past the first year. What changed were his son's abilities to coordinate his responses to conditions that elicited the emotion. Interestingly, Major asked himself a question about these observations of anger that researchers continue to ponder. He wondered why he had not noticed "vicious" behavior in his son since the work of other observers of children had led him to believe that vicious behavior was normative. Perhaps, suggested Major, his son's temperament mitigated against such behavior; on the other hand, he considered the possibility that little R had not been unduly frustrated, nor had he had many opportunities to learn by imitation. Major's inquiry about individual differences and possible biological and social influences remains unanswered, although investigations by contemporary researchers have suggested that, indeed, temperament, learning, and environmental context all affect children's emotional development.

Another early writer with very definite ideas about the biological bases of behavior was Compayre (1914). Strongly influenced by Darwin's writings on emotion, Compayre argued that anger has both internal and external outcomes. He believed anger represents the foundation of hatred within the self and that it causes the individual to strike out at others. Compayre's ideas are important not only because they were an early example of the application of Darwinian theory to child development but also because they contrast with earlier Victorian writing about children that was extremely sentimental, attributing only innocence to the young. Compayre's image of the child was far more rooted in popular Darwinian views of nature— "red in tooth and claw." Depicting children's motives, Compayre (1914) wrote: "In his heart there are seeds of malignity, of hatred, of evil inclinations, a certain need of destructiveness. To disturb, to undo, to tear, to destroy, to kill—these are his daily joys..." (p. 211).

Children, however, could differ from one another in what today we would call temperament. Noting individual differences by age and sex (young ones were angrier than older ones, with girls more timid than boys), Compayre also observed that certain families appeared to produce angry, aggressive children more than other families. "In some mysterious way, bad parents bequeath their own faults to their children" (p. 212). Not willing to attribute this bequeathal entirely to heredity, Compayre noted that environmental influences were just as significant. We will observe that Compayre's concerns about familial influence on anger, both hereditary and environmental, echo through research conducted in the 20th century, reflecting the scope of concern about the nature–nurture issue, which has framed so much psychological research during this century.

Aside from the well-known laboratory studies of Watson and the lesser known work of Major and other early baby biographers, few systematic data about anger in infants and children were collected until the 1930s. In that decade, several important studies took place that had a profound effect upon understandings of the development of anger.

Anger in Bridges's Genetic Theory of Emotion

As we have already detailed in Chapter 4, Kathryn Bridges developed a theory of emotion ontogenesis during the 1930s that proposed that discrete emotions differentiate out of an infant's general state of excitement. Her observations of children in a nursery school and two foundling hospitals led her to conclude that the emotion of anger differentiates from excited distress at about 6 months. She claimed that by the time the child reaches school age, anger differentiates into disappointment, anger, jealousy, and envy (Bridges, 1930, 1932). We have noted the methodological problems in the observations Bridges made; the circumstances under which the children in the foundling hospitals lived almost certainly influenced their emotional lives, as Bridges herself recognized.

Florence Goodenough's Study

Florence Goodenough (1886–1959) was raised in a rural area of Pennsylvania, attended a teacher's college, and later taught at the Vineland School for mentally retarded children. After receiving her master's degree from Columbia, she went to Stanford to work as Lewis Terman's chief research assistant on his studies of gifted children. In 1925, she came to the Minnesota Child Guidance Clinic and later was instrumental in the founding of the Institute of Child Welfare at the University of Minnesota. Her work at Minnesota is well known among psychologists, particularly those interested in the assessment of individual differences. Her much-cited study of anger was, in part, motivated by her interests in individual differences and the need for normative data relevant to age and sex differences. Goodenough's book, *Anger in Young Children*, published in 1931, has achieved "classic" status in the literature on children's emotions. For example, Willard Hartup (1974), of the renamed Institute of Child Development at the University of Minnesota, commented that "again and again, social psychologists come back to Florence Goodenough's data about age differences in children's angry behavior" (p. 336). We are thus invited to examine carefully the work that Goodenough did in determining age changes in anger.

Goodenough argued that there was insufficient evidence to demonstrate that facial expression alone was an accurate indicator of emotion. She believed that in order to interpret and not simply describe emotional behavior, one had to know the precipitating stimuli. Therefore, she was persuaded to obtain data about children's anger from observations made by mothers in their homes. She recruited mothers to be trained in observation and then to submit reports on their children's behavior when angry. Not only did the mothers have to describe their children's behavior, they also had to note the following: the frequency and duration of angry outbursts; the general conditions apparently leading to the increase in irascibility; the activities occurring at the same time as the anger; the immediate causes of the anger; the ways the mothers attempted to control the behavior; and the nature of the parent–child relationship in general.

The mothers kept detailed records for 1 month and out of this Goodenough obtained data on 1,878 anger incidents in 45 children ranging in age from 7 months to 7 years 10 months. She commented that many of her reports were incomplete and difficult to interpret, despite her efforts to train the mothers in systematic observation. Moreover, behaviors tended to happen too rapidly; one observer could hardly record every important aspect of a transaction. Despite these limitations, she managed to draw some authoritative conclusions.

Like Major, Goodenough (1931) concluded that with age and increasing motor coordination, anger behavior changes. She wrote:

> With advancing age, the forms of behavior displayed during anger become more definitely directed toward a given end, while the primitive bodily responses of the infant and young child are gradually replaced by substitute reactions commonly of a somewhat less violent and more symbolic character. (p. 69)

Furthermore, Goodenough observed that the frequency of anger outbursts reaches its peak around age 2, although the average duration of angry episodes (5 minutes or less) changes little until age 8. Sex differences appeared throughout her data, most notably the fact that after age 2, boys seemed to display anger far more frequently than girls. She noted that hunger, fatigue, and illness as well as the presence of older siblings, all appeared to increase the probability of children's angry behavior.

Goodenough made a number of intriguing comments about anger control. Her study had given her insight into the "average" number of angry incidents in different-aged children. As a response to those who thought that parental management regulated children's emotions, Goodenough (1931) replied that some children appeared to demonstrate more anger than others due to "an inherited predisposition or because of poor health. Likewise, environments differ greatly in their anger-provoking qualities" (p. 215). Thus, unlike scores of "experts" on child psychology who followed her, Goodenough was reluctant to give advice on the control of children's anger because so many variables could be operative.

She did, however, observe some trends in the types of control exerted by the families she studied. For example, she believed that children's age and gender affected adults' responses to their angry behavior. Girls' anger tended to be ignored, while for boys "bribery, spanking, threatening, and isolation" (p. 216) were the typical parental reactions. Further, Goodenough observed that as children grow older, use of physical force by adults to control their angry episodes declines. In an observation that would come as no surprise to B. F. Skinner and other advocates of behavior management, Goodenough noted that "giving in" was used more often by parents of children who had frequent outbursts of anger. Finally, Goodenough discovered what many researchers on parent–child relations have confirmed: there is very little agreement between what methods parents *say* they use and those they *actually* use. For example, she wondered how aware these mothers were of their own behavior. Self-professed "gentle and kind" mothers sometimes had children whose behavior indicated otherwise. Also, inconsistent discipline appeared to incite more anger in children as well as more resentment. Resentment, said Goodenough, breeds in children who come to believe that nothing they can do will be met with parental approval.

Florence Goodenough (1931) did not hesitate to remark that the major factor that elicited anger was the "home atmosphere" (p. 242). Parents whose children showed the least amount of anger were the ones who did not spend a lot of time attempting to categorize "bad" and "good" behavior. They maintained a sense of humor in the home; they were consistent in their responses to their children's behavior; they set standards appropriate for their children's ages and abilities. Despite being consistent and maintaining certain standards, these parents were not inflexible. If changes had to be made in the daily schedule that might be upsetting to children and provoke their anger, these parents did so in recognition of their children's needs and did not act capriciously on the basis of "the convenience or mood of the adult in charge" (p. 248). Goodenough appeared to be describing, in her straightforward, common-sense approach, what Diana Baumrind would later call the "authoritative" parent (Baumrind, 1971).

The importance of Goodenough's work cannot be too strongly emphasized. As we have stated, her observations of anger in children are still highly respected by contemporary researchers in child development. Additionally, her advice about child rearing appears to have been incorporated into American understandings and expectations of parenthood. For example, in the first edition of *The Common Sense Book of Baby and Child Care*, Benjamin Spock (1946) reiterated many of the ideas Goodenough emphasized. While it is impossible to know if Goodenough's work directly influenced Spock, his statements about how the meanings of children's behavior vary according to their ages resemble the empirical data she gathered. Further, his remarks about temper tantrums being associated with fatigue, hunger, or illness certainly reflect Goodenough's data.

THE MIDDLE YEARS

In 1948, a conference modeled on the 1927 Wittenberg Symposium on Feelings and Emotions was sponsored by the Loyal Order of Moose. This conference, the Mooseheart Symposium, was organized by M. S. Reymert, director of the Mooseheart Laboratory for Child Research, which was associated with the University of Chicago. Reymert later edited the conference papers in a book called *Feelings and Emotions*. One contributor, J. E. Anderson (1950), summarized the standing of emotion in psychology at the time by stating:

During the last two decades emphasis has shifted from analysis in terms of the traditional categories of fear, anger, and love to one in terms of frustration and aggression, attachments and detachments, and adjustment and maladjustment. (p. 418)

Two papers in this volume reflected developmental concerns. Anderson's contribution amply demonstrated how psychologists were viewing emotion as a function of learning and problem solving. He observed that as children grow, their early emotional responses are replaced by a "mechanical or routine" (p. 422) response to situations that earlier had produced emotion. He believed that the nature of adjustment could be evaluated on the basis of how many situations elicited emotionlike responses with the "more secure person" (p. 422) showing emotion in very few, if any situations. Emotion terms may have troubled Anderson, for he repeatedly spoke of "negativism," which his descriptions revealed to be anger.

The other paper concerned with developmental issues presented at the Mooseheart Symposium was by the well-known child psychologist Arnold Gesell. Gesell (1950), remembered for his theory of maturation and his detailed illustrations of children's development at various ages, called emotion the "feeling of a motor attitude (and its systemic, biochemical correlates)" (p. 393). He viewed emotion solely as resulting from changes in the organism's "action system" (p. 395), although he did state that children's affective life is influenced by cognitive growth and adjustment to the social environment. Hints of the later emphasis on the interrelated development of cognition and emotion can be found in Gesell's work. Furthermore, he, like Anderson, appeared to be aware of patterns of socialization that varied by class. Anderson (1950), for example, had observed that "differential controls over emotion. . . are related to social status" (p. 423); and he supported this by saying that boys in lower classes were encouraged to fight when challenged, whereas middle-class boys seemed to be taught to conform. This effort to differentiate emotion socialization patterns by class would later be continued by researchers in the 1980s.

Many of the papers at the Mooseheart Symposium addressed the question of frustration and its sequelae. Given the widespread influence of the frustration–aggression hypothesis in the 1940s, this is not surprising. The Yale group—Dollard, Doob, Miller, Mowrer, and Sears—had presented a theory which, combined with developing behaviorism, dissuaded researchers from studying emotional reactions. Another example of work involving the elicitation of emotion in children but which instead emphasized frustration was G. E. Chittenden's (1942) doctoral research on preschool childrens' social play. Conducted at the University of Iowa, this work sought to demonstrate that children could be categorized according to two types of assertiveness: dominative and cooperative. Chittenden's descriptions of dominative assertiveness, in terms of direct force applied to another either to influence or resist being influenced, sound very much like what we would today call aggression. Although she observed hitting, kicking, pinching, and other forms of physical force in addition to threatening verbal statements, nowhere in her lengthy paper does she mention aggression or anger. How children learned to respond to frustration continued to interest researchers in the

1950s (Davitz, 1952; Otis & McCandless, 1955). Reflecting upon our observations about the influence of sociocultural conditions on views of anger and aggression, we can perceive a growing concern during the 1950s with how children learn various social skills and how they might be taught to modulate their aggression. This was the time of the "baby boom." The increasing numbers of children being educated in schools with limited space seemed to call for further understanding of social cooperation. Although these studies functioned within the theoretical framework of the frustration/aggression hypothesis, they are forerunners of the work by Bandura and Walters (1963), which rejected the hypothesis and emphasized the effects of social modeling.

Although little attention was paid to emotion during this time, support for psychological research on other topics was strong. With the surge in the birthrate psychologists became ever more focused on child-rearing practices and their sequelae. The popular media as well convinced Americans of the crucial importance of parent–child interactions. Influenced (though perhaps not convinced) by psychoanalytic insights that had permeated the culture, Americans of the Eisenhower era were ready for "objective" information about the best way to raise moral children.

In 1957, Robert Sears, Eleanor Maccoby, and Harry Levin published a book that attracted considerable attention. They sought to replace "expert opinion" on child rearing with research-based observations, and their data on childhood aggression became widely known. Analysis of this work demonstrates the problematic status of emotion in American psychology at that time. The reader who checks the index to find where anger is discussed is advised to "see aggression" instead. Similarly, there are no references to "emotion," though there is a reference to "emotional disturbance" and under that entry, direction to pages covering "toilet training" and "weaning." Despite the lack of attention to emotion per se, the Sears et al. work had a significant impact on other researchers, and its findings were disseminated in the larger culture by child-rearing "experts."

Child Rearing in the 1950s and the Control of Anger

Sears, Maccoby, and Levin conducted their study under the auspices of the Laboratory of Human Development at Harvard University. Their motivation for conducting the study was doubtless multifaceted but one influence must have been the increasing support for psychological research in the 1950s. During World War II, psychologists had demonstrated the utility of their research methodologies. The American public had come to admire scientists and believed that science could provide answers to all manner of perplexing questions. Chief among the questions for the Sears team was the nature of child-rearing practices, their influence on personality development, and the source of these practices. Sears et al. believed that their data could offer more to parents seeking accurate information about their tasks than could the expert opinion of previous decades, which had been largely anecdotal. As researchers affected by the intellectual climate and politics of their times, they believed that data about child rearing could be collected by interviewing only mothers.

In order to gather information about the three central questions, Sears et al. enlisted the aid of 10 volunteer interviewers who conducted interviews with 379 mothers living in the Boston area. The interview schedule was carefully designed to be comprehensive and as unbiased as possible. All of the mothers who participated in the study had a child who was about 5 years old. During the interview, they were asked to reflect upon their interactions with their children since birth. The mothers described how they had weaned and fed their children, their methods of toilet training, the ways they had dealt with dependency, how they controlled sexual activity, and their responses to their children's aggression.

Robert Sears, the first author on this project, had been an author for the very influential book, *Frustration and Aggression*, published in 1939. Therefore, it is not surprising to find in the 1957 work an emphasis on the way frustrating situations elicit aggressive responses. Further, both studies addressed the problem of controlling aggression, with this later book suggesting that various child-rearing practices influence the ways children learn to regulate aggressive behavior. For Sears et al., the key variables that affected responses to frustration were the sex of the child (less aggression was permitted in girls), the socioeconomic standing of the family (lower socioeconomic groups punished aggression more severely), and the personality of the mothers.

The mothers who reported the greatest amount of aggression in the home were judged to have more anxiety about child rearing, lower self-esteem, greater dissatisfaction with their life circumstances, more conflict over their roles as mothers, less esteem for their husbands, and more disagreement with their husbands over child-rearing practices. The authors equivocated on the possible reasons for the strong relationship between the amount of aggression displayed by children and their parents' own feelings of dissatisfaction. Sears, Maccoby, and Levin suggested that such mothers were hypersensitive to the hint of hostility due to their own negative feelings about their lives; on the other hand, perhaps their negative feelings produced more frustrations in their homes to which their children responded with aggression. (This approach in effect blames mothers for producing high levels of frustration in children. Somewhat later, Patterson [1980] would observe that temperamentally labile, "out-of-control" children may create dysphoria in mothers which then affects their marital relationship and produces increased frustrations in family interactions.)

Sears et al. cautiously interpreted their results. They were aware of the problematic nature of the data-gathering process in which mothers had to recall interactions with their children over a 5-year period. Also, the authors noted that some mothers were probably motivated to present a portrait of family life that may not have been fully accurate. Finally, the researchers recognized the limitations of their scaling of answers and the problems that existed when comparing scores on different scales (e.g., between permissiveness and punishment). Nevertheless, they did draw some tentative—and important—conclusions from their data.

They pointed out what later came to be widely known as the "self-fulfilling prophecy" effect in psychology. That is, mothers who expected their children to be more aggressive had children who met those expectations. On the other hand, mothers who had a nonpermissive attitude about aggression expected that their children would not behave in such a fashion. When aggression did occur in these families, mothers had various ways of responding. Severe punishment appeared to be related to an increase of aggression, most likely due to the child's feelings of frustration in response to punishment. This led Sears et al. (1957) to predict that "the mothers who were most permissive but also most severely punitive would have the most aggressive children; those who were most non-permissive but least punitive would have the least aggressive ones (p. 260). Data on both sexes confirmed this prediction, leading the researchers to conclude that "punishment by the mother bred counter-aggression in the child" (p. 261).

Looking at these data from the perspective gained through recent studies of child abuse, we can only wonder what occurred in the families described by Sears et al. as using "severe punishment." Those children who received severe physical punishment tended to be far more aggressive than the other children studied. Later we will examine recent studies involving abused children in which a similar high level of aggression obtains.

The Development of Aggression

In his review of the psychological research conducted on children's aggression during the 1940s and 1950s, Buss (1961) commented that there may be no developmental changes of note. The research he examined produced contradictory findings, with some finding an increase through preschool and others finding a decrease. Buss suggested that there may be no overall developmental trends but rather many forms of aggression that develop at different rates and at different times in the child's life. The question of developmental trends was also addressed by Seymour Feshbach (1970) in a major review article appearing in *Carmichael's Manual of Child Psychology*. Feshbach noted the lack of normative data on the development of aggression in children but urged psychologists to consider aggression in the context of general developmental theories. In particular, he argued that researchers must begin to study the way the child's *interpretations* of events interact with their biological preparedness to experience anger when threatened or frustrated. This emphasis upon cognition as a mediator between a stimulus (such as a threat or a frustration) and a response (a retaliative act) is a good example of how the cognitive revolution in psychology was beginning to have an effect on researchers in the early 1970s.

Another psychologist calling for developmental data on aggression about this time was Willard Hartup of the Institute of Child Development at the University of Minnesota (Hartup, 1974; Hartup & DeWit, 1974). He, too, could find little in the research literature indicating normative trends in the ontogenesis of aggression. Although he did not emphasize the cognitive component as much as Feshbach did, Hartup called for a functional analysis of aggression in children. This functional approach would later become more important for psychologists studying socioemotional development (see, e.g., Malatesta & Wilson, 1988), for it provided insights into several issues that have long perplexed psychologists.

First, it enables one to understand how the function of aggression might vary according to social setting and thus be either encouraged or discouraged by parents and other agents of socialization. Second, a functional analysis allows one to avoid the either/or argument that has so long raged in psychology: either we must see aggression as an inevitable, biologically determined aspect of human experience or we must view it as learned and thus potentially eliminated from human experience. Hartup's position differed from early researchers who believed that aggression in children had to be extinguished. Rather, he moved the discussion onto a different plane by stating:

> Neither the child who lives in the poorest ghetto nor the child who lives in the most affluent circumstances can survive unless he acquires a harm-doing repertoire and some capacity for coping with aggressive affect. Social and cultural evolution will hopefully continue in a direction which will lower the necessities for interpersonal aggression, but it is neither ethical nor feasible, at present, to counsel that pacifism must be encouraged at all costs. The appropriate aims of childhood socialization are to establish clearly articulated and highly conservative values with respect to the expression of aggression and to provide appropriate aggressive training within such a moral scheme. (Hartup & DeWit, 1974, p. 616)

Despite Feshbach's turn toward cognitive psychology and Hartup's functional approach, researchers were unable to explicate clearly the relation between the emotion of anger and acts of aggression. The terms anger and aggression were no longer being used interchangeably; indeed, Feshbach (1970) had stated that although anger could act to energize behavior that sometimes was aggressive, "the aggressive drive may be rooted in other antecedents than those fostering anger" (1970, p. 162).

The pioneering work of both Feshbach and Hartup revealed that psychologists had not yet resolved the question of normative trends in the development of aggression. Insistence on theoretical orthodoxy in previous years had diverted attention from the search for these trends. Florence Goodenough, who pledged no allegiance to a particular theoretical worldview other than the scientific one of objectively gathering valid data, had begun the search for these trends. By the early 1980s, two authors were willing to examine research on aggression to try to uncover information about developmental patterns in aggression.

In 1983, Ross Parke and Ronald Slaby published a major paper on the development of aggression in the *Handbook of Child Psychology*. Here they addressed theories of aggression, biological data on aggression, the question of sex differences, the stability of aggressive behavior, and developmental patterns. By far, the greatest amount of attention was directed to the social determinants of aggression, including the family, peers, and the media. Parke and Slaby reported a few studies on physical environmental influences on aggression such as temperature and crowding, and they concluded their paper with a review of the literature on the control and modification of aggression.

Concerning developmental trends, the authors noted that surprisingly little information existed. They reviewed many of the early nursery school studies discussed earlier in this chapter and concluded that between the ages of 1 and 2 children begin to demonstrate aggressive behavior toward peers and, somewhat less frequently, toward adults. After age 2, these behaviors tend to decline, just as Goodenough had said. Some authors argue that with continuing development of cognitive abilities, the form of aggression changes between ages 2 and 4. Physical aggression decreases while verbal aggression increases. Another way of differentiating forms of aggression was offered by Hartup (1974), who discriminated instrumental aggression (in the service of repossessing an object, territory, or privilege) and hostile aggression (directed against another person). Hartup found that younger children (between ages 4 and 6) employ more instrumental aggression, while older children (ages 6 to 7) show more hostile aggression.

Parke and Slaby found that preschool children do not reciprocate insults, while school-age children do. However, when goals are blocked, preschool and school-age children respond in similar ways, with the proportion of hostile reactions not varying. The increase in overall hostile behavior by school-age children is attributed to their ability to infer intentionality on the part of those who block their goals.

In later development (9–12 years of age), children's ability to discriminate intent influences whether or not they respond with aggression. Furthermore, in contrast to younger children, 12-year-olds inhibit aggressive responses when the frustration is verbal, while physical provocation continues to elicit aggressive reactions.

Parke and Slaby (1983) concluded their review of the literature on normative trends in the development of aggression by commenting on the increasing importance of a cognitive perspective. However, they cautioned researchers not to abandon the study of emotion, for "it is unlikely that simple cognitive models alone will suffice" (p. 573).

With so much social concern being expressed about aggression from the 1950s onward, the psychological study of *anger* in infants and children risked being overlooked. Nevertheless, Jerome Kagan, whose longitudinal study of children is a landmark in the field (Kagan & Moss, 1962), reintroduced to the study of aggression in children both developmental considerations as well as speculations about anger. In a paper that appeared in an important book edited by DeWit and Hartup, *Determinants and Origins of Aggressive Behavior*, Kagan (1974) argued that aggression can only be understood from a motivational perspective that accounts for the intention behind the act. He implied that anger occurs after the individual has been able to judge the cause of a frustration and thus Kagan appears to fall into the camp of those arguing that cognition precedes emotion. This conclusion is, however, too hastily drawn, for Kagan has a far more complex and holistic approach to the relations among cognition, affect, and motivation.

Developmentally, Kagan suggests that aggression occurs in most American children between the ages of 18 and 28 months. At this time, the child has a rudimentary ability to discern intention. However, much of the behavior labelled as aggressive in earlier studies, Kagan (1974) argues, must be reexamined in light of his insistence that an act is aggressive only if there in an "intention, conscious or unconscious, . . . to inflict psychic or physical harm on another" (p. 107). In other words, whether or not an act is judged as aggressive depends on the motivation for that act. For example, consider the studies of preschool children in which efforts to wrest a toy from another child were interpreted as aggressive. Kagan reinterprets these common encounters between children as often having no hostile intentions or anger as motivators; rather, the child simply desires the toy and thus Kagan would not call one child's pushing another child an aggressive action.

THE SECOND WAVE

The Psychology of Anger in a Changing Culture

The 1980's witnessed a veritable explosion of research papers on anger and aggression. Many factors, proximal and distal, contributed to the increasing numbers of psychologists asking how anger and aggression develop in children, how children learn to manage their angry feelings and their aggressive acts, how they use emotion expression to regulate both their own behavior and the behavior of others, and how environmental variables shape the emotional lives of humans who appear to be born prepared to express and experience emotion.

Social forces unleashed in this culture due to rapid social change caught the attention of psychologists organizing research agendas. National concern about the apparent increase in child abuse stimulated funding of studies on the anger and aggression of children subjected to extremes of adult anger and aggression. The effect of television viewing was also targeted for research funding. Television was no longer perceived as a benign form of entertainment, for studies began to show relations between the amount of television viewing, the types of shows watched, and children's subsequent angry acting out (Eron, 1987; Eron et al., 1983; 1987; Singer & Singer, 1985). Concern was also voiced about latchkey children, who lacked adequate supervision. Dual-career families increasingly became the norm and yet the government still failed to rally to the need for increased quality day care (Silverstein, 1991).

All of the above factors served to heighten concern about children's development, especially their unregulated aggressive proclivities. The old question of nature and nurture has consequently returned and is particularly apparent in recent longitudinal studies of aggression.

Nature and Nurture: Stability of Aggression

The enduring question of how much variance in behavior can be attributed to biological differences and how much to differential learning gets played out specifically in the recent literature on socioemotional development. However, by the 1980s, many psychologists seemed to have wearied of the perennial argument about "which comes first," thinking or feeling, and "which is more important," heredity or environment. Emotions researchers recognized the role of cognitive development in the child's emerging emotional repertoire. Researchers emphasizing the cognitive aspects of emotion acknowledged the possibilities of innate, biological determinants of affect (see, especially, Berkowitz, 1989; Berkowitz &

Heimer, 1989). A difference in emphasis became particularly evident in longitudinal studies of aggression that showed remarkable stability in individuals in various cultures, including those like China, discouraging aggressive acts by children (Ekblad, 1989). Was this due to inborn temperamental differences? Was the stability a result of consistent reinforcements from the environment? Or was there some kind of complex interplay between temperament and environment? These were the kinds of difficult, and still largely unresolved, questions that animated a number of longitudinal studies of the 1980s.

Longitudinal studies pose many challenges for psychologists, although their rewards in terms of data on developmental trends are rich. One study (Cairns, Cairns, Neckerman, Ferguson, & Gariepy, 1989) has noted that longitudinal studies of aggression need to acknowledge that the meaning of aggression may be different given different developmental contexts. Typically, researchers have used the same operational definition of aggression throughout their study regardless of the age of the children. With the current emphasis on context, however, we will probably begin to see a new approach to longitudinal analysis. As suggested by Cairns et al. (1989), "at each developmental stage, the construct [aggression] reflects the social judgments of society, the social attributions of researchers, and the social constructions of the self" (p. 329).

Leonard Eron has documented how theoretical advances influenced his thinking during the course of a 22-year longitudinal study of aggression. While his work always emphasized the learned aspects of aggression, Eron observed how the central thrust of his interpretations has changed from drive-reduction theory to cognitive theory. Persistence of aggressive behavior over time is now viewed by Eron (1987) as resulting from the cognitive elaboration of drive, cue, response, and reward. In other words,

> it was what the subjects were saying to themselves about what they wanted, what their environment would permit or expect, what might be an effective or appropriate response, and what were the likely consequences of such action that helped determine how aggressive they are today. (p. 441)

Eron noted the influence of identification with parents and parental punishment on boys' aggressive behaviors. Like Sears et al. (1957), he found that the more children with moderate or little identification with their fathers were punished, the more they aggressed against others. Loeber (1982) also believed that persistent aggression must somehow be related to the family environment, although he could not find definitive factors underlying family management (or lack thereof) in terms of its influence on children's behavior. He reviewed a number of studies on the stability of children's antisocial behavior—those "acts that maximize a person's immediate personal gain through inflicting pain or loss on others" (p. 1432). Clearly, aggression must be seen as a type of antisocial behavior, although Loeber was interested in a more global description of these children's frequently delinquent behavior. Loeber concluded that children rated as highly antisocial in middle childhood become even more antisocial as they passed through adolescence. Although Loeber could not describe specific family-management skills of parents of children showing chronic antisocial behavior, he did suggest that such a child's behavior tended to alter radically parents' attempts to intervene to stop the acts. These children could easily coerce their parents into abandoning efforts to control their behavior.

One of the best-known researchers exploring the long-term stability of aggressive behavior is Dan Olweus of the University of Bergen in Norway. In a review of 16 studies, Olweus (1979) determined that researchers had found a substantial amount of stability in aggressive behavior and concluded that such stability contradicts claims by some psychologists that personality cannot be meaningfully studied because behavior is situation specific. On the contrary, Olweus, found a high degree of stability in the research he reviewed despite changing peer groups, schools, family situations, and the like. The rewards for aggressive behavior in the immediate environment do not appear to be all that is responsible for maintaining a high level of aggressive behavior over time. Rather, Olweus (1979) argued, "relatively stable, internal reaction tendencies are important determinants of behavior in the aggressive-motive area" (pp. 872–873). Olweus prefers to see these "reaction tendencies" as aspects of personality and not simply the result of biologically defined temperament. While temperament plays a role in the development of personality, Olweus suggests that the latter—personality—is what emotions researchers need to be studying in order to advance our understanding of anger and aggression.

Like Eron and Loeber, Olweus is convinced that the family environment plays a major role in maintaining children's level of aggression. Even more than temperament, Olweus points to negativism in the mother (characterized by hostility and rejection) and the mother's permissiveness of aggression as being the key variables in the development of boys' aggression (Olweus, 1980). In a study of two groups of Swedish boys (median ages 13 and 16), Olweus found nothing to suggest that socioeconomic status related either to levels of aggression or to child-rearing behaviors within the family. Others, however, believe that socioeconomic status plays an important role because of varying attitudes about aggression and also because of different approaches to the socialization of emotion.

Anger in South Baltimore: The Influence of Class

The normative trends Goodenough sought in her research in the 1930s continue to intrigue psychologists; now, however, these trends are understood within a context of increasing appreciation of individual differences. Not only do children differ biologically in "temperament, in facial neuromusculature, in arousal levels, and in perceptual discrimination ability" (Lewis & Saarni, 1985, p. 13), they also differ in the patterns of socialization to which they have been exposed within their families and the culture at large. Sex differences in affective development have received considerable attention; further, social class and culture also shape emotional expression and experience. In the introduction to their book *The Socialization of Emotions*, Michael Lewis and Carolyn Saarni (1985) wrote that these individual differences "can occur at any level of our analysis of emotion:

which stimulus elicits what response, what is the nature of the expressive behavior, and which is the appropriate emotional state for a particular situation" (p. 13). Early studies of anger in children occasionally suggested that class differences may be important determinants of children's affective responses but most of this research was based on observations of middle-class children attending university preschools. Sears et al. (1957) noted class differences in how mothers interpreted and responded to their children's aggression but they did not explicate specifically the processes through which class shapes socialization within families. One major ethnographic study that did examine how social attitudes about emotions are communicated to children was conducted in South Baltimore by Peggy Miller and Linda Sperry (1987).

Miller and Sperry's intensive longitudinal investigation of three young girls and their mothers depicted how class shapes socialization not only through immediate events in the environment but also through personal histories that parents bring to the task of child rearing. Miller and Sperry were particularly interested in collecting data about how language molds the socialization process that occurs between mothers and young children just beginning to learn how to talk. Toward this end they videotaped interactions between three mothers and their 2-year-old daughters over a period of 8 months. They also conducted extensive interviews with the mothers. In much of this conversation, anger and aggression were prime topics of interest.

Numerous examples provided in the report demonstrate the attitudes of this class of women regarding anger and aggression. The children ranged in age from 18- to 25-months when the study began; despite their youth, little about a world of random violence was kept from them. The mothers believed it necessary to "toughen" their daughters and did this through teasing and by telling graphic tales of daily violence encountered in their neighborhood.

They also spent a great deal of time discussing how those who had transgressed deserved what they got. To be in a situation of aggression and not stand up for oneself was deemed "sissy behavior." Thus the children learned early not to reveal weaknesses of any kind.

Anger was frequently expressed in home; in fact, Miller and Sperry stated that all the other emotions were played out against a backdrop of anger. Sometimes the mothers accepted their daughters' anger; sometimes they deliberately provoked it through teasing; sometimes they attempted to suppress it. Through varying responses to anger, these mothers were teaching their children a set of rules about emotion:

(1) When another child hurts you physically, or takes your toy, or wrongs you in some other way, defend yourself. (2) But don't respond angrily or aggressively without reason. (3) When mother teases you, assuming the role of an older, bullying child, show that you can stand up for yourself. (4) Otherwise, do not direct anger or aggression at your mother or other parental figures; comply with their standards. (p. 23)

The first and third rules warn the child about being a sissy; the second and fourth prohibit spoiled behavior. These rules so carefully described by the authors open their analysis to a social-constructivist approach to anger. As Averill (1982) argues, children do not necessarily learn specific responses for specific situations; rather, like Amy, Wendy, and Beth in Miller and Sperry's report, they learn rules that "help constitute and regulate behavior" (Averill, 1982, p. 333). It is thus significant that Miller and Sperry began studying these three young girls just as they were learning language and could, therefore, better understand the information they were acquiring about emotion.

Miller and Sperry (1987) noted the same expressions of anger in these children that Goodenough had observed: facial, vocal, postural, gestural expressions. In addition to these nonverbal behaviors, Miller and Sperry described the ways anger and aggression became expressed linguistically through a "distinctive set of lexical items" (p. 28). Interestingly, these children did not tend to talk about feelings of anger but rather spoke of aggressive acts. Miller and Sperry believe this reflects a "childrearing ideology focused more on the goal of self-protection and defense than on the expression of angry feelings as such" (p. 28).

The above research, though limited to the study of three families, highlights the broader contextual focus that is needed to bring a more complex analysis to bear on the socialization of anger and aggression, and sets a model for others who would pursue the question further.

SUMMARY AND COMMENTARY

In the present chapter we chose to survey the literature on anger (rather than some other emotion) as our prototype of how the field has studied affect because of the dense concentration of literature on this emotion. There has been far less research on Watson's two other primary emotions—fear and love—although one might argue that the recent upsurge in literature on attachment comes as close to studying love as we have come in this century. There has been precious little developmental research on any of the other basic emotions (see Izard, 1991, for discussion of other emotions and some of the scattered studies on the development of these emotions).

During our current literature review, we noted that discussions of research on anger have tended to dwell on its negative properties and to focus on finding ways to curtail its manifestation in behavior. Despite the wealth of research on anger and aggression, the field has not advanced very far in its understanding of the dynamic properties of anger in social and personality functioning. Much of the research we reviewed was normative/developmental in nature. After what has amounted to a century's worth of research on the topic, one must conclude that we know only rather mundane things about the course of anger expression in childhood. While anger expression itself seems to become more muted, aggression increases between the the first and second years of life, and there is an increase in "hostile" versus instrumental aggression at school age (Goodenough, 1931; Hartup, 1974).

In terms of differential development, a few studies examined variables associated with anger/aggression during childhood. To summarize the results of these studies, low anger/aggression in children is associated with a maternal personality that is flexible and humored (Goodenough, 1931). Variables associated with high rates of anger/aggression are temperamental lability (Peterson, 1972), permissiveness for aggression (Olweas, 1980), marital conflict, severe punishment, maternal anxiety about child rearing, maternal low self-esteem, maternal conflict about role as mother, maternal low esteem for husband (Sears et al., 1957), severity of punishment combined with low or moderate identification with fathers (in the case of boys) (Eron, 1987), maternal negativism, that is, hostility and rejection (Olweas, 1980), and exposure to teasing (Miller & Sperry, 1987).

Important as the above findings may be, we are nevertheless faced with the observation that even if we added all of the variables together and entered them in a grand multivariate model, it is unlikely that such a model would help us predict differential personality development—a goal that is implicit in much of the research on anger and aggression. As adults, some individuals are clearly more "anger-prone" than others; that is, anger functions as a prominent part of their personalities. What accounts for this consolidation of personality around anger? Research this century has pointed to differing levels of frustration, punishment, abuse, unstable family life, and neurotic personality traits in parents. But we have always known or suspected this, and a list of variables hardly amounts to a theory of individual personality development. Does the literature we reviewed help us predict individual development and behavior? Is it even very useful in an explanatory sense? Let us consider the case of John Watson, whose biography is detailed in Chapter 4.

Watson's background included exposure to marital conflict, violent eruptions by his father (accompanied in all likelihood by severe punishment), and low identification with his father. Yet although Watson was combative in high school (as required to defend himself), he did not grow up to become unusually aggressive or antisocial. Instead, he grew up to be eminent. If he harbored anger as a personality disposition, and there is reason to believe that he did, it did not impede his professional advancement, and perhaps even assisted it. How does emotions theory, or genetic personality theory, for that matter, help us explain this particular personality?

One of the problems with single-emotion approaches to the psychology of emotion development is that personality development involves all of the primary emotions as they are differentially developed in the individual. One or two emotions may eventually come to dominate a personality, or may be especially salient in a particular individual, but it is the configuration of personality and the array of emotions and how they are differentially activated that needs to be considered. Part IV takes up the issue of personality organization and its development in greater detail.

Before we leave the present chapter let us consider one final issue. In the opening of the chapter, we speculated that one might be able to extract general principles of emotion socialization or of personality from the example of anger. Reviewing the literature above, one sees that anger/aggression is enhanced under conditions where it is severely punished. This finding both defies social learning theory as well as suggests a counterintuitive prediction for other emotions. In social learning theory terms, punishment is any action that suppresses a behavior it follows. With anger, parental actions that we classically think of as being punishing do not seem to be effective. As indicated above, punishment tends to augment anger/aggression rather than decrease it. Perhaps punishment suppresses other kinds of behavior, but not emotional behaviors. Or perhaps it is the case that severe punishment has a general reinforcing effect on emotion, anger as well as other emotions. Unfortunately, there is no research that speaks to this issue. Even if we were to find an additional association between severe punishment and extreme anger, for example, we still would be at a loss to explain why one child's experience of severe punishment leads to an anger-prone personality while another child's experience of the same leads to a depression-prone personality. Part IV addresses this issue as well as other enigmas in detail. Before we turn to personality theory however, we consider research on empathy—a research literature that is almost as voluminous as that on anger and aggression, and perhaps represents this culture's hoped-for antidote to aggression.

Empathy and Prosocial Behavior

How could it be possible to feel no interest in other people and because
of an ivory tower of indifference, detach yourself from the life they
bring with their open hands?

PICASSO, *Les Lettres Françaises*

In 1972, Lauren Wispé introduced an issue of the *Journal of Social Issues* by
suggesting that a subtle change in the Zeitgeist had resulted from the wrenching
experiences of social disorder in the 1960s. In particular, Wispé (1972) cited the
Kitty Genovese case as instrumental in motivating social scientists to explore the
dynamics of human altruistic behavior. Largely as a result of that well-known
example of the inhibition of altruism, social scientific research began to shift its
emphasis from "negative" behaviors to an exploration of the motivational origins
of positive, prosocial behaviors. In order to chart this change, Wispe assembled a
collection of papers all devoted to the examination of positive forms of social
behavior. According to Wispé, one of the keys to understanding these forms of
behavior lay in the fundamental human capacity for empathy and sympathy.
Thus the stage was set for the tremendous outpouring of research on empathy,
sympathy, and prosocial behavior that emerged in the 1980s. Wispé, whose many
writings on empathy, and particularly sympathy, have always contained a
historical perspective (1968, 1986, 1987, 1991), accurately predicted an important
new direction for social scientific research, one in which developmental
psychologists have fully participated.

One indication of the shift foreseen by Wispé is the number of dissertations on empathy in infants and children written in the 1980s. As we have already noted, this decade marked a major turning point for psychology's acceptance of emotion as a legitimate focus of study. Additionally, by the end of the 1980s, more and more psychologists were understanding that psychology itself must approach its central defining questions developmentally.

At the forefront of this new research were Norma Feshbach, Helen Borke, Nancy Eisenberg, Janet Strayer, Martin Hoffman, Carolyn Zahn-Waxler, and Marian Radke-Yarrow. These individuals led the way in articulating the definitional issues involved in empathy, sympathy, personal distress, and projection. They also rose to the challenge of measuring these variables and they have steadfastly maintained a developmental orientation in their work, seeking to understand the ontogeny of empathy, its relation to prosocial behavior, and the primary influences on the emergence of "fellow-feeling" in children's experience of their social environments. Because many excellent reviews of the literature already exist (Barnett, 1982; Eisenberg & Miller, 1987; Eisenberg & Mussen, 1989; Eisenberg & Strayer, 1987b; Moore, 1990; Radke-Yarrow, Zahn-Waxler, & Chapman, 1983), we will only briefly review these topics before turning to important issues not fully examined in this work.

DEFINITIONAL ISSUES

Definitions of empathy can be broadly categorized in terms of how much emphasis is placed on cognition and affect. That is, some view empathy as a cognitive process involved in understanding another person's feelings, while others emphasize the affective component of empathy by stressing the vicarious experience of emotion. One definition that has acquired wide acceptance in recent years is found in the work of Nancy Eisenberg. While not excluding the cognitive component, she argues that empathy is primarily an emotional response involving a vicarious affective reaction to another person's state or condition, a "feeling with" that person (Eisenberg & Strayer, 1987a; Eisenberg & Mussen, 1989; Eisenberg & Fabes, 1990). More specifically, Eisenberg and Strayer (1987a) define empathy as "an emotional response that stems from another's emotional state and that is congruent with the other's emotional state or situation (p. 5)." Significantly, this definition implies that empathy can be a response to a wide variety of emotions and it avoids more narrow conceptualizations that view empathy solely in terms of the emotional response to another person's distress.

The terms "sympathy" and "empathy" have often been used interchangeably, although recent work attempts to differentiate them. Eisenberg and Strayer (1987a) contrast the "feeling with" of empathy with the "feeling for" of sympathy. That is, the individual who sympathizes is not only aware of another person's distress but also wishes to take action in order to alleviate whatever is causing that distress (Wispé, 1991). Although empathy can be a response to a wide range of emotions—positive and negative—sympathy is most properly thought of as a response to a negative emotional state. Wispé (1991) notes that the word *sympathy* literally means a "suffering with" another person and he argues that it would be "inappropriate and insincere" (p. 69) to sympathize with another's happiness.

In attempting to draw distinctions between empathy and sympathy, some authors note the difference implied in the two German terms *Einfuhlung* and *Mitfuhlung*. The first use of the term *Einfuhlung* is generally credited to Theodor Lipps's late nineteenth-century work on aesthetics, although Gladstein (1984) notes earlier references. Lipps spoke of *Einfuhlung* as representing the process by which a person "feels oneself into" a work of art (Gladstein, 1984; Goldstein & Michaels, 1985; Wispé, 1987). The actual word "empathy" was coined by Titchener who was attempting to explain how people "humanize" non-human forms and was seeking an analogy to sympathy. As an example of what he meant by empathy, Titchener wrote: "a column seems, according to its proportions, to stretch up easily to its load, or to plant itself doggedly under a too heavy pressure,—precisely as a man might do" (Titchener, 1910, p. 333). This description along with Titchener's other writings about empathy led Wispé (1987) to remark that it is rather unclear exactly what Titchener meant by empathy. As explained by Buchheimer, *Mitfuhlung* does not imply this kind of "merging into" process that Titchener attempted to describe with the word "empathy." Rather, *Mitfuhlung*, or sympathy, is more a matter of feeling along with another person without the implied convergence of emotions (Buchheimer, cited in Goldstein & Michaels, 1985, p. 7). Although recent work has by and large accepted this distinction between empathy and sympathy, some writers continue to call for a broader view of empathy that would include sympathetic responses (e.g., Barnett, 1982). Moore's attempt to provide such a perspective has led him to refer to the "empathy-sympathy complex" (Moore, 1987, 1990).

Some authors believe it is important to differentiate empathy and sympathy from feelings of personal distress. In his work on altruistic behavior, Batson has shown that personal distress is an egoistic reaction, which, when it motivates helping behavior, does so only to relieve personal distress and not to improve the other person's situation (Batson, 1981; 1987; Batson et al., 1981). Thus personal distress is self-oriented, while sympathy (or empathy—the two being undifferentiated in Batson's work) is other-oriented. While Batson's work has primarily focused on adults, Eisenberg and her colleagues (Eisenberg et al., 1989) studied second- and fifth-grade children and found that measurement of heart-rate patterns, facial expression, and self-report information could differentiate empathic responses to another's sad situation from responses of personal distress. Children who were more empathic were also more willing to help, thus supporting Batson's position.

Projection is another psychological concept sometimes confused with empathy. Eisenberg and Strayer (1987a) note that the usual definition of projection involves the ascription of one's own feelings to another and thus they conclude that projection is primarily a cognitive process initiated in the self and not in the other person, as is empathy. This difference between projection and empathy, while clear with regard to abstract definition, has long been recognized as problematic in the measurement of empathy (Hastorf & Bender, 1952; Strayer, 1987).

Before we turn to the problem of measurement, we pause to consider an assumption that is strongly implied in much recent conceptual and empirical work on empathy. Because recent interest in empathy has arisen in large part as a result of efforts to determine the parameters of prosocial behavior, psychologists often treat empathy as if it were some kind of "magic elixir that automatically produces social competence and prosocial behavior" (Feshbach, 1982, p. 320). As we have seen, there is considerable conceptual ferment over how empathy should be defined. Feshbach (1982) believes it is often defined too broadly so that it "takes on the property of an all-embracing 'good'" (p. 319). This raises the question, Can empathy be "bad?" Yes it can, according to some thoughtful observers. For example, Barnett (1987) cites situations where empathy about others' feelings might be counterproductive. If a second grader is participating in a spelling bee, she may not want to do well out of concern that a friend would then feel sad about losing. This example cuts to the heart of American concerns over competition and how much experience children should have with it. Therefore, given a society where individual competition is encouraged and rewarded, empathy for others might be viewed as problematic.

Zahn-Waxler and Radke-Yarrow (1990) also suggest that empathy can be maladaptive for children when it is overdeveloped. Overidentification, long a concern of psychoanalysts (see e.g., Ekstein, 1972), can lead to a fusion between persons, making it impossible for individual development to occur. This is a problem for children relating to one another and is also a problem when parents overidentify and overempathize with their children, making it impossible for parents to engage in appropriate disciplinary behaviors (Feshbach, 1987). As another example, consider a mother so fused with her child that she cannot bear to have the child feel pain. She could refuse to have the child immunized, thus putting that child at great risk. Psychoanalyst Christine Olden (1958) offered several case examples of how such maternal fusion prevented normal ego development in children and argued that this kind of narcissistic closeness cannot be called empathy.

In an intriguing paper entitled "Contagious Sneezing and Other Epidemics of Empathy in Young Children," Lesley Koplow (1986) noted another problem that can occur when empathy is too forcefully encouraged by parents and teachers. Koplow works with disturbed children (the exact diagnosis was not provided) who have difficulty with ego boundaries. That is, when one child gets excited or sneezes or laughs or cries, an empathic contagion sweeps through the classroom. Teachers must walk a fine line with the children in teaching them to be sensitive to one another's emotions while at the same time enabling them to retain a secure sense of the self without constantly being distracted by others' feelings.

Although empathy is typically viewed as positive, particularly when it leads to prosocial helping behavior, nevertheless, sometimes empathy can exacerbate the original emotion, possibly leading to antisocial behavior. Campos et al. (1983) remark that empathic anger might escalate an already volatile situation. Likewise, empathic sadness and even helping behavior might be unwelcome. Sometimes people refuse help aggressively.

Finally, and tragically, there is an issue of safety regarding children's empathy. Mark Barnett (1987) notes that child molesters sometimes entice the intended victim by telling the child that help is needed for a wounded puppy or that a relative is ill and calling for help. Such ruses play on children's empathic reactions to their detriment. Barnett suggests that children need to be taught situation specificity regarding empathy: sometimes empathic responsiveness is not desirable.

These caveats are rarely mentioned in the burgeoning empathy literature. They point to the need for continued fine tuning of the research on empathy with regard to its conceptualization and measurement.

MEASUREMENT

Janet Strayer (1987) has noted that the affective and cognitive components of empathy "have been difficult, if not impossible, to dissociate in empirical attempts to measure empathy" (p. 230). Thus, she argues that if one holds a definition of empathy that emphasizes affect, then one must measure empathy using methods that actually tap emotion. These would include self-report and measures of facial expression and physiological arousal. To use measures of role-taking or cognitive perspective-taking to study empathy defined primarily as affective is to confound definition and measurement.

One of the earliest and most widely used measures of empathy in children was developed by Norma Feshbach (Feshbach & Feshbach, 1969; Feshbach & Roe, 1968). Using a procedure that has come to be known as the Feshbach Affective Situations Test for Empathy (FASTE), Feshbach and Roe showed slides and told stories about children to their subjects. After each picture and story, the subjects were asked to tell how they felt. The affects shown in the slides were happiness, sadness, fear, and anger. Feshbach and Roe asked some of their subjects to tell how the child in the slide/story felt in order to differentiate subjects' empathy from their social comprehension. Feshbach and Roe found no difference between boys and girls in socially comprehending the emotions of either boys or girls; on the other hand, they found significantly more empathy in children responding to a slide/story about a child of the same sex.

Marcus, Roke, and Bruner (1985) have argued for the use of multiple measures in research attempting to link empathy to prosocial behavior. They maintain that both verbal and nonverbal measures of empathy should be employed because of their differing relations to measures of cooperation among children. Strayer (1987) has also called for a multidimensional approach to empathy that would tap its cognitive as well as affective components. In a study using self-report and facial/gestural indices, Eisenberg, McCreath, and Ahn (1988) reported a relation between prosocial behavior and facial/gestural indices but little relation between preschoolers' self-reports and their altruistic behavior. Thus, they concluded that some of the difficulties in determining the relation between empathy and prosocial behavior may result from the use of self-report measures alone.

Multiple approaches to measurement have also been implicated in the differentiation between empathy and personal distress. Eisenberg et al. (1988) employed facial, heart rate, and self-report indices and found consistency among them. In their study, heart rate decelerated when children responded to a stimulus film with sympathy, while it accelerated when the film evoked anxiety and self-orientation.

Although nonverbal measures of empathy have shown promise, their use requires inference on the part of the researcher regarding the phenomenal experience of the subject. Therefore, today it is generally accepted that the "elusive phenomenon of empathy" (Eisenberg & Strayer, 1987b, p. 398) can be most effectively studied through the use of multiple measures.

THE DEVELOPMENT OF EMPATHY

Efforts to understand the development of empathy have been complicated by differences between researchers regarding both the definition and the measurement of empathy. On the one hand, those who take a cognitive-developmental approach (see, e.g., Lewis & Michalson, 1983) tend to argue that role-taking ability represents the critical dimension of empathic response. Using this approach, Wilson and Cantor (1985) found that preschool age children could *recognize* the emotion of another (in this case, fear) although they did not report *feeling* that same emotion as did the early school age children. On the other hand, those for whom the affective element of empathy is central, find that very young children do indeed respond with empathy to other people's feelings (Eisenberg et al., 1988; Lennon, Eisenberg, & Carroll, 1986).

A model of empathy that takes into account both cognitive and affective factors has been proposed by Norma Feshbach (Feshbach, 1979). Feshbach's three component model asserts that in order for a child to respond with empathy, he must first have rudimentary cognitive skills such that the emotions of others can be discriminated, an ability she calls an "elementary form of social comprehension" (Feshbach, 1982, p. 320). The second component involves perspective- and role-taking, an ability that emerges after the child learns about different emotions. These two cognitive components work together with the affective component, namely, the ability to experience the emotion being witnessed. Feshbach (1982) notes that during the 1970s, debate raged over the degree to which cognition and affect shape empathy. Researchers continue to disagree over where they place their emphasis and this influences their views of developmental issues, as we will see below.

In addition to varying emphasis placed on the affective and cognitive components of empathy, a related conceptual issue that also has developmental implications involves the amount of differentiation involved between the person feeling empathy and the individual whose emotional situation has prompted the empathy. Eisenberg (Eisenberg & Fabes, 1990) assumes at least a minimal amount of differentiation is necessary before one can truly say a child has experienced empathy. The question of differentiation between the self and the other is important because of the number of studies that have demonstrated empathic distress in infants who have yet to attain an understanding of subject–object distinction (Martin & Clark, 1982; Sagi & Hoffman, 1976; Simner, 1971). Are those infants who cry in response to hearing another infant cry experiencing empathy? Most authors—including Hoffman, whose research on this issue is most widely cited—view this infantile response as a precursor to more mature forms of empathy (Barnett, 1982; Eisenberg & Strayer, 1987a,b; Hoffman, 1984). In his writings on the formation of character, Bertrand Russell (1926) termed these responses examples of "instinctive physical sympathy" (p. 200), the foundation of more elaborate forms of sympathy (or empathy). Russell was particularly concerned to note the sensitivity of young children to others' emotions and connected this with their development of character. Thus, he advised that "if the father shouts or the mother speaks rudely to the maids, the child will catch these vices" (p. 200).

Although the nature–nurture question has in many ways defined psychology since its inception, the drive to ascribe nearly all forms of human behavior to instinct waned in the early part of the twentieth century. Evidence of this is clearly seen in Paul Guillaume's (1926/1971) *L'imitation chez l'enfant*. In that book, to which Piaget referred frequently in his *Play, Dreams, and Imitation*, Guillaume argued against those who held that sympathy is a human instinct, saying instead that children learn to assimilate others' emotions that are consonant with their own. The dynamics of this process challenge researchers today as they endeavor to describe and explain the socialization of empathy while at the same time holding that there is a fundamental biological contribution to the human capacity for empathy.

Factors Influencing the Acquisition of Empathy

Writing in the issue of the *Journal of Social Issues* edited by Lauren Wispé, psychoanalyst Rudolf Ekstein (1972) stated categorically: "Good mothering . . .makes for good empathy" (p. 79). The last 20 years have brought considerable social critique to the subject of parenting and, in particular, the different contributions of mothers and fathers to the raising of children. Feminist critique of the psychoanalytic literature's tendency to blame mothers for all of children's behavioral and emotional problems, combined with emerging awareness of the role of the father (Silverstein, 1991), has led psychologists to tread carefully when they write of maternal influences on development. Nevertheless, considerable evidence exists to show that Ekstein was correct in his statement about empathy. Unfortunately, much less is known about the attributes of good fathering and their effect on the development of empathy.

What exactly constitutes the kind of good mothering that produces good empathy? In a summary of findings about the development of empathy in the critical second year of life, Zahn-Waxler and Radke-Yarrow (1990) note that mothers who are affectionate and sensitive have children who express more empathic concern for others. In addition, those mothers who take the time to explain others' feelings, to elicit caring responses, and to reject harmful behaviors, have children who score high on empathy measures. Zahn-Waxler and Radke-

Yarrow also noted stressors in family life that may contribute to an inhibition of empathic responsiveness. For example, parental depression may influence children initially to display too much empathy, leading to an aversion to other persons' distress. Likewise, marital discord and a familial environment shaped by anger can affect children by creating such high levels of arousal that withdrawal is the child's only recourse. Finally, children who are maltreated are less likely to develop empathy since they are never able to form secure attachments with their caregivers.

Research on the relation between attachment and empathy/sympathy has shown that children rated as securely attached at 15 months were rated as more sympathetic to peers at age $3\frac{1}{2}$ than those children who were anxiously attached (Waters, Wippman, & Sroufe, 1979). More recently, Kestenbaum, Farber, and Sroufe (1989) found the same relation between secure attachment and empathy in preschool-age children. Secure attachment means that children can be freed to explore their environments, environments which include other persons registering a range of emotions. Being securely attached and developing the basic trust (Erikson, 1963) that one's own needs will be met may then liberate children to be able to respond to the needs of others (Strayer, 1985). Despite research evidence showing a relation between secure attachment and empathy, Barnett (1987) cautions that one must take care not to assume direct, causal links between any single variable (like attachment) and empathy, since multiple factors influence attachment and some may be more important than others in shaping the development of empathy.

Caregivers who are sensitively attuned to their infants' emotions not only encourage secure attachment but also enable infants to acquire the ability to turn to others for assistance in regulating emotion, particularly distress. Evidence from a study by Ungerer et al. (1990) points to the relation between infants' self-regulatory abilities and the development of empathy. Externally oriented self-regulatory strategies at age 4 months were shown by Ungerer et al. to predict primitive empathic responding at 1 year. By contrast, those infants who showed poorer self-regulation (measured by employing the still-face procedure) at 4 months responded at 1 year with personal distress (indexed by arousal-dampening sucking of body parts or clothing) when viewing a videotape of another infant fretting and crying. Personal distress at 1 year was predicted by a self-oriented regulation strategy at 4 months when infants could not turn their attention to the environment in order to cope with a stressful situation. Inability to contain arousal by attending to the environment results in poor coping in infants, and it has been suggested that this is in part due to early interactions with caregivers who respond inappropriately to infant distress (Gianino & Tronick, 1985). The findings of Ungerer et al. connect self-regulation to empathy in an important way and suggest a new direction for research on empathy and individual differences.

Other data reveal related variables that either discourage or encourage the development of empathy. A meta-analysis of studies of empathy and aggression indicated that children growing up in abusive situations show low levels of empathy and tend to respond to peers' distress with aggression (Miller & Eisenberg, 1988). Abusive parents themselves score lower on indices of empathy. By contrast, responsive, warm parenting, inductive discipline, and acceptance of a child's emotional life are related to high scores on various measures of empathy. In other words, parental empathy is strongly related to the development of empathy (Feshbach, 1987) as shown in a retrospective study of college students (Barnett, Howard, King, & Dino, 1980) and in research on children ranging in age from 5 to 13 (Eisenberg et al., 1991; Fabes, Eisenberg, & Miller, 1990).

The studies by Eisenberg et al. (1991) and Fabes et al. (1990) are notable for their use of multiple methods in the measurement of empathy (including heart rate) and their differentiation of empathy from personal distress. Both studies found a correspondence between maternal empathy and the empathy of girls. Like other research showing gender differences in empathy (see, e.g., Feshbach, 1982; Lennon & Eisenberg, 1987), both Eisenberg et al. and Fabes et al. found that maternal expressions of sympathy and perspective-taking were associated with more sympathy and less personal distress in girls. Although the relation was weaker for boys, Fabes et al. did find boys being more willing to help a distressed person when they had mothers who showed more sympathy. Eisenberg et al. (1991) suggest that these gender differences may result from parents expressing fewer negative emotions around boys than girls. It is important to note, however, the conclusion drawn by Lennon and Eisenberg (1987) from their review of the literature on gender and empathy: Many of the reported differences appear to be artifacts of the types of measurement used since some studies report large, significant differences between boys and girls and others show negligible differences.

A study that found a marginally significant gender difference with girls scoring higher than boys on empathic concern is more important for its findings with regard to the parental antecedents of empathy in adulthood. Using data on 5-year-olds collected by Sears et al. (1957), Koestner, Franz, and Weinberger (1990) administered a measure of empathy to 75 of these individuals 26 years later. They found that 36% of the variance in empathy could be explained by parental behaviors that had been assessed by Sears et al. The two most important contributors to adult empathy were paternal involvement in child care and maternal tolerance of dependent behavior. Koestner et al. (1990) called the discovery of the importance of fathers' involvement "quite astonishing" (p. 713), and in the midst of their scientific discussion of their results, expressed profound concern regarding the number of children presently being raised apart from their fathers. Maternal tolerance of dependency, another variable strongly related to adult empathy, may also be in short supply today since single motherhood may require that children behave more *independently* at earlier ages. The Koestner et al. analysis also showed a weaker but significant relation between empathy and maternal inhibition of aggression in childhood and mothers' satisfaction with their maternal roles.

Although parental—especially maternal—interactions with children have consistently been cited as being highly important in the development of empathy, other variables have also been studied. For example, Mark Barnett (1984) has explored whether empathy is moderated by the similarity between a child's own personal experience and the situation that has aroused emotion in another person.

Working with 3- to 5-year-olds, he found that children who had encountered a situation similar to that of the person they later saw as distressed showed significantly more empathy on both self-report and facial expression measures than the children who had not undergone a similar experience. Other studies have demonstrated an increase in empathy when there is similarity between the subject and the protagonist with regard to variables such as age, race, and sex (Feshbach & Roe, 1968; Gibbs & Woll, 1985). Howes and Farver (1987) demonstrated that toddlers were more likely to respond to a crying friend in a day-care situation than to a crying acquaintance.

What needs to be clarified about the effect of similarity on empathy is whether it is true for all persons at all ages. This is an old question, pondered by Jersild (1933) when he commented that "sympathy . . . seems to be quite specific in young children: a child may protest and cry when his father is injured, and yet appear undisturbed if he sees a stranger similarly hurt" (p. 390). Since most recent research on empathy employs pictures shown and/or stories told about strangers to the child, Jersild's observation cannot be verified empirically. Jersild also believed that time moderates empathy; that is, the more time that has passed between experiencing an event and observing another person responding to a similar event the more the degree of sympathy evoked in the observer may be lessened. Jersild even suggested that this is one reason why adults may have trouble understanding children's emotional responses to their experiences since adults are far removed from childhood. Again, this is an issue that has received little empirical attention.

Age and Empathy

Today, as we have noted in earlier chapters, there is considerable evidence to demonstrate a biological foundation for infant receptivity to emotions, particularly the emotions of the primary caregiver. Babies recognize and respond to angry, sad, fearful, and happy maternal expressions with similar expressions. Infants thus acquire considerable information about the world via their ability to read and respond to emotion signals. This ability is clearly adaptive, and thus it is not surprising that recent research has pointed to empathic-like behavior in animals (Plutchik, 1987) as well as evidence for the heritability of the affective component of empathy (Zahn-Waxler, Robinson, & Emde, 1992).

James Mark Baldwin (1894) called infants' ability to recognize differences in the emotional makeup of others "one of the most remarkable tendencies of the very young child in its responses to its environment . . . Its associations with personality come to be of such importance that for a long time its happiness or misery depends upon the presence of certain kinds of "personality suggestion." (p. 334).

Baldwin's views on the development of sympathy/empathy anticipated current positions. Baldwin believed that the organic, instinctive tendency to respond to another's emotional state underlies the later development of reflective sympathy/empathy, which can only emerge once the child has realized the distinction between the self and the other. This position, which greatly influenced

Piaget's ideas on egocentrism and perspective-taking (Gladstein, 1984), is seen most clearly in Hoffman's developmental model of empathy (Hoffman, 1975, 1978, 1982a,b, 1984, 1987, 1990).

Hoffman's Model of the Development of Empathy

Martin Hoffman has introduced a model of empathy that is an important contribution to the literature—though it is oriented primarily toward distress since he is ultimately interested in children's moral development. Hoffman describes six specific modes of empathic arousal that appear at different developmental points. The first type of empathic arousal, and the earliest to appear, is the reactive cry of the newborn. Hoffman suggests three possible mechanisms underlying this behavior: an innate response; a primary circular reaction in which the infant cries in response to another infant's cry and then in response to the sound of his or her own crying; a conditioned response in which a second infant's cry functions as a conditioned stimulus, the sound of crying having been previously associated with distress (e.g., at birth).

More developmentally advanced than the simple reactive cry is the classical conditioning of crying. Hoffman claims that empathy can be classically conditioned in situations where another feels distress and the young child is also feeling distress. In this case, the other person's distress cues take on significance as conditioned stimuli that in the future can evoke distress in the self. For some early developmentalists like Jersild (1933), empathy/sympathy as a conditioned response was the only appropriate explanation.

The third form of empathic arousal noted by Hoffman has long been viewed as an important component in empathy. Hoffman calls it "direct association," meaning that another person's distress evokes memories in an individual of his or her own past feelings of pain or discomfort. For some early writers, this was the only genuine form of empathy/sympathy. For example, one of the first papers written by Scottish psychologist Alexander Bain dealt with sympathy. Bain later considered the topic in his textbook, *Mental Science: A Compendium of Psychology and the History of Philosophy*, published in 1868. In that book he wrote:

> We cannot sympathize beyond our experience, nor up to that experience, without some power of recalling it to mind. The child is unable to enter into the joys and griefs of the grown-up person; the humble day-labourer can have no fellow-feeling with the cares of the rich, the great, the idle; the man without family ties fails to realize the feelings of the domestic circle. (p. 277)

Though he offered an associationistic explanation of sympathy, Bain (1868) did not believe that sympathy was simply a cognitive assessment of another's condition. Rather, he spoke of the "infection" (p. 280) of sympathy in which one is "forcibly possessed" (p. 277) by the same feelings the other is experiencing. The significance of Hoffman's contribution is evident when comparing his work to some earlier writings on empathy/sympathy that held an either/or position, saying it had to be either an instinct *or* "classical conditioning" *or* a more general learned association. Hoffman claims "all of the above," and in so doing has influenced researchers on empathy to view it as complex and multidimensional.

The fourth mode of empathic arousal noted by Hoffman is mimicry. Earlier writers had been concerned about motor mimicry and the evoking of empathic responses. This approach fits well with theories of emotion proposed by William James as well as Silvan Tomkins: when one mimics another person's facial expressions and gestures, one then feels the same emotion due to the kinesthetic cues produced.

Language-mediated (Hoffman, 1984) or symbolic (1982a) association represents the fifth form of empathic arousal, only now the child has acquired language to the degree that the written word—such as in a personal letter—can evoke empathy. Hoffman also says that this fifth type of empathic arousal can occur in response to seeing a picture of someone in distress, although Hoffman would probably offer another interpretation to Baldwin's (1894) claim that his 22-week-old child wept "at the sight of a picture of a man sitting weeping, with a bowed head in his hands and his feet held fast in stocks" (p. 333).

Hoffman describes these five forms of empathic arousal as largely involuntary and minimally cognitive. The sixth form—role-taking—involves a deliberate cognitive act of imagining oneself in the place of the other. Emotion arises from this act of imagination because of past experiences of conditioning and association. The difference, however, between this form of arousal and the other five is that no person need be present to offer emotion cues; the evocative stimulus is the imagination itself.

Regarding the developmental sequencing of these forms of empathic arousal, Hoffman is unwilling to argue that they represent "stages." Although reactive crying diminishes with age, probably due to learned inhibition, the other forms of empathic arousal all continue throughout life, though certain persons (parents, teachers, therapists) may employ role-taking more than others.

These six forms of empathic arousal represent, according to Hoffman, the affective component of empathy. The cognitive component is introduced when the child can begin to experience separation and individuation. Whether one takes a Piagetian, cognitive approach to this process or a more clinical approach (e.g., Mahler, 1975), the acquisition of a sense of the other as having inner states independent of one's own is one of the most significant—if not the most significant—milestones of development. Hoffman's important contribution to the empathy literature has been his discussion of how empathic responses change as cognitive development occurs. Although we as yet have no complete lifespan account of the development of empathy (i.e., one that would incorporate insights about postformal operational thought), nevertheless, Hoffman has taken steps toward a lifespan account by theorizing about how increasing cognitive complexity affects empathy through adolescence.

In Hoffman's model, the earliest form of empathy, before the child has developed "person permanence," is global empathy. Children less than a year old sometimes demonstrate that they cannot discern the difference between something happening to them and something happening to another person. Should another child be hurt and cry with pain, the 10- or 11-month-old might respond as if he or she had been hurt.

Once the child has become aware of the self and the other as separate physical entities, "egocentric" empathy emerges. At this point, the child may understand that the other is separate and permanent as a physical being, but psychologically, there is still enmeshment to the degree that the other's inner state may be confused with one's own inner condition. Hoffman is careful to note the quotation marks around the word he uses for this second phase of empathic development: Although the child cannot discern the difference between inner states of the self and the other, nevertheless, the child still recognizes distress in the other, and, even as young as age 13 or 14 months, may make an effort to provide comfort. The comfort, however, may be what comforts the self, as when a child proffers a favorite stuffed animal to his weeping mother. Thompson's (1987) review of the literature on empathy in infants and very young children suggests that children even at this young age may have a rudimentary sense of the self-other distinction, although they may not be able to express it clearly.

Between the second and third year, when children learn that other people feel differently than they do, role-taking becomes possible and the child may then show "empathy for another's feelings." Hoffman claims that because children now understand that others may experience difference emotions from their own, they are freed to be even more responsive to emotion cues. In addition, language offers other routes to understanding emotion besides facial expressions and gestures. Because of the linguistic and cognitive development occurring around age 4, a broader range of possible empathic responses is possible. For example, Hoffman states that a child of this age not only feels empathy for another person's fear but may also have an inkling about that person's shame at feeling afraid.

Hoffman calls the final form of empathy "empathy for another's general plight." This form begins to emerge in later childhood, when children acquire a sensitivity to the fact that people have their own personal histories. Thus, the older child not only empathically feels the distress of the moment registered by another person but also feels empathic about past difficulties, or what Hoffman (1982a) calls the "general life condition" (p. 288).

Hoffman's model predicts that age should produce increases in children's empathy due to increased cognitive ability, just as Saxby had suggested in 1925. A recent study of 5- to 13-year-olds by Janet Strayer (1993) confirmed Hoffman's prediction by finding age increases in empathy continuum scores. Strayer's scoring method combines affect match and cognitive attributions regarding the nature of the stimulus person's emotion. Her findings showed "increases in overall affect match (with age controlled) as cognitive attributions become increasingly other-person-centered" (p. 198).

Limitations of Hoffman's Model

Although Hoffman's model has been widely embraced, not all aspects of it have been tested empirically. For example, Strayer (1987) suggests that more work needs to be done to identify the cues that elicit the different modes of empathic arousal; the ages at which these cues have the most salience also need to be considered. In addition, researchers need to identify potentially different outcomes when more than one form of empathic arousal is present and to assess whether this changes with age. To be fair, it should be noted that much of Hoffman's work ties empathy to moral behavior, a connection that has not been specifically addressed in this chapter although it has received much attention from researchers. Therefore much of the richness of Hoffman's model has not been captured here.

Because Hoffman's approach has become a widely accepted view of empathy, it is important that we examine it not only for what it contains but also for what it omits. Like many psychological models, it does not fully account for the biological substrate of empathy, nor does it take into account the biological patterning of specific emotions that might evoke empathic responses. Hoffman's theory of empathy is actually a theory of empathic distress. As a result of Hoffman's work and the work of others specifically interested in the relation between empathy and prosocial behavior, psychological approaches to empathy have become narrowed.

Another problem with the research on empathy inspired by the theoretical work of Hoffman, among others, is that it has paid scant attention to contextual effects on empathy. Although a few of the studies cited above attempted to discern how the similarity between children and their situations affected empathic responding, other variables such as the size of the group, the number of strangers in the group, and the goals of the group have not been examined with regard to the evocation of empathy, although these variables have been investigated as moderators of prosocial responding. Furthermore, social and cultural teachings about empathy have received little attention with regard to their moderating effects on children's expressions of empathy. The kind of ethnographic work done by Miller and Sperry (1987) on the socialization of anger in South Baltimore needs to be conducted to learn more about social learning with respect to empathy. Finally, recent work on empathy has not accounted for the historical period and dominant ideologies about how human beings should treat one another and what they should teach their children about interpersonal interaction.

Discrete Emotions and Empathy

As we have seen, research on empathy has typically employed distress as the target emotion due to the theorized links between empathy and helping behavior. As noted by Zahn-Waxler (1986), distress itself can be viewed as a combination of various negative emotions such as concern, sadness, tension, and fear. When these emotions are combined under the rubric of "distress," one cannot tell what aspect of the empathic response has motivated the resultant behavior. In addition, the different emotions might be felt with different intensities, thus making it even more difficult to predict exactly how empathy impacts upon behavior.

Consider the example of a 3-year-old child observing another child who is crying because someone has grabbed a toy from her. If there is affect match, what is being matched? If the observing child begins to cry or shows some other behavioral indication of empathy, she might be doing so out of sadness because of the loss of the toy, or anger that her friend has been treated badly, or fear that such bullying behavior might happen again. Any one or even all three emotions could be registered by the friend whose toy was taken; to which one or ones will the observing child be most likely to respond? We believe that empathy research at this time cannot answer this crucial question because it has failed to take into account affect biases in personality. For example, the individual whose personality is organized around anger might be more likely to empathize with anger and respond accordingly.

Even though widely used measures such as the FASTE (Feshbach & Roe, 1968) include happiness, fear, anger, and sadness, the empathy score is usually reported as a combination of responses to these emotions. Thus, it is difficult to discern differential empathic response to discrete emotions. When Strayer (1993) examined children's responses to vignettes characterized as showing the four emotions of the FASTE measure, she found empathy continuum scores to be higher for happiness in 5-year-olds than for the other emotions, although this finding held for only one of her conditions. Strayer comments that investigations of empathy in response to euphoric as well as dysphoric emotions need to employ equal stimuli for each, instead of the common current practice of emphasizing the dysphoric emotions.

In an earlier, naturalistic study of empathic behaviors occurring in a preschool setting, Strayer (1980) found that happy affect produced the greatest amount of affect matching in children, significantly more than any of the other emotions observed. This is an important observation, especially since Marcus's (1986) meta-analysis of naturalistic studies of empathy and prosocial behavior showed that happy affect has a strong facilitating effect upon cooperation, helping, and sharing. In addition, Strayer found that children who more frequently showed happy affect were more likely to be empathic than those children whose affect was dominated by sadness. However, we should note that this may represent a contrast effect between a positive and negative affect. Sadness at low levels may enhance empathy more than anger or fear, as other research suggests (see Chapters 9 and 10).

The use of naturalistic observation might be one way to begin to develop a broader view of empathy. As Zahn-Waxler (1986) states, "pure, laboratory assessments of empathy . . . do not always help in understanding behavior in the real world" (p. 314). Interestingly enough, it is in a body of relatively early work—that of Lois Barclay Murphy—that we encounter insights on the relation between empathy and personality based on naturalistic observation. Murphy's work also reflects an attempt to present personality as the result of a complex interaction between biology and culture. Finally, Lois Murphy's writings reveal a basis on which to make predictions about how affect biases in personality might shape differential empathic responding.

Studies of Sympathy: The Life and Work of Lois Barclay Murphy

Lois Barclay Murphy (b. 1902) was asked to contribute to O'Connell and Russo's (1983) fascinating collection of reflections of eminent women in psychology, and thus we have access to the details of her life. Lois grew up in an intellectual family, the eldest of five children of a father who traveled the world as a Methodist minister and a mother who had been strongly influenced by two students of William James who taught at the University of Iowa in the late 1890s—Carl Seashore and G. W. H. Patrick. Born in Lisbon, Iowa, in 1902, she moved to Chicago when she was 5 years old. Spending many happy summers at her grandparents' farm in Iowa provided her with a "deep sense of growth in many areas of life" (Murphy, 1983, p. 91). Being the eldest, she also had many opportunities to care for her younger siblings. This gave her a deeply rooted sense of individual differences as well as a strong feeling for the needs of children.

She attended Vassar College where she studied with Margaret Floy Washburn although she did not major in psychology. In fact, she says that Washburn's strong opinions on what was *not* proper psychology (Freud, for example) led her to become even more curious about psychologists labeled by Washburn as unscientific. Reading the work of Watson had led her to believe that "psychologists were not really interested in people or human life" (Murphy, 1983, p. 95) so she explored the writings of Freud, Morton Prince, Walter Prince, and F. W. H. Myers, author of a book published in 1903 called *Human Personality and the Survival of Bodily Death.* She became interested in comparative religion, particularly the religions of India, and in 1928 received a Master of Theology degree from Union Theological Seminary in New York City. She was appointed to the faculty of Sarah Lawrence College in 1928 to teach religion; she remained on the faculty at Sarah Lawrence until 1952, when she left to become a research psychologist at the Menninger Foundation.

Lois Murphy's ideas about psychology changed considerably after a friend introduced her to Gardner Murphy, her future husband, when she was 22 years old. Here was a psychologist who conducted psychic research at Harvard, had studied the work of Myers, and was a friend of Walter Prince. She writes that she was "thunderstruck by this psychologist who bucked the establishment so courageously" (Murphy, 1983, p. 96). His ideas about psychology, along with her very gratifying experiences as a mother of two children, led her to pursue the study of child psychology. During the 1930s, she began teaching courses on child development and obtained her Ph.D. from Columbia University in child psychology in 1938.

During the 1930s when she was beginning her study of child psychology, she observed that the field tended to focus upon aggression and conflict in children. She believed, however, that psychologists should also be looking at "positive aspects of their social development, especially sympathy" (Murphy, 1983, p. 97), in part because she had carefully observed the empathic behaviors of her two children. She writes that she was ridiculed by the "nursery school establishment" (p. 97) for wanting to study sympathy but, nevertheless, she obtained support from the Macy Foundation and published the results of her research in 1937 in *Social Behavior and Child Personality.* At the time, however, other developmental psychologists had not yet discovered the study of prosocial behavior and they "ignored [her] work for a decade" (p. 99). An important element of all of Murphy's work is her sensitivity to the effects of culture on personality.

In the 1930s, she and her husband participated in a seminar on anthropology taught by Ruth Benedict. Margaret Mead was a member of the group. As a child, she had been fascinated by the subcultural differences between her grandparents in Iowa and her grandparents in California. Thus, she said, "the emphasis on the cultural setting of behavior was absorbed into my bones; it is impossible for me to write anything about development without attention to the subcultural context" (p. 97). In 1950, she actually had the opportunity to work in another culture when she helped to plan the B. M. Institute of Child Development and Mental Health in Ahmedabad, India.

When Gardner Murphy accepted a position as director of research at the Menninger Foundation in 1952, she realized that this would provide her the opportunity to study normal development in preschool children. She argued that there were numerous studies of pathology in children but no one was studying how children coped with their everyday lives. Will Menninger supported her desire to study this, but when she spoke with a representative of NIMH to explore the possibility of a grant to support her research, she was met with ridicule. Coping was not listed in the Psychological Abstracts index at the time. Through persistence, she was able to obtain funding from NIMH, which supported her work through 1969. Coping, by that time, had entered psychology's lexicon.

During the 1960s she became very involved with the development of the Head Start program. She recalls how her interest in children of poverty had been piqued in childhood when she accompanied her father on pastoral visits to families living in substandard housing. She participated in Head Start "at all levels, from that of national planning, training at the state level, and consultation one morning a week over three years with the local Head Start Center" (Murphy, 1983, p. 101).

Gardner Murphy retired from the Menninger Foundation in 1967 and went to teach at George Washington University. Lois Murphy continued her writing while also consulting at Children's Hospital on infant studies. She traveled widely, presenting her work at national and international conferences. All the time, interest in prosocial behavior was growing. In 1979, after Gardner Murphy's death, she accepted an invitation from Marian Radke-Yarrow to be a guest scientist at the Center for Child Health and Development at NIH where, she reports, she greatly enjoyed working with young researchers exploring prosocial behavior.

Lois Murphy's Work on Sympathy

At the time she began to study sympathy, in 1932, she could find no scientific information on the subject. Nor did she find writings about cultural and personality factors in sympathy. But, as we noted above, she was determined to study positive social responses and so obtained the support she needed from the Macy Foundation. Not only did she want to learn about different forms of sympathy (empathy being its affective component, in her view) but she also felt it was important to study individual differences in how children responded to others' distress. She gathered her information by observing children at Columbia's Child

Development Institute. She watched children in class as well as on the playground, surveyed teachers regarding their evaluations of children's sympathy, interviewed parents, studied diaries of children's daily activities, and conducted informal experiments.

At all times in her research on sympathy, Lois Murphy kept the "big picture" in view; that is, she wanted to see how sympathy functioned in "the total personality in its cultural setting" (Murphy, 1937, p. 17). Perhaps as a result of her experience of psychology at Vassar, she objected to the atomistic approaches to personality that she believed were prevalent at the time. She argued that the quantitative insights of the empirical psychologists ought to be mutually supportive with the interpretive insights of the more clinically inclined but instead psychologists pitted them against one another. Her desire was to collect data scientifically but then to relate them to a conception of the whole personality.

Her interest in grounding a conception of personality within a broad view of culture led her to consider the historical moment in which she was conducting her research on sympathy in children. Surely, she wrote, these were times that called for more sympathy but, instead, American ideals of individualism created a competitive environment where people hesitated to express sympathy for one another's condition. Further, she recognized that the psychology of the time viewed emotion with considerable skepticism. She also noted how progressive women felt an aversion to being seen as sentimental. Following the advice of Watson, among others, educated women of the time wanted to raise their children scientifically. She termed this the professionalization of personal relationships and noted how the middle-class mothers she observed at the Columbia school rarely hugged their children as they left them for the day. These middle-class parents may not have expressed direct aggression toward their children through physical abuse but Murphy believed a kind of emotional abuse was occurring. She commented that the rigid schedules espoused by the child-rearing authorities of the time were a kind of indirect aggression. These parents were influenced by the "tooth-brush and building blocks school of present education which . . . emphasized toilet habits and motor activity to the exclusion of emotional development" (Murphy, 1937, p. 36).

Before proceeding with a description of Murphy's view of sympathy and personality, we should pause to examine exactly what she meant by sympathy since, as we have seen, this is a term with shifting definitions. Like today's researchers, Murphy (1937) viewed empathy as "the induction of feeling in response to expression of feeling by another person" (p. 287). This, she believed, was the simplest form of sympathy, present at birth in the reactive cry of the infant. Sympathy not only includes an emotional match with another person's distress but is behavioral in that the sympathetic individual responds to "sympathy stimuli" with positive social acts. In her observations of children, these acts included helping, removal of the cause of distress, comforting, punishment of the cause of distress, protection and defense, warning (e.g., "you might hurt yourself"), telling an adult or another child of the other's distress, and questioning ("why are you crying?").

We should note her inclusion of punishment of the cause of distress on this list since she, unlike many contemporary researchers, observed sympathetic and aggressive behaviors in the same children. In fact, she believed that individual differences showed up in varying ratios of sympathy and aggression. Some persons would be more inclined toward sympathy, others toward aggression. Further, she argued that there is a transaction between the individual personality and the environment since some environments (like crowded, small play spaces) seem to elicit more aggression than sympathy even in those children who showed more sympathy than aggression in other environments. She also observed the effect of different teachers' personalities on the children's sympathetic and aggressive behaviors. Thus, Murphy (1937) concluded that although there was "unimpeachable evidence of a 'sympathetic trait'" (p. 191), nevertheless the behavior resulting from this trait depended upon the "functional relation of the child to each situation" (p. 191).

Many of Lois Murphy's insights about sympathy have been confirmed by recent research, although one has to be careful about making comparisons due to differences in terminology. Her notion of sympathy included a behavioral element, whereas today's approach to the subject tends to split the affective/cognitive response to the other from the behavioral response. For Murphy, feelings, thoughts, and acts are part of a whole in terms of the way the child negotiates his or her way through social experiences. One striking similarity with today's research findings is her distinction between those children who showed sympathy because they truly felt concern for the other child and those who appeared to be motivated by their own feelings of insecurity and anxiety—personal distress, as researchers use the term today. This difference, which has been predicted in children on the basis of self-regulatory behaviors observed in early infancy, appears to be robust.

In the course of reviewing the empathy literature we noted that contemporary research pays scant attention to issues of personality. But for Murphy, personality was the central question. She hinted at the notion of affect bias in personality and suggested that it would influence the way children express sympathy. For example, Murphy (1937) stated, "children with predominant tendencies to be fearful would be apt to express sympathy in different ways from children with a predominantly aggressive [angry] tendency" (p. 317). Likewise, she stated that the verbal child will sympathize with words; the physically active child will do so with actions. Why one child would behave in one way and not another was a question neither Murphy nor her teacher and mentor, A. T. Jersild, could answer at that time.

SUMMARY AND COMMENTARY

This chapter indicated that there has been a tremendous amount of research on empathy, sympathy, and prosocial behavior over the past three decades. In part this reflects the funding realities of governmental policy concerned with problems of social decay. It may also reflect concerns in the public mind that our society is all too often saturated by violent images and surfeited with anger, crime, and aggression.

Developmental research during this time has been largely age graded. Theoretical models, such as that of Hoffman, have been proposed to account for normative milestones in the growth and development of empathy and prosocial behavior, and these models have guided much contemporary research on empathy. However, there has been less explicit attention to issues of individual differences. Jersild, writing in 1933, wondered about differences in the expression of sympathy:

> Why one is more catholic in his sympathies than another is often difficult to tell. A person may seem very sympathetic when another is in physical pain and yet appear to be quite unaffected by another's worries and fears. He may sympathize with one who is in need of food but fail to respond when this same friend seems to feel inferior. (Jersild, 1933, p. 390)

In the time since Jersild reflected upon this question, scattered studies have provided information on some of the factors that promote empathy and account for individual differences in empathic responding. This literature indicates that empathic children have developmental histories characterized by positive affect, secure attachment patterns, and good self-regulatory abilities, and have parents who are relatively sensitive, empathic, unstressed, happily married, and who use inductive disciplinary strategies. And yet, as in the case of the literature on anger and aggression, a list of variables does not a theory of personality make. We are still left to consider the question of how empathy operates in personality so as to promote prosocial behavior. Why should the above list of variables be associated with empathic tendencies? Is empathy a "type" of emotion like anger, fear, sadness, and happiness? That is, is it organizing, sensitizing, and does it operate like a personality trait in individuals in whom it is well developed?

It will be useful to keep these questions in mind as we turn to the literature on the role of emotion in personality development. Although the present authors do not as yet have well-formulated ideas about the above questions, we believe that the tendency to *behave empathically* is different from the *capacity for empathy*. We also believe that the behavioral tendency is linked to a particular pattern of emotional organization, one that is relatively balanced in terms of access to the full range of human emotions. We believe that the empathic personality is one in which positive emotions such as joy and interest predominate, but with mild biases toward shame/shyness and sadness. Moreover, we think that a predominance of anger in personality actively quells empathic tendency. At the time of the now famous Kitty Genovese case, bystanders—a crosssection of middle- and working-class individuals—failed to come to her aid despite cries of distress and her obvious plight. In this case empathy was apparently not activated. A more troubling trend is evident in contemporary culture, especially that of inner-city life as indexed by a case that made the news more recently. In Oakland, California, a woman by the name of Dione Wells was fleeing an attacker who had beaten and stabbed her. She happened to pass a group of teenagers. Instead of observing impassively as did the bystanders in the Kitty Genovese case, these teens actively knocked her down and kicked and stabbed her, all the while yelling "kill her." Inner-city life has become solitary, nasty, brutish, and short. As the Miller and Sperry study indicated, anger and aggression may be adaptive under certain environmental conditions. But what does it do to the quality of human mercy and interpersonal kindness, either within families or in the larger social context? Unfortunately, the bulk of research this century on empathy has been on middle-class children from intact families. A different picture of empathy and its relation to anger and aggression might emerge from more representative research, and research that was oriented to an understanding of individual differences in the development of these emotional dispositions. At this point we turn more directly to a consideration of differential personality and the role of emotions in development, organization, continuity, and change.

Emotion and Personality Development

The previous two chapters show how intensively developmentalists have studied children's anger and empathy, especially over the past two decades. Oddly, however, though one comes away from these two literatures well informed about normative age-graded changes in these expression/feeling domains, there is a dissatisfying sense that the field knows less about how these behaviors and feelings relate to personality and differential development. Unlike the literature on attachment, which has capitalized on the coherency of Bowlby's theory for understanding personality difference, the field of emotions research still appears to be seeking an overarching theoretical framework that can accommodate not only the observations on anger and empathy, but other socioemotional behaviors as well. Do the principles of development and socialization discovered for the emotion of anger hold for sadness and shame as well, or do the latter emotions obey different principles? Parental use of physical punishment tends to heighten anger and aggressivity in children (Chapter 6); does it have a similar impact on other emotions? What is the socialization history of the individual who is depression-prone rather than anger-prone? How does empathy interact with depression and anger? How do the various emotions cohere within individual personalities to account for the remarkable diversity of human individuality? Does emotion consolidate in personality by early adulthood and remain essentially unchanged throughout the lifespan, or are there occasions for change and transformation? These are some of the questions that are addressed in the remaining chapters of this book.

In Chapters 8–12 we attempt to show how an organizational approach to the topic of socioemotional development can provide the kind of larger framework that is needed to accommodate the various and disparate facts that have accumulated in the research literature over the years. In Chapter 8 we present a historical backdrop to some of the more recent models of personality, as well as critically evaluate these models. In Chapters 9 and 10, we consider a discrete emotions, functionalist analysis of personality and its development, as first articulated in Malatesta and Wilson (1988) and elaborated in Malatesta (1990) and Magai and Hunziker (1993). We also show how attachment theory and emotions theory can be reconciled to one another. Chapters 9 and 10 are primarily concerned with the role of emotion in organizing and structuring personal experience and individual behavior and in the establishment of emotional traits and dispositions. In Chapter 11 we consider the forces that disrupt established personality patterns and propel change in personality organization. The Afterword offers some concluding comments and reflections.

8

The Role of Emotion in Personality

Organizational Models

An alternative to the single-emotion approach to personality is the "organizational" approach. Earlier in this volume we considered one organizational model of emotional development—that of attachment theory—but found that emotions per se did not figure prominently in the original theory. Psychoanalytic theory also constitutes an organizational approach, but only indirectly deals with emotions and tends to be centered on one broad emotion—anxiety—and its various derivatives. In Chapters 9 and 10 we consider a discrete emotions functionalist approach, which both addresses the full range of emotions and speaks to differential personality development and the emergence in personality of distinct organizations around particular emotions.

What all organizational models have in common is the assumption of a core structure or core dynamic that provides the coherence to behavior. The organizational structures in psychoanalytic theory are constructs such as the id, ego, and superego. The organizational forces in attachment theory are "internal working models." Beyond the developmental literature, organizational constructs live on in the form of personality "traits." In recent times trait theories of personality have gained the ascendancy within personality psychology. Another organizational model, that of affect theory (Tomkins, 1962, 1963, 1991, 1993), revolves around the concept of unique affective organizations that propel and characterize individual personality.

219

PERSONALITY THEORY: PAST AND PRESENT

Concepts of personality date back to the early Greeks. A particularly viable and long-enduring theory of personality is the notion of traits. Traits were seen as being unique, enduring dispositions that both characterized individuals and predisposed them to behave in certain predictable ways. In the following discussion we trace the historic origins of trait theory. We then consider the contributions of Gordon Allport and the more recent taxonomic approach of present investigators, and finally consider the view from discrete emotions theory, with particular attention to the affect theory of Silvan Tomkins.

Trait theories of personality have an ancient heritage and have had a strong representation within the field of personality psychology. In the earliest days of the field, trait ideas were subsumed within the context of character or temperament theories of personality. The early Greeks referred to types of men that were characterized by more or less of the four bodily humors (phlegm, yellow bile, blood, black bile) as phlegmatic (slow, apathetic), choleric (irritable), sanguine (energetic, happy), and melancholic (depressive). Later on Von Haller (the physiologist), Cabanis (an early physiological psychologist), and Kant (the philosopher) suggested temperament versions of personality based on the four humors of the Greeks. In France a number of authors were also assembling lists of character types. Ribot (1903), for example, discerned three main types—sensitive, active, and apathetic—and then went on to describe a plethora of "species" and "varieties" subsumed within the three more basic "genera." The theory did not have much of an impact on the field, possibly because it was long on taxonomy and short on dynamics. Further taxonomies were generated by other psychologists with about the same degree of success.

A more interesting treatment, and a forerunner of contemporary emotions theories, is found in a work by A. F. Shand (1914) entitled *The Foundations of Character.* Shand faulted his contemporaries for their taxonomic approaches:

> such lists of qualities do not tell us anything of their inner connection, and to what limitations they are subject, and what are the chief systems of the mind which elicit, develop, and organize them, whilst allowing other qualities to perish. (p. 26)

In contrast to other writers of the time, Shand proposed a theory of personality that tied character types to the properties of, and development of, the affect system. As such he considered the primary emotions as the root forces of character.

In Shand's system, emotions were differentiated from emotional systems. The latter contained the "primitive" instincts and other tendencies associated with particular emotions, whereas emotions per se involved perception and apprehension and thus were more psychological in nature. Shand spelled out the instinctive tendencies associated with each emotion, certain laws of development, and their nature and function. He stipulated the range of events that could elicit a particular emotion and maintained that these kinds of experiences could give rise to typical characters.

Shand viewed temperament or character as the sum of the innate tempers of a person's different emotions. Each emotion was linked with different innate tempers that could be differentially expressed in different individuals. Shand also maintained that different emotions were associated with different activities or "conduct." Because emotions were linked to certain kinds of instinctual activities, knowing the basic emotion in the character of an individual should enable one to predict behavior. For example, the person whose mood/temper was of repugnance would be inclined to "detect the faults of its objects" and find "satisfaction in the criticism of human nature." Shand (1914) also found that emotional dispositions influenced information processing. For example, when a person was in an irritable mood, he or she would be likely to

> get angry on the smallest pretexts, and to find justifications for our anger on all sides. Our sensibility to anger is increased both in range and in delicacy. Things and persons seem contrary. We are ready to blame them and to exaggerate their defects. (p. 151)

Shand was less successful in delineating the origins of emotional dispositions, although he ascribed importance to constitutional differences and habit formation. His treatment of this topic was more superficial and somewhat obscure.

It should be obvious from the above that Shand was influenced by the Darwinian theory of evolution and by American functionalism. His theory was complex and quite advanced for the time. It deserves credit for attempting to move beyond the mere classification of character types to that of explanation and prediction. However, in the decade that Shand was writing, Watson was preparing the groundwork for the subsequent behavioristic revolution, and functionalism was rapidly eclipsed (Beilin, 1983).

Before the behaviorist revolution had gotten very far, however, Gordon Allport, who had been influenced by European philosophy and psychology, began to formulate his ideas about individual personality. His work, in turn, was influenced by the German structuralists. Work in that vein includes Kretschmer's *Koerperbau und Charakter: Untersuchungen zum Konstitutionsproblem und zur Lehre von den Temperamenten*, Rorschach's *Psychodiagnostik*, Spranger's *Lebensformen*, Jasper's *Psychologie der Weltanschauungen*, Mueller-Freienfels' *Persoenlichkeit und Weltanschauung*, and Jung's "psychological types." Walther Jaensch's (1926) *Grundzuege einer Physiologie und Klinik der psychophysischen Persoenlichkeit* is illustrative of the approach taken by the early German structuralists. Jaensch discerned two basic character types in children—T-type and B-type— on the basis of galvanic and mechanical irritability in sensory and motor tasks, as well as by performance on eidetic (optical) phenomena. T-types were reserved, morose, and serious, whereas B-types were lively, good-natured, and emotional. Prototypes of T-type and B-type personalities were said to be Johannes Mueller, the famous physiologist, and Goethe, respectively. The author pointed out that Mueller's face was austere and serious. Goethe's face, by contrast, reflected his spirited personality and sociability. The focus on the face as an expression or mirror of character was well represented in the research of the time. However, some of the scholarly work of German *Ausdruckspsychologie* (expression psychology) sadly was coopted by Hitler's regime for its own ideological purposes and led scholars to temporarily abandon this vein of research.

In England, the German émigré, Hans Eysenck began to develop his own structural model of personality founded on two main dimensions: extroversion/introversion, and neuroticism. These dimensions not only lent themselves to personality types but defined dimensions of personality or traits.

In American psychology, the name most closely associated with the concept of traits is that of Gordon Allport. His long, productive career and influential theory of personality was deeply affected by American functionalism and German structuralism. One example of the joint influence of both strands of research is reflected in his work on expressive behavior. It was Darwin who originally suggested that a lifetime of expressive behavior could etch telling lines on a person's face. German expression psychology pursued the thesis that personality conveyed itself in expressive behavior, most notably in the face, but also in voice and in movement. After his return to the States, following study in Germany and England, Allport conducted his own series of investigations on expressive behavior. He found that expressive behavior was an integral component of personality, and in 1933 he and Vernon published an important volume, *Studies in Expressive Movement.* We turn now to a more complete introduction to Allport's life, his times, and his work.

MODERN TRAIT THEORIES OF PERSONALITY

Gordon Allport (1897–1967)

Gordon Allport is considered the founder of American personality psychology; he is perhaps most well known for his insistence that psychology focus on that which is unique in human personality versus that which is general. In their biography of Allport, Atwood and Tomkins (1976) suggest that the task of individuation was particularly salient and difficult for him. Although Allport grew up in a relatively affluent family, his youth was stressed by a certain degree of social isolation. He was the youngest of four children and there was a significant age discrepancy between himself and his next older brother; he was also somewhat socially awkward, noting in his autobiography (Allport, 1968), "I never fitted the general boy assembly." On top of this, he was faced with the problem of finding how to distinguish himself in a family of singularly accomplished individuals. Allport's father was a physician, a hospital administrator, and a pharmaceutical entrepreneur. His three elder brothers all achieved professional distinction.

A large part of Gordon's early development took place in the shadow of his brother Floyd, who grew up to become a well-known social psychologist. Like Floyd, Gordon attended Harvard for his undergraduate degree; Floyd even taught the younger Gordon experimental psychology in his role as teaching assistant to Herbert Langfeld. Again, like Floyd, he took his Ph.D. at Harvard, and both became academic psychologists. After Gordon received his A.B. degree in economics and philosophy he spent a year in Istanbul teaching sociology and English. He returned to the States to take up doctoral studies, which he completed in 2 years. The subject matter of his thesis was unique for his time and was regarded by the august Titchener as unbefitting a Harvard student. The thesis, entitled "An Experimental Study of the Traits of Personality: With Special Reference to the Problem of Social Diagnosis," represented the first American dissertation written explicitly on the issue of the component traits of personality. Allport also received a travel award from Harvard and spent two intellectually formative years studying in Berlin, Hamburg, and Cambridge. His subsequent work clearly shows the influence of German structural psychology and the various movements that reflected the *Strukturbegriff* such as *Gestalt*, Stern's personalistic psychology, Krueger's complex qualities, and the school of *Verstehen*. He was also influenced by William McDougall from England, in his emphasis on motivational variables and in the acceptance of the biological basis of some aspects of behavior. He was also much taken with the work of William James, especially his humanistic orientation and concerns about the ability of psychological methods to capture the essence of humanity in a veridical way.

Allport returned to teach at Harvard for a short time, then went to Dartmouth, and finally returned to Harvard in 1930 to teach in the Department of Social Ethics. He was to remain at Harvard until his death in 1967.

Early in his professional career, Allport moved beyond Floyd's shadow as he began to stake out the territory of personality. Prior to this time, personality issues were subsumed within the general branch of social psychology, at least in America. In his writings, Allport stressed the importance of the unique qualities within the individual, taking a lead from the German philosopher, Windelband, who had made a distinction between nomothetic (generalizing) and idiographic (particularizing) approaches in the sciences. Having studied in Germany after his degree, Allport was much taken by Stern's personalistic psychology (*Ueber Psychologie der individuellen Differenzen, Zur Psychologie der Aussage, Die differentielle Psychologie, Studien zur Personwissenschaft*, and *General Psychology from the Personalitistic Standpoint*), with its idea of the unique configuration of personality, the centrality of personhood (*"keine Gestalten ohne Gestalter"*), and the importance of feeling in terms of the salience of Gestalten. The dimensions of feeling that personalistic psychology focused on "are exceedingly numerous, and more distinctions are turned up than other schools of psychology ever dreamed of. Wundt's tridimensional framework is made to look like a bony scarecrow" (Allport, 1968, p. 288). Allport was also influenced by the German *Charakter* approach to personality, for example, as personified by the work of Eduard Spranger. In his work *Lebensformen (Types of Men)* (1928), Spranger described six dimensions of value (ways of looking at life) in personality corresponding to separate and distinct ideal types: the theoretic, economic, esthetic, social, political, and religious. Regarding these dimensions as traits, Allport proceeded to examine whether they could be tested and validated, and he answered in the affirmative (Allport, 1966; Allport & Vernon, 1931).

Allport also specialized in developing a psychology of personality that applied to normal rather than disturbed individuals. He furthermore objected to the psychoanalytic idea that human behavior was almost entirely driven by unconscious needs and past experiences. Instead, Allport championed the view that a person's motives could be assessed by asking individuals directly what their goals were, rather than by resorting to projective media. He believed that behavior is generally under the control of largely conscious motives and that the individual is a valuable source of information regarding his or her own motives and behaviors. In his autobiography, Allport (1967) tells the story of his galvanizing first and only encounter with Freud. Having made an excursion to Vienna when traveling on the continent, he decided to call on Freud. On actually meeting him, in order to overcome an initial period of awkwardness, Allport made small talk about a young boy who was concerned with cleanliness and his obsessive mother, whom he had encountered on the train coming to Vienna. To Allport's consternation, Freud proceeded to interpret the anecdote as Allport's disguise for an expression of his own feelings—"And was that little boy you?" Allport was aghast; this was taking the idea of unconscious motivation too far.

Allport received various honors during his professional life, including the presidency of APA. His most well-known works include: *Personality: A Psychological Interpretation* (1937), *The Nature of Prejudice* (1954), *Becoming: Basic Considerations for a Psychology of Personality* (1955), and *Pattern and Growth in Personality* (1961).

Allport's Contribution to Trait Theory

Allport began his career, and continued throughout, trying to educate his colleagues about the centrality of traits in the organization of personality. His doctoral dissertation was on the topic of traits and his first professional paper, offered at the IX International Congress in 1929, was entitled "What Is a Trait of Personality?" He took up the theme again 36 years later in his Distinguished Scientific Contribution Award lecture, entitled "Traits Revisited," at the 1965 APA convention. In his various writings Allport emphasized the diversity and uniqueness of individual personality. Allport and Odbert (1936) calculated that there were nearly 18,000 words denoting personality traits in the English language. If one eliminated clearly evaluative terms like "adorable," as well as references to transient or temporary states of mood or activity, the number of relatively stable traits could be reduced to 4,000 or 5,000 traits. Such is science that in the several decades from the birth of personality psychology—usually designated as 1937, when Allport published *Personality: A Psychological Interpretation*—the concept of personality was heralded, challenged, declared dead, and finally resurrected. In transit it lost some 4,000 descriptors, being reduced from Allport's 4,000–5,000 to the current "robust five" of the five-factor model of personality (McCrae & Costa, 1985). Nevertheless, personality theory is once again a thriving enterprise. In a recent issue of the *American Psychologist*, Lewis Goldberg (1993) reflects that "the past decade has witnessed an electrifying burst of interest in the most fundamental problem of the field—the search for a scientifically compelling taxonomy of personality traits" (p. 26). Notably, however, none of this research is developmental, nor do questions concerning the origin or ontogenesis of personality traits seem to occur to personality researchers, although some writers believe that traits spring from original temperamental dispositions.

For its own part, developmental theory has only had an occasional flirtation with the notion of personality traits. Watson alluded to the formation of enduring "habits" based on emotional conditioning, but did not succeed in elaborating this beginning into a full-fledged theory of personality development. Research on "temperament traits" has seen sporadic treatment in the developmental literature (Bates, 1987; Thomas, Chess, & Birch 1968) but the bulk of work has been empirically rather than theoretically grounded. There have also been strands of research on isolated traits such as "dependency" (Sears et al., 1957), "ego resilience" (Block & Block, 1980), and "cognitive styles (Kogan, 1976), but these are research foci rather than trait theories of personality development. In point of fact, there currently are no trait theories of children's personality development emanating from either the personality or developmental literature. Later on, in Chapters 9 and 10, we consider a trait theory based on emotional organizations. Before we do so, however, it will be important to examine how the notion of trait has been treated in the adult personality literature.

The Five-Factor Model of Personality

Theorists and researchers within the trait tradition have argued about the number of basic traits inherent in human personality. For example, Eysenck (1947) asserts that there are only three major dimensions—extraversion, neuroticism, and psychoticism. Cattell (1947, 1957) reduced a compendium of 18,000 traits down to 16, and these traits were subsequently represented in the Sixteen Personality Factor Questionnaire (16PF; Cattell, Eber, & Tatsuoka, 1970). Most recently, a five-factor model of personality has been hailed as one of the most important theories of personality to emerge in recent times. The first evidence of a five-factor model of personality came from Fiske (1949) and the subsequent work of Norman (1963). The suggestion that there are five major "axes of personality" has since been replicated in a large number of studies (Costa & McCrae, 1980; Digman & Takemoto-Chock, 1981; Digman & Inouye, 1986; McCrae & Costa, 1985; Norman, 1963; Tupes & Christal, 1961). What these studies found is that factor analyses of personality test items tend to produce five-factor solutions in which certain types of items reliably cluster together; moreover, this pattern obtains across a variety of personality tests, item pools, and subject populations. Across studies, the five factors tend to load on the same clusters of items; the labels applied to the individual factors are also similar. For example, Norman (1963) originally identified the factors as Surgency (talkative, sociable versus reclusive, adventurous), Agreeableness (good-natured versus irritable, mild and cooperative versus negativistic, not jealous versus jealous), Conscientiousness (responsible, persevering, fully scrupulous), Emotional Stability (calm versus anxious, composed versus excitable, not hypochondriacal, and poised versus nervous, tense), and Culture (imaginative, artistically sensitive, intellectual, polished). Costa and McCrae have labeled the results of similar factor yields as Extroversion, Agreeableness, Conscientiousness, Neuroticism, and Openness to Experience. Digman and Takemoto-Chock (1981) found similar factors which they called Introversion-Extraversion, Friendly Compliance versus Hostile Noncompliance, Will to Achieve, Ego Strength versus Emotional Disorganization, and Intellect. Subsequently, Digman and Inouye (1986) proposed that the fourth factor be labeled Anxiety since the factor has high loadings on such items as nervous, fearful, concerned, and tense.

At the empirical level, there appears to be good support for the argument that there are basically five major dimensions of personality. In reviewing these various factor-analytic studies of personality, one is struck by the similarity and convergence of factors and the domains that they tap. However, as Digman and Inouye (1986) wryly note, the advent of computers and computer programs has turned the task of factoring large correlation matrices into child's play, but there "is still no program that will tell us what the factors mean. . ." (p. 120). The point is well taken. In multivariate research, interpretation is best guided by theory. But trait-analytic work is typically empirical and tends to be devoid of a theoretical framework. Indeed, the current literature has been more successful in generating lists of traits than in identifying a theoretical basis for the tendency of personality scales to have items that cluster together in certain ways. There are a few exceptions to this general observation. Eysenck (1967; Eysenck & Eysenck, 1985) has proposed a biologically based explanation for his three factor theory. Hogan (1983) has attempted to relate the five factors that have emerged in recent research to a sociobiological explanation for individual differences. There is obviously room for further theoretical analyses.

The alternative framework we would like to suggest places emotions at the core of the analysis. This framework is further supported by our analysis of how items dealing with the emotions load within the "big five" of the five-factor model. Contemporary emotions theory has stressed that there are a limited number of primary or basic emotions and that they each have unique properties. Some emotions theories, most notably those of Tomkins, Izard, and our own (elaborated in Chapters 9 and 10), suggest that emotions can become structuralized in the personality in the form of personality traits. Izard has developed a emotion-trait scale to measure such personality dispositions—the Discrete Emotions Scale, or DES (Izard, 1972). The separate emotions and individual scales on the DES are as follows: Interest, Joy, Surprise, Anger, Sadness, Guilt, Shame/Shyness, Fear, Disgust, and Contempt. In theory, one's personality can become structured around any one of these emotions or around a particular pattern of emotions.

Although not all of Izard's (1977) 10 fundamental emotions are represented in the item pools of the tests that have made up the substrate of the factor analytic studies, those emotions that are well-represented tend to load in different factors. Factor 1, for example (Surgency, Extroversion), loads on items that can be construed as indexing general *happiness* and ebullience. Factor 2 (Agreeableness, Friendly Compliance versus Hostile Noncompliance) represents items that can be seen as biased toward the *hostile* triad of emotions (Izard, 1972)—anger, contempt, and disgust. Factor 3 (Conscientiousness) may relate to guilt, or avoidance of guilt, or to the defensive avoidance of other emotions. Factor 4 (Neuroticism, Anxiety), as already mentioned, loads on *fear*: fearfulness, nervousness, and tension. Factor 5 (Culture, Intelligence, Inquiring Intellect), to the extent that it taps dimensions of imaginativeness, creativity, and inquiring intellect, seems to pick up items that evaluate an individual's general *interest* and involvement in the world. To the extent that a low score on Factor 1 implies the converse of happiness, that is, unhappiness, this factor may also detect personalities of a *sad* or depressive nature. The same factor may also subsume *shame/shyness*, since these tendencies are likely features of the introversion pole of the extroversion scale. Thus, four factors of the five-factor model are capable of identifying an array of personality types based on emotion traits.

Interestingly, Izard's own factor-analytic study of emotions using the DES yielded a pattern of results validating the uniqueness of the different emotions and their linkages to specific personality organizations (Izard, 1972). A more recent study by Izard and colleagues (Izard, Libero, Putnam, & Haynes, 1993) examined the pattern of correlation between the discrete emotions identified in the DES and three other personality tests. Although they did not correlate DES items with the items of the Neuroticism–Extroversion–Openness (NEO) scale of Costa and McCrae—which taps the five dimensions of personality of the five-factor model—they found, as predicted, that the positive emotions of joy and interest were positively correlated with Eysenck's Extroversion Scale, and that all the negative emotions were positively correlated with the Neuroticism Scale. Other discrete emotions were positively correlated with individual dimensions of Jackson's Personality Research form, and Zuckerman's Sensation Seeking Scale. Some of the personality dimensions did not correlate with discrete emotions traits; Izard et al. (1993) suggest that this is as expected, since some traits may reflect defensive coping strategies aimed at avoiding unpleasant affect.

Some emotion/personality types may be more prevalent than others. Clinical psychology has long recognized traits that are organized around anger, fear, and sadness. Indeed, the most ubiquitous types of personality scales measuring emotional dimensions in personality tend to be centered on hostility (e.g., the Cook Medley Hostility Scale, the Framingham Scale, the Anger-In/Anger-Out Scale), anxiety (the Taylor Manifest Anxiety Scale; the State–Trait Axiety Inventory), and sadness-depression (Beck Depression Inventory, the Hamilton Scale, the Zung Depression Inventory). Positive emotions such as happiness and interest, in contrast, are obviously of less clinical significance, and thus are not well represented in diagnostic inventories. However, when it comes to ordinary personality, all of the primary emotions, including joy and interest, are likely to be incorporated in some way. For example, both joy and interest figure prominently in the constellations that describe Factor 1 and Factor 5 of Norman's (1963) five factors.

One of the biggest shortcomings of the five-factor model is that it is more a taxonomy of personality than a theory. While it is interesting and remarkable that the five factors identified by Norman and others are found repeatedly in factor-analytic studies of the items from personality scales, such replicability may have more to do with the technique of factor analysis than with human personality.

Certainly there has been little attempt to explain why human personality should be organized according to five dimensions, and why—the functionalist question—around these particular dimensions? What is missing from these inductive approaches to personality is a guiding theoretical system—one that is capable of explaining the how, why, and wherefore of human personality. A theory is needed that not only describes individual differences as measured by personality inventories, but can relate character "structure" to the observables of behavior, and can link structures with developmental history. Such an enterprise clearly requires a theory of human development and of human motivation. Theoretical analyses are patently missing from research and writing concerning the five-factor model of personality.

If, as we contend, the five dimensions of personality rendered by factor-analytic studies are more legitimately seen as being related to emotion traits, we would be well on our way to a motivationally based account of human personality (an account that is more fully developed in Chapters 9 and 10). Such a thesis is not new. Almost all contemporary emotions theorists maintain that repetitive emotional experiences generate emotional traits or biases. The most well-articulated theory is found in Silvan Tomkins's four-volume work, *Affect, Imagery, Consciousness* (1962, 1963, 1991, 1993). In the following section, we present a biographical sketch of Tomkins and then present the basic tenets of his theory.

SILVAN TOMKINS AND AFFECT THEORY

Biography of Tomkins (1911–1991)

Silvan Tomkins was the firstborn child of a family of Lithuanian descent, who grew up in Philadelphia. His father and grandfather had been dentists, and Silvan's mother hoped that her son would also take up dentistry as a profession. However, this was not to be his fate, for Silvan found himself attracted to the study of play writing, to philosophy, and eventually to psychology.

Tomkins's lifelong quest was nothing less than the pursuit of "a psychology of the human being." In the course of this venture, and throughout his life, he struggled to bring affect and cognition together for the field of psychology and, one suspects, for himself. Tomkins had grown up in a family that placed an extraordinary emphasis on intellectual matters. Silvan, as a young boy, was early identified by his family as being gifted and he was often referred to as "the genius." He suffered from what was apparently a delicate physical constitution, which resulted in heightened maternal concern about the state of his physical well-being (Tomkins, 1987). In combination, his family's emphasis on mind and corporeal being may have been a developmentally formative experience foreshadowing Tomkins's keen interest in emotion later in adult life. Once, in another context (a discussion of how philosophers and biologists have been drawn to the emotions), he commented, "A deep concern with either mind or body or both appears historically to lead to concern with affect" (Tomkins, 1981, p. 310). The dualism implied by the mind/body split in the organization of experience (and possibly the mind–emotions split) may indeed have been predisposing for a dualistic view of the organization of experience. Tomkins saw the world as consisting of what he called "polarities" and developed a scale that reflected this version of the world (the Tomkins Polarities Scale). In his writings he distinguished between negative emotions and positive emotions, between masculine and feminine emotions, between humanistic versus normative values, and, perhaps most importantly of all, between affect and cognition.

With respect to the latter, Tomkins devoted his life to placing the emotions in proper perspective with respect to the other human faculties. In the Hullian and Freudian psychologies of the day, the human organism was a drive-ridden creature in original development; ideally, and with maturation, cognition would come to prevail. Tomkins scorned this pallid version of the human—"sicklied over with the pale cast of thought." In his own view, being fully human called for a reinstatement of emotion. He believed that the reunion of affect and cognition would be salutary since, in his own words, "out of the marriage of reason with affect comes clarity with passion."

Tomkins attended the University of Pennsylvania where he received his bachelor's degree, an M.A. in psychology, and a Ph.D. in philosophy. He worked as a research assistant at the Harvard Psychological Clinic from 1936 to 1943, where he came into contact with and was influenced by Henry Murray. He held various teaching and research appointments at Michigan State University, Harvard, Princeton, the Graduate Center of the City University of New York, the University of Pennsylvania, and Rutgers University.

He helped develop (along with his wife, Elizabeth J. Tomkins) the scoring system for the TAT, and was the author of affect theory, a theory of human motivation, and script theory, which explains how emotions shape personality and culture. He received APA's Clinical Division Distinguished Contribution Award in 1971, a Career Investigatory Award from NIH in the late 1960s, and the Bruno Klopfer Distinguished Contribution Award of the Society for Personality Assessment in 1975.

What follows is a brief introduction to his affect theory and script theory, and admittedly a vast simplification of the original work. We take the risk of oversimplifying Tomkins's complex formulations at the service of achieving the more important goal of communicating the most seminal ideas that emerge from what amounts to a body of very acute observation and theory. In the account of his theory, Tomkins was wont to generate original linguistic constructions—new words and phrases and new meanings for common expressions. This was probably his way of startling readers and forcing them to abandon their conventional ways of thinking about affect. In any case, in the present treatment we use some of his own vocabulary but provide our own understandings of what he meant.

Affect Theory: A Theory of Human Motivation

During the 1950s, general systems theory had emerged as an interesting heuristic for psychology. We have already discussed how it affected the writings of John Bowlby. Tomkins also was taken by certain aspects of systems theory, as well as by cybernetic science, and this influenced the way in which he began to think about the human organism and the organization of mental faculties. Tomkins began to consider emotions as one of several interacting intraorganism subsystems. His model of the nervous system was an assembly model in which different systems and various mechanisms are differentially engaged and combined. These subsystems included the motor, the cognitive, the drive, and the emotions systems, among others. In his model, information from these systems converge on a "central assembly," which is an executive mechanism. The power of the affect system resides in its flexibility. It can be called up by central or peripheral sources (direct emotional stimuli, or memories) and be coassembled by the central assembly with any other subsystem to boost the power of these systems. It can function independently, dependently, and interdependently. For example, emotions can control cognitions or be controlled by them or be integrally interconnected with them. "This permits one person to become truly more 'cognitive' and another to be much more 'affective' via the differential affective magnification of other mechanisms, including affect magnifying itself" (Tomkins, 1991, p. 72).

The notion that affect, cognition, and drives are separate systems was a radical idea for psychology (though early Greek philosophers recognized such a distinction). Before Tomkins, affects were typically regarded as synonymous with, or derivatives of, drives. In one of his more startling propositions, and contrary to Western philosophic tradition, Tomkins maintained that emotions played a more powerful role in human motivation than biological drives such as hunger, thirst, and sex.

> Contrary to Freud, I do not view human beings as the battleground for their imperious drives, which urge them on blindly to pleasure and violence, to be contained only by a repressive society and its representations within—the ego and the superego. Rather, I see affect or feeling as *the primary innate biological motivating mechanism*, more urgent than drive deprivation and pleasure, and more urgent even than physical pain. Without its amplification, nothing else matters, and with its amplification anything can matter. (Tomkins, 1987, p. 137)

In this framework, emotions became the basic "wants" and "don't wants" of the human condition—the real factors in motivation, drives aside. In the short history that is psychology, drives have frequently enjoyed a special status. Freud, Hull, Mowrer, and others made them central constructs in their theories of motivation since drive-related behavior appeared "urgent." However, according to Tomkins, drives gain the quality of urgency only by virtue of their coassembly with the affective system. Drives are merely directional vectors, steering us to engage in this or that activity in the service of individual and species survival. However, it is affect that is the real motivating or propelling factor in behavior; it supplies the "oomph" by amplifying drive. Tomkins illustrated the difference between drives and affects using two classic drives: respiration and sex. Breathing is a drive in that it is crucial for survival. The condition of anoxia has life-imperiling consequences, but it does not in itself motivate. The manner in which one responds to lack of oxygen will depend on which of several affects has been activated. One may become anoxic, for example, under conditions of being suffocated by someone intending homicide—the potential victim will struggle fiercely in order to recover his ability to breathe. But, as Tomkins reminds us, World War II pilots who lost oxygen gradually at high altitudes simply slowly lost consciousness and went to their deaths with smiles on their faces. Thus, the drive of respiration coassembled with fear creates a vastly different motivational product than respiration coassembled with pleasant light-headed sensations. Tomkins offers another example involving the sexual drive. Although this is a drive that seems quite urgent, at least to anyone who has ever been an adolescent in the back seat of a Chevy van, the motivating quality inheres in the affect that accompanies the sex drive, not in the drive itself. Sexual desire without excitement "is a limp penis."

Since the distinction between drives and affects had often been blurred by earlier writers, Tomkins took special pains to differentiate between the two. In particular, he spelled out a number of characteristics that differentiate them. Drives, unlike emotions, have a cyclic character; they are time-locked. We have to eat, drink, breathe, urinate, defecate, and sleep periodically. (Sex and attachment are drivelike behaviors that do not require such time-locked periodic satisfaction, though they have most of the other features of drives.) Drives must also be satisfied in specific ways and they are noninterchangeable. For example, the hunger drive is not satisfied by urinating or sleeping, but by consummatory behavior. There is also a stereotypical or universal quality to drives. People eat in the same way all over the world. The sequence of behaviors is universal—one puts food in the mouth, masticates, and swallows. In contrast to drives, emotions can occur at any time, there is flexibility in what elicits them, and they can be expressed in any number of ways.

Tomkins distinguished nine fundamental emotions, each with its own specific motivating properties and functions. Joy is intrinsic to the formation of social bonds. Interest/excitement is fundamental to orientation, attention, arousal, and exploration; it readily attaches to a variety of objects and then draws further engagement with those objects. Surprise is a general interrupter of ongoing activity and has a "channel-clearing" function; it allows us to reorient and thus change attentional investments. Distress/anguish is an emotion that is most closely associated with crying; it lets the self and others know that all is not well and motivates self and other to do something about it. Fear motivates fight or flight in dealing with an imminent danger. Anger is focused on the removal of barriers to goals. Shame, contempt, and disgust are affect auxiliaries. Disgust and contempt are innate defensive responses auxiliary to the hunger, thirst, and oxygen drives. Their function is to repel or eject things that have a noxious quality. Shame is auxiliary to interest and enjoyment. It is recruited only after interest or enjoyment has been activated, and serves to inhibit these emotions.

Each of the fundamental emotions is elicited by specific innate activators; however, they are also very conditionable, which means that they can be activated by any number of previously neutral objects or situations. For example, interest is innately activated by novelty. However, interest as an activator of sustained attention and investment can attach to nearly any object under the sun, as in Allport's functionally autonomous goals.

Basic Human Goals

In addition to the specific motivations of specific emotions, Tomkins perceived that there were certain more overarching goals or "blueprints" for human behavior. According to Tomkins, humans are ruled by the "general images" of (1) maximizing positive affect, (2) minimizing negative affect, (3) keeping affect inhibition to a minimum, and (4) maximizing the power to achieve the foregoing goals (i.e., affective balance). In this formulation, Tomkins is going beyond the psychoanalytic formulation that man is ruled by only two motives—the avoidance of pain and the pursuit of pleasure. What Tomkins means by the third principle is that humans *need to feel*, to experience and express their feeling, and that the suppression of emotion is in itself punishing or unpleasant. Emotion that is blocked continues to press for release and may become transmuted by lack of release. Humans *like to feel*—life without affect would be incalculably boring. Affect makes us feel alive and makes us *care* about how we are living. The fourth goal is about having a sense of balance and efficacy with respect to emotion regulation. We want to feel that we have the power to avoid negative affect, to achieve positive affect, and to live fully and intensely as emotional beings. The idea that we are most human when we are fully emotional is a radical idea for psychology, since Western philosophical, religious, and literary tradition, not to mention modern psychology, has been heavily invested in the ideology that affect is primitive and disorganizing. Tomkins instead emphasized the organizing, adaptive qualities of emotion, and the unique emotion/cognitive interface that makes us human and enriches our experiential lives.

Role of the Face

Tomkins identified 13 components of the total affect system (Tomkins, 1962), but placed special emphasis on the face as the primary site of the affective response. Tomkins regarded the face as "the organ of affect," much as the lungs are the organ of breathing.

The centrality of the face first became apparent to Tomkins while caring for his newborn son during a sabbatical year. Watching his infant cry, he was struck by the massiveness of the response, which he labeled distress (rather than anxiety, as per Freud). This was not just an "expression" of affect, but the central phenomenon. Here Tomkins would depart from Darwin's original formulations. Darwin had viewed facial expression as a reflection of emotion going on somewhere else and which got forwarded as a communication to the social surround. Instead, Tomkins viewed the activity of the face (and to a lesser extent, that of the voice) as the primary source of subjective affective experience. At first he thought that the sensory experience of differential affect was based on the contraction of muscles associated with the different expressions, but more recently (Tomkins, 1991) he has stressed that it is feedback from the skin of the face and its specific receptor and differential blood flow that is the locus of emotion. Thus, in this system, emotion is "skin deep."

Personality

In Tomkins's theory, personality is the net cumulation of "ideo-affective" structures. These are organizations of affect and cognition that sensitize the individual to process and interpret the world in particular ways and which determine strategies of affect regulation. These structural properties of the personality orient to the affective meaning of information and the informational content of affect in the social surround. In this system affects are always associated with ideas and ideas with affects, hence the hyphenated treatment of the term. The affect/cognitive coherences that constitute ideo-affective structures can undergo various kinds of development and transformation. Below, strong and weak affects, and strong and weak affect theories are described first. Developmental models of personality that feature various ideo-affective structures, as described in the second volume of *Affect, Imagery, Consciousness,* are then presented. (A much more elaborated theory of personality was published in 1987 and 1991, which Tomkins termed "script theory.")

Strong and Weak Affects. Strong affects involve intense feelings of long duration and are associated with a high "density" (saturation) of experience. Weak affects involve low-density organizations of feeling and are associated with experiences that generate little feeling and little thinking, or if the feeling and thought are intense, they are not of long duration. Whether positive or negative, "they must seize the individual's feelings and thoughts to the exclusion of almost all else" (Tomkins, 1965b, p. 273).

Strong and Weak Affect Theories. "Affect theories" are ideo-affective organizations that serve as filters and regulators of information and experience. They predispose us to perceive the world in certain emotionally tinged ways and to assimilate information to preexisting affect-laden schemata. Strong affect theories control a great deal of a person's day-to-day activities, whereas weak affect theories come into play only occasionally or only at weak levels. Strong and weak affect theories are largely the products of socialization, though constitutional factors may also play a role. Two examples of this principle, involving anger and shame, are given in Chapters 9 and 10.

Socialization of Emotion

Biology guarantees that the emotion system is prewired for function even before birth and that there is a set of innate activators of emotion as part of our biological heritage. Early in development the elicitors of emotion tend to be connected with the physical parameters of stimuli: their intensity, color, form, rise time, and so on. With development, other objects and events in the environment become capable of eliciting emotions. It is these learned elicitors, and the modification of innate emotional responses, that constitute the core of what gets transformed or socialized in development.

Tomkins distinguished between four kinds of emotional organizations or affect theories:

1. Monopolistic, in which a single emotion tends to dominate the affective life of the individual (as in the hostility-prone or chronically depressed individual).
2. Intrusion, in which a minor element in the general structure of personality intrudes and displaces a dominant affect under specific conditions (e.g., shame on an occasion when one's intelligence is impugned).
3. Competition, in which one emotion-based structural aspect of personality perpetually competes with others in the interpretation of information (as in the narcissistic personality, where contempt and shame often alternate).
4. Integration, in which no single affect theory is permitted to dominate the personality in a monopolistic way.

According to Tomkins, the most developmentally favorable outcome (involving the affectively balanced personality) results when affect socialization is "rewarding" rather than "punishing." Affect socialization is rewarding when a child's parent helps the child avoid negative affect situations, but does not teach the child to suppress negative affective experiences when they occur. In the latter case the parent helps attenuate negative affect by empathizing with the child's experience, and helps the child cope with the sources of negative affects so as to avoid their unnecessary provocation. Punitive socialization of affect is just that—unpleasant and punishing. This occurs when the caregiver amplifies negative affect rather than helps reduce it. For example, a parent may upbraid a child who has difficulty solving a homework problem, thereby adding more shame to the original humiliation. Such a parent also fails to help the child cope with her suffering and moreover may provide an ideology that teaches the child to be vigilant for occasions of negative affect and thus maximizes their occasion.

Personality organization is not impervious to change; it can undergo transformation over time. Tomkins has identified four temporal models that speak to the issue of continuity and discontinuity in affective organization over time. The first is called the *Snowball* model. In this model pivotal early experiences recur developmentally and contribute to emotional organizations that come to dominate the personality over time, even if they were not monopolistic in early life. This is essentially a continuity model. The *Iceberg* model is the analogue across time of the intrusion model. Here, the adult personality is vulnerable to intrusions from the past, but under specific, limited conditions; moreover, the intrusions tend to be alien to the present affective life of the adult (e.g., shame from an early childhood experience, say from a sexually exploitive and abusive relationship, may intrude in the life of the adult who is not particularly pervaded by shame as a characteristic of personality, but who may experience intense shame if an intimate relationship suddenly turns abusive). The *Co-extensive* model, which is the temporal analogue to the competition model, is a model of discontinuity and flux, in which two or more emotions compete for experience and produce temporal disequilibrium, as in the case of contempt ruling one set of experiences, alternating with a run of shame (see, e.g., Malatesta-Magai & Dorval, 1992). The temporal analogue to the integration model is the *Late Bloomer* model, where previously warring aspects of affect theories may be engaged to successful resolution and eventually achieve an integration (e.g., during the course of psychotherapy).

Script Theory

Script theory constitutes Tomkins's most mature version of a personality theory. *Scripts* in Tomkins's system are analogous to what others have called schemas except that Tomkins more than any other writer has emphasized the role that affects play in organized patterns of behavior. Scripts are composed of scenes. The scene is the basic element in life as it is lived and it is imbued with affect. Two of the earliest scenes, developmentally, are (1) birth and (2) the novel face of the caregiver, scenes which engender the most primitive scripts of fitful flailing in the case of the birth experience, and excitement-driven visual tracking in the case of the novel face.

Certain scenes occur with some degree of frequency and become more salient and dominating. Tomkins called this phenomenon *psychological magnification*; it involves the process of connecting one affect-laden scene with another. As similar scenes occur repeatedly and are concatenated with one another they become "magnified scenes," which are prominent features of personality. Scripts are sets of rules for ordering, interpreting, evaluating, predicting, and controlling scenes. They tend to be selective, incomplete, and, in varying degrees, accurate and inaccurate; that is, they are subject to various kinds of distortion. Because they are often inaccurate they are subject to disconfirmation and thus scripts are intrinsically capable of change.

Another feature of scripts is their modularity, which means that they are variously separable, combinable, recombinable, and decomposable. Different modules become coassembled over time and with development. As any particular modular component becomes magnified through the process of psychological magnification, it looms ever more important in personality, since it will tend to override weaker modules.

There are several major classes of scripts. One of the earliest sets of scripts, *nuclear scripts*, involves early scenes that are repetitive, affectively dense, and developmentally important. The scenes are typically organized around significant social objects and involve the individual's "most urgent and unsolved problems" (Carlson, 1981, p. 502) and as such are particularly important in understanding personality structure. These particular organizations, in turn, affect how the individual perceives and manages future scenes involving similar social objects. A more detailed description of nuclear scripts is found in Tomkins (1987), and Carlson (1981) provides an extended illustrative example.

Relation between Scripts and Affects

Toward the end of his life, Tomkins made what he felt was an important discovery about the relation between different kinds of scripts and different kinds of emotion organization. In an invited address at the annual meeting of the International Society for Research on Emotions, in June of 1990 entitled "Emotions and Reverse Archaeology," Tomkins told the audience,

> one day a light bulb went on in my head, that each of these [major kinds of] scripts, while very complex in affect structure and composition, nonetheless had a primary affect which matched extraordinarily well my understanding of the nature of each of the primary affects.

The mapping between scripts and affects is described below. Recall that scripts are sets of rules for ordering, interpreting, evaluating, predicting, and controlling scenes—that is, structures of personality that affect information processing and behavioral patterns and thus regulate ongoing affect.

Affluence scripts, which are basically aesthetic in nature and involve things of intrinsic value to the individual, are associated with the positive affects of joy and interest—beautiful scenes in nature, the infant's perception of the mother's face, and so on.

Damage repair scripts involve good scenes that have changed from affluence to damage but which can be repaired, and engender the affect of shame. In Tomkins theory, shame is automatically triggered when positive affect is interrupted, for example, when a child runs to greet what she thinks is her mother, only to find that it is a stranger. The abrupt cutoff of joy and interest prompts shame and a turning away. Since shame can only occur within the context of an established relationship—i.e., where a bond already exists—there is always the lingering hope that the bond can be repaired. Thus shame exists in relation to social bonds where the original investment is positive.

Limitation remediation scripts are those in which the individual confronts aspects of life that are less than optimal but that can and must be confronted, for example, ongoing pressures that must be endured and coped with, such as a less than challenging job, a stressful relationship with a spouse. etc. These kinds of scripts involve the affect of distress. They are situations of ongoing duress, which can potentially be ameliorated and improved.

Decontamination scripts involve scenes that have become tainted in some way, but which can be purified or decontaminated. The affect associated with decontamination scripts is disgust, and it involves rejection and repulsion.

Toxic and antitoxic scripts involve scenes of intolerable punishment that must be avoided, escaped, attenuated, or eliminated. They are scenes that humans find intolerable and engender feelings and defenses around the primary emotions of fear, rage, and contempt. Each involves affects that are sufficiently punishing that they cannot be endured (as can distress) for any great length of time.

The ramifications of the above may not be immediately obvious, but the theory suggests that an analysis of affect structure may provide one of the more illuminating approaches to understanding personality. It suggests that once one has identified an individual's salient emotion traits, one is a long way toward understanding the scripts that organize the individual's daily activities, as well as having some insight into the nature of original nuclear scripts. In a graduate seminar on human development led last year by the first author, after an introduction to the idea of discrete emotions but before affect theory was discussed, the class members were asked to record some of their earliest memories and, then, shifting to adulthood, to record the emotions that they experienced most frequently in their everyday lives. The first part of the exercise provided what we hoped would be "nuclear scripts"; the latter provided a window on affective organizations. When the class had completed the task the material was set aside for the time being and Tomkins's theory was introduced. After that, we returned to the personal material recorded by the students (the material was submitted without student names). We found that the most prevalent negative affective experiences of these students revolved around the affects of sadness/distress and guilt, and, more importantly, that the early memories almost all involved limitation remediation scripts of some sort or another. A relevant footnote is that in this small class of eight students, seven were aspiring clinical psychologists—whose professional lives would someday be devoted to repairing and limiting the distress of others. In the next two chapters we consider in greater detail how an analysis of affect structure may be applied to the task of understanding individual personality and the organization of behavior.

Summary and Evaluation of Tomkins's Theory

Tomkins's theory of the human is almost commensurate with the complexity of its subject. His theory comprises a comprehensive, creative, and penetrating account of human consciousness, affect, and behavior. However, because the theory is so detailed and complex, and the prose style so dense and idiosyncratic, the uninitiated reader can find the work quite daunting. This may explain why the theory has not found a wider readership, although it must also be admitted that during the time Tomkins was writing psychology was just emerging from an era that was particularly antagonistic to the emotions—behaviorism—and moving towards another that was also inhospitable—the so-called cognitive revolution. Affect was nowhere in sight in these agendas, and Tomkins's first two volumes languished in virtual obscurity save for the work of Izard (1971, 1977) and Ekman (1972, 1984). Given that Tomkins was especially sensitive to the world's regard of his intellectual products, he took the lack of receptivity to these volumes personally. In fact, the lack of attention to his theory following the publication of Volumes 1 and 2 was so distressing to Tomkins that he could not bring himself to complete the projected four-volume work until 30 years after the original publication. Fortunately, the climate of contemporary psychology is much less hostile to scholarship concerning the emotions. Indeed, the tide appears to have finally turned for Tomkins, as witnessed by increasing attention to his work in clinical psychology (Kaufman, 1989), sociology (Scheff, 1988), psychiatry (Nathanson, 1992), and developmental psychology (Magai & Hunziker, 1993; Malatesta, Culver, Tesman, & Shepard, 1989).

Influence on the Present Work

The above summary cannot hope to do justice to the theory in its enormous complexity, but it may serve as an introduction for those who would read further. Tomkins's work has been deeply influential in the work of the first author, and will be clearly in evidence in the elaboration of our discrete emotion, functionalist analysis of personality development, presented in the next two chapters. We are indebted to the genius of Tomkins's ideas, and to his spirit of perseverance in the face of early critical neglect.

The introduction to Tomkins's work serves as a bridge to the next chapter. From the foregoing we can extract an important principle that will be useful in organizing that chapter, namely, the notion of ideo-affective organizations—those dynamic structures of personality that are inherent in Tomkins's generic scripts. Ideo-affective organizations are equivalent to what Izard (1971, 1977) has called affective/cognitive structures, and what we term affect biases or emotion traits (Malatesta, 1990; Malatesta & Wilson, 1988). What we wish to do in the following chapters is show how these organizations play out in personality in an affect-specific, trait-specific way. To do this, we draw from the large volume of empirical work on the emotions that has proliferated over the past decade and a half, most of which has, hither-to-fore, not been subsumed within an overarching theory of personality or affect.

What is embedded in script theory, and what Tomkins saw so clearly, is that affective biases acquired in the course of development affect information processing and behavior in pervasive ways: in the quality of a person's perceptions, in their interpretations, judgments, attributional styles, in their decision-making, social preferences, and behavioral styles. In the following, we also go beyond Tomkins's tantalizing but limited description of social and developmental process, to the presentation of a theory of emotional development that subsumes more of the dynamic properties of the developmental process as we now understand them.

A Discrete Emotions, Functionalist Analysis of Personality Development

Part I: The Fundamentals

The model of personality development described in this chapter draws its theoretical inspirations from several of the sources mentioned earlier in this volume, attachment theory (Chapters 2 and 3), trait theory (Chapter 8), and affect theory (Chapter 8). Although each of these theories is seminal, each suffers certain ellipses—one because it emphasizes individual personality at the expense of the interpersonal, one because it concentrates on interpersonal process to the neglect of the individual, and one because it focuses on adults and does not consider early development and the origins of individual differences. To be specific, attachment theory is mainly an interpersonal theory; until fairly recently it focused almost exclusively on the dyad in early development and its sequelae in later intimate relationships. The individual is treated less adequately. By contrast, affect theory and trait theory focus almost exclusively on the individual, neglecting relationships, and both give fairly superficial accounts of early development.

With respect to affect theory, the first two volumes of Tomkins's opus were published before attachment theory had gained much attention (Tomkins, 1962, 1963), and thus he can be excused for failing to treat this issue. However, some 30 years later, by the time he had completed Volumes 3 and 4 (1991, 1993), there was still not a single word on attachment. To be sure, there is a chapter on the emotion of distress in Volume 2, and a lengthy discussion of the infant cry. However, consideration of the cry as a phenomenon critical to parent–infant bonding receives little play in his work. Moreover, although Tomkins talked about the centrality of nuclear scripts in Volume 3, little of his theoretical writing here or in the earlier volume was devoted to elaboration of critical relational events in infancy. This is because the purpose of his exposition on human crying and distress was to delineate certain affect principles rather than to explore the dynamics of social relationships. As such, he did not elaborate on the different types of cry and the development of individual differences in the propensity to express emotional upset.

Trait theory is also neglectful of developmental process, and in general fails to deal with the origins of individual differences. In the present chapter we elaborate on the promising construct of trait but go beyond the presently fashionable taxonomic approaches. Here we argue that a comprehensive theory of personality must solve the problem of motivation, map out the domains of influence, specify the occasions for the elicitation of the trait, and deal with person–situation interactions. Moreover, and perhaps most important, it must deal with ontogeny and engage the central issues of human development. It must specify the interpersonal origins of personality traits, account for individual differences, and address the issue of continuity and change over the life course. Here we consider a motivationally based account of human action and human development based on a discrete emotions, functionalist analysis of personality. Since we have introduced the term functionalism, let us pause to consider its meaning with respect to that of discrete emotions theory.

NEOFUNCTIONALISM AND DISCRETE EMOTIONS THEORY

As Beilin (1983) has pointed out, a new functionalism began to influence psychology in the 1970s, cutting across the various disciplines of linguistics, cognition, and emotion. In William James's time functionalism was used to describe a Darwinian or psychoevolutionary view that regarded mental events as adaptive acts that are meaningfully studied in their natural biological context. Today, it is the social context (as part of the larger biological context) that is critical for analysis of the development of language, thought, and emotion.

Theoretical models of emotion have themselves undergone considerable transformation. The dimensional models of emotion of the 1950s, which tended to focus on hedonic tone or level of activation, gave way to an assortment of typological, or "discrete emotions," models in the 1960s, including those of Ekman, Izard, Plutchik, and Tomkins. What all of these models had in common was the assumption that human emotions could be described in terms of a basic set of emotions, limited in number, but each with unique properties in terms of phenomenology, physiognomy, motivation, and neurophysiology. Each emotion could be seen as having a functional or adaptive property specific to the changing and ongoing demands of the environment. In Izard's (1971, 1977) theory, in particular, the ontogenesis of emotions was analyzed from the perspective of its relation to ongoing adaptation to the social surround.

In the present chapter we consider the ontogenesis of personality traits organized around the fundamental emotions in a manner that is theoretically consistent with Tomkins's affect theory and Izard's differential emotions theory, but in a fashion that details the importance of relationships in establishing the original core of affective organizations, and which is much more explicit about the relations between attachment propensities, affective organizations, psychological process, personality, and behavior.

AN AFFECTIVE ANALYSIS OF EARLY ATTACHMENT PATTERNS

Within the context of affect theory (Tomkins, 1962, 1963), attachment behavior qualifies as neither drive nor primary affect, and thus it appears to fall between the cracks, as do two other motivated behaviors discussed by Tomkins—those related to sex and pain. However, as in the case of the latter two phenomena, attachment behavior has qualities of both affect and drive, a point to which we return momentarily.

Within attachment theory, affective signals—smiles and cries—are attachment behaviors; they are part of an instinctual, biologically-based behavioral system. Infant attachment behaviors are preadapted evolutionary propensities designed to keep caregivers within close proximity. Reciprocity between the two partners' behaviors is preprogrammed in the human organism, and attachment develops in the context of the responsiveness of one partner to the signals of the other. The "purpose" is the child's survival. Affect per se, as in the case of "felt security," is incidental—a by-product of proximity-promoting tendencies.

In the case of affect theory, however, feelings and emotions (felt security or otherwise) are not epiphenomena; they are the main event (Tomkins, 1963). Recall that Tomkins distinguished between drives and affects; drives supply the information, that is, the kind of behavior required—breathing, eating, sleeping— but affect supplies the motivation; that is, it amplifies the drive. Thus, if we may bring interpretation to bear, attachment is a drive-like behavior in that it instigates a particular class of behaviors. Attachment behaviors are directional in nature and involve the business of getting attached, a source of protection and individual survival. But an infant devoid of emotion will not become attached. This is a defect that can be seen in autistic children. As infants, they may cry, cling, and track with the eyes, but their behaviors are muted and curiously vacant. Haviland (1976) describes an infant whose only developmental defect appeared to be her lack of affective tone; by 8 months of age the child, who was being cared for in a high school nursery, began to deteriorate. Unlike other children in the nursery, she was tended only for basic needs and was otherwise neglected. A consultant noted that she failed to engage her caregivers and sustain their attention because she did not reward them with looks and smiles and excitement. Happily, an intervention program designed to deliberately shape up more affective behavior on the part of the infant was effective. The little girl gained in alertness and responsivity, and finally started to look and act more like other children her age. Haviland speculates that they had intervened in the life of a child who might have become autistic, or at the least was on her way to being severely developmentally compromised.

In most infant–caregiver relationships, affect serves to sustain contact and nurture the development of the child. It is fundamental to the attachment process in that it draws the caregiver into sustained engagement. Moreover, the particular character of the interaction will produce particular kinds of coping behaviors and emotions in the child. Caregivers who are intrusive and overstimulating (Belsky et al., 1984) will produce avoidant children. The critical feature for our analysis is the quality of affect experienced by the child. Bowlby, Ainsworth, and colleagues have surmised that anxiety is at the base of avoidant and ambivalent attachment styles, and we would not refute this. However, as subsequent research has shown, anger is also stimulated in the relationships of both avoidant and ambivalent children, although it is expressed subversively in the case of the avoidant child. Here we contend that much more can be made of these emotional experiences. In our discrete emotions functionalist analysis, emotions associated with attachment experiences are the earliest, though not the sole, contributions to affective organizations. Other elements will be considered later on.

Suffice at this point to stress that emotions are the motivational sine qua non of attachment. Emotions connected with attachment make the infant care, and care in particular ways. When an infant's safety is jeopardized, fear promotes proximity-seeking and, typically, comforting from the caregiver. When infant behaviors provoke anger in the caregiver, the infant's perception of threat produces anxiety that cannot be satisfied by seeking social contact, but must be sedated with avoidance. When infant attachment behaviors are thwarted, anger promotes protest. And so forth. Affect makes the child care about outcomes and care in particular ways, with anxiety, excitement, contentment, anger, distress, and shame. With each of the types of caring comes particular motivations and behavior patterns.

Affect theory (Tomkins, 1963) for its part, focuses mainly on one particular attachment behavior, that of the cry. Crying is seen as an organized behavioral activity whose fundamental communication is about affect. In addition to the information about distress that is communicated, the affect itself is motivating. Unrelieved crying is punishing for both infant and caregiver. The infant is motivated to find relief from its distress since the feedback of crying is unpleasant. If the crying is prolonged the distress is magnified. As Bühler and Hetzer (1928) and Sagi and Hoffman (1976) have shown, the distress of crying is contagious; infants exposed to the cries of other infants begin crying themselves.

In terms of the caregiver, evolutionary theory teaches that caregivers are motivated to respond to the cry simply because they are preprogrammed for this response. Affect theory focuses on the affect that the cry provokes in the caregiver. If the cry is particularly harsh and grating, as is the case with some preterm and other developmentally compromised infants, or if the caregiver is already in a state of irritation, the cry may be perceived as angry and demanding and provoke similar anger in the caregiver. He or she may then turn away or react with violence—a reaction that is unhappily not rare, as we know from firsthand accounts of parents who have killed their own children because they could not get them to stop crying. Under more normal circumstances, the cry is perceived as "distress" and an empathic response is elicited, followed by caregiving that is sensitive to the needs of the child. The child's experiences around crying are obviously developmentally important. It is in the context of how the cry of distress is answered that the infant learns that distress need not be interminable and that other human beings can assist in the alleviation of distress. Under less favorable circumstances, the infant may learn an altogether different lesson, namely, that distress is a painful experience that one must learn to cope with on one's own, or even that distress becomes keener in the presence of another.

During the period of infancy, and over time, the child learns (or does not learn) that others can be counted on to help alleviate her distress. Apart from this, she also learns that others are (or are not) gratifying in other regards. The bond between caregiver and child qualifies as an example of what Tomkins has described as a "psychological addiction." The concept is meant to apply to love relationships as well as to other kinds of social commitment. At the heart of all psychological addictions is a dynamic that is grounded in properties of the affect system. Psychological addictions are formed in the context of repeated alternation between strong positive affect and strong negative affect, which produces magnification of the affective experience, making it keenly felt and resonant in quality. In the context of face-to-face play and affectionate contact, the child experiences intense delight. When the caregiver leaves, distress is precipitated. From this perspective, attachment, or bonding, results from the alternation between affectively positive and negative experiences, whose contrasting effects only serve to heighten the positive value of the caregiver for the child.

The nascent affective organization associated with attachment styles, however, is but a beginning. Other aspects of personality organization are forged and compete for representation as new developmental demands are made on individuals, as family circumstances change, and as children enter the larger community in which their families live. One of the things that Tomkins was insistent about in terms of the development of ideo-affective organizations, was that in order for a scene to become magnified and part of a larger script, the scene had to be repeated a number of times. However, mere repetition was not sufficient for the consolidation of a magnified scene. While the experiences had to be sufficiently similar to invoke preexisting screens or templates with which to match the experience, the scenes also had to have some variance in them or they would lack psychological distinctiveness.

A DISCRETE EMOTIONS, FUNCTIONALIST ANALYSIS OF DEVELOPMENT BEYOND EARLIEST INFANCY

Our discrete emotions theory of personality assumes that persons are organized around particular patterns of emotional experience and that these are functionally related to early and continuing emotion regulation strategies. We also believe that they operate in a trait-like way and continue to play a functional role in everyday experience. The notion of emotion biases or emotion traits is captured in the idea that some people are morose by habit, others carefree, still others belligerent, supercilious, self-effacing, or high-strung. These folk descriptions of personality are ways of synopsizing the salient emotional dispositions of people. In discrete emotions vocabulary we would say these individuals were organized around the particular emotions of sadness, happiness, anger, contempt, shame, and anxiety, respectively. Folk descriptions of personality also show an awareness that personality is uniquely configured, organized, and predictable. In our framework we refer to such affectively toned descriptions of personality as *emotion traits* or *affective biases*. The former term already has some currency in the literature. However, that term is also closely associated with notions of personality stability. In fact, the reason that contemporary trait-analytic theories of personality do not address developmental issues (see Chapter 8) is traceable to the early taxonomic approaches at the turn of the century and assumptions that traits were grounded in temperament or constitutional differences and therefore relatively immutable (see discussion by Whitbourne, Zuschlag, Elliot, & Waterman, 1992). Although we will use the term emotion biases interchangeably with the term affective biases, our preference is for the latter because it is less laden with connotations of developmental stasis. Our first task is to show that emotion traits or biases are *relatively* stable and therefore have characteristics associated with structural and organizational status. But as we also discuss and illustrate in Chapter 11, these organizations are not immutable; they are sensitive to stage-linked developmental demands, new threats and challenges, and ongoing learning.

To return to the original thesis, affective biases, as we conceive of them, are dispositions that have both structural and dynamic features, and in that respect resemble Allport's original formulation. For Allport (1937), a trait was a "generalized and focalized neuropsychic system (peculiar to the individual), with the capacity to render many stimuli functionally equivalent, and to initiate and guide consistent (equivalent) forms of adaptive and expressive behavior" (p. 295).

What is interesting about this description is that Allport recognized that traits are structural/organizational, but that they also have dynamic properties. The idea that they "render stimuli functionally equivalent" implies active cognitive processing that somehow alters incoming information in a preferential and consistent way. The idea that traits "initiate and guide" adaptive and expressive behavior suggests that these traits predispose individuals to behave in particular ways that will be consistent across time.

Two other critical features of Allport's analysis are his emphasis on expressive and adaptive behaviors. Expressive behaviors—facial expressions, body language, tone of voice—have communicative value and therefore the potential to influence others. The dyadic aspect of expressive behavior is especially important in development. Adaptive behavior implies coping, and coping of a particular nature. Although Allport was not talking about emotions per se, he might well have been, because, as our discrete emotions, functionalist analysis of personality shows, emotion traits alter information in affect-specific ways, are evident in affect-specific expressive behaviors, and have specific adaptive functions. Here we suggest that when individual emotions become crystallized in personality traits, they will bias behavior in several affect-specific ways, namely:

1. In information processing (perception, memory, interpretation, judgment, attribution)
2. In intrapsychic and behavioral processes (coping and defensive strategies)
3. In interpersonal behaviors

Emotion traits should be manifest in all of the above areas, and differentially so for different affects/emotion traits. We first consider how mood/personality traits affect each of the above domains of functioning, and then turn our attention to a more concentrated focus on the affects of anger and shame/shyness, in order to consider the socialization and development of these two traits over time. In the following we show how affect can bias (1) information processing, (2) coping styles, and (3) interpersonal process.

Affect Biases Information Processing

Let us first examine the data on mood-based (i.e., affect-based) biasing in information processing. Within recent times, there has been growing recognition that emotions may influence information processing and perception in important and specific ways. The concept, of course, is not new; the first serious experimental analysis of the phenomenon was tackled by the "new look" psychology of the 1940s and 1950s (Bruner, 1957). Current interest in the problem has been revived by the emergence of cognitive psychology, which has been particularly interested in the mechanisms of information processing (encoding, storage, retrieval), and from within social psychology, especially those interested in "social cognition." Research on social cognition focuses on the processes by which persons make judgments of social objects and situations.

Much evidence now exists to substantiate the fact that a subject's affective state can influence that subject's performance on a range of evaluative judgments; the effects appear to be fairly robust (Schwarz & Clore, 1983, 1988). Two major explanations have been advanced to account for the effect, namely, the mood congruency hypothesis (Bower, 1981), and the feelings-as-information hypothesis (Schwarz & Clore, 1983, 1988; Clore & Parrott, 1991).

In brief, the mood congruency hypothesis asserts that mood affects retrieval of information and subsequent task performance (in learning situations and judgment tasks) through the mechanism of mood-congruent recall. Essentially, the thesis is that being in a particular mood can enhance the retrieval of "mood-congruent" information or make mood-congruent thoughts more readily available to consciousness (Bower, 1981; Isen, 1984); that is, being in a positive mood should make positively valanced memories more accessible to recall than negatively valanced memories and being in a negative mood should allow the opposite to occur. In the classic test paradigm, subjects in neutral or "emotional" (i.e., positive, negative) moods learn certain materials at Time 1 (T1) and are tested for recall in congruent or noncongruent moods at Time 2 (T2). Though early studies seemed to indicate that congruency of moods at T1 and T2 facilitates recall, the effect has subsequently been found to be limited, being strongest for relatively unstructured material and for material that is self-referential. The effect is also somewhat fragile and not altogether reliable.

In an attempt to explain some of the inconsistencies in the mood-congruency literature as well as account for other data showing that mood affects a range of evaluative judgments, an alternative explanation has been advanced by Schwarz and colleagues (Clore & Parrott, 1991; Schwarz & Clore, 1983, 1988). These investigators have proposed an affect-as-information hypothesis. In contrast to the mood-congruency effect whereby emotion has an indirect effect on evaluative judgments through selective recall, the alternative theory proposes that emotions have a direct effect on social cognition by routing attention along certain paths, and via the information the emotion itself supplies during information processing; that is, emotion is itself an important source of information when making decisions and judgments. For example, feeling good or bad in the presence of certain situations may inform one about the advisability of continued contact or serve to help one make judgments about satisfaction with one's life. Emotional states may also direct one's attention and make certain features of a situation more salient than others. In two studies that pitted a mood-congruency explanation against an affect-as-information explanation for the effects of mood on judgment, Schwarz and Clore (Clore & Parrott, 1991; Schwarz & Clore, 1983) were able to determine that moods themselves have both directing and informational functions and that the informational function is distinct from the selective retrieval action of mood-congruency effects. Subjects were found to report more happiness and satisfaction with their lives overall when a good mood was induced (either by finding planted money or in the context of being asked questions on a sunny day) than when a poor mood was induced (no found money, rainy day), and this effect held even when the subjects were induced to attribute their present feelings to transient external sources.

Schwarz and Clore's (1988) mood-as-information explanation is an important construct, one that was originally suggested by differential emotions theory and affect theory (Izard, 1971, 1977; Tomkins, 1962, 1963), and is now apparently well-supported. However, the data covered by Schwarz and Clore (1988) deal mainly with positive versus negative emotion and, in fact, the authors feel that the effect of moods on information processing is limited to these more global states. "One can have 'good moods,' ' bad moods,' 'irritable moods,' 'cheerful moods,' but perhaps not a great many others" (Schwarz & Clore, 1988, p. 46). To the extent that affect biases may function very much like moods, it is possible that the effects of "negative moods," as studied in experimental studies that do not assess specific emotions, may actually obscure very specific information processing effects. According to differential emotions theory, affect theory, and our own discrete emotions, functionalist account, the mood-as-information thesis should extend to emotional traits in personality, and differentially so, depending on type of trait-related mood, as discussed in Malatesta and Wilson (1988). In that paper, we suggested that each of the emotions had specific self-cuing functions and that these were linked to particular kinds of motivated behavior. Table 4, presented earlier, specifies the self-cuing information as well as the motivated behavior that should be associated with each of the basic affects. The above linkages between emotions, self-cuing function, and motivated behavior are as predicted in the theoretical literature. They may seem self-evident and almost banal. However, the implications of these observations for personality functioning are not trivial; indeed, they have important ramifications. If one experiences anger on an ongoing basis, one should be predisposed to interpret others as angry, hostile, and withholding. McCown, Johnson, and Austin (1985) found that delinquents made more errors in an affect decoding task than non-delinquents, most notably in the case of two emotions that are considered part of the hostile triad by Izard (1972)—anger and disgust; these delinquents apparently expected and found hostile intentions in the facial expressions of others.

If one experiences predominantly sad mood, one should be more sensitive to the disappointments and losses of others, that is, be more inclined to see the downside rather than the positive side of things. Studies show that persons with depressed affect can be characterized by a perceptual set known as depressive realism. What this means is that depressed people interpret situations less positively than their nondepressive counterparts. Persons who are somewhat dysphoric but not clinically depressed may also have greater sensitivity to the disappointments and losses of others, as evident in their empathic responses. Tomkins's research (1963) on the relation between humanistic and normative ideologies and that of affect indicated that the true humanist tends to have sadness and interest as dominant affects, whereas contempt/disgust is more typical of normatives. To provide another example, graduate students in clinical psychology, selected on the basis of personality variables such as verbal ability, capacity for insight, and empathic tendencies, in addition to high GRE scores, are informally observed to have mild depressive tendencies. In a broader range of subjects, a study by Magai, Distel, and Liker (1994) showed that securely attached adults, who are considered to be the most psychologically healthy individuals, had mild elevations on sad affect by self-report, but not anger, contempt, fear, disgust, or shame.

People who are anxious should be vigilant for threatening stimuli. Research using the Stroop test has shown that it takes longer for anxiety disorder patients to color-name threat words than nonthreat words, while controls are not affected. In dichotic listening tasks, anxious subjects have longer reaction times to probes following threat words in the "unattended" ear, probably as a result of attention being caught by the threat words (see Mineka & Sutton, 1992, for a review of relevant studies).

The above effects are not "negative mood" effects, they are affect-specific effects and congruent with the self-cuing properties of these particular emotions.

Affect Biases Coping Styles

Emotions have evolved to assist individuals in coping with threats and in achieving goals. Intrinsic to each emotion is a particular manner of coping with environmental contingencies. Under ordinary circumstances, emotions are prompted by specific environmental events, deployed in coping, and then subside. These adaptive responses are affect-specific. Anger assists the person whose efforts have been thwarted in overcoming obstacles. Fear instigates behavior that removes the individual from situations of threat. Shyness helps protect the vulnerable person from further violations of his or her privacy and diminishes exposure and vulnerability. As Haviland and Lelwica (1987) have shown, infants as young as 10 months of age are capable of differential coping responses. In this case the environmental stressors involved exposure to intense maternal emotion expression. Mothers were instructed to simulate sad, angry, and happy affect in both tone of voice and facial expression as they interacted with infants. The babies appeared affected by these manipulations in affect-specific ways. They responded to maternal simulations of sadness with downcast eyes and an increase in mouthing movements, which suggests self-soothing. They responded to maternal simulations of anger with an increase in gaze aversion and in no-movement responses (possibly a freezing reaction indexing fear). The response to maternal joy involved an increase in joy expressions.

In the well-developed personality (cf. Tomkins's integrated personality), the full repertoire of emotions is available to the individual and specific emotions are deployed for specific adaptive purposes. However, in the course of development many individuals develop affective biases such that certain affects are preferentially employed in coping and defense. When the biases are not extreme, they merely constitute individual differences in personality. Various coping styles have been demonstrated with respect to different emotions. For example, with respect to the experience of sadness, Nolen-Hoeksema and Morrow (1991) have shown that some people can be characterized as having a "ruminative" coping style, whereas others have a "distractive" coping style. In the case of shame, Lewis (1971) differentiates between styles of coping with shame that take the form of "by-passed" shame or "overt, undifferentiated" shame. Harburg, Gleiberman, Russell, Cooper, and Lynne (1991) differentiate between anger coping styles of "anger-in," "anger-out," and "anger-reflective." Brown, O'Keefe, Sanders, and Baker's (1986) research on children disclosed various styles of coping with anxiety, including "self-talk," "distraction," and "catastrophizing."

Developmental experiences surely come into play in fostering one type of style over another. A child can learn to cope with anxiety in a passive manner or in an active, problem-solving way. She can also establish personal habits that help avoid the occasions of anxiety. Such differences probably account for the development of either a personality favoring conscientiousness, punctuality, and studiousness—an anticipatory strategy that helps avoid occasions of anxiety, or a reactive personality plagued by phobias, anxiety attacks, and psychosomatic problems. Here we can see that anxiety coping defenses may lie at the heart of two of the five-factor dimensions of the taxonomic approach to personality (i.e., Conscientiousness and Neuroticism). Similarly, a developmental analysis of anger indicates that when dependency needs are frustrated, the resulting anger can be channeled into independence, avoidance, and achievement strivings, whose rewards may in some way compensate for dependency need deprivation. The frustration of autonomy needs, by contrast, can lead to anger that gets channeled into continuous interpersonal struggle, which gives overt anger a chance to crystallize in personality. This analysis also indicates that because people learn to regulate emotion in different ways that lead to different outcomes—conscious versus unconscious shame (overt versus bypassed shame), conscious versus unconscious anxiety (anxiety versus repression), conscious versus unconscious sadness (rumination versus distraction), personality analysis based purely on self-report will not adequately capture emotion stylistics, or will summarize them but conceal the underlying dynamics, and thus rob the analysis of greater predictive power. For example, the five-factor dimension of Conscientiousness may adequately predict conscientious behaviors such as neatness and punctuality. But a trait of anger or shame—which includes the manner in which anger or shame is managed—predicts a much wider range of behaviors related to the accuracy of information processing and the kinds of distortion that may occur, which in turn may bias personal and social behavior in distinctive ways.

Carrying the notion of coping styles further, we can see that when affective biases operate in a monolithic, inflexible way, they incur defensive coping and become associated with psychopathology. Two analyses, one by Kellerman (1990) and one by Malatesta and Wilson (1988), place emotions at the core of psychopathology and particular defensive coping styles. For example, Kellerman suggests that the paranoid defense of projection is based on the emotion of disgust, that repression in the passive personality is based on fear, displacement in the aggressive personality is based on anger, and regression in the impulsive personality is based on surprise.

Malatesta and Wilson (1988) differentiate between "surfeit biases" and "deficiency biases" corresponding to the overuse and underuse of particular emotions in personality functioning. In the extreme form they become "surfeit pathologies" involving the excessive activation of a particular emotion or set of emotions, and "deficiency biases" that involve inadequately expressed emotions and which can take one of two forms. In one form, an emotion or set of emotions is "warded off" or absent in the affective repertoire through dynamic mechanisms of conflict and defense. In the "undeveloped" type, the person shows an absolute absence of the capacity for the emotion. Tables 5a and 5b summarize the surfeit and deficiency pathologies that are associated with particular emotions.

In summary, surfeit and deficit pathologies involve failures in affect regulation; affects are either overexpressed or underexpressed. Within the context of emotion-trait theory, affect biases also involve overexpression or underexpression of certain types of emotion (surfeit and deficiency biases, respectively), but not to the extent that they cripple a person's ability to negotiate the trials and tribulations of daily life. However, they do alter a person's behavior in biased ways, both in coping strategies and in a broader context. For example, children reared in an environment in which one or both parents are depressive tend to develop biases around the emotion of sadness and behavioral strategies that are congruent with this background affect. Research shows that such children display parentified responses that involve hypertrophied empathy. They are alert to depression and misery in others, and are acute at identifying it and in offering assistance (Zahn-Waxler & Kochanska, 1990). Zahn-Waxler and Kochanska's (1990) research, as well as the study by Haviland and Lelwica (1987), illustrates another facet of emotion-based personality traits—the impact of emotion on interpersonal proc-

Table 5a. Emotion Traits in Pathological Form

Emotion	Surfeit pathology	Associated cognitions or cognitive framework
Anger	Violent, aggressive behavior; antisocial personality	Others intend to obstruct or harm me and I can be effective against it
Sadness	Depression (anaclitic type, after Wilson, 1986)	Valued objects have been lost; one's efforts are fruitless
Fear	Anxiety neurosis; phobic	Anticipations of danger; others intend to harm me or events will harm me and I will be ineffective
Contempt	Pathological narcissism	
	1. Pseudograndiosity (defense against feelings of inferiority)	1. I feel superior to you but fear I am not
	2. True grandiosity (diffuse, narcissistic, egocentric, grandiosity)	2. I am superior and you cannot also be superior
Guilt	Depression (guilt-ridden type, after Wilson, 1986)	Something bad will happen and there is no escape. I have done something for which I will (should) be punished.
Disgust	Avoidant reactions (e.g., anxious)	Something (e.g., food) is repellant and needs to be kept away.
Shame/shyness	Pathological shyness (Zimbardo, 1977)	I am extremely fragile and others may easily hurt me; I am inferior to others.

Source: Malatesta & Wilson, 1988.

ess. The latter is especially important because it suggests how and why individuals develop different styles of emotion regulation and how different emotions may come to dominate in personality.

Affect Biases Interpersonal Process

In addition to the self-cuing properties of emotion, emotions have signal value for others in that they communicate response tendencies. Exposure to affect also tends to motivate similar or complementary response tendencies in the observer. Anger signals that an attack (verbal or behavioral) may be imminent; the astute social partner understands that she must prepare to defend herself. Sadness signals that the individual has experienced loss, and the responsive social partner is motivated to offer nurturance and succorance. Shame/shyness signals a need for privacy. Fear signals submission and serves to ward off attack. Contempt signals dominance to others, which may provoke either submission or countercontempt. Guilt signals acknowledgment of blame, and the social partner expects reparation. Disgust communicates repulsion of the social partner,

Table 5b. Emotion Traits in Pathological Form

Emotion	Deficiency pathology: Undeveloped	Cognitive framework	Deficiency pathology: Warded off	Cognitive framework
Anger	Inadequate personality	My assertive abilities are nonexistent	Avoidant personality	I don't know how to respond when others threaten me.
Sadness	Schizoid	Others don't strike a responsive chord in me; their problems do not touch me.	Hypomania	Being sad is too painful; it is better to look on the bright side of things.
Fear	Antisocial personality	There is nothing to fear; there are no constraints on behavior.	Counterphobic	There is nothing to fear about what I am afraid of and I will prove it.
Contempt	Loss of ego-identity	There is no "I" that exists.	Identity diffusion (failure to see different individuals as separate selves with an ordered or organized relationship to one another).	People are all the same.
Guilt	Sociopathy	Nothing I do is wrong.	Paranoia	You did something wrong and should be punished.
Disgust	Indiscriminate oral compulsions	Everything is attractive and I can't discriminate my own likes and dislikes.	Obsessional neurosis	The symbolic equivalent of something disgusts me.
Shame/ shyness	No sense of social hierarchy; people are all basically interchangeable.	There is no "I" that exists separate from "thou" that organizes our relationship to one another. Clinically manifest as a lack of discrimination among people or, in children, as an absence of stranger anxiety.	Uninhibited personality style (as an overcompensation for warded-off shyness)	Nothing embarrasses me and it is important that I demonstrate this to you.

Source: Malatesta & Wilson, 1988.

whereas interest signals receptivity. Joy promotes social bonding through the contagion of good feeling.

When emotions become incorporated in personality in the form of emotion traits, they bias the nature of social interactions in ways that act to sustain certain patterns. The angry, hostile individual will tend to have antagonistic encounters with others; in cases where the social partner is in a position to escape or attack in return, she can arrange to avoid further encounters. When in the context of a structurally stable, long-term relationship, as in work, marriage, or family, social partners can become locked in cycles of dysfunctional interaction. One such dysfunctional pattern has been described by Retzinger (1991) in her book on marital quarrels. In brief, Retzinger demonstrates the dynamic and reciprocal relationship between shame and rage and the role it plays in the escalation of conflict. When one partner criticizes or shames the other, anger and humiliation are experienced; such feelings tend to provoke shaming counterattack, which provokes further shame, humiliation, and rage. Similarly, Scheff (1987) has explored the shame–rage spiral in the context of a therapy session; he shows how a slight by a therapist initiated a sequence of shame–anger responses that escalated over the course of the session.

The reciprocal influence of affect biases in interpersonal process can be detected as early as infancy. Infants of depressed mothers are at risk for affective disturbances and developmental problems. Observations of depressed mothers and their infants show how parents may unwittingly socialize a predisposition for depression in their offspring. Research by Bettes (1988) indicates that depressed mothers take significantly longer to respond to the signals of their infants, that their utterances are more variable, and that they are less likely to adjust their behavior to that of their babies. Thus the mothers violate the usual mother–infant contingency patterns and do so on a chronic basis, setting up early conditions for learned helplessness in their infants. Field and colleagues (Field, Healy, Goldstein, & Guthertz, 1990) found that depressed mothers and their infants matched negative behavior states more often and positive behavior states less often than well mother–infant dyads, suggesting that infants as young as 3-months of age may be acquiring affect patterns similar to those of their mothers. We will have more to say about the intergenerational transmission of affect biases in the last two chapters.

In summary, our discrete emotions, functionalist analysis of personality is based on the notion that the fundamental properties of emotion make them susceptible to structuralization within the personality. Once established in the personality they influence information processing, behavioral patterns—including coping and defensive strategies, and interpersonal process. These basic propositions are expanded upon in the next chapter as we present a more in-depth analysis of emotion traits by focusing on two particular kinds of affect bias—those involving anger and shame. We engage in this more extended analysis so as to illustrate the extraordinary pervasiveness of affect biases, and in order to shed light on a developmental process singular to the emotions of anger and shame.

A Discrete Emotions, Functionalist Analysis of Personality Development

Part II: Illustrations from Biography and Empirical Research

In this chapter we consider how two emotions, those of anger and shame, become structuralized in the personality. Two emotions were chosen rather than one so as to highlight the differential nature of these two affects as they operate in personality. We also wanted to stress that there are both common principles involved in the processes through which emotions become structuralized in the personality and differences that stem from the unique properties of these emotions. In developing the case, we draw from two sources of data—biography and more traditional empirical research.

A VIEW OF PERSONALITY FROM BIOGRAPHY

There is no more compelling way to demonstrate the organizational nature of emotion traits in personality than by the simple description of personality. In the present chapter we choose to illustrate the workings of affective biases with two personalities rather than one, so as to highlight the differential properties of different kinds of emotion traits.

Here we present two personalities who are already somewhat known to the reader—John Watson and Carl Rogers—both eminent psychologists, but with personalities as different as night and day. We could have just as easily chosen figures other than psychologists who are well known to the public—for example, a rock star, or newscaster. Instead, we chose individuals whose written work, as well as biographical material, is available for inspection, because we wanted to illustrate just how pervasive emotion traits are in personality, even to the point of affecting the structure and content of theoretical visions. Both Rogers and Watson have written extensively about psychology and human nature. Although their views on human nature are quite divergent, both ideologies are integrally related to each man's own unique emotion organization and personality.

John Watson gave science an understanding of human nature that was optimistic as well as troubling, and which was essentially reactive and reductionisic. In Watson's writings, human nature was infinitely shapeable and a person could become anything under the sun—doctor, lawyer, mortician, beautician. At the same time, humans were bound by an environmental determinism—that is, shackled by whatever environmental contingencies befell one through the vicissitudes of fate.

Carl Rogers, whose name is most closely associated with the humanistic movement in psychology and client-centered psychotherapy, gave us a model of human nature that was active and growth oriented, a model refreshing in its ebullience concerning the intrinsic goodness and potential of the human being, though perhaps too idealistic and naive by today's jaded standards.

For Watson, emotions were primitive and somewhat dangerous, the loose cannons of personality, in need of restraint, and preferably utter subjugation. For Rogers, emotions did not need containment, but rather realization and expression. How do we account for such vastly different views of the human? What were their origins?

Given the emphasis, above, on dealing with early development and the impact of interpersonal exprience, we need to begin at the beginning and make certain assumptions about the attachment histories of these two men. In Chapter 4 of this volume we presented a somewhat detailed biography of Watson in the context of his role in the genesis of American behaviorism. As indicated in the biographical sketch, Watson was an only child and subjected to what we may construe as a strict upbringing. The reconstruction of his attachment history is of necessity speculative. There is little actual description of the mother's behavior toward her son or of his toward her during his early development. However, we do know that he displayed little overt emotional response when his mother died. His relationship with his father must surely have been conflicted, given that the elder Watson was alternately abusive and absent; when his father sought a reconciliation later in life, Watson turned his back. In adulthood, Watson's relationships with women seemed to get off to a passionate start, often reflecting a rebellious streak vis à vis the conventional morality of the day, but then degenerated into open disregard. Given the above facts, and from the vantage point of the cumulative data from attachment research, we may speculate that Watson had an avoidant attachment pattern.

In the case of Rogers, an analysis by Magai and Haviland (in preparation), suggests that Rogers had a secure attachment style, though there were some minor avoidant features. He spoke warmly of his parents; he had a stable, communicative relationship with his wife over the many decades of their marriage; he showed extraordinary commitment to his students.

That said, how do attachment relationships figure into the larger scheme of things? How is attachment related to affect and emotional organization? How does it relate in the particular instance of these two psychologists? Do the different attachment styles of these two men have a bearing on the way they approached their theoretical works, on their particular perspectives and ideologies? Attachment is one place to start, but the true kernel, we submit, is not attachment itself, but is embedded in the emotions that attachment strivings provoke and in the emotional quality of the response of caregivers—that is, within the larger emotions behavioral system. These experiences leave emotional residues that then interact with later emotional experiences as the affect system is activated time and time again.

As indicated earlier, in most infant–caregiver relationships, affect is the central "pull" in the context of dyadic interaction. Affect serves to sustain contact and nurture the development of the child. In optimal attachment scenes, the child shares in an animating, enjoyable interactive dialogue with the caregiver; similarly, during occasions of stress or challenge, the child finds relief from distress through the caregiver's ministrations and is not forced to suffer on his own. The experiences of interactive joy and excitement, on the one hand, and relief from suffering, on the other hand, are some of the most rewarding experiences a child can have.

In the case of Rogers, these experiences may have been especially rewarding. Carl had been sickly as a child and his parents feared that he might not survive infancy. His parents and siblings appeared to have been particularly solicitous of him until school age when he was out of danger. Then, like the rest of the children in the family, he was expected to abide by the rather strict codes of behavior dictated by the family's Midwestern and fundamentalist values. Love prevailed, but became contingent on good behavior. Such a contrast between the unstinting and intense pleasures of infancy and the harsh restrictions and contingencies of childhood, by Tomkins's theory, would have laid the groundwork for a "psychological addiction" for human social contact. However, one wonders whether these experiences alone would have sufficed to propel Rogers toward a career as a clinical psychologist with a "passionate" interest in people (Kirschenbaum, 1979). One looks to other developmental events of emotional consequence. One also looks for repetition, variance, and psychological magnification (Tomkins, 1963, 1987).

Despite Rogers's relatively secure attachment, he was acutely shy as a child, as described by his wife—who knew him in childhood—as well as by his own account. Shyness is part of the superordinate affect category of shame, and shame is linked to, but not necessarily always a concomitant of, attachment. It is linked to attachment in that an emotional bond is a necessary precondition for the experience of shame. Rogers's fragility as an infant promoted special solicitude on the part of his parents and siblings. This heightened degree of attention likely contributed to both a feeling of privilege and uniqueness as well a feeling of being damaged. In fact, a sense of vulnerability may have been one of Rogers's earliest introductory experiences with shame.

In isolation, this experience of infancy might not have mattered very much and might not have contributed to a shame-biased affective organization. However, other subsequent experiences were concordant. The grounds for shame/shyness magnification existed in other significant family circumstances and developmental events, including the family's self-imposed aloofness from others, and by their several moves. Socially isolated, and trained to think of himself and his family as different, Rogers probably found it difficult to acquire the usual peer social skills children learn during the elementary years, thus further contributing to a sense of ineptitude and discomfort. Rogers was also exposed to what he regarded as particularly brutal teasing from his many older siblings, which would have heightened his sense of shame and vulnerability as well. Thus, in addition to positive affect (joy and interest in social objects), another aspect of his emotional organization became crystallized around shame/shyness. In Rogers's case there were multiple, continuing, and various sources of shame socialization in his life, but he was also acutely drawn to people, seeking in them the kind of intense communion and affectivity experienced in his infancy. The centrality of positive affect, as well as shame, in Roger's affective organization is substantiated by an analysis of his personal and social life (as extracted from several biographies), his expressive behavior (affect coding of filmed interviews), his philosophy of human nature, and the ideology behind his psychotherapeutic practice (Magai & Haviland, in preparation). It is noteworthy that the latter was designed to provide clients with relief from their own negative self-evaluations (i.e., feelings of shame), and to stimulate positive affect and positive self-esteem in the context of what Rogers termed "unconditional positive regard"—a phrase that seems to conjure up the idyllic and idealized period of Roger's early infancy before the realization of damage and inferiority and the conditionality of love.

We turn now to consider a very different personality. For John Watson, the recurrent affectively charged experiences of his life revolved around the affect of anger—his father's violent outbursts, the likely frustration produced by his mother's strict fundamentalism, and anger prompted by the taunting of his classmates. Unlike Rogers, who turned inward in the face of the teasing of his siblings, Watson lashed out at those who would torment him. He was always embroiled in fights in school, and his aggressiveness was rewarded by success in defending himself, which probably added to an abiding sense that he could overcome just about any obstacle. His rebellious disregard of conventional morality, as well as his apparent contempt for women, betray an underlying hostility. However, his rebel's identity and confrontational nature helped forward his professional ambitions and enabled him to assert and establish his behavioristic empire. Later in life, in the aftermath of the ignominy of being thrown out of academia, and finding himself clinging to the lower-echelon rungs of the Walter J. Thompson advertising company, he says he learned to find joy in the analysis of sales curves. This is either brave stoicism or the psychological defense of denial. Denial is a feature of the avoidant personality. Watson was avoidant in his personal relationships—distant with his wife, aloof with his children, withholding of physical affection, and, beyond the immediate family, socially somewhat of a loner.

Watson's avoidant attachment and anger organization is reflected as well in his theoretical writings, both in the content and in the structure of his thinking. He wrote that parental affection was vastly overrated, in fact, that it spoiled children and was to be avoided. The structure of his thinking patterns appears to have been almost exclusively absolutistic, versus relativistic or dialectical (in the nomenclature of the post-Piagetian cognitive theorists). As Haviland has noted (Haviland & Kramer, 1991; Haviland, in Magai & Haviland, in preparation), absolutistic thinking tends to predominate in individuals who are charged with angry affect. The more positive side of an anger organization is that it fuels an aggressive drive, a drive that was clearly in evidence throughout Watson's professional career.

The above affective analysis of the lives of two well-known individuals is of necessity limited due to considerations of space. As well, the presentation of biographical material supporting the analysis was necessarily brief. For a more complete examination of the data and source of interpretation, the reader is referred to the original biographical material (Buckley, 1989; Kirschenbaum, 1979) or to Magai and Haviland (in preparation). Here, it was not our intent to prove our point via biography, but to provide an illustration.

Moving to another level of data, we can examine laboratory studies of affect involving direct observation and/or experimental manipulation. The case for the pervasiveness of affect organizations on thinking, behavior, and social relationships is well supported by the empirical literature on emotion. In the following discussion we examine the literature on anger once again, and that of shame/shyness, each from the perspective of a discrete emotions functionalist analysis. We begin with a reexamination of the literature on anger, thus time with a view to examining the role of this emotion in personality process. We then consider shame/shyness.

ANGER AND PERSONALITY PROCESS

Certain individuals tend to be irritable, sensitive to slights, cynical, and argumentative. They are described by others as being "hostile," and are viewed as having a relatively enduring personality disposition. On any given day, such individuals can be expected to be angry about one thing or another.

In our view, when anger affect predominates in personality we say that the individual is organized around the trait of anger or has an anger organization. The theory predicts that anger as a trait is an enduring dispositional tendency and that evidence of such will be found pervasively across wide domains of information processing, behavior, and interpersonal process. Let us first examine the evidence for an anger organization. Are anger biases wide or domain-specific? And what is the relation between affective state, thought, and action? How pervasive is the anger bias and how insistently and subtly does it insinuate itself into the personal lifestyle and interpersonal relationships of individuals?

The Anger Organization

Based on the self-cuing properties of anger emotion described in Table 4, we would expect a person organized around the emotion of anger (1) to feel angry and resentful more frequently than others, (2) to have a perceptual bias that sensitizes the individual to identify occasions for anger with more than average frequency (i.e. to be vigilant for hostile provocations), (3) to have a tendency to interpret ambiguous social scenes as ill-meaning (i.e., to infer that others want to thwart, humiliate or otherwise provoke the individual), and (4) to behave readily in an aggressive fashion. Three personality configurations that have been identified in the literature seem prone to hostile emotion: (1) The Type A Behavior Pattern of the adult literature and, within the developmental literature, (2) insecurely attached children, and (3) aggression-prone children.

Type A Behavior Pattern (TABP) is a personality configuration that was identified over 20 years ago, when it was called "hurry sickness" because of its association with a fast-paced, hard-driving personality and with cardiac disease. Over time the cardinal features of TABP were defined as impatience, hard-driving ambition, time urgency, and hostility; in fact, an irritable voice and explosive speech pattern are the key clinical features in classifying subjects during the assessment procedure of the structured interview. More recently, it has become evident that it is the hostility component that features most prominently in the personality and which is the variable most closely associated with cardiac disease. In our own study of the emotional expressivity in TABP (Malatatesta-Magai, Jonas, Shepard, & Culver, 1992), Type A individuals scored higher on trait anger and trait aggression than did their Type B counterparts. It is important to note that Type A's did not differ on other emotional dimensions, as suggested by Friedman and Booth-Kewley's 1987 meta-analysis; Types A and B were equivalent on measures of anxiety and depression. Thus, the negative emotion bias was restricted to anger. Another important finding was that not only were younger Type A males (the classic coronary-prone individual) angrier, they were more likely to show evidence of attempts to *suppress* anger. Clinical psychology suggests that suppressed emotion often finds an outlet in projection or other defensive coping styles. Indeed, results of a subsidiary study, not yet published, provide support for this phenomenon. The first author developed a projective test that consisted of a series of ambiguous socioemotional situations that could be resolved in favor of angry, sad, or fearful interpretations and responses. Type A subjects selected angry resolutions of the ambiguous social scenes significantly more often than did Type Bs.

Anger as an organizing force in personality is also found within the child developmental literature. Attachment research has identified two types of insecurely attached children, both of whom show anger organizations. Avoidantly attached children in general show a tendency to suppress their emotions; however, they show a disposition to engage in unprovoked attacks of aggression directed at their mothers and have been described as covertly hostile.

In contrast, ambivalent children tend to be temperamentally irritable and to display their anger openly. This difference in the display of anger—covert versus overt—raises the issue of how anger or any emotion trait may be structured within the personality. Earlier we drew a distinction between two types of emotional bias—a deficiency bias and a surfeit bias. The surfeit condition involves the case where a particular emotion or set of emotions monopolizes the person's repertoire—the emotions are excessively activated and expressed. In the case of the deficiency bias, emotion expression is restricted—either because the emotion is warded off due to unconscious conflict, or because the emotion is insufficiently developed. Avoidantly attached children appear to be anger deficient—apparently due to unconscious conflict rather than inadequate exposure to social models who express this emotion, as we will see. Ambivalently attached children appear to be surfeited with anger in that they have a low threshold for its activation.

Berlin (1993) found that avoidant preschoolers were significantly less likely to acknowledge angry affect than ambivalent children, who had the highest scores among avoidantly, securely, and ambivalently attached children. Working with school-age children, a student from the first author's laboratory, Joan Adickman (1993), found that 6- to 8-year-olds who were identified as insecurely attached (mainly avoidant) on the basis of the Separation Anxiety Test made more errors in an emotion decoding test that involved the projection of hostile emotion (anger, disgust, and contempt) than did securely attached children.

Another group of children who have been intensively studied in recent times are aggression-prone children. Although such a label describes a behavior rather than a personality type, the literature indicates that this behavior pattern is indicative of an anger organization in that it is biased toward hostile perceptions, attributions, and unfriendly interpersonal strategies. For example, Rubin and Clark (1983) interviewed aggressive and nonaggressive preschoolers about reactions to a variety of hypothetical situations. Aggressive children offered as many solutions as nonaggressive children to problems involving the acquisition of objects or access to desired activities, but were more likely to rely on coercive strategies—agonistic and bribe strategies—and were less likely to offer prosocial strategies. Aggressive elementary school children (Rubin, Moller, & Emptage, 1987) also were more likely to suggest bribe and affect manipulation strategies and less prosocial strategies than their nonaggressive counterparts across a range of scenarios. In help-seeking vignettes, aggressive children were more likely to use bizarre strategies and to say they would bully their targets rather than offer prosocial strategies such as asking politely. In friendship initiation situations, aggressive children produced fewer relevant strategies and were more likely to offer abnormal strategies and fewer invitations to potential friends. Finally, a study by Walters and Peters (1980) showed that aggressive children preferred aggressive responses as a first-choice strategy across a range of social situations.

The foregoing early studies suggest that aggressive children engage in a restricted range of strategies and more atypical patterns of information processing than their nonaggressive counterparts when it comes to conflict resolution, friendship initiation, and object acquisition, and favor aggressive and nonnormative strategies for dealing with interpersonal goals. Subsequent research indicates that the above information-processing biases and deficiencies are causally implicated in *behavior* patterns. The work of Dodge and colleagues (Dodge, Pettit, McClaskey, & Brown, 1986) and Lochman (1987) shows that the aggressive behavior of aggressive versus nonaggressive children during real social interchanges is linked to specific perceptual and attributional biases. Dodge et al. (1986) found that aggressive children were more likely than matched nonaggressive peer controls to attribute hostile intentions to a peer provocation, to access aggressive responses to this stimulus, and to behave aggressively when provoked. Lochman (1987) assessed differences in self-perceptions, peer perceptions, and attributions of relative responsibility in aggressive and nonaggressive boys under experimental conditions of competitive dyadic discussion. The aggressive boys had distorted perceptions of their own aggressiveness; despite equivalent levels of aggression in aggressive and nonaggressive peers during the interaction, aggressive boys perceived their partners as being more aggressive than themselves.

Aggressive children also apparently have a lower threshold to anger arousal. For example, Underwood, Cole, and Herbsman (1992) found that aggressive children reported more anger in response to anger-eliciting videos than did nonaggressive children. This lower threshold apparently holds under ambiguous situations as well. In a study by Graham, Hudley, and Williams (1992), aggressive and nonaggressive adolescents were exposed to negative outcome scenarios; when the scenes were ambiguous, aggressive subjects assumed more malicious intent on the part of pictured children, reported greater anger, and said they would respond in hostile ways more often than nonaggressive subjects.

It is important to note that the above effects tend to be of small magnitude under relaxed testing conditions, and to increase during real or simulated events that involve threat or challenge (Dodge & Somberg, 1987). Thus we cannot expect biases to be in evidence at all times. Emotion biases may be camouflaged under ordinary circumstances and in the context of polite social intercourse. They are activated when they can assist at the performance of goal related behavior, and thus are likely to be called into play mainly during occasions of challenge.

The tendency for emotion biases to be elicited selectively and to interact with situational context is nicely illustrated by an analysis of regional differences of aggressive behavior in adult males. Nisbett (1993) analyzed the contrasting behavioral and attitudinal qualities of Caucasian males in various parts of the United States. He found that homicide rates for Southerners are substantially higher than those for Northern males. Examining a wide array of data, he systematically ruled out competing explanations and concluded that the rates are linked to regional differences in the harshness of parental disciplinary practices, as well as regional differences in attitudes about the legitimate and proper provocations to aggression. Specifically, Southerners report more severe beatings by parents than Northerners, and Southern men are more likely than Midwestern subjects to strongly endorse spanking as an appropriate discipline policy. For other attitude items, although Southerners do not endorse violence across the board, they do for certain items related to protection of self, family, and one's honor. For example, Southerners versus non-Southerners are twice as likely to endorse killing as justified when it comes to defending the home; they are also significantly more likely to agree that a man has the right to kill to defend his family, and that police should shoot rioters. Southern white men are also twice as likely to report having guns for protection as rural Midwestern white men. In one of the few experimental studies to test the regional disposition to aggression and violence, college students were deliberately challenged by a confederate's rude and insulting behavior. The subjects were observed during the experimental manipulation and their affective behavior coded; they also completed several projective measures. Southern versus non-Southern subjects displayed significantly greater anger in response to the provocation. However, the anger did not affect the quality of their responses on all the projective measures. An elevation in anger content was evident in only one of the three projective media, the one involving affront and sexual challenge, with Southern versus non-Southern men more likely to respond with violent imagery. Here it is important to note that the projective scenario resembled the experimental manipulation in that it involved an offensive insult, although the real-life insult was directed at the subject rather than protagonist's romantic partner. Thus, background variables of regional upbringing interacted with situation-specific anger priming to produce a significant bias in information processing.

In summary, an anger-prone personality configuration is well documented and described in the literature. Individuals with an anger/hostility bias are likely to experience more anger on a day-to-day basis, to have a lower threshold for anger provocation, to perceive more stimuli as requiring hostile or aggressive responses, to more readily interpret other individuals as having hostile intentions or as behaving in a provocative manner, and to actually behave in a more aggressive, hostile manner. Thus the bias appears to be pervasive and widely influential across psychological domains of perception, information processing, and behavior.

To return to the five-factor theory of personality for the moment, we note that interpreting the agreeableness/antagonism dimension as a measure of trait hostility does much to clarify why the items on this scale cluster in the way they do. People who are angry, that is, who experience the world as frustrating, will of necessity be mistrustful and contentious. Other terms that load on the agreeableness/antagonism factor—selfish, stubborn, unfair, suspicious, cold, stingy, critical, headstrong, negativistic, and jealous (McCrae & Costa, 1985; Digman & Inouye, 1986)—are interpretable within this framework as well. This granted, we still need to inquire as to the origins of such a personality trait.

Ontogeny of the Anger Organization

A critical question for personality theory is how do children acquire affective biases and how do they become structuralized within the personality? Although it is somewhat remarkable, the voluminous literature on the Type A personality, spanning almost three decades, has only recently begun to investigate the developmental origins of the Type A personality. There is some evidence for a "hypertensive" family style characterized by gaze avoidance and the communication of contempt, sarcasm, and criticism (Baer et al., 1980, 1983).

Karen Matthews and colleagues have been studying an analogue Type A Behavior Pattern in children using an instrument called the MYTH. Children who score high on this scale are more aggressive in their interactions with others and experience more frequent aversive life events than children who score low (Murray, Matthews, Blake, & Prineas, 1986). Type A Behavior Pattern in children has been found to be moderately stable between 5 to 11 years of age, suggesting that the personality pattern may develop relatively early in life. Matthews, Manuck, and Saab (1986) found that trait anger, but not Type A, predicted increases in diastolic blood pressure in 15-year-olds during a natural stressor (having to give a speech in an English class), indicating that like adults, anger and hostility may be the crucial variables in the development of cardiovascular disease. In another study, McCann and Matthews (1988) found that in contrast to global Type A, one component—potential for hostility—affected children's cardiovascular response, independent of parental history of hypertension. Children with high scores on potential for hostility showed exaggerated systolic and diastolic blood pressure in one of several stress tasks.

What is clear from the above review is that children begin to show Type A behavior patterns early in life, that the pattern is stable over time, and that TABP, and especially predisposition to anger/hostility, is associated with the kind of cardiovascular patterns seen in adult, coronary-prone Type A individuals. What is not yet known is how the Type A pattern in children originates, although Type A boys tend to have Type A mothers and fathers (Matthews, Stoney, Rakaczky, & Jamison, 1986). Rosenman and colleagues (Rosenman, Rahe, Borhani, 1974; Matthews, Rosenman, Dembroski, Harris, & MacDougal, 1984) established that there was no significant heritability component of global Type A behavior as assessed by the structured interview, although some self-report scales did have heritable components. A reanalysis of a subsample from the original Rosenman study using tape-recorded interviews with 80 monozygotic and 80 dizygotic twin pairs (Matthews et al., 1984) suggested that certain clinical ratings involving expressed hostility might have a heritable component. However, other ratings that appeared to index the tendency to suppress or inhibit anger were either not evaluated or did not show such a pattern. Thus, it is possible that certain aspects of emotionality—for example, arousability or irritability—might have a genetic loading, but also that styles of emotion management (open expression versus controlled) introduce a source of learned variance that may be etiologically significant.

In summary, the limited children's literature on TABP suggests that temperamental irritability, parental modeling of Type A behavior (including, assumably, anger and hostility), and a critical family climate may be important biological and environmental factors predisposing children to develop a hostile personality.

In terms of the literature on insecure attachment patterns, there appear to be different sources of contribution to the angry disposition of ambivalently and avoidantly attached children. As reviewed in Chapter 3, ambivalently attached children are more irritable as infants; this has not been found to be the case for avoidant children. Parenting factors appear to play more of a role than constitutional differences, especially in the case of the avoidantly attached children. Mothers of avoidant children have been described as covertly hostile, as insensitive to their infant's signals, and as overstimulating (Belsky et al., 1984; Gaensbauer et al., 1985; Main, Tomasini, & Tolan, 1979; Malatesta, et al., 1986). Thus there are three facets of parental behavior implicated in avoidant attachment that are potential contributors to a defensive anger organization. Let us look at these variables more closely.

On fine-grained analysis, it appears that what has been described as covert anger may not be especially covert. A graduate student from the first author's laboratory, Joanna Tesman (1992), did a detailed behavioral analysis of the vocal and facial behaviors of mothers during face-to-face play in early infancy. She found that what is typically described as covert hostility is more accurately described as mixed signals that involve masked anger—for example, the combination of a smile and irritated voice. Another graduate student, Connie Jones (1990) did a content analysis of the speech of mothers during mother–infant interactions sessions at $2\frac{1}{2}$, 5, 7, and 22 months, and found that mothers of insecure infants (most of whom where avoidant) used more angry content words than did mothers of secure infants during face-to-face play. Exposure to angry words, facial expressions, and tone of voice, even when partially masked, conceivably sets the stage for negative affective contagion. As Haviland and Lelwica have shown (1987), infants as young as 10 weeks of age are capable of differentiating sad, angry, and happy affect expressed by their mothers, and, more importantly, they are differentially responsive; under the anger condition, protest and anger are recruited.

In terms of insensitivity to infant cues, this feature of maternal behavior means that the children of these mothers will not learn the normal contingency patterns between their signals and the responses of partners. Infants in the first 2 to 8 months of life are capable of contingency learning, and react to noncontingency as though they are frustrated by the violation of their expectation—that is, they react with anger (Lewis, Alessandri, & Sullivan, 1990).

As for exposure to overstimulation, infants appear to have an inverted U-shaped arousal threshold, and react to extremes of arousal with distress (Field, 1982). Even young infants have strategies to deal with distress and discomfort, including defensive crying and gaze aversion (Stern, 1974).

In summary, mothers of avoidant children appear to be angrier, less sensitive, and overstimulating early in their infant's development. Later in development, the combination of avoidant attachment and exposure to maternal coercive disciplinary techniques is associated with the overattribution of hostile affect to nonhostile social stimuli (Adickman, 1993). Thus an early anger disposition may become further consolidated in personality.

Ambivalently attached children and their mothers show a different developmental history. Ambivalently attached children express more overt anger than securely attached children when they are separated from their mothers in the context of the Strange Situation, and express more anger on reunion (Cassidy &

Berlin, 1994). They also show more anger under conditions of a mastery motivation task (Frodi, Bridges, & Grolnik, 1985). According to Cassidy and Berlin's review (1994) and the work of Lyons-Ruth et al. (1984) and Belsky et al. (1984), these mothers are not described as particularly angry, but rather as inconsistent or neglecting. Inconsistency of maternal behavior means that an infant's patterns of expectancy will be built up only to be dashed, producing conditions of *frustration*, a classic trigger for anger.

Comparing the behaviors of mothers of ambivalent and avoidant infant provides a clue as to the covert versus overt nature of these children's anger organization. The overstimulating interactive style of mothers must make them aversive partners, but if angry protest by the infant is met by anger on the part of the anger-prone mother, other defensive strategies for dealing with discomfort must be acquired—such as avoidance. There is also evidence that mothers of avoidant children may actively discourage the overt expression of negative emotion, at least according to mothers' self-report (Berlin, 1993). This constellation of behaviors may explain why avoidant children are more subversive in their anger expression.

Studies of abused children, reviewed in Chapter 3, indicate that these children are predominantly insecurely attached; they are typically classified as avoidant or as showing a mixed avoidant/ambivalent pattern. Thus, the literature on maltreatment is germane to the issue of emotion socialization for anger biases in avoidant and ambivalent children. Lyons-Ruth et al. (1984) found that maltreating mothers were more likely than nonmaltreating mothers to exhibit hostility toward their infants in subtle ways, and tended to interfere in their infants' activities. Mothers who behaved in a covertly hostile manner (e.g., exhibiting behaviors such as smiling while speaking in a sharp voice) tended to have children who were avoidantly attached, and who showed a pattern of mixed avoidant and resistent behavior in the context of the Strange Situation. Crittenden (1981) found that abusing mothers interfered with their infant's goal-directed behavior (i.e., frustrated them), and displayed mixed emotional signals often involving covert hostility. During mother-infant interaction, infants of abusive mothers reacted to their intrusive, hostile, and confusing signals by fussing, averting their gaze, and refusing to interact. Other studies have shown that abusive mothers distort the affective value of emotion signals. For example, Kropp and Haynes (1987) found that abusive mothers tended to label negative affect as positive. In addition, Oldershaw and Walters (1989) found that abusive mothers perceived their children more negatively than controls, even when their children's behavior did not differ from that of other children. Abusing parents and their children are also characterized by low empathy (Miller & Eisenberg, 1988).

Interpersonal Process Develops and Sustains the Organization

Above we described some of the factors that come into play in forging an early anger organization. Here we consider the forces that aid in the consolidation of behavior patterns.

Thus far in the present developmental analysis, our infants have developed their attachment styles and are well on their way to their unique emotional organizations. The fussy, ambivalent child of infancy may now be the demanding toddler with a whine in her voice. The inexpressive, avoidant child of infancy now makes occasional "unprovoked" attacks against his mother, and seems to behave in a resentful way. Will these nascent tendencies begin to crystallize or will they be diluted and leveled with further growth and development? In point of fact, both kinds of outcome are possible. Here we consider the forces that help to maintain and consolidate early anger organizations in the case of some children.

From the above, it is easy to see why infants who find their mothers insensitive and overstimulating would become avoidant. Obviously, this is an adaptive strategy—at least in the short run—since it reduces the chances of further discomfort. However, it also deprives infants of important social learning experiences, namely, experiences contributing to knowledge about the expressive, communicative qualities of the human face. Such infants will develop their own kind of insensitivity. A longitudinal study by Crockenberg (1985) supports this prediction. Crockenberg found that mothers who expressed greater than average anger during the toddler period had less responsive attitudes during the prenatal period than mothers who expressed little anger during the toddler period. There was no significant degree of relationship between early infant irritability and maternal anger, nor between early irritability and later toddler empathy, and thus a constitutional explanation is largely ruled out. Most important for our thesis, during the toddler period maternal anger expressed toward children was found to have a unique effect on empathy. When maternal anger (versus other negative emotions) was directed toward the child, toddlers showed less concern for others more concern for the self, were less compliant, and displayed more angry defiance toward others. The lack of empathy in these children is traceable to a developmental history specific to anger socialization. The link here, between maternal anger and children's lack of empathy, is interpretable within the framework of a discrete emotions, functionalist perspective. A child exposed to greater than average parental anger will necessarily orient to the implicit threat of physical abuse or abandonment. As such, defensive strategies will be mobilized and the child's cue sensitivity will be narrowed; there will be less vigilance toward cues indicative of others' needs. Indeed, as mentioned earlier, abused children have been found to do more poorly than nonabused children on emotion recognition tasks. Other facets of parent-child interaction promoting anger biases in this context are related to modeling factors. Parents with poor anger control ostensibly deprive their children of opportunities to observe appropriate anger modulation; moreover, given the monopolization of anger in the parents' repertoire, they also deprive their children of opportunities to observe other emotions, and to observe empathic responses to others.

We can envision how children's own anger organizations may become consolidated over time. Exposure to angry affect tends to reproduce anger in others because of the principle of affect contagion; that is, the affect of one person has a tendency to spread to that person's social partners (Izard, 1972). The spread of anger among those exposed to the angry affect of others is illustrated in a series of studies by Cummings and colleagues (e.g., Cummings, 1987; Cummings, Ballard, El-Sheikh, & Lake, 1991; El-Sheikh, Cummings, & Goetsch, 1989). Children were exposed to background anger while they were alone or playing with other children. The anger occurred in the context of arguments between adults, either parents or unfamiliar individuals. What Cummings and colleagues have shown, convincingly enough, is that mere exposure to angry affect, even when it is not directed at the child, produced feelings of anger and distress in those children who overheard it; in some children it even instigated aggressive behavior. Children are apparently also sensitive to the patterns of emotion exchange between their parents and are differentially affected. For example, Katz and Gottman (cited in Gottman, 1993) examined the effect of parental marital interaction on children's emotional development. They identified two marital interaction patterns on the basis of cluster analysis; one was symmetrically hostile (called the mutually hostile pattern), and the other was an asymmetrical pattern in which the wife was angry and the husband was withdrawn (called the pursuer–distancer pattern). The investigators found that marital behavior sampled when the children were 5 years of age predicted their emotional problems 3 years later. The mutually hostile marital pattern predicted externalizing behavior problems in the children (e.g., aggressiveness), as assessed by teachers' ratings on the Child Behavior Checklist, whereas the pursuer–distancer marital pattern predicted children's internalizing problems (e.g., depression).

In terms of parent–child interactions, more will be involved than contagion of parental anger, though this is surely a component. As Crockenberg (1985) has pointed out, there is likely a reciprocal relation between maternal attitudes and behaviors and children's behaviors that helps to maintain maternal anger, such that mothers who are less responsive characterologically may set the stage for children's noncompliance, which in turn may stimulate more maternal anger and further noncompliance from children.

Development beyond early infancy will also be affected by parental child-rearing styles of discipline and conflict resolution. Parent–child conflicts are emotionally charged, salient, and repetitive; they are conceivably an important crucible for the development of emotion organizations and for learning affect management strategies and defenses (Malatesta & Wilson, 1988). Magai et al. (1994) found that adult subjects who reported that their parents used coercive disciplinary styles (including physical punishment) to a significant extent had emotion-trait profiles organized around the hostile emotions. Adickman (1993), studying 6- to 8-year-olds, found that the combination of insecure attachment and coercive disciplinary styles was associated with hostile biases in the children's emotion projection.

Language is another vehicle for the elaboration of an anger sensitivity. As Jones (1990) has shown, the mothers of children destined to be avoidantly attached engage in more anger narrative than the mothers of those who develop secure attachments. Miller and Sperry's (1987) ethnographic study of the socialization of anger and aggression in children from the urban, working-class neighborhood of South Baltimore was reviewed in Chapter 6. Recall that the children were 18 to 25 months old at the start of the study and they and their mothers were studied over a period of 8 months. What Miller and Sperry found from interviews and tape-recorded interactions was that the mothers were preparing their children for the street-tough life of South Baltimore by teasing them and inciting anger. In addition, mothers' narratives were structured so as educate their children in the proper response to provocation—that is, to be angry rather than sad—and included instruction in the instrumental strategies for dealing with both one's own anger as well as the anger and aggression of others. Dodge et al.'s (1986) analysis of the information-processing strategies of aggressive children also suggests some of the reasons why angry patterns may be maintained over time and become consolidated in personality. These researchers found that aggressive versus nonaggressive children had more hostile information-processing biases. More important, they were also more likely than average children to receive negative and ignoring peer responses when they attempted to enter a group, thus probably reinforcing their sense of needing to screen the world for the hostile intentions of others.

It is clear from the above that children can develop emotion-specific biases—in this case, an anger organization—in their behavior at a very young age. In fact, such biases may develop as early as the first year of life. Shiller, Izard, and Hembree (1986), who coded the emotional response of 13-month-olds to separation from the mother, found that some expressers of high-negative emotion displayed predominantly anger, whereas others showed mainly sadness. Anger biases may persist over long periods of time. Caspi, Elder, and Bem's (1987) analysis of data from the Berkeley Longitudinal Study, tracking development from early childhood (8–10 years of age) until 30–40 years of age, indicates that ill-tempered boys become ill-tempered men and ill-tempered girls grow up to have marriages characterized by dissension and conflict, and which tend to dissolve.

An examination of the literature on the Type A personality configuration begins to shed light on what kinds of circumstances and processes help to maintain the organization over time. The latest research indicates that a key feature of the Type A personality is not only that Type As experience anger more frequently, but that their emotion management style is one of suppression (Malatesta-Magai et al., 1992). According to clinical observation, suppression of anger should result in projection. And, indeed, as indicated earlier, in our own research we were able to empirically confirm the tendency of Type A's to project anger onto the protagonists of ambiguous vignettes. Projection of anger, interpersonally, is a primary vehicle for interpersonal antagonism and the maintenance of friction and animosity.

The above literature illuminates the origins and some of the factors involved in the maintenance of anger organizations over time. One factor, of course, is constitutional irritability. Other factors involve exposure to social agents who are frustrating, overly intrusive, and insensitive to infant cues, who lack empathy, who display excessive anger, who use coercive disciplinary strategies, who elaborate an angry worldview, and/or whose regulation of anger is poorly performed. Early emotion biases are then sustained through the mechanisms of either interpersonal avoidance or regular angry interchanges. Repetitive emotional experiences also affect cognitive function in pervasive ways, including perception and appraisal, encoding, memory, interpretation of information, and attributions. Over time, these experiences help to create the development of informational "structures" that are conditioned to process information in preferential ways. Such cognitive biases then come to sustain particular kinds of emotion. In the case of anger, perceptions, appraisals, and attributions are inclined to find the world a hostile, frustrating, and humiliating place. This in turn generates behaviors whose products confirm the hostility of the world. Thus, emotion, cognition, and behavior interact in a synergistic way such that perceptions and feeling sustain one another in a recursive loop.

From the above discussion we can distill some general principles of emotions socialization, but certain features will be idiosyncratic to the unique functional and signal properties of anger. General principles include constitutional predispositions, affect contagion, self-regulation and defensive coping, and emotional–cognitive–behavioral loops. Anger-specific processes involve the emotion-specific properties of anger as a motivational signal to the self, and as an informational/motivational signal to others. Experiences with frustration will provoke anger, not fear or happiness. Interpersonally, displaying an angry face and voice will provoke aggression in others; displaying a fearful, sad, or interested face and voice, likely will not. And so on. In order to illustrate this more forcefully, we now turn to an examination of the shame/shyness trait and its development.

SHAME/SHYNESS IN PERSONALITY PROCESS

Certain individuals are introverted, somewhat self-effacing, and socially shy. Unlike the hostile individual, they are not inclined to be aggressive. Here we consider the personality trait that relates most closely to shame, that of shyness and social sensitivity. By all accounts shyness is a common affliction. Zimbardo (1986) found that 55% of students identify themselves as being shy (15% were situationally shy, whereas 40% were "dispositionally shy").

Although shyness can be described as involving "social anxiety," and although shy people tend to report substantial levels of anxiety, it is clear that shyness is not synonymous with general anxiety or fearfulness. For example, Jones, Briggs, and Smith (1986), using several measures of dispositional shyness, have demonstrated that the personality trait of shyness is either uncorrelated or weakly correlated with nonsocial fears.

Shyness, theoretically, is a derivative of shame (Tomkins, 1962, 1963), though few shy people will admit that they are shame conflicted. Scheff (1984) has maintained that there is a taboo on the acknowledgment of shame in contemporary Western culture; we are ashamed to acknowledge shame. However, if shyness is indeed linked to shame, shy people should report being susceptible to embarrassment, and, indeed, the correlation between measures of shyness and the tendency to be easily embarrassed range from .57 to .70 (Jones, Briggs, & Smith, 1986). Dispositionally shy persons should also show other features of personality linked to the shame-relevant feelings of exposure, vulnerability, and failure, and to the behaviors of avoidance, hiding, and self-protection, as we will see as the analysis proceeds.

Within the framework of our discrete emotions, functionalist analysis of personality, when shame predominates in personality we say that the individual is organized around the trait of shame. The theory predicts that shame as a trait will be an enduring dispositional tendency and that evidence of such will be found pervasively as biases in information processessing, behavioral dispositions, coping, and interpersonal relations.

The Shame/Shyness Organization

Table 4 indicates that the fundamental self-cuing properties of shame are that one is exposed, has failed, or is inferior. The behavioral tendency associated with shame is retreat and hiding. As such, we would expect a person organized around the emotion of shame (1) to feel exposed, vulnerable, and less socially competent than others, (2) to have a perceptual organization biased toward self-consciousness, (3) to perceive others as having a negative evaluation of the self, (4) to see the self as one thinks others do (i.e., as inadequate), (5) to lack facility with social skills, including assertiveness, and (6) to avoid occasions of social exposure. As a behavioral organization, a shame bias finds expression in three characterological descriptions in the literature: "behaviorally inhibited" infants, "withdrawn" children, and "shy" and "socially anxious" adults.

Kagan and his colleagues (Kagan & Snidman, 1991; Kagan, Snidman, & Arcus, 1992) have been studying the behavior of "behaviorally inhibited" infants for the past several years. This research indicates that 15–20% of healthy Caucasian children living in stable families can be classified as being temperamentally inhibited and 30–35% as uninhibited. The traits were found to be stable through the eighth year in 75% of the children. Four-month-old infants were originally classified as "high reactive" or "low reactive" on the basis of their motoric responses to a variety of stimuli, including a tape-recorded human voice. Motoric responses of the high-reactive infants included spastic motions, vigorous limb activity, and back arching. High-reactive infants also fussed and cried during intense motoric activity. Motoric responses of the low-reactive infants were much less intense and not accompanied by distress. Observations of the infants interacting at 14 months with both social and nonsocial unfamiliar stimuli indicated that the high-reactive infants responded with high fear and the low-reactive infants responded with low fear. A similar assessment at 21 months showed the same results. The high-reactive children of infancy became the behaviorally inhibited children of school age. As assessed at 4, $5\frac{1}{2}$, and $7\frac{1}{2}$ years of age in the context of exposure to an unfamiliar setting, unfamiliar peers, and novel objects, behaviorally inhibited children tended to be cautious, shy, emotionally reserved, and remained close to their mothers. Kagen's research thus suggests that there is a group of children who are physiologically predisposed to shyness as a trait, although he acknowledges that there are probably two types of shy children. One group is shy because their physiology biases them to develop a reserved style around people and to be avoidant of other types of unfamiliar stimuli. Another group may become shy because they have experienced rejection by their parents or peers.

In their Waterloo Longitudinal Project, Rubin and colleagues studied the interpersonal problem-solving skills of extremely withdrawn children in early elementary school (summarized in Rubin & Rose-Krasnor, 1992). In contrast to nonwithdrawn children, withdrawn children tended to rely on more adult-dependent, nonassertive problem-solving strategies with respect to object conflict and friendship initiation dilemmas. In play with nonwithdrawn peer partners, socially withdrawn children were more likely to modify their initial requests to partners after failure, i.e., to be accommodating or deferential.

Much of the research on shyness and social anxiety has been conducted with adult subjects. In adults, shyness has been defined by the "propensity to respond with heightened anxiety, self-consciousness, and reticence in a variety of social contexts" (Jones, Cheek, & Briggs, 1986, p. 630). In terms of perceptual biases, shy persons are inclined to see themselves as being more self-disclosing than they actually are (Meleshko & Alden, 1993), ostensibly because they may already feel particularly exposed and vulnerable. The negative thoughts of shy people tend to center on personal inadequacy and desires to withdraw and escape from social interaction (Brodt & Zimbardo, 1981; Jones & Russell, 1982; Zimbardo, 1977). Shy versus nonshy people report substantial social anxiety, and they are more likely to make self-protective, internal, and stable attributions for their social distress (Arkin, Appelman, & Burger, 1980; Girodo, Dotzenroth, & Stein, 1981).

Shyness/shame is behaviorally evident in any number of verbal and nonverbal markers. Malatesta-Magai and Dorval (1992) describe the verbal and nonverbal markers of shame, contempt, and affiliation during interpersonal process. Markers of shame include facial indicators of blushing and "abashed look," hiding behaviors such as covering the face, averting the face or body, gaze aversion, lowered head, and slumped or lowered posture, and self-grooming behaviors. Verbal indicators include self-contempt or defensiveness, statements of submission, embarrassed or self-conscious laughter, low or lowered voice, trailing voice, and marked speech disfluency.

Shy persons are perceived by others as having low social and interpersonal skills. Shy versus nonshy persons are typically rated as less friendly, less assertive, less relaxed, less talented, less poised, and more shy in both conversations and monologues (Cheek & Buss, 1981; Jones, Cavert, & Indart, 1983; Pilkonis, 1977).

In terms of coping and defense strategies, our functionalist analysis indicates that the adaptive goal of shame/shyness is to protect the vulnerable person from further violations of his privacy and to reduce exposure and vulnerability (see Table 4). We would thus expect the coping responses of shy persons to be organized around avoiding social disapproval. One could achieve this goal by being congenial, noncontroversial, nonconfrontational, and agreeable. Interestingly, the literature indicates that shy persons are particularly vulnerable to social persuasion and attitude change. For example, Souza and Silva (1977) found that shy versus nonshy subjects were more readily persuaded to change their attitudes to match those of a speaker. Another way of avoiding social disapproval is to adopt conventional behavior and attitudes (Arkin et al., 1980) and to limit the opportunities where one's behavior can be observed and evaluated, such as public speaking (Jones, Briggs, & Smith, 1986). Interpersonally, shy persons initiate fewer conversations and talk less than those low in shyness (Pilkonis, 1977), are less self-disclosing (Jones & Briggs, 1984), and avoid social encounters (Leary, 1986). They are less assertive interpersonally, tend to experience more dating and sexual problems, and suffer from loneliness (Zimbardo, 1986). The shyness trait is sustained by an anxiety-inhibition cycle (Leary, 1984) as well as by the dynamics of interpersonal process. Being with others makes the shy person feel anxious; retreat reduces the anxiety but reinforces the isolation. Interpersonally, loneliness is sustained because shy people are less open and outgoing. As such they tend to seek out social partners less often. By the same token, shy people are judged to be less friendly and likeable (Jones & Russell, 1982; Zimbardo, 1977) and thus are less likely to be sought after as social partners. Even in the midst of a social relationship, their self-protective behaviors, such as low self-disclosure, reduce the chances for intimacy and guarantee further social isolation. They are also deprived of corrective social feedback. Thus, the social isolation of shy people is interpersonally reinforced and sustained over time. Research indicates long term stability of the shyness pattern. Kagan's work shows that behaviorally inhibited infants become behaviorally inhibited children. Morris, Soroker, and Burruss (1954) found that 24 individuals who had been classified as shy and withdrawn as children still displayed this tendency 16 to 27 years later. Caspi, Bem, and Elder's (1988) analysis of the Berkeley Longitudinal Study found that men with a history of childhood shyness tended to delay marriage, fatherhood, and establishment of a stable career. Shy women spent significantly less time in the labor force than other women.

In summary, the shy/shame-prone individual is well identified in the literature. Individuals who are behaviorally inhibited or shy appear to experience more social anxiety on a day-to-day basis, are self-conscious and preoccupied on a more regular basis, and are more likely to perceive others as critical and judgmental, to see the self as inadequate, to be socially and politically conventional, to be socially avoidant and low on intimacy, to be unassertive, and to suffer a variety of interpersonal problems. On the other hand, since shame is intrinsically a social emotion, and is relevant because the person cares about others (for their opinions and interest in the self), when levels of shame are not dysfunctionally high, they sensitize the person to social cues, make him more socially observant and responsive, and foster empathy. For example, Rubin and colleagues (Rubin & Rose-Krasnor, 1992) found that grade-school children who were shy were more likely than nonshy children to modify their initial requests to partners after failure, and concluded that shy children can thus be viewed as responsive to feedback from social partners and quite resilient in following initial social failure. To give another instance, persons who enter the clinical field, such as Carl Rogers, are often likely to be shame sensitive. In fact, Magai and Haviland (in preparation) suggest that shame was a significant precondition for Rogers's success in psychotherapy and for the elaboration of his theory of psychotherapy. According to Lewis (1971), the shame-sensitive individual has permeable self-boundaries and can readily travel between the self and social partner. Coincidentally or not, this is a hallmark of empathy. In addition, shame fosters introspection and self-reflection, attributes that are essential for the "examined life" that is worth living and for personality change in psychotherapy. Affect is in general very contagious, especially shame. One cannot help but imagine that some of Rogers's legendary success with clients resided in his approachable, non-threatening persona, in the shame-relevant affect that he radiated, and in client contagion of shame and consequently closer inspection of the self. Once shame is induced in the client it has the capacity, by virtue of its self-cuing function, to foster or enhance self-consciousness and self-awareness. Of course, not all therapists are characterized by shame-relevant affect, nor are all therapists equally empathic. Fritz Perls, for example, was more dominated by contempt; he was notably sarcastic, aggressive, and confrontational. He tended to ignite anger in clients but then was able to have them use these experiences therapeutically. In any case, the above review indicates the presence of a distinct personality bias for shame/shyness, and that its influence is pervasively found in perception, information processing, intrapsychic dimensions, and interpersonal behavior. We turn now to a consideration of the origins of the shame/shyness personality disposition.

Ontogeny of the Shame/Shy Organization

Kagan's research on behaviorally inhibited infants and youngsters indicates that at least some shy children may be inclined toward shyness by genetic predisposition. Since other shy children did not show a history of high motoric reactance in infancy, we may conclude that shyness may be acquired by other means as well. Moreover, a biological predisposition for behavioral inhibition does not guarantee that one's fate is irrevocably linked to shyness, since some 25% of the children studied by Kagen were no longer behaviorally inhibited by their eighth year (Kagan et al., 1992). To further our discussion we consider social factors that may interact with biology or that may initiate the beginnings of a shy/shame organization.

Darwin (1872) suggested that shame can be seen in the child as early as the second year of life. Recent research confirms that the capacity for shame is in place by at least $2\frac{1}{2}$ years of age. Barrett, Zahn-Waxler, and Cole (1993) found that 80% of $2\frac{1}{2}$-year-old children display shame behaviors in the context of a mishap. Stranger wariness at 9 months may be the developmental precursor of social shyness at a later age (Lewis, 1992).

Lewis (1992) has suggested that certain parental disciplinary practices also predispose the child toward the development of shame. The child-rearing literature of the 1950s and 1960s distinguished between several styles of parental discipline: coercive discipline involving the use of physical punishment and deprivation of privileges, love-withdrawal, and induction. Magai and Hunziker (1995) have further distinguished between inductive approaches that involve guilt-manipulation, and matter-of-fact induction which involves reasoning. Lewis (1992) suggests that love withdrawal is relevant to shame socialization because the parent's withdrawal of love generates a very powerful internal global attribution of failure. A recent study (Magai & Hunziker, 1995) that looked at the emotion-trait profiles of individuals as a function of their rearing histories confirmed that there was a significant correlation between self-reported shame and the parental child-rearing styles of guilt induction and love withdrawal, but not matter-of-fact induction or physical punishment.

Tomkins (1963) devotes almost all of Volume 2 of *Affect, Imagery, Consciousness* to shame/humiliation and its socialization. As he indicates, some shame experiences are inescapable and linked to human development. For example, children cannot help but note the difference in stature and in motoric, linguistic, and cognitive abilities between themselves and adults, and the comparisons are intrinsically shaming. Shame is also fostered in the child by the experience of failure and defeat—events that can hardly be avoided in the course of development—and by critical comments from social agents—also hardly to be avoided within the context of most families. However, not all children develop a shame/shyness bias. Tomkins suggests that shame in children is fostered by the punitive socialization of that affect. By this he meant that instead of minimizing the exposure to circumstances that could result in failure, and attenuating the child's experiences of shame through empathic responding, the parent magnifies the experience of shame. Shame magnification can take many forms—both behaviorally and through the inculcation of beliefs and attitudes. Tomkins felt that shame was promoted when a parent showed contempt for a child who acted ashamed, thereby amplifying the child's original shame experience. The parent also sensitizes the child to shame by continually drawing the child's attention to shameful acts and objects and by screening the world for humiliating and shameful events, pointing them out, and expanding upon them. When a child continually hears an ideology that supports the elicitation of shame, such as "children don't know any better" and "children ought to be seen and not heard," she eventually comes to believe this ideology. If a child hears comments to the effect that "people are basically selfish and not to be trusted," she can develop a deep suspiciousness of human nature and anxiety about intimacy and self-disclosure. A child exposed to such an ideology will naturally seek verification that people really are that way; with such a bias and selective vigilance, it should not be difficult to locate confirmation, which would then reinforce the validity of the ideology.

Finally, exposure to contempt and criticism is intrinsically shaming. Therefore, if the parent has a monopolistic contempt organization, he or she will be especially critical of the child, as with all other social objects. Tomkins suggested that a child exposed to such a shame-saturated culture can respond in several ways. He may submit, render deference, and thereby reexperience shame; over time, shame will crystallize. Alternatively, he may fight back by turning contempt against the parents. This will normally lead to a struggle between parent and child, with further parental criticism and attempts to dominate and control the autonomy of the child, and with rebellion and counterattack on the part of the child, leading to a contempt/shame/contempt/shame spiral. The above begins to shed light on how interpersonal process generates and sustains this particular kind of emotion organization. It bears further examination.

Interpersonal Process Develops and Sustains the Organizations

Thus far we have described some of the factors that contribute to a bias towards shame/shyness. Here we consider the forces that act to reinforce and sustain that pattern.

Initial shame/shyness tendencies may be reinforced by continued experiences with criticism, failure, exclusion, or exposure. More typically, they are sustained and amplified within dynamic social systems such as families, where there are repetitive and mutually influential exchanges over long periods of time. This kind of dynamic is well illustrated in an affective and sociolinguistic analysis of the speech and interaction patterns of a family that was filmed during the course of a study of language development (Malatesta-Magai & Dorval, 1992).

The family in question consisted of a father, a mother, and a 12-year-old son; the family was videotaped in their home and was asked simply to spend some time talking to one another as they normally would. The talk activity consisted largely of a discussion of the family's plans for the upcoming week and making arrangements for them.

Despite the banality of the topic at hand and the relatively stress-free and neutral conditions under which the filming was done, the interchange was saturated with affective communication. Informal inspection of the 24-min clip disclosed that the predominant affects displayed by this family were shame, contempt, and, to a more limited extent, affiliation. A subsequent microanalytic analysis of speech and of verbal and nonverbal markers of affect indicated that the mother had a predominant shame organization and the father a predominant contempt organization. The father expressed a certain superiority and disdain via aloofness during most of the filming, and by various critical comments directed at the wife; the comments were subtle but their contemptuous nature was readily detected by our coding system, and the wife's contingent reactivity validated the affective content of these communications. The verbal and nonverbal communications of contempt and disrespect provoked attempts by the wife to defend herself as well as to countershame her husband and expose him before his son and the camera person. Over the course of the 24-min interaction, the husband continued to express his resistance by alternately withdrawing and participating in a disruptive manner, and by periodically contradicting his wife, belittling her, and failing to agree with agendas she had constructed for the family. Moreover, the son colluded with the father in undermining the mother's objectives.

The wife's nonverbal behavior suggested intensified shame as the session proceeded. She did not, however, confront her husband or challenge her son, but kept forging ahead with issues of various social obligations, trying to enlist her family's cooperation in discussing the issues and making resolutions. In so doing, she ignored (bypassed) and contained her shame. The son's participation during this session consisted of playful mockery and occasional affiliative gestures toward his father, but was more often characterized by rebellion and overt contempt toward both parents, particularly his mother; for example, at one point he gestured to paintings on the wall and derogated his mother's taste in artwork.

However, he also showed runs of shame when the father's critical commentary was momentarily diverted to him, when either parent attempted to exert domination of him, and in empathic response to some of his mother's more obvious reactions to the belittling comments of her husband.

Given the mother's exposure to her son's resistance and thinly veiled sarcasm, the husband's withholding stance, and the mother's exclusion from the occasional bouts of repartee enjoyed by father and son, it is likely that the mother experienced intermittant shame, distress, and frustration. The father and son colluded in their resistance and contempt, and in the process excluded the mother. Nevertheless, the mother accepted much of this in apparent good humor and without open rebellion, and continued to forward the process of family agenda-making. What is of note here is the mother's bypassed shame and singular pursuit of the family agendas. The bypassed shame apparently permitted her to cope with the immediate situation and was adaptive in this context. However, if the coping style we observed is characterological and not simply situationally elicited by the presence of the experimenter in the home, she is at risk for insensitivity and the reinforcement of alienation. By disattending to her own shame she at least partially deflects the experience of anger. But the avoidance of confrontation means continued isolation and tacit permission for the father and son to behave in a distancing, exclusionary way, thereby perpetuating the familial cycle of contempt, shame, and alienation.

An analysis of the son's affective behavior revealed runs of both shame and contempt. He experienced shame by virtue of parental domination, by exposure to the contempt of his father, and by his empathic identification with the shame of his mother. He absorbed and learned a contemptuous style of relating as well, both in defense against shame and through identification with his father. His out-of-family narratives—mockery of a doctor's assistant and ridicule of classmates—indicated that his disdain and rebellion was not prompted solely by the family's attempt to restrict his behavior. In the latter instances he was not being coerced, yet contempt was a dominant posture. This impression is reinforced by a collateral film in which the son is observed having a conversation with a school friend; his patronizing mannerisms and derogatory comments closely resemble those of his father, but he also displays clear markers of shame as well, and alternates between the two.

In summary, shame is forged within family systems and reinforced by systemic features that sustain it over time. The above study also illustrates another point made earlier. An individual's shame experience can be conscious or bypassed (Lewis, 1971). In the case where it is conscious, the painful affect experienced by the individual can motivate anger and confrontation and can also motivate reparative interpersonal actions as described within Tomkins's framework. Shame that is unconscious and bypassed, however, has different ramifications both intrapsychically and interpersonally, as illustrated above. The socialization literature is not sufficiently elaborated to determine which factors influence the development of conscious versus bypassed shame. However, the Magai, Distel, and Liker (1994) study found that conscious shame was reported only by those individuals exposed to guilt induction and love withdrawal. Although Lewis (1992) has suggested that coercive discipline is also shaming, the Magai et al. study failed to disclose an association between subjects' report of parental reliance on coercive discipline and elevations on subjective shame. As such, it is possible that coercive, punitive discipline fosters a defensive coping style that results in the routing of shame from consciousness.

Experiences beyond the family can neutralize an emerging shame pattern or may amplify it even further. A recent study conducted at the Max Planck Institute in Berlin examined the impact of differential teaching styles on children's self efficacy and academic performance in the former east and west sections of the city before the political unification of the two Germanies (Oettinger, Little, Lindenberger, & Baltes, 1994). The teaching style in East Germany, congruent with a collectivist ideology, consisted of providing individual performance feedback to children in front of the whole class as early as the first grade; moreover, other teacher evaluations—expressed both verbally and nonverbally—were given throughout the school day, and further public evaluations were held during parent–teacher assemblies, at parents' workplaces, and at meetings of state-organized youth organizations. In contrast, in the West, performance feedback was given privately and teaching was more individualized to suit the needs and talents of children. As expected, East German children were found to have lower personal agency and self-efficacy beliefs and these predicted school grades. What is interesting about the East–West differences from a discrete emotions point of view is that the children in the East Germany schools were exposed to massive shaming tactics. Thus, it is possible that the oberved differences in control beliefs and in school performance may be mediated by differential internalization of shame. As indicated above, public exposure and criticism is innately shaming in character, and produces feelings of inadequacy. Although there has not been a follow-up of these groups of children since the East converted to the Western system, discrete emotions theory would make the prediction that there will be shame residues in the personality structures of the children from the East, which may be manifest in continuing feelings of greater vulnerability, a lowered facility in social skills, heightened self-consciousness, lower assertiveness, greater social isolation, lower guilt (versus shame), less intrinsic motivation, and continuing compromise of self-efficacy beliefs. Of course, not all children would be expected to show this pattern, in particular, those exposed to the buffering effects of certain family circumstances—secure attachment patterns and parental disciplinary styles favoring induction (reasoning) rather than coersion or love withdrawal. We would also predict that children with insecure attachments who were exposed to coercive disciplinary practices at home and shaming and criticism in school, under the less repressive milieu of Western style education, would begin to more overtly express an inner rage that had previously been sequestered. Since the shamed self naturally responds with anger under conditions in which anger is not restricted, the repetitive exposure to angering circumstances in the lives of these children (insensitive and coercive child rearing at home, shaming in school) creates conditions that are ripe for explosive, rebellious, and antisocial behavior. Longitudinal follow-up of the children of this "experiment in nature" would provide invaluable data for the testing of developmental models of branching life courses (Magai & Hunziker, 1993).

The above literature sheds light on the origins of some of the factors involved in the maintenance of shame organizations over time. One factor is clearly a constitutional predisposition. Other factors involve exposure to parental affect biases, experiences with failure, parental disciplinary practices, socialization that involves criticism, teasing and taunting, and exposure to a familial shame ideology or to interpersonal process centered on contempt within the family. Early biases are then magnified by subsequent interpersonal experiences and sustained through social avoidance and isolation. Repetitive experiences such as these result in shame becoming structuralized within the personality, and with the elaboration of informational structures that are conditioned to process information in a shame-vigilent way. Shame-prone individuals are inclined to be self-conscious, to be vigilant for other's criticism or disapproval, and to be dissatisfied with the self. These traits, in turn, cause individuals to be socially reticent and to be selective in their self-disclosure patterns. If the shyness is extreme, such a personality will reinforce in others the impression of unapproachability and unfriendliness, which may further support the individual's social isolation.

From the above we can extract some general principles of emotion socialization, but once again, as in the case of anger, certain features will be idiosyncratic to the unique functional and signal properties of shame. General principles include constitutional predispositions, affect contagion, identification, defensive coping, and emotional–cognitive–behavioral loops. Shame-specific processes involve the emotion-specific properties of shame as a motivational signal to the self (signals that communicate exposure, vulnerability, and inadequacy), and as an informational/motivational signal to others (desire for privacy and unassertive interpersonal style). The shy/shame-prone child will be a ready target for schoolyard bullies and others with a penchant for domination (Olweas, 1980).

On the more positive side, shame-prone individuals may have more harmonious social relationships with their immediate circle of friends and colleagues in that they will tend to be more conciliatory and accommodating. The heightened social sensitivity of such individuals may also make them more interpersonally responsive and predispose them for careers in the helping professions, as in the case of Carl Rogers.

In the following section we turn to a more extended discussion of the factors that are involved in the development of emotion biases.

EMOTION BIASES, SOCIALIZATION, AND PERSONALITY

Earliest Developmental Influences

In this section we consider genetics, basic parental warmth and empathy, and early learning processes.

Genetic Influences

It should be obvious from the above material that constitutional differences play a role in biasing personality development. A general discussion of the contributions of temperament can be found in the series of roundtable discussions that appear in the April 1987 issue of *Child Development* (pp. 505–529). A summary of findings from a longitudinal study of twins that is especially relevant to a consideration of emotion biases is described in an article by Emde et al. (1992). In brief, this study of 200 twin pairs found, based on observational ratings, a modest heritability for behavioral inhibition and shyness, significant heritability for activity level, but not task orientation, and a significant heritability for empathy. The heritability for general positive and negative hedonic tone was not significant. In terms of parental ratings, there was significant heritability for sociability, shyness, attention, activity, and emotionality. There was little genetic influence for frustration, as assessed by the child's reaction to restraint and toy removal. These data suggest that there may be a greater heritability for affect biases of shyness over anger. The fact that there was not a significant heritability for general positive and negative affect is not surprising from the point of view of discrete emotions theory. General ratings risk obscuring significant findings with respect to individual negative emotions, which have different properties and probably different heritability quotients.

Heritability estimates do not account for all of the variance in emotion traits, and thus we must turn to the contribution of socialization experiences. Here we consider factors such as parental input, affect dynamics, and information-processing phenomena.

Parental Warmth, Empathy, and Affective Balance

As Tomkins (1962, 1963) originally suggested, children are likely to acquire emotional organizations or affective biases under conditions that involve the punitive socialization of emotion (Malatesta et al., 1989). In contrast, under rewarding socialization of emotion, children develop a balanced repertoire, one in which no particular emotion dominates the personality; such individuals experience and use affects flexibly in the organization of goal-directed behavior, and possess general socioemotional competence. It is now apparent that parental warmth and sympathy are important conditions for the rewarding socialization of emotion. For example, Roberts and Strayer (1987) found that parental warmth was significantly related to the encouragement of negative affect expression, and that warmth and responsiveness accounted for 61–69% of the variance seen in children's general socioemotional competence. Parental warmth is also correlated with children's empathy (Barnett, 1987), and parental sympathy is correlated with children's self-reported situational sympathy, at least for girls (Fabes et al., 1990). Eisenberg et al. (1991) found that family cohesiveness, a variable assumed to provide the kind of emotional support believed to facilitate empathy and sympathetic responding, was associated with reported sympathy, as well as sadness in reaction to a sympathy-provoking film. Parents who are characterized by greater than average personal distress or anger had children with less dispositional sympathy (Fabes et al., 1990) and empathy (Crockenberg, 1985).

In summary, having a warm, sympathetic parent whose own emotional organization is well-balanced and not constricted by the monopolization of any particular emotional bias, will likely encourage the development of the child's full emotional repertoire, general socioemotional competence, and disposition toward interpersonal sympathy and empathy. In contrast, the parent whose own personality favors some emotions to the exclusion of others is likely to create an emotional climate that fosters the development of emotion biases in his children. But the issue of parental influence raises several other even more basic principles, the first of which is mutual accommodation in dyadic influence.

Mutual Accommodation

Emotions have evolved phylogenetically within the context of mammalian developmental needs and the properties of gregarious social organizations, as noted in Chapter 2. Emotions are thus intrinsically social, although they serve individual goals, needs, and ultimately individual survival. A principle of emotion socialization that is closely associated with this property and with the signal function of emotions is that which we will term "mutual accommodation."

One of the first psychologists to tie mutual regulation of dyadic behavior to signal exchange between interactants was Karl Bühler (1927). During the 1920s, Bühler was drawn to the then emerging science of cybernetics, and was quick to discern its application as a model for certain aspects of human behavior. In a three-volume work on language, expressive behavior, and the state of psychology as a science (*Sprachtheorie, Ausdrückpsychologie, Die Krise der Psychologie*), Bühler mapped out his conceptualization of how members of a community (no matter how large or small—a dyad is a small community or system) regulate one another's behavior through the exchange of signals.

Bühler (1927) makes a distinction between three terms with respect to the development of signals. Early expressive behaviors are "symptoms"; they may or may not be goal directed. When symptoms are interpreted by another person as goal-directed communications, they become "signals." When interpretations of signals are specific to the receiver they are called "representations." Representations are said to depend on the nature of the relationship between the sender and receiver, and thus add a distinctly qualitative aspect to the communication. Interactants in a dyad, or in any other community of interactants with a history of relationship, interpret the expressive symptoms within the framework of that history. The behaviors of a "community" of interactants therefore are never independent from one another; rather, they are interdependent. Individuals regulate one another's behavior through the ongoing exchange of signals. The term Bühler actually used was *gegenseitige Steurung*, which literally translated means mutual control or mutual regulation. This term has somewhat of a mechanistic ring to it, consistent with its cybernetic derivation. Today we might prefer to view the process he described as one of *mutual accommodation*, a term that captures the more dynamic and reciprocal quality of the phenomenon, as well as the organismic aspect of human interaction.

Mutual accommodation is a fitting description of the kinds of behaviors that characterize the parent–infant interaction. Stern (1984) speaks of the developing mother–infant accommodation to one another's behavior as "attunement." The mother is said to adjust her behavior to match that of her infant in terms of the form, intensity, and temporal features of the baby's expressive behavior; the infant also responds to the mother's activities. Affect attunement is said to involve matching not only of overt behaviors, but of internal states as well. Sometimes this synchrony does not prevail. When one or the other of the partners fails to respond to the other in a way that maintains harmonious mutual regulation, "misattunement" occurs. If misattunement persists, the child is said to be at risk for subsequent behavioral problems. There is much in the empirical literature to support these assertions. The constructs of attunement and misattunement relate readily to the principle of mutual accommodation.

Mutual accommodation is achieved when members of a dyad appreciate dyadic contingencies. If contingency does not obtain, synchrony of interaction is impossible. Once mutual accommodation is achieved, a breakdown in the pattern of contingency produces visible disruption to the dyad and to the behaviors of the individual interactants; moreover, the breakdown in pattern is accompanied by evidence of emotional distress and internal dysregulation.

It is now well established that interactions between caregivers and their infants are characterized by a high rate of exchange of emotional (expressive) signals. Malatesta and Haviland's (1982) study of the contingency patterns between mothers and their 3- to 6-month-old infants during face-to-face play showed that maternal responses are immediate, contingent, and specific to the kinds of signals that infants emit. Both mothers and infants display a high rate of emotional expressions to their partners; each partner emits about 8 expressions per minute. This average, however, obscures individual differences of considerable magnitude. In the Malatesta and Haviland study, when infant rates were lower than this average, maternal rates were also low; correspondingly, when infant rates were higher than average, maternal rates were higher as well.

Maternal responses to infant affect changes have an intrinsic rhythm that appears to mirror the rhythm of the child. Infants occasionally become overstimulated, which precipitates crying and gaze aversion. In such instances, typically, mothers quickly modify their level of stimulation. Field (1982) found that mothers tend to keep their levels of activity at a rate that maintains the infant at an optimal level of arousal.

For their part, infants are also responsive to the signals of their mothers and will alter their behavior accordingly. For example, Cohen and Tronick (1983) found that 3-month-old infants of healthy nondepressed mothers, who simulated depressed affect in a laboratory manipulation, engaged in behaviors that appeared oriented toward eliciting responsivity from their mothers so as to restore more normal patterns of interaction. The mothers were asked to simulate depression by adopting an unresponsive, frozen facial expression, and to resist responding to their infants when the infants reacted. The babies initially responded with brief positive expressions; when this failed to elicit a response, they began to fret and cry, and finally turned away and withdrew.

In summary, infants and caregivers come prepared to react to their partners' emotional signals in a way that reveals sensitivity to patterns of contingency between them, and that involves ongoing adjustment and accommodation. Infants are acutely sensitive to the emotional signals of their social partners. Haviland and Lelwica's (1987) study of 10-week-old infants, mentioned earlier, showed that infants are not only responsive to emotional signals of social partners but differentially responsive; sad maternal expressions elicited self-soothing behaviors, angry expressions elicited motor freezing, and joy elicited reciprocal smiling.

The emotional signals of social partners also have the capacity to affect interactants at a physiological as well as a behavioral level (Field, 1987). For example, Field monitored heart-rate changes in high-risk infants and their mothers during face-to-face interaction. Heart-rate curves of the mothers and infants mirrored one another during the interactions, with increases in heart rate during stressful, disturbed interactions, and decreases during more synchronous interactions (Field, 1982).

Mutual accommodation as a regulatory process is generally adaptive. However, such a process can go awry due to disturbances in one or both of the partners. In certain cases, the form of accommodation that is achieved between infant and caregiver is skewed, leading to maladaptation in subsequent development. In the Cohen and Tronick (1983) study cited above, mothers simulated depressed affect to their infants for 3 minutes. Infants reacted to the breakdown in normal interactive exchange and lack of contingency initially by increasing their rate of positive bids (brief smiles, vocalizations); however, in the face of their mothers' continued nonresponsiveness, the positive interactive bids gave way to cycles of negative behavior involving protest (crying), wariness (head aversion, sober or sad face), gaze aversion, and withdrawal.

Two additional points concerning the above study are worth mentioning. First, infants rapidly displayed an alteration in their own behavior following the onset of maternal nonresponsiveness. Second, 25% of the infants cried steadily for 30 seconds or more and were clearly upset (there was no comparable upset in a control condition); moreover, these infants remained distressed and significantly more wary for the first minute following restoration of the mother's normal behavior. These data provide an impressive demonstration of how exquisitely sensitive young infants are to alterations in their caregiver's emotional signals, and how rapidly their own behavior may deteriorate under conditions of nonresponsivity. It is apparent that there may be long-term consequences of exposure to this kind of environment for socioemotional development. Studies of endogenously depressed mothers indicate that infants are at risk for developing a depressed style of responding themselves (Field, 1987). This development may be due to the failure of contingency (which is known to produce "learned helplessness" in animals [Seligman, 1975]), or it may relate to direct contagion of affect (see below). While failure of contingency may be directly relevant to the formation of affective biases around sadness and depression, the broader principle of contagion can account for other kinds of affective bias as well.

Contagion, Imitation, and Self-Regulation

Emotional contagion involves the spread of emotion from one individual to another, and can be seen in the phenomena of mob panic and "group glee" as well as in the more limited context of dyadic interaction. In early development emotion contagion is difficult to distinguish from imitation.

Classically, imitation is considered a voluntary, deliberate process. Piaget believed that children only became capable of imitation at about 10 months of age. However, infants have been observed to make expressions resembling those of their social partners as early as the neonatal period (Melzoff & Moore, 1977), and their activities appear directed and effortful. The literature on the proclivity of infants to match the facial and vocal expressions of social partners is now quite substantial. Malatesta and Izard's (1984) review indicated that even very young infants are capable of matching elements or whole facial expressions of models with similar expressions of their own. Whether the phenomenon in question is "imitation" or something else is moot. However, it is clear that during their first 6 months, infants are capable of quite specific facial appearance changes—brow, lip, and tongue movements—and they accommodate their responses over time to match a model, all without self-observation or external reinforcement (Malatesta & Izard, 1984). The implications for infant development are obvious and significant. They indicate that young infants are capable of adopting the vocal and facial mannerisms of anyone with whom they spend substantial time and simple exposure is all that is required. We turn now to a discussion of contagion.

Hatfield, Cacioppo, and Rapson (1992) define contagion as "the tendency to mimic another person's emotional experience/expression (his or her emotional appraisals, subjective feelings, expressions, patterned physiological processes, action tendencies, and instrumental behaviors) and thus to experience/express the same emotions oneself" (p. 151).

Contagion thus appears to differ from imitation in that the behavioral matching is assumed to be accompanied by an affective reaction, and one that is similar to that experienced by the social partner. In early development, contagion is considered the precursor or forerunner of empathy. Infants exposed to other infants who are crying will begin crying themselves (Sagi & Hoffman, 1976). The infants in Cohen and Tronick's (1983) study began to show depressed-like affect after exposure to simulated depression in their mothers within 3 minutes of maternal unresponsiveness. On a more sanguine note, Malatesta et al. (1986) found that mothers who smiled a great deal and showed a lot of interest in their interactions with their infants had infants who showed increases in joy and interest over time. Malatesta and Izard (1984) have commented that mothers typically tend to avoid the expression of negative affect in the presence of their infants as though they were aware of the contagion principle. In the study by Malatesta and Haviland (1982) infants were found to display a wide range of emotional expressions including a good mix of positive and negative expressions;

mothers, in contrast, had a much more restricted range centering on positive affect. They rarely emitted anger expressions and these were limited to "mock anger" usually directed at a doll rather than the infant. Expressions of sadness were seen in the context of a "concerned" expression usually in response to an infant's expression of distress. But these expressions were rare, fleeting, and quickly replaced by more positive expressions. This is a good strategy if infants are vulnerable to contagion. An empathic mother will not continue to reflect the infant's negative mood state if by reflecting the infant's feelings the infant becomes more distressed. Mothers in the Malatesta and Haviland (1982) study appeared to believe Spinoza's dictum that an affect cannot be restrained nor removed unless by an opposite and stronger affect: when infants modeled sadness, mothers modeled happiness.

Based on the research of Bühler and Hetzer (1928) and Sagi and Hoffman (1976) on the spread of neonatal distress, and the related research reviewed above, the period of infancy may be one that is particularly vulnerable to the effects of contagion, though contagion is not limited to this stage of development; contagion phenomena have been described for adolescents and adults as well. Students in dormitories who are exposed to the depressed affect of their roommates begin to show depressive symptoms themselves over time (Howes, Hokanson, & Lowenstein, 1985). Many other examples are cited in a review article by Hatfield et al. (1992).

One of the mechanisms involved in contagion is what an earlier German scholar, Lipps (1906), referred to as "motor mimicry," that is, the tendency for observers to unconsciously mimic the expressive movements of their social partners. A review of the empirical support for motor mimicry is found in Bavelas, Black, Lemery, and Mullett (1987). The mimicry of facial expressions of emotion is particularly germane to the issue of the contagion of emotional feeling. Facial expressions of emotion are said to directly contribute to the subjective awareness of emotion (Tomkins, 1962, 1963; Izard, 1971, 1977). This is known as the facial feedback hypothesis, the idea being that it is the contraction of facial musculature or the skin of the face that leads to differentiated emotional experience. To paraphrase James, a frown is the face's way of telling the self that all is not well with the world.

The constraints of space to do not allow us to discuss the issue of "facial feedback" in detail; moreover, several good reviews already exist (e.g., Lanzetta & McHugo, 1986). It will suffice to note that there is substantial research supporting the thesis that the unconscious mimicry of facial expressions of emotion leads to congruent emotional experience. Thus, mere exposure to the affect of other individuals is sufficient to induce a similar emotion in the observer, and one assumes that the same principle applies to infants (although see Chapter 5 for the controversy surrounding infant feelings).

The issue of whether infant responses to caregiver affective expressions are based on imitation or contagion cannot be decided here. However, the obvious sensitivity and responsivity of infants to caregiver displays has important developmental implications. Malatesta and Haviland's (1982) microanalytic study of mothers and young infants during face-to-face interaction found that mothers display an average of 8.05 emotion displays per minute; infants attend to their mothers' expressions about one quarter of the time (Hittelman & Dickes, 1979). At those rates, assuming that a mother spends about 3 hours a day in caregiving interactions with her awake infant, the average infant is exposed to 362 exemplars of emotion per day, or about 32,580 during the third to the sixth month, a period of time identified as the peak period in face-to-face play (Field, 1979). This is obviously not a trivial learning opportunity for the infant. It also should be noted that mothers in face-to-face play with their infants display highly articulated, exaggerated expressions of emotion. Friedman and Riggio (1981) have suggested that people who are especially expressive are more likely to provoke contagion in others than are inexpressive people. If contagion is as powerful an influence as Hatfield et al.'s (1992) review suggests, or if the tendency for infants to imitate is as compelling as James Mark Baldwin (1894) originally speculated and the review by Malatesta and Izard (1984) indicates, the high rate of maternal expressive behavior displayed to infants is of no minor significance. Since we know that adults have pronounced expressive biases (Malatesta, Fiore, Messina, & Culver, 1987) over which they have little awareness and control, the potential to bias infant expressive behavior early in life is considerable.

The existence of this kind of powerful social influence in infants before the development of strong regulatory controls might make the process of emotion socialization seem inordinately passive for the recipient. However, there is growing evidence that infants are capable of rudimentary emotion regulation within the opening months of life.

Haviland and Lelwica (1987) have made a point of distinguishing between contagion and self-regulation of emotion in young infants. According to these authors, self-regulation is more differentiated than imitation or contagion. Both the latter involve matching the expressions of social partners. Self-regulation, in contrast, can involve either matching or nonmatching responses. Haviland and Lelwica's (1987) study suggested that infants did not automatically take on the sad, angry, and happy moods of their mothers' simulated affects. Instead, their behavior appeared to be directed at altering their mother's behavior; failing that, they became distressed and attempted to cope with their distress. This was also evident in the Cohen and Tronick (1983) study, where infants worked through positive maneuvers and protest before succumbing to distress and withdrawal. However, we must note that both studies involved temporary, experimental manipulations. In more naturalistic settings and in everyday life, the rudimentary coping and self-regulatory strategies of infants may be overridden and neutralized by the potency of high-frequency affect biases of caregivers, as the literature on endogenously depressed mothers has shown (Field, 1987).

Processes in Later Development

In this section we consider the developing child's growth in linguistic and cognitive competence and the dynamic learning processes that may be involved in the acquisition of emotion biases.

Language

Most discussions of the relation between language and emotion explicitly or implicitly assume that language replaces overt expression early in development and that it is a vehicle for the subordination and control of emotion. Various theorists have described emotion as going "underground" developmentally as part of a fundamental maturational process (Krystal, 1977; Piaget, 1952, 1971; Vygotsky, in Rieber & Carton, 1987), using such terms as desomatization, interiorization, and centralization. Linguistic expression of emotion is also thought to be more subtle and to drain affectivity of some of its rawness and intensity. Krystal (1977), for example, talks about the way that language assists in the "desomatization" and taming of emotion.

Developmentalists also view language as one of the primary ways that children learn to manage their emotions. For example, Kopp (1989) indicates that

> language offers young children a multipurpose vehicle for dealing with emotions and moving toward more effective ER [emotion regulation]. With language children can state their feelings to others, obtain verbal feedback about the appropriateness of their emotions, and hear and think about ways to manage them. (p. 349)

Children obviously use self-talk to reassure themselves when they are anxious or upset. For example, a child left alone in a waiting room might sooth herself by verbalizing that the mother is coming right back. Self-talk was found to be an important means of regulating anxious affect among grade-school children (Brown et al., 1986). The motor act of speech itself can serve to shunt emotion in particular directions and also to obfuscate affect in social interaction. Speech production involves using the muscles of the mouth in a coordinated fashion, and in early development the motor coordination required to produce recognizable speech means that interest affect must be deployed for concentration and effort, and other emotions must be suppressed. Later in development, speech can be used to mask emotion being expressed in the lower half of the face. Interestingly, fast speech is often found in people who have something to conceal about their feelings, as in the glib speech patterns of con artists and certain politicians. Fast, propulsive speech is also found in the anger-inhibited Type A personality.

The above observations emphasize the obfuscatory and dampening effects of language on affect. Before continuing further we would like to make two important points. First, language can assist at both the amplification of emotion as well as its attenuation. Second, language not only describes affect (among its many other functions) but is intrinsically saturated with affect; here we refer to the paralinguistic features of speech. When we speak, we reveal not only our thoughts, but also our feelings. Affect is overdetermined; that is, it is duplicated in several channels—in the tonal quality of utterances, in our facial expressions, in body language, and in the words we use to articulate our feeling states. In the following we consider how both features of speech assist children in expressing their feelings and where individual differences (affect biases) may be found.

Affect in the Emotion Lexicon

Emotion expression is found in the affect lexicon—that is, in the active affective terminology or vocabulary that individuals use in their everyday conversations. Children acquire the ability to describe their internal states relatively early. Bretherton, McNew, and Beeghly-Smith (1981) report that infants begin expressing emotions linguistically as early as 18 months. There are a number of stylistic features of affective language that are permeable to socialization effects: affective range, frequency of affective terms, use of display versus internal state words, use of certain types of emotion words, and so on. The research of Connie Jones (1990), using our longitudinal data base (Malatesta et al., 1986, 1989, 1994), documents individual differences in several of these dimensions. Jones sampled the speech of mothers at four points in early infancy and correlated dimensions of maternal speech with dimensions of child speech when the children were 5 years of age. Maternal language was found to predict child language, differentially so for securely and insecurely attached children. Specifically, Jones found that for securely attached children there was a significant positive correlation between maternal frequency and range of affect words, with the frequency and range of their children, and a near significant correlation for "feeling" (versus "display" and "physiological") terms; for insecurely attached children, the mother–child correlation for range was nonsignificant, and the correlation for frequency and use of "feeling" words was negative, though marginally so. A study by Dunn, Bretherton, and Munn (1987) looked at similar parameters during the initial language acquisition stage, that is, between 18 and 24 months of age. These investigators found that there were stable individual differences in the way caregivers talked to their children across time. Individual-difference dimensions that showed stability were total number of maternal utterances about feeling states, the proportion of maternal conversation turns concerned with feeling states, and the frequency of maternal causal statements about feeling states. More importantly, and in accord with Jones's data on older children, maternal speech to infants was found to predict children's speech; that is, child feeling-state utterances at 24 months were positively correlated with maternal feeling-state utterances and feeling-state conversation turns 6 months earlier.

Affect in Intonational Patterns

As indicated above, affect saturates all utterances, not just the affect lexicon. Arguing contrary to prevailing opinion, Bloom and colleagues assert that children acquire language at the service of expressing their internal states rather than to achieve purposes or goals (Bloom & Beckwith, 1989; Bloom, Beckwith, & Capatides, 1988; Bloom, Beckwith, Capatides, & Hafitz, 1988). These researchers studied the expressive behavior of young children by having mothers keep diaries and by audio- and video-recording children for later speech analysis and for the coding of affective behavior (facial, intonation, bodily). They found that early and late word learners differed in their development with respect to affect expression from 9 to 21 months. All of the infants showed increases in their emotional expressivity over the period of language acquisition. However, one group of infants gained in expressivity because they learned to say words relatively early, whereas the other group increased in their frequency of emotional expression. The investigators also noted that infants who acquired language early spent more time in what they termed "neutral affect" than infants who acquired language later. It should be mentioned here that the first author of the present volume was invited by Dr. Bloom to view the videotapes for confirmation of their coding system. For the most part, there was good agreement. However, it was clear that Bloom et al.'s "neutral" category contained many expressions of "interest." Although some theories of emotion do not specify interest as an affect, it is considered a primary (positive) affect within Tomkins's affect theory and within Izard's differential emotions theory. Thus, it appears that interest is deployed in the service of the mastery of language; in fact, Bloom and colleagues note that a state of quiet alertness and attention (focused interest) supports cognitive activity. In another analysis of their data, Bloom and Beckwith (1989) found that when children first began acquiring language, neutral (i.e., interest) intonational patterns prevailed over positive (joy) or negative (distress) patterns. However, by the time the children reached a vocabulary spurt toward the end of the period of single-word speech, words were more likely to be said with positive (joy) intonation. The differences in affective tone during the first and second stages of language acquisition are interesting and, in our interpretation, reflect on the different functional significance of joy and interest affects. Joy serves play and emotional bonding, whereas interest involves concentrated attention and serves learning. During the initial acquisition of language, attention and concentration are required in order to understand the mapping between receptive and productive language. Once some facility has been acquired, language can be practiced and used more playfully.

The first author's research on affect in speech has been focused on individual differences in affective expression (Malatesta-Magai et al., 1994). Specifically, we investigated the relation between affect in language and affect in the voice (during speech) as sampled during the second and third years of life. Inflectional characteristics and other phonological aspects of speech were prominent; we found both general developmental patterns as well as idiosyncratic patterns specific to dyads. One important finding was that children remained affectively fluent in the facial channel between the second and third years of life and, moreover, that they actually augmented their expressivity using the vocal channel; that is, their vocal affectivity increased even when controlling for increased speech production in the third year. The increases were mostly in the domain of positive affect (interest, surprise, and joy), but one negative emotion—anger—also showed an increase.

These studies suggest that what children learn in development is not to switch from one channel of emotion expression to another, or to dampen affectivity altogether, but greater flexibility in the use of different systems of affective expression, and greater facility in modulating expressivity according to context.

With the mastery of language, children become more vulnerable to the affective ideologies of parents and other social agents. This is grossly apparent at the level of culture as described by several studies from cross-cultural research.

Cultures impose constraints on how parents use language to promote social goals. For example, cultures dictate which emotions can be described in feeling terms and how elaborated each emotion is. In the context of Whorfian linguistic theory, cultures with a wider affective lexicon should have greater awareness of distinctions among emotions. Certain emotion categories may be well or poorly elaborated in any particular culture, which also affects how parents socialize affect and restrict or encourage emotion expression. Levy (1980) has noted that, in any particular culture, the number of words that pertain to an emotion is a good index of how important an emotion is to that culture. An emotion with an extensive array of terms to describe it is said to be hypercognized, whereas an emotion with relatively few terms is said to be hypocognized (Levy, 1980). A hypercognized emotion is readily brought into the social domain where it can become the focus of community regulation; this can serve either to sensitize or desensitize children to a particular emotion. On the one hand, emotion that is endlessly described may lose its potency; on the other hand, if there are innumerable shadings to an emotion, and important contingencies associated with the nuances, a fine sensitivity may develop. The fact that an emotion is hypocognized does not mean that it is not socialized. However, it does mean that the emotion will be less distinct and less available to reflective consciousness.

The distinction between hypo- and hypercognized emotions is an important construct for our understanding of emotion socialization at the family level as well, although there has been little examination of individual differences in maternal styles with respect to this distinction. In the Malatesta and Haviland (1982) study, mothers' affective speech to their children was analyzed. The authors distinguished three types of maternal affect commentary: the first consisted of "affect encouragement" ("Come on, smile for Mommy), the second consisted of "discouragement" (e.g., "Don't be sad," "Don't be cranky"), and the third type was a nondirective "Rogerian" sort that reflected the child's apparent feeling ("You're feeling unhappy, aren't you?"). However, there was no attempt in that study to determine how the distinctions related to later development and there was no analysis of whether the differing styles were applied differentially to different kinds of emotion either in the overall sample or for particular mother–child dyads. The data base was too limited for that kind of analysis, although such an analysis would be important in addressing issues of emotion socialization.

Distinctions in maternal responses of the sort noted above could conceivably contribute to individual differences in affective biases. In a more recent study we have attempted to examine parental ideologies about affect management. We first generated a set of 30 vignettes concerning emotional events, 3 for each one of Izard's 10 fundamental emotions (Izard, 1977), and keyed them to his descriptions of these affects on the Differential Emotions Scale (Izard, 1972). We then gave the vignettes to mothers of 6- to 8-year-olds ($N = 14$) and asked them to indicate what they would do if these experiences happened to their child. For example, one vignette was, "You have company to the house and you ask your child to come in and say hello to your friends. Your child stands in the room looking shy and uncomfortable. Later you talk to your child about how he/she might have felt. What do you say to your child?"

An empirically derived coding system was developed and applied to the data. Three main categories and nine subcategories of maternal response were discriminated. The first five related to Category A, which dealt with the rewarding socialization of emotion, and included (1) praising or affirming what the child did or said, (2) affirming the child's feelings (empathy), (3) comforting or consoling, (4) helping the child to cope by taking action, and (5) offering explanation. The next two, in Category B, involved disregarding the child's emotional state, and included (6) abstract statements about the way things are, and (7) offering a rule of conduct or social convention. The last two, in Category C, involved the punitive socialization of emotion, and included (8) shaming, and (9) guilt induction.

Our analysis of the mothers' responses indicated that the various affects attract certain modal responses from mothers, indicating that this culture encourages certain emotions and discourages others. For example, shaming was the modal response to children's expression of contempt and anger. Children's disgust experiences were responded to equally with empathy and offering a rule of conduct. Shame evoked comforting, shyness evoked empathy, guilt experiences evoked both guilt induction and comforting equally. Surprise and joy evoked affirmations of the child's feelings, and interest and sadness evoked parental active participation or helping the child. Superimposed on these modal responses were large individual differences, with some mothers showing a tendency to use more punitive socialization than others, and with some mothers applying punitive socialization to different emotions. These data are some of the first to look at affective socialization as conveyed by affective ideology. They are limited since only 14 subjects were involved, but the procedure appears to offer a promising way to assess parental affective biases that may be instrumental in shaping the affect biases of their children.

Other Cognitive Processes in Later Development

It is clear that children develop more sophisticated and more well-articulated understandings about emotions and their uses as they mature. For example, several studies by Saarni (1993) and colleagues and by Harris (1993) and colleagues have provided compelling evidence that over the grade-school years children acquire increasing sophistication with respect to several dimensions of emotional knowledge, which includes growing awareness of the child's own internal states and the ability to describe them linguistically, the ability to discern others' emotional states, the assignment of meaning to expressive behaviors, the awareness of cultural display rules, knowledge that emotional states can be dissimulated (i.e., uncoupled from expressive behaviors), abstractions about the unique emotion traits of others, knowledge about self-presentation, and knowledge about how to regulate one's emotions and cope with stress. The above abilities, among others, constitute children's knowledge base with respect to emotions and contribute substantially to their "emotional competence" (Saarni, 1993). Saarni (1993) indicates that the first five skills will be learned by all or nearly all children, whereas the latter abilities may be learned more variably, with some children acquiring greater skill in them than others.

In recent times there is growing interest in individual differences with respect to the above knowledge-based skills and their relation to affect regulation. For example, Saarni and colleagues (reviewed by Saarni, 1993) have identified gender differences in display rule use, and Brody and Hall (1993) summarize the data on gender differences in the knowledge of display rules. Harris (1993) and colleagues have studied children's comprehension of causes of emotions, the use of display rules, and the existence of mixed emotions. Emotionally disturbed children attending special schools were found to differ from normal children in their understanding of display rules. Whereas normal children recognize that one should conceal one's feelings both in order to protect oneself or to protect others, emotionally disturbed children had particular difficulty with the latter category, possibly because they have difficulty recognizing the impact of their emotions (if expressed) on others. Another study showed that emotionally disturbed children were more likely than normal children to insist that emotion is an autonomous process and as such cannot be changed and redirected.

Differential socialization does not always lead to skill deficit, but can lead to special sensitivity, for example, in the heightened empathy/parentified behavior of children reared in families where one or both parents are depressive. For example, Zahn-Waxler and colleagues (reviewed in Zahn-Waxler & Kochanska, 1990) found that children of depressed parents show certain kinds of precocious behavior patterns that are thought to be linked to heightened and internalized guilt. In one laboratory-based study, depressed and well mothers were asked to show their children a photograph of a crying baby and then to show her own sadness and concern. The depressed mothers tended to bypass the infant's sadness and instead focus on their own problems and distress or they identified their child as the cause of their sadness (as in, "You really make me sad when you disobey"). These kinds of patterns are referred to as forms of guilt induction. Children exposed to such patterns apparently fall prey to the inductions; they show precocious, excessive, and unrealistic responsibility for the problems and concerns of others.

One cognitive process that is particularly interesting with respect to individual differences in emotion expression and regulation is that of defensive strategies. Cassidy and Kobak (1988) discuss the process of defensive avoidance of affect in infants in the context of the attachment relationship; some infants learn that certain emotions (anger, distress) cannot be expressed because they threaten the attachment bond. The dangerous emotions are then curtailed behaviorally and the painful affect associated with them is shunted from consciousness.

Fischer and colleagues (Calverley, Fischer, & Ayoub, in press; Fischer, Shaver, & Carnochan, 1990; Fischer & Ayoub, in press) have provided a more detailed model of emotion/cognition development that examines how defensive processes originate and become organized. According to their theory, emotions are processed at different stages of development as different kinds of appraisal capabilities become available to the child. Emotions are said to begin with the perception of notable change, followed by evaluative appraisal related to "concerns" or goals. If events interfere with goals, they are appraised negatively and negative emotion results. With the development of self-monitoring capabilities, emotions are processed through additional appraisal loops and children acquire the ability to exercise self-control of action tendencies. At this point emotional action tendencies become the events appraised, causing emotional reactions to emotions, or emotion loops. It is at this juncture, we hypothesize, that information "cut-off" and "take-out" loops can develop. Normally, for example, if a child's goals are thwarted, anger is expressed; however, if experience has taught that anger is severely punished, fear may result instead, leading to a suppression of anger around particular persons or around people at large. In the latter case the child learns to segregate anger from the rest of his/her experiential/expressive repertoire. As experiences are repeated and development proceeds, children develop complex emotion loops that may be activated readily and automatically; they also acquire emotion-related concerns, which function at an organizational level and affect the nature of subsequent interactions and appraisals in emotion-specific ways. Over time, the individual develops emotional scripts around actions/objects/events and emotions.

One fundamental developmental principle with regard to affects involves the polarity between positive and negative affects. Children naturally distinguish between positive and negative events, persons, and situations based on their positive or negative emotional experiences with them; this is called normal splitting. Splitting is also involved in self-concepts; that is, people develop positive and negative self-perceptions and these become organized as more or less basic to the self. For most individuals, positive self-descriptors are more central than negative self-descriptors. Early in development individuals also acquire basic social/behavioral scripts that are organized around particular emotions, such as love/affection for caregivers and fear/avoidance of strangers. Over time the individual learns to coordinate and integrate disparate views of self and others. Under traumatic circumstances, the normal process of segregating positive and negative experiences becomes hypertrophied; disparate views, attitudes, and scripts are strictly segregated and marked by sharp affective divisions. What is unique about Fischer's theory is that it accords important learning to emotions, themselves, as experienced products. It highlights the self-cuing motivational properties of emotions; when intense traumatic emotions are experienced and the child does not yet have the capacity to defend the self, more sharply defined splitting is required, and can contribute to dissociative phenomena.

In subsequent research, Calverley, Fischer, and Ayoub (in press) have explored dissociative phenomena in individuals exposed to repetitive emotional traumas. Subjects were young adolescent women hospitalized for depression who had been sexually abused as children on a continuing basis and a control group who had not. The results illustrated significant differences in the splitting of cognitive scripts. Negative self-descriptors were more central and positive self-descriptors more peripheral to the core identity of abused women, whereas the reverse pattern was true of nonabused women; the abused women also produced an unusually large overall number of negatives. The abused women showed a form of complex dissociative coordination or "polarized affective splitting" not found in the nonabused women; they showed a sharply negative representation of self-with-mother and a sharply positive representation of self-with-father, even when the father was the perpetrator. Moreover, particular emotions were segregated within particular relationships, such as rage for one relationship, and affection for another. Interestingly, the abused women did not evidence a lower developmental profile, indicating that the phenomenon is related to cognitive processing effects, and not to fixation or regression, phenomena linked to developmental delay and failure.

Jantzen and colleagues (Jantzen, 1992; Jantzen, Magai, & Allen, 1993) studied a nonhospitalized sample of sexually abused women who were attending college. Unlike the depressed, hospitalized women Calverly et al. (in press) studied—who showed marked dissociative phenomena—these women showed another kind of impairment. Jantzen and colleagues examined the coping styles of their abused and nonabused subjects using Weinberger, Schwartz, and Davidson's (1979) repressive coping style scale, which discriminates four styles of coping with anxiety: repression, low anxiety, high anxiety, and defensive high anxiety. They found that the the nonabused subjects were significantly more often characterized by a repressive coping style, whereas the abused subjects were predominantly characterized as highly anxious. It is difficult to compare the subjects in the Calverly et al. and Jantzen et al. studies because we do not have comparable measures on the extent of abuse and age at onset, though it appears that the women in the Calverly et al. study were more disturbed. We hypothesize that repression is a common coping mechanism for most people; when trauma occurs the normal defensive processes become impaired. If the trauma is moderate rather than extreme, it may result in high conscious levels of anxiety; in extremity it may lead to dissociative phenomena.

The empirical study of defensive processes in emotion management is one of the newest and most exciting frontiers in emotions research. Phenomena long observed in clinical practice can be profitably explored using theoretical models such as the one articulated by Fischer and colleagues. Such analyses will enhance our ability to understand the development of idiosyncratic styles of emotional organization, and the forces that propel and sustain them both in normal development and in psychopathology.

The above principles highlight some of the most important contributions to emotion socialization and the origins of individual differences. In the process, we have emphasized the development and consolidation of emotion traits as organizing principles in personality and as the source of individual continuity over time. However, it is important to note that emotion traits do not function inflexibly in personality, except under conditions of psychopathology. In normal development and normal personality functioning, although moods and emotion traits are relatively stable (see review by Malatesta, 1990), there are two conditions under which traits are modified or moderated: (1) according to context, and (2) in response to significant life challenge. We defer a discussion of the latter to Chapter 11. Here we briefly consider context moderators of affect traits.

Traits do not operate monolithically but are often modified in consideration of particular environmental contingencies. This is well illustrated in a series of research studies by Pervin and colleagues (summarized in Pervin, 1993). In one study, Pervin (1988a) had drug abusers—who are known to use a wide assortment of drugs—generate a set of situations in which they used or wanted to use drugs, and a set of emotions experienced. The Situation × Affect data were then factor analyzed (the list of situations included representative situations associated with each drug). Collectively, data from the study confirmed that drugs are used to sedate painful affects, that some drugs were generally associated with relief from specific affects, and that individuals established a pattern of preferred drugs to deal with unique constellations of painful affects.

In another series of studies (Pervin, 1988b), students rated the relevance of a set of affects to representative situations and people, and each affect was rated in terms of its association with each of the other affects. Situation by person by affect data indicated that (1) all subjects had a major positive affect factor and a major negative affect factor—which, in many cases, could be further subdivided, (2) the more specific organization of affects appeared to depend on the situational content, and (3) there were large individual differences in the means for the affects, in the rank ordering of affects, in the relations between the affects, and in the kinds of situations that were associated with specific affects. Also of note was the finding that for some individuals, people seemed more important than situations in determining the organization of affects, whereas the reverse was true for others. Collectively, Pervin's studies provide compelling support for both the existence of unique affective organizations as well as data on the sensitivity of affect biases to context.

In summary, we have described the conditions that contribute to the development of individual differences in emotion biases and have illustrated how the biases operate in personality across wide domains of psychological functioning. Thus far, we have mainly addressed the period of infancy and childhood. Traditionally, these are the periods thought to be the most permeable to environmental influence. However, as we will see in Chapter 11, the story of development does not cease with the onset of adolescence and adulthood.

Emotion and Personality Change

In the middle of the journey of my life,
I came to myself within a dark wood
Where the straight way was lost.
DANTE, *Inferno*

OVERVIEW

If poetry, biography, and fiction are any guide, salient changes of mood and emotion often represent turning points in people's lives and in their personality development. In fact, emotional upheaval and personality change are often intertwined themes. In life and in literature, the turning points catch us by surprise; they are unexpected. They are salient because much of our lives are organized so as to preserve continuity. Disruptions in our everyday routines are experienced as general annoyances, or "hassles" (Lazarus & Folkman, 1984). Change is also threatening. People whose lives are governed by conformity, tradition, and the reliability of events—however boring—can cling tenaciously to their routines. An off-Broadway play by A. R. Gurney, *Later Life*, about a couple who meet 30 years after a separation, promotes the theme that people do not change even after three decades; they just become "more so." Indeed, the hero, who is a staid, reserved, Bostonian Brahmin, and who resisted a passion 30 years ago on the Isle of Capri, once again, at the age of 50, equivocates about pursuing the woman who excites him. The woman herself, who is portrayed as somewhat more adventurous, also ultimately succumbs to the inertia of her life in the decision to return to an abusive husband from whom she is presently separated.

When the two protagonists first met—back on the Isle of Capri—the man alluded to a dread that at some point in his life he would be brought down by some unnameable catastrophe. Thirty years later the woman inquires if the prophesy had been fulfilled; he shrugs his shoulders that unaccountably it had not. Nevertheless, it becomes clear to the audience in the course of the play that the catastrophe of his life was not some active event, but the passivity and inaction of his own personality. Thus the themes of continuity and doom are linked in this play as they are in several other works of fiction.

However, in real life, the constants in our lives often provide comfort in a chaotic world. Stability, continuity, and routines all guarantee that not every situation we confront will be new. For the most part, we are comforted by routines and by familiarity. Routinized social conventions allow us to reduce uncertainty when we meet unfamiliar persons. Well-learned motor skills and automated behavioral patterns permit us to devote more of our "limited capacity" resources to the more demanding cognitive and emotional decisions that life's complexity forces upon us.

By contrast, the possibility of change also excites the imagination, as some of our great literature shows. The tale of *Parzival*, for example, as told by Wolfram von Eschenbach, is the story of a young boy raised by his mother in an idyllic, pastoral wood secluded from the larger world and kept in a state of naïveté. A chance encounter with a cousin reveals to him his true identity and lineage in the royal family; he subsequently tumbles into maturity as he ventures forth in life, propelled by the tale of a murdered uncle whose life must be avenged.

A more recent example from literature depicts personality change as more gradual, though it is once again associated with powerful emotional experiences. In *The Color Purple* (Walker, 1982), change evolves slowly against a backdrop heartache and abuse. The protagonist, Celie, is described by herself and others as dull, slow-witted, unattractive, and useful only for her willingness to do chores that no one else cares to do. The book relates her growth into adulthood and reveals an awakening to self-worth that emerges from her sorrow over a blighted love affair. By the end of the book the reader realizes this is a different and more mature Celie, a woman who is unafraid to experience the full range of emotions and who possesses a hard-won wisdom about herself, her family, her friends, and her race. Personal change is not imposed from without but emerges from inner struggle. As Celie says, "Well, I say, we all have to start somewhere if us want to do better, and our own self is what us have to hand" (p. 230). This woman—who endured scorn, rape, and physical abuse from the time she was a young girl—can say on the last page of the book, "But I don't think us feel old at all. And us so happy. Matter of fact, I think this the youngest us ever felt" (p. 244). A personality originally flooded with negative emotions and internal struggle has nevertheless found inner peace in later life, and a coherent and almost joyous sense of self.

In the middle ground between works of fiction and biography are various "legends" that embellish upon historical and biographical events so as to accentuate the natural drama of life. Some of these involve glorious and heroic attainments. For example, there is the story of Prince Hal, the empty-headed, idle playboy who is transformed by the demands of his royal ascension to the throne of England into the valorous Henry V. Another example is found in the life of

Boudicca, the first-century Celtic queen of the Iceni tribe of Britons. In this case, Boudicca's domestic tranquility was rudely crushed and her personal circumstances irrevocably changed in the aftermath of the rape of her two adolescent daughters by Roman soldiers. Beside herself with outrage, hatred, and the lust for revenge, she turned to her people, ignited the already festering discontent of the Iceni, and led them in an uprising. Transformed into a fierce and aggressive warrior, she and her troops organized themselves for combat and proceeded to sack and burn the first Roman settlement at Camulodunum (Colchester) in what was described as a particularly brutal battle, with no Roman man, woman, or child left alive. This event guaranteed her immortalization as The Warrior-Queen in the pantheon of British heros and heroines.

The life stories of the world's great religious leaders all seem to involve discontinuities as well. Moses, for example, lived comfortably in the land of Midian until he was summoned to lead his people through the desert to freedom, a task for which he thought himself completely unsuited, being ashamed of his speaking abilities and reluctant to abandon the secure continuity of his life. Siddhartha Gautama, a wealthy Hindu prince, had been raised to delight in luxury and was sheltered from witnessing events and people that could occasion distress in him. As he left the confines of his sequestration at adulthood, he fell upon his first sights of aged, sick, crippled, and destitute persons, and was so startled by these examples of human suffering that he fled the city, as legend has it. He then retreated to the desert to ponder what he had seen and after 49 days of meditation in the shade of the Bo tree had a spiritual awakening; the emergent understandings transformed his life and anticipated the founding of Buddhism. The prophet Mohammed, though orphaned in childhood, in adulthood achieved well-being, wealth, and power, only to cast it aside at midlife to preach the love of Allah even though his teachings brought him persecution.

As well, tales of religious conversion regularly describe personal histories of transformation and rebirth—many involving renunciation of a priviledged and nominally happy life for one of travail and self-abnegation. In Christianity, the "Lives of the Saints" portray case after case of this kind of change. St. Paul, for example, who is literally "blinded by the light," left behind a life of prestige and power to become a wandering missionary, often scorned and imprisoned for his new-found beliefs. St. Augustine described himself as lusty, impulsive, and largely carefree in his preconversion life. He underwent a dramatic change, according to legend, and emerged as one of the most influential of all Christian theologians. St. Francis of Assisi was a wealthy youth with a life of ease virtually guaranteed by his family's position in society. He abandoned all in order to found a new religious order devoted to ministering to the lowliest persons in his social world. These stories are consistent with a central tenet of Christianity that advocates the necessity of "rebirth"—the idealization of radical change in personality encompassing new beliefs, emotions, and behaviors.

In Judaic tradition there is the story of Moses, mentioned above; a more contemporary example is of Theodor Herzl, the founder of Zionism. Herzl was a cosmopolitan Austrian Jew who was an ardent proponent of assimilation through conversion as an answer to "the Jewish question"—the much discussed European issue of whether Jews could be accommodated in modern Western European culture. However, the events of the Dreyfus affair in France so disgusted and frightened Herzl, according to his own account, he renounced his former assimilationist position, became, if you will, a born-again Jew, and began to formulate his ideas about an independent Jewish state—which, of course, was eventually actualized in the State of Israel.

The skeptical and secular world can dismiss tales of religious transformation as being exaggerations at best and fabrications at worst; and indeed, such tales have been used instrumentally to inspire, convert, and induct individuals into various religious communities. We will look more carefully at empirical research on religious conversion presently as a means of elucidating the emotional dynamics that are involved in the process and to address the question of whether religious conversions or other significant life changes entail real personality change, and whether such changes endure. At this point suffice it to acknowledge that stories of personality change seem at once startlingly unreal, yet somehow credible. They seem believable because they are found everywhere, not just in religious tradition.

Modern biography and autobiography is the next level at which we find accounts of significant personality change. Although biographical and autobiographical accounts of lives extend back in time to the beginnings of recorded history (viz., *Plutarch's Biographies*), they have been given new impetus in recent times as the **self** of Western culture, which, once knit into the broad community of tribe, ethnic group, clan, and neighborhood, has become the "divided self," the "alienated self," and the "empty self" of modern and postmodern times. As such, hunger for greater fullness and embeddedness, at least according to one account (Cushman, 1992), has led to the incredibly successful expansion of the psychotherapy industry, from the lonely beginnings of a single individual—Freud—just about a century ago, to a booming clinical enterprise. As Cushman (1992) notes, in California alone, there are 10,000 psychologists, 6,500 psychiatrists, 11,000 clinical social workers, and 19,000 marriage, family, and child therapists. As well, one may also speculate that isolation of the individual in modern times was one of the sources that gave rise to the confessional poetry of midcentury (including that of Robert Lowell, Anne Sexton, John Barryman, Delmore Schwartz, and Sylvia Plath), to its tremendous success, and to the subsequent diffusion of confessional autobiographies that now fill our bookstores.

Biographical and autobiographical accounts of lives from modern culture (see, e.g., Liv Ullman's *Changes*) offer ordinary citizens prospects for change and therefore ignite the popular imagination. Many of them also appear to inspire hope for regeneration. One of the most famous accounts of lives transformed is found within a volume by Bill Wilson and Robert Smith, the founders of Alcoholics Anonymous who triumphed over dissolute and wasted lives to reinvent themselves in sobriety (Alcoholics Anonymous, 1976). The "big book" of A.A., *Alcoholics Anonymous*, is filled with personal narratives of individuals claiming to have experienced similar personality change. Although early editions of the book (written "anonymously" by Bill Wilson) gave the impression that such personality change occurred suddenly and spectacularly, later editions testified that such transformations did not always occur so dramatically (Alcoholics Anonymous, 1976).

As indicated above, the "idea" of personality change excites the imagination; examples are found in diverse literatures. From these stories and others, it is obvious that life change offers opportunity in addition to threat. However, as fascinated as our literary cannon and biographical literature is with issues of both continuity and change, as psychologists, we know surprisingly little about the conditions that prompt and support change. Indeed, developmental psychology and personality theory are both solidly grounded in continuity models of human development (Whitbourne et al., 1992). Freud, for example, hypothesized that people's lives were motivated by a relentless "repetition compulsion," based on his observation that individuals frequently played out earlier themes and traumas in their current lives. More recent authors, analytic and nonanalytic alike, espouse similar principles. Epstein (1993) indicates that the preservation of personal habits, styles, and beliefs are governed by a "coherence principle," the idea being that there is a central motivating drive in humans to preserve a stable sense of self. Caspi and Moffitt (1993) have proposed that individual differences in personality tend to be preserved over time, even during points of transition; moreover, they suggest that it is precisely during the unsettling times of transition that personality traits are accentuated.

Developmental psychology, in particular, appears to be especially taken with notions of stability, coherence, and predictability. In fact, historically, the field has been captivated by two central romances—the notion of "early experience" (pedogenesis) and the doctrine of "continuity." *Pedogenesis* refers to the expectation that early events are particularly formative, and later events less so. Basic personality traits are thought to be forged during the first 2 to 5 years of life and the continuity principle instructs that these traits will be carried forward into adulthood and beyond. Freud, in particular, thought that 5 was the bellwether year, but Spitz and Bowlby felt that certain core developmental phenomena, such as attachment, started to establish themselves in the personality as early as 6 to 8 months of life, and were well lodged by the second to third year. Contemporary attachment theory stresses that the mental elaboration of an "internal working model" ensures that early attachment patterns will be forwarded and will form the foundation for all other subsequent interpersonal relationships.

While it is true that our developmental research paradigms are oriented toward the examination of how things change or remain the same over two or more developmental epochs, our bias is clearly for continuity, as observed in the reporting of stability coefficients. Although variance estimates include stability, change, and error, in using the term "stability coefficient" psychologists emphasize the continuity implied by any Pearson correlation coefficient over .30.

In the 1950s and 1960s the primate research of Harry Harlow and colleagues offered the first serious challenge to the romances of pedogenesis and continuity. Although the earlier research had indicated that infant monkeys reared by unresponsive wire-frame mothers were doomed to social and sexual dysfunction, subsequent research showed that the effects of surrogate mothering were not irreversible and that the monkeys could be rehabilitated; some of the more debilitating effects could be offset by experiences with peers. These initial studies, as well as those of a different sort in physiology and embryology, inspired a raft of "stimulus addition" and "stimulus subtraction" paradigms within psychology (Thompson & Grusec, 1970) designed to partial out what was immutable in development and what was not. However, the larger picture has sadly been lost in all the carefully controlled animal studies of enrichment and deprivation and in the heated polemical arguments around the early experience literature of the 1960s and 1970s.

From a broader perspective and from the vantage point of the compelling stories of our great and profane literatures, pedogenesis and continuity are not the definitive or only rules in life. Lives and personality patterns do appear to change, though we know little about the mechanisms or processes involved in such change. They are dark and formidably opaque to judge by the lack of theory with respect to life change. (Here we are not talking about the kind of stage sequential normative change described by Freud or Erikson.) What is particularly startling is that the two branches of psychology that should have the most to say about the topic are largely silent.

Clinical psychology is grounded in the very notion that psychotherapy produces behavioral and intrapsychic change; if not, the practice of the profession is one of the greatest hoaxes of the century. However, a large proportion of its practitioners refrain from the kind of documentation of change that is used in academic psychology—clinical psychologists in major training institutes notwithstanding (Strupp & Howard, 1992). For example, out of all the psychologists and therapists from related disciplines in the country—see the figures above for California alone—the Society for Psychotherapy Research has attracted a membership of only 1,000.

Part of the reason that clinical psychology at large has not paid more attention to the documentation of change has to do with the fact that change in clients is patently obvious to the clinician and does not require "empirical verification." Clinical psychology operates from its own hermeneutic and obeys its own principles of verification. Another reason that practicing therapists actively eschew academic research on the profession is that they view themselves as more closely allied to the humanities than the sciences, and thus represent a culture apart from the rest of psychology (viz, C. P. Snow). Additionally, in early training, there is the tension created by having to live as a citizen in both of C. P. Snow's two cultures during graduate education, and beyond, if one becomes an academic. Even those who dared to open the door of the therapy office to the recording technology of laboratory science were deeply conflicted about scientific analysis of therapy, as Haviland's (in preparation) analysis of Carl Rogers's theoretical and research writings shows. The fact that clinical psychology thrives, despite various assaults to the "empiricism" of its therapeutic claims, is testimony to the strong will to believe that change is possible, both on the part of therapists who devote years of their lives to training and practice as well as on the part of patients and clients who pay mightily in time, money, and agonizing introspection. Yet the field has remained largely inarticulate about the processes involved in the transformation of personality, even when the topic is considered on its own turf and in its own journals.

There is some limited research on psychotherapy change—called psychotherapy outcome research. However, "change" is often vaguely defined, and research in this area can be particularly problematic (Strupp & Howard, 1992). Here we suggest that part of the difficulty in substantiating significant personality change resides not so much in the fact that people do not undergo change, but because clinical psychology has failed to grasp how emotion "works" and the mutative importance of emotion to personality change. Indeed, the field of clinical psychology has failed to develop its own coherent theory of emotion and emotional development to guide research—a problem that is still noted and regarded as a problem by at least some clinicians (e.g., Greenberg, 1993).

There is a long legacy to the neglect of emotion in psychodynamic psychology. Freud's first forays into psychotherapy convinced him that emotion was central in personality development, that neurosis was due to "strangulated affect," and that personality change was mediated by emotional catharsis. But in his later work, as he became more convinced of the centrality of sexual repression and symbolic process, his success in psychotherapy deteriorated, and he became more pessimistic about prospects for personality change, as reflected in his work, *Analysis, Terminable and Interminable* (Lewis, 1971). In attachment theory as well, although the emphasis has been on continuity, there are some observable discontinuities that remain unaddressed. Though by and large the stability coefficients for attachment type over a 1- to 5-year period range from .60 to .70, such figures come from studies of attachment with intact, stable, middle-class families, and thus we have no way of knowing if the coefficients are high because of stable attachment/personality patterns and internal working models or because of the stability of life circumstances. We do know that in studies involving poor and disadvantaged families living under more stressful and chaotic conditions, the stability coefficients drop precipitously. Even in research with stable, intact families, there is a significant amount of variance that is unaccounted for in attachment classification stability coefficients. However, there is relatively little comment on the individuals whose profiles change, and little in the way of explanation. Here, again, we propose it is because developmental psychology has no (explanatory) theory of discontinuity.

In this chapter we argue that it is emotions that provide both the thread of *continuity* in lives—in the form of personality traits, as well as the dynamic motivational force behind personality *change*, whether that process takes place in the context of psychotherapy, in the context of life crisis, or in other especially meaning-laden life events. In the present chapter we elaborate on the role of emotion in branching life courses, as first introduced by Magai and Hunziker (1993). But before doing so, let us return to the lives of Watson and Rogers. In one man we see that continuity in life structure and personality prevailed, in the other, that there was notable discontinuity.

John Watson was confronted with a significant crisis in his life in his mid-thirties. His affair with a graduate student was exposed and he was excommunicated from academia. Such a profound change in his fortunes and attendant emotional turmoil could have prompted a reexamination of his life, his rebellious-confrontative motives, and his pattern of interpersonal relationships. Instead, although he can be accorded some respect for his tenaciousness and stoicism, and the ability to survive such an ignominious defeat, he did not pursue a path that would lead to change. Instead, he appears to have become even more cynical, confrontative, and sexually exploitative. Although he landed temporary jobs teaching at Clark and the New School, his contract was eventually not renewed at the New School for reasons that appear once again to involve complications related to sexual liaisons (Buckley, 1989). Watson persisted in thumbing his nose at academia by publishing pieces on child development that were unsubstantiated by research. He continued to be dismissive of human attachments, and escalated his ideological battle against emotions and emotionality in his advice to parents.

In the case of Carl Rogers we have different conditions and a different resolution, one that takes advantage of emotional disequilibrium at the service of growth and personality change. We pause first to elaborate on other aspects of Rogers's personality that have not yet been mentioned. In addition to prominent interest/joy and shame components to his personality, other aspects were undeveloped, namely, his toleration for and ability to express anger. The disinclination or inability to express anger had early origins and persisted over time as a feature of his personality—as he himself became aware of and articulated in autobiographical material written later in life. The lack of affect tolerance for anger was pivotal in a personal crisis that occurred in his 40s.

At midlife, Rogers had become deeply involved in his work on client-centered psychotherapy, in the promotion of his therapeutic ideas, and in the mentorship of his students. Absorbed with his growing reputation and professional recognition (he was elected president of APA and received other prestigious awards), and experiencing a great deal of professional and media attention, Rogers was directly in the public eye—exposed and vulnerable. In the process of trying to apply client-centered psychotherapy to more severely disturbed clients, in a new ambitious program of research, a borderline client he had been treating responded with extreme hostility and soon thereafter had a psychotic break. Rogers experienced a severe crisis and withdrew from his work.

Magai and Haviland's (in preparation) analysis of his life and work suggests that it was the exposure to strong negative affect, which Rogers had always sought to avoid, and for which he had little modulatory control, in combination with anticipation of professional exposure of this disastrous therapy that ignited a massive shame/failure/exposure response that in turn precipitated crisis. He underwent 2 years of personal psychotherapy that apparently had a healing effect on him. The crisis, as well as the reexamination of self engendered by therapy, are credited with leading to a reduction in shame as a central and controlling force in his life narrative, to a greater ability to express and tolerate anger from others, to a more emotionally elaborated construction of experience, and to the production of his later and more mature theoretical works.

Both men suffered crises in midlife; one underwent change and one did not. The above material suggests that two of the mutative agents in life change are *emotion* and *self-reflection*, and that both components may be required in the case of positive personality change. Where self-reflection is negated as in the context of defensive denial, or is compromised by splitting, the energy for change is either dissipated or gets bound up in an intrapsychic Gordian knot. We will have more to say about this later on.

As indicated above, crisis is one such juncture at which intense emotion is activated and released for either productive personality work or for constriction and conservation of pattern. In fact, there has been growing interest in the issue of personal crises in lifespan developmental research. The idea of crisis as a turning point in individuation was originally advanced by Jung in the context of his own midlife crisis and has been subsequently pursued empirically by Levinson and Gould in their biographical examinations of midlife crisis in groups of men. In addition, the recent work in anthropological, literary, and masculine critique studies shows a growing interest in examination of individual lives. The latter field has been especially interested in changes in masculine identity and behavior. What is interesting about what some writers have observed as apparent shifts in masculine identity is that they appear mediated by a prior period of crisis (emotional turmoil) that dismantles an earlier emotional structure. Midlife may be an especially vulnerable period for personal crisis because of physical, familial, and work-related changes and challenges. A particularly good example is given by David Jackson (1990). In an autobiographical account, Jackson describes the disorientation, disequilibrium, and emotional turmoil instigated by a physical collapse at the age of 46. He recovered in a hospital only to find that he had a damaged heart valve and endocarditis. The consequent loss of his sense of "masculine invulnerability," combined with the out-of-control experiences encountered in dealing with an objectifying, dehumanizing medical establishment, so unsettled him that his stance with respect to his masculine identity and position vis à vis women (which was acknowledged as being particularly exploitative) was, in his account of events, radically altered.

Levinson and Gould's analyses of adult lives (Gould, 1978; Levinson, Darrow, Klein, Levinson, & McKee, 1978), and the above-mentioned masculine critique literature, deal exclusively with men's lives and men's transitions, although Levinson has been at work on a study of woman's lives and David Gutmann's (1975) work suggests that women face a similar midlife challenge. In Gutmann's work, women have shown evidence of personality change (at least with respect to older cohorts born earlier in the century before the most recent wave of feminism in the 1960s) in terms of greater comfort with assertiveness and aggression in later life. Gutmann believes that this represents a reemergence of aggression that is submerged during the child-rearing years; aggression is driven underground earlier, according to Gutmann, because it would be lethal to the marital relationship and emotional security of children. A study by Malatesta and Culver (1984) clarifies the relations among apparent changes in women's personalities, role contingencies, and experienced affect. The investigation used narrative material from Abigail Stewart's Longitudinal Study of the Life Patterns of College Educated Women, archived at the Henry Murray Center, Radcliffe College, which had followed women for 19 years over four waves of measurement. The four time periods coincided with the transition to college, and with three stages of marriage and family life. Malatesta and Culver performed a content analysis of the major themes and affects mentioned in the narrative material and found that the women, as a cohort, underwent thematic and affective changes over the several waves of the investigation. Salient during the first wave—at late adolescence—was the presence of anger and aggressivity, which related to thematic content of success and domi-

Figure 3. Emotions beyond the childhood years.

nance; this is perhaps not an unusual finding given a cohort of particularly bright young women entering their freshman year at an elite and intellectually prestigious college. During the second wave, when most of the women had very young children, the dominant affect became depression and thematic material revolved around issues of independence and lack of success. At the third wave, when children were mostly of school age, depression themes receded and themes of affiliation with children increased, but depressed affect was replaced by anxiety, and this affect was now linked with lack of success themes. At the fourth wave, success had once again become the top-ranking theme, as it was in the first wave when these women were college freshmen; however, at this point many had since resumed careers and now were describing feelings of pride at recent accomplishments: Developing skill in a new job as a therapist, opening a law firm, publishing a book, receiving an advertising award. Depression and anxiety were both down from the last wave, though anxiety still constituted the chief negative affect experience and the occurrence of anxiety themes in the narrative were positively correlated with both affiliative and success themes. Over one third of the sample had divorced or separated, and many had established new relationships with men though these were commonly fraught with ambivalence.

From the above we observe that women's lives undergo a series of changes as they engage new roles and task demands. The kinds of challenges that this particular cohort of women confronted—raising children, putting careers on hold, enduring isolation, and, for some, contending with disintegrating marriages and new intimate relationships—generate emotional turmoil of crisis proportion. For example, one woman described a current relationship as generating "violent unhappiness." Since the study used a nomothetic level of analysis, and we did not perform in-depth interviews with the women but relied on extracting material from accounts of "highs and lows" of the preceding years, we cannot test the crisis hypothesis for any single individual, nor determine if and how crisis affects the structure of personality. The study also raises questions about the nature of personality "change." Are we to regard the observed changes in the contents of thought and emotion in the women we studied over the four waves of measurement as personality changes? Can personality really be all that variable? Or are the observed patterns more accurately described as context-controlled adaptations to changing role requirements? The question of what constitutes personality change will be taken up again later on. In any case, to the extent described, the cohort of women encompassed by Gutmann's analyses and by Malatesta and Culver's study show evidence of change in their salient experiences at different points in the lifespan.

The impact of role demands in defining developmental crisis and adaptation is not singular to women as Levinson's and Gould's research with men has shown. In fact, there is some reason to believe that crisis may precipitate greater instability and personality disruption in men. Hess' (1979) analysis of friendship patterns in men and women indicates that women may be less vulnerable to precipitous life change because their social support networks make them better equipped to handle adversity. It may also be that women's greater readiness to express their emotions (Brody & Hall, 1993) averts reliance on "stoicism" and denial in which emotional distress is contained within the self and may then build to a crisis proportion. To be sure, at this point these are merely impressions, and certainly require research for their verification.

In this chapter we distinguish between two types of personality change, gradual, almost imperceptible change, and dramatic, radical change. Biographical and autobiographical accounts of personality transformation tend to showcase the latter kind of change because of its great dramatic character. The developmental literature orients more toward the former kind of change, if it discusses change at all, and discussions are typically limited to reigning paradigms. The child developmental literature focuses on normative age-graded change, and while the lifespan developmental literature deals with both normative and nonnormative change, there is a tendency to *report* on discontinuity rather than to explain it. For example, Whitbourne et al.'s (1992) 22-year sequential study of psychosocial development in adulthood found that there was an increase in trust, intimacy, and identity in the third decade of life, but there is little discussion of what developmental processes lay behind this change. Moreover, we have little idea of what this looks like in any single individual, or how it is accomplished in any individual life. Similarly, we have Zimbardo's (1977, 1986) finding that 20% of his sample of college students who were formerly shy were no longer shy. Who were these people? What happened to them to produce this transformation? As West and Graziano (1989) indicate, it is only recently that psychologists have begun to consider why and how people change or remain the same and to pursue the ultimate goal of "developing empirically based theoretical perspectives that elucidate the processses underlying stability and change in personality" (p. 184).

In trying to solve the riddle of developmental continuity and change in our own work and in this chapter, we have taken three approaches. One is to question ourselves. The second is to examine the literature for any research that relates powerful emotional experiences to personality change. And the third is to analyze biography and autobiography for further clues and evidence.

We begin with a personal account. When the idea for this book first germinated—about 10 years ago—psychology had just barely awakened to the idea that there was a pressing need to study emotion as a fundamental process. As the field expanded, work on emotions proliferated at an astounding rate. Much of it was solid and established an important base for the field. And some of it was original and creative. But a large portion of it also involved the rehashing of old controversies that did not materially advance our understanding of some of the more dynamic issues.

The first author's own attempt to understand processes related to the development of individual differences in personality led to the formation of a discrete emotions, functionalist analysis of personality, summarized in Chapters 9 and 10. This treatment of the development of emotional organizations was necessarily limited to the description of extraordinarily salient, monolithic, and readily identifiable, personality patterns, since we required at least some empirical literature to put our case together. The literature on TABP and aggressive children suited our purposes perfectly, as did the literature on shyness.

Our sense of satisfaction at having identified coherent patterns and ones that subscribed to a theoretical understanding was, however, somewhat tainted. These versions of personality seemed too pat and seamless. They described prototypes or "ideal types" (cf. Spranger, 1928) and seemed somewhat removed from our experience of real people, even those who conformed to a particular prototype. To that extent, we realized we unwittingly had been caught up in the occupational hazard of "shrinking human nature" to fit the needs of paradigms.

Indeed, as we reflected on the logic and coherence of the patterns we had described, we became somewhat wary of the powerful image of immutability that such a conceptualization seemed to convey. There was something rather disconcerting about the fixity implied by the idea of emotion traits. To think of personality as crystallized for all time was tantamount to a kind of American heresy. We knew at that point that there had to be an eleventh chapter, which wrestled with the issue of personality change, and which engaged the issue of more complex personality organizations. Apropos, we turned to several sources of meditation on the issue, one being the literatures outside of psychology's domain. What, we wondered, did our great and profane works of literature tell us about personality change? Here, we thought, we might tap into the prevailing ethnopsychology of change. G. A. Kelly was one of the first to take advantage of folk psychologies in the construction of theory. More recently, Bruner (1990) has avocated that ethnopsychology be more actively exploited by psychologists, and be accorded the same kind of status as ethnoscience and ethnobotany in anthropological research. In Bruner's view, autobiographical and biographical materials constitute primary instruments of culture, instruments through which humans learn to assign meaning to their world. As such, we turned to the literary cannon as an adjunctive source of theory on personality change.

Allusions to personality change in Western literature were not so difficult to find, although somewhat more difficult than we at first imagined. We were surprised that accounts of personality change in great literary works were not all that common. People we approached with our observations who were experts on the literary cannon suggested to us that great literature does not often feature drastic personality change because the art of literary creation relies on character *development*, which, to be believable, and to be well crafted, must take place over a substantial period of time. And although personality change is not *often* immortalized in works of fiction and poetry, various authors have written about the issue, and have taken quite disparate opinions. For example, in "The Age of Anxiety," W. H. Auden writes:

> We would rather be ruined than changed
> We would rather die in our dread
> Than climb the cross of the moment
> And let our illusions die.

And Kafka's *Metamorphosis*, of course, is the quintessential horror story of change. Change is disorienting, creates disequilibrium and estrangement from others, and, ultimately, death.

In contrast, Henri Bergson thought for a conscious being to exist is to change, to change is to mature, to mature is to go on creating oneself endlessly (*Two Sources of Morality and Religion*, 1932). Another author, the poet John Donne, thought that "Change is the nursery of musicke, joy, life, eternity" ("To His Mistress Going to Bed," Elegy XIX).

In contrast to fiction and poetry, where reports of personality change are somewhat sparse, in autobiography and biography they are almost the order of the day; moreover, they tend to involve changes that are more precipitous than those found in fiction and poetry. This genre of literature is, by all indices, extremely popular and makes a salient impression. Almost everyone we consulted could cite at least two or three lives they knew of through biography and autobiography that supplied the kinds of accounts we were looking for. We heard of Clive of India, the undistinguished British civil servant of the 1800s who played Russian roulette as a game to test whether he was destined for great things. Since he survived the experiment, he took it as a positive omen; he grew in confidence and, as history records, went on to conquer India. We were reminded of Lawrence of Arabia, whose military conquests during the first world war made him a hero at home, but who experienced a trauma that shook him to his foundation. During one military escapade Lawrence was captured by the Turks and was brutally tortured and sodomized. Biography has it that this experience released latent homosexual tendencies in Lawrence, the realization of which drove him into a reclusive existence from which he never fully recovered. In this account, an adventurous spirit was turned into an introvert, the obverse life trajectory of Clive of India. And so forth. These stories all seemed of a seamless piece: dramatic, complete, enduring change of both a positive or negative sort. While interesting and compelling, they seemed bereft of the kind of mixedness and complexity one actually experiences in real life. Was there significant "narrative smoothing" (Spence, 1986) going on at the service of an ideology of transformation? Biographical accounts involve significant interpretive work, and even the reading of someone else's biographical interpretation lends itself to various theoretical and hermeneutical assimilations. One could use the life of Anne Sexton, for example, to illustrate either discontinuity or continuity. That is, Middlebrook's (1992) biography of Sexton can be read as an account of a mad housewife who changed into a famous poet, or as a depressed, borderline housewife who grew into a depressed, borderline poet. Alternately, one could use the same document to show how her life course involved personality development that featured the incorporation of experience in epigenetic development (Magai & Hunziker, in press). Suffice it to say at this point, the very "heroic" nature of many of the tales of personality change made one want to examine the thesis more closely.

One approach to analyzing what people mean by personality change and its circumstances is to look for patterns over an array of instances. In doing so, we found that almost all tales of personality change—fiction, nonfiction, and what is today called "faction" (embellished biography)—involve key or turning points that pivot on emotionally charged contexts, as examined below.

LITERARY AND BIOGRAPHICAL EXAMPLES OF LIFECOURSE CHANGE AND THEIR RELATION TO AFFECT

In scanning an array of literature, it became obvious to us that there were prototype occasions for reports of personality change. They all involved highly charged and emotionally salient events and encounters that served as the galvanizing context for change. Some of the categories that occurred with greater than average frequency were the following:

1. *Stories of passionate love.* These accounts typically describe love affairs featuring "coup de foudre" experiences or as involving particularly great difficulties and anguish for the lovers. Out of these lightning storms and maelstroms come tales of dramatic change, oftening involving heroism (*Mort d' Arthur*), or, alternatively, tragedy—that is, tales in which the hero/heroine is driven mad or to despair and isolation. An example of the latter is found in Racine's play *Andromaque*, where Orestes goes mad, after the woman he loves, Hermione, pursuades him to kill Pyrrhus, only to renounce him for the murder and to commit suicide. Another is that of Giovanni Boccaccio, the fourteenth-century Italian author of *The Decameron*. Later in life he wrote *The Corbaccio*, a satire aimed at women in general and more specifically at the rich and pretty widow who rejected him; it marks a transition point in his life, for it is at this time that he renounces worldly pleasure.

2. *Religious conversion experiences.* There are numerous examples of this particular genre. Later we explore religious conversion experiences in more detail because of the sheer density of literature that is available on this topic.

3. *Political conversion experiences.* The process of adopting a new political or ideological commitment has much in common with religious conversion according to Glicksberg (1976), who has written a very penetrating account of political ideology. The new political commitments that people adopt tend to be described as precipitous, compelling, and transforming. "The emotional needs that drove many intellectuals to embrace Communism was largely religious in character, though in public they explained their motives as part of a world-historical movement" (Glicksberg, 1976, p. 277). Political conversion is vividly brought to life in a series of books by Arthur Koestler (*Scum of the Earth, Dialogue with Death, Darkness at Noon*) that were fictionalized accounts of his experiences during the Spanish Civil War, and prior to and during the second world war. Koestler was an influential European journalist when he discovered Communism in 1931 and embraced it enthusiastically. This ideology appeared to offer the hope of resolving deep philosophical and political doubts he had about culture and society; it also gave him a locus for expressing his stormy and passionate nature. Koestler had a number of passionate ideological commitments that he embraced throughout his life, but what is of interest here is that highly charged emotional events were typically involved in commitment experiences as well as in the destabilization of positions he had previously and fervently adopted. One example from his life will suffice. Though Koestler was a zealous Communist for several years, as a prisoner during the Spanish Civil War about to be executed and witness to the executions of innocent persons, he "discovered" that the means do not always justify the ends; he eventually renounced Communism and made other changes in his life.

4. *Wartime experiences.* Wartime experiences have been described as having a profound impact on both general development and on personality. *All Quiet on the Western Front* (Remarque, 1929) shows how the brutality of basic training thrusts adolescents into manhood (i.e., advances the developmental timetable), and how the brutality of war so numbs young men that it makes them feel alien and unfit for civilian life. "We became hard, suspicious, pitiless, vicious, tough—

and that was good; for these attributes had been entirely lacking in us" (p. 20). Under extreme conditions, the stress of war can produce psychic trauma of such magnitude that individuals are plagued for years with flashback experiences that seize them suddenly and unexpectedly and flood them anew with fresh terror. Several literary and screen works give flesh to these descriptions. Celine's *Journey to the End of Night* is a vivid description of how war drives people insane. Singular and particularly horrific experiences of war and their consequences for personality have been graphically portrayed in a number of post–Vietnam War films, including *The Deerhunter*.

5. *Personal traumas (torture, bodily injury, rape, incest).* The biography of Anne Sexton (Middlebrook, 1992) illustrates the psychological consequences of sexual abuse in childhood. In the Sexton biography we learn of a woman so traumatized by the sexual abuse of an alcoholic father and a spinster aunt that both the events and associated anger were split off from consciousness for a long time; however, the sporadic bouts of depression that she was subject to, and the odd, catatonic "trances" that overcame her and which could last for hours at a time, may have been the turbulent expression of the earlier traumas. Calverley et al.'s (in press) empirical investigation of childhood abuse documents similar features of splitting and dissociation in a more representative group of sexually abused women.

6. *The flight from boredom.* Though little has been written about boredom as an emotional experience, there is much in literature to suggest that extreme boredom is both painful and motivating. Saul Bellow's *Herzog* is a novel whose quintessential issue is of the pervasiveness of twentieth-century boredom and the ways that it afflicts, in particular, the story's protagonist. Stultifying boredom may also have played more of a role in certain cases of religious conversion or "spiritual awakening" than has been acknowledged. To be specific, one can envision that it may have been more the boredom of a priviledged and cloistered life that drove Gautama to the desert than his encounters with sick and old people. As well, there is also biographical evidence in the life history of George Orwell that suggests his experimental immersion in lower-class life (which became material for several of his books) and subsequent commitment to Communism were a partial reaction to his own comfortable bourgeois life and the boredom that it engendered.

In the wake of any of the above experiences, the individual is motivated to fill the oblivion, cope with the exigency, or secure the love object. All of these motivations entail behavioral and cognitive commitment and of necessity entail life change, and, apparently, personality change. We pause here to examine the nature of personality change. Most of the instances encountered in literature and biography involve the adoption of new ideologies (religious, political, secular) or circumstances of life (e.g., marriage, career change). Sometimes the emotional underpinnings of the change are masked and the change is cast as purely intellectual or sociological, as in the case of Wiersma's (1988) study of women who took up careers after raising families. In the course of interviewing these women, Wiersma became frustrated by the stereotyped stories they told of growth prompted by sociological changes in the culture, and of their enormously gratifying experiences of self-discovery. Wiersma dubbed these "press releases"—stories told for public consumption. Subsequently, she probed more deeply and discovered the personal/emotional circumstances that lay behind the process for each individual woman, and how difficult the transition had been given resistant husbands, critical relatives and friends, and sexist work environments.

Passionate love also often encourages individuals to make dramatic changes in their lives and as well may introduce them to philosophies and ideologies that they explore and sometimes adopt. Henry Murray is a particularly good example. Although he is most well known as a personality psychologist, Murray had another career before he discovered psychology (Anderson, 1988). He received an M.D. from Columbia and a Ph.D. in biochemistry from Cambridge, and had published 21 articles in leading medicine and biochemistry journals before he underwent profound affective upheaval. The circumstances of this upheaval have only recently come to light (Anderson, 1988), and include an extramarital affair with Christiana Morgan. Torn between his commitment to his family (his daughter was but 2 years of age when the affair first began) and this new-found love, he began exploring the works of Jung—which he had just discovered—with Morgan. She already had an intimate acquaintance with his work and even arranged to have Murray meet Jung. By his own account, it was Murray's subsequent conversations with Jung and Morgan, and his in-depth readings in psychology, that finally convinced him to renounce the life of a medical researcher for that of a psychologist. Let us now turn to a component analysis of the process of such change.

Surprise, Emotional Disequilibrium, Appraisal, Reflection, and Change

From examination of these and other materials we have discerned a pattern that suggests some of the mechanisms and processes involved in personality change. Both cognition and emotion are involved in the process, in a sequence that can roughly be described as follows: surprise/shock, emotional disequilibrium, appraisal, reflection, and, at least potentially, personality change.

First, something has to occur that shakes or shatters the prevailing way of seeing and relating to the world, self, and others; that is, there must be an occurrence of something that disrupts preconceived ideas and generates acute emotional feelings. The person described in fiction and biography typically encounters someone or something that surprises, startles, or shocks. From a theoretical point of view, this is an important observation. Surprise, in Tomkins's formulations, is the channel-clearing affect (Tomkins, 1963). It clears the sensory channels for the reception of new information and puts on hold the information-processing strategies that are uppermost in the personality repertoire. Experientially, surprise is personally startling; an event is experienced as preposterous, totally "other," contradicting all of the individual's usual expectancies. With the individual's fundamental expectations shaken, there is a greater openness to new ways of appraising the world and for a potentially new organization of experience.

Surprise can be generated by persons or events, but almost always takes place in an interpersonal context. Surprise will typically take the form of some great enchantment (falling in love, or having a religious or political conversion experience), a great disenchantment (falling out of love, becoming disillusioned with a religious or political ideology), or the experience of terror (war, other personal traumas), which will profoundly alter one's sense of fundamental security. Surprise thus becomes allied with other emotions; one can be surprised by joy or surprised by grief or terror.

We say that surprise almost always takes place in an interpersonal context because there is nothing that is innately more enchanting, disenchanting, or terrifying than another human being. In fact, the prototype for original disenchantment is found in everyone's childhood, according to Tomkins (1963). Constituting an obverse of original sin—the discovery of the individual's own flawed nature—the child's first disenchantment involves the upsetting discovery that the parent is not all that he or she at first seemed. In the course of experiencing delayed and imperfect gratification, the idealized parent of infancy is discovered to be less than perfect, disappointing, and deeply flawed. This is the prototype for disgust, which in Tomkins's script theory involves scenes where "something good turns bad." The parent is unmasked as flawed and disenchantment is experienced— with a number of ramifications which we need not go into here. The acute emotional feelings that are generated by an enchantment, disenchantment, or terror produce a kind of psychic disequilibrium during which old patterns of thinking and feeling are disrupted and new learning and new modes of information processing are facilitated.

The speculation that it is the phenomenology of feeling that is galvanizing and intrinsic to change is found in the works of a number of early psychologists, most notably William James (1902/1961). In fact, we can pause here to consider two types of personality change from among the several mentioned above for closer inspection. Religious conversion and war experiences are chosen because there is now substantial empirical work on these areas that speak to personality change.

Religious Conversion as a Prototype of Personality Change

William James addressed the issue of religious conversion and personality change in his book *The Varieties of Religious Experience* (1902/1961); this work also points to the centrality of emotional experience in personality change. At the time that he was writing there was little in the way of personality theory and he hoped that his work might offer a "crumb-like contribution" (p. 100) to such an effort. Indeed, he viewed the book's central goal as elucidating some of the origins of individual differences as represented in basic character or personality. The diversity of character structure, he believed, resulted from differences in emotional organization. James (1902/1961) wrote: "...the causes of human diversity lie chiefly in our *differing susceptibilities of emotional excitement*, and in the *different impulses and inhibitions* which these bring in their train" (p. 212).

James believed that people are predisposed to view the world in two primary ways and he called the personality types associated with these temperamental dispositions the healthy minded and the sick soul. The first way of experiencing the world—the healthy minded—is represented in the personality in which happiness dominates. He remarked that for some individuals, this is an "involuntary" response, for they have a "way of feeling happy about things immediately" (p. 85). Other persons, also having this disposition, have developed it into a systematic, philosophical outlook upon the world in which all events are viewed as having some element of goodness. James (1902/1961) clearly communicated his bias that such persons, while apparently happy and satisfied with their lives, nevertheless have embraced an inadequate philosophy,

> because the evil facts which it refuses positively to account for are a genuine portion of reality; and they may after all be the best key to life's significance, and possibly the only openers of our eyes to the deepest levels of truth. (p. 140)

James felt his own character to be of the "sick soul" variety and identified with such persons whose personalities tended to be organized more around the negative emotions. Nevertheless, he recognized the difficulty of living with these emotions. These individuals, he claimed, had to be "twice-born in order to be happy" (p. 143). Although he recognized that most people "are intermediate varieties and mixtures" (p. 143) of these two types, he believed it was important to portray them in their extremity in order to elaborate upon their differing dynamics.

Drawing from many examples ranging from ordinary, undistinguished citizens to the most famous of his times, like Leo Tolstoy, James offered portraits of the kinds of discontinuities of personality that can redirect adult lives. Specifically, he focused on change that occurred as a result of religious conversion, though he recognized that religion did not always have to be the key to such change. In fact, James (1902/1961) said that

> the new birth may be away from religion into incredulity; or it may be from moral scrupulosity into freedom and license; or it may be produced by the *irruption* into the individual's life of some new stimulus or passion, such as love, ambition, cupidity, revenge, or patriotic devotion. (p. 150)

In all of these cases and including those with a religious theme, the change could occur suddenly or gradually but the key idea was that fundamental changes in human personality were indeed possible.

When the sick soul—Tolstoy being a prime example—undergoes a rebirth, happiness as a vital aspect of personality emerges. However, this is not the naive happiness of the healthy-minded individual who refuses to come to terms with suffering and evil. Rather, a balance is achieved wherein the personality is no longer dominated by negative affect, nor is it given wholly over to positive affect. Neither, says the old functionalist, is an adaptive position vis à vis the realities of human life and experience. Rather, he states, the happiness of the religiously twice born

> is not the simple, ignorance of ill, but something vastly more complex, including natural evil as one of its elements, but finding natural evil no such stumbling-block and terror because it now sees it swallowed up in supernatural good. (p. 135)

Here James is describing an individual who can experience happiness as well as sadness and not be overwhelmed by either; this is a person who has experienced what he called the unity of the self and what Tomkins (1963) would have referred to as the integrated personality, in which no single affect dominates (see Chapter 8). What James (1902/1961) does not mean, however, is that positive affect and negative affect cancel one another, resulting in affective neutrality. Rather, he describes how the array of emotions, freely experienced in the "heterogeneous personality," produces a "series of zig-zags, as now one tendency and now another gets the upper hand" (p. 145), and how these experiences become unified at a deeper level when religious ideas take a central position in consciousness and religious aims "form the habitual centre" (p. 165) of a person's life. Although James goes on to present numerous examples of how religion provides this unity in diversity, his statements about other motivators of change suggest that his treatment of regligious conversion experience is to be taken as but one example of a larger dynamic process. Whatever the "habitual centre" of personality energy becomes—religious, political, artistic, scientific, or otherwise—the change is charged with emotion. As James says, an idea "grows hot and alive within us" (p. 165). This is not merely an intellectual decision for change; it is one in which emotional experience ignites change that becomes integrated within the personality. Another way of saying this is that the individual has achieved a measure of "wisdom" (Baltes, Smith, & Staudinger, 1992; Staudinger, Marsiske, & Baltes, 1993). This is not the purely speculative wisdom of the philosopher; rather, it is the wisdom of human experience, an admixture of insight into one's own ways of thinking and of feeling.

James gained his insights from both his own experiences and through biographical analysis. We turn now to research on religious conversion that is grounded in more contemporary empirical methods, namely, that of Chana Ulmann. In *The Transformed Self*, Ullman (1989) describes her research with a large number of religious converts using semistructured interviews and standardized and nonstandardized paper and pencil measures of emotions and attitudes. The study was not limited to one or another religious group, but included subjects from Christian, Jewish, Baha'i, and Hare Krishna faiths, and consisted of 40 religious converts and 30 nonconverts who had religious affiliations and who came from similar socioeconomic backgrounds.

Ullman had anticipated that the conversion experience would pivot around a change in ideology, but what she found was something more akin to a falling in love experience (what we have called a major enchantment); that is, a common feature of religious conversion was a sudden infatuation with a real or imagined figure. More important for our thesis is that the conversion experiences typically took place aginst a backdrop of great emotional turmoil. Fully 80% of the sample described considerable distress during the 2-year period prior to their conversions. The emotional states most frequently described were distress-anguish (67%), anger-rage (25%), and fear-terror (22 %). By and large, the pre-conversion lives were absorbed in issues of self, not ideology or altruistic concerns about others. They instead were dominated by personal "despair, doubts in their own self-worth, fears of rejection, unsuccessful attempts to handle rage, an emptiness, and an estrangement from others" (Ullman, 1989, p. 19). Contrary to expectations, the emotion of guilt was mentioned only 15% of the time, and only 27% of the converts described preoccupations with what could be designated as "objective," "existential," or "other-oriented" precursors of their conversion experience. The personal relationships that emerged as central to the conversion experience tended to involve (1) a father figure who supplied order and protection, (2) a peer group that offered a community of unconditional love, and/or (3) an all-loving, transcendental object that served as an attachment figure. The new attachment figure or group appeared to be attractive because it offered a promise of relief from isolation or distress.

Another salient commonality among religious converts was the tendency to have experienced a troubled youth. Of the nonconverts, 73% described a happy childhood, whereas only 6% of the religious converts described such histories. Approximately one half of the sample of religious converts described extremely unhappy childhoods (versus 13% of the nonconverts), and two thirds described an extremely difficult adolescence, typically filled with unhappiness and pain (versus only 6.7% in the control group).

What is especially interesting about this pattern of findings is that the profile fits prototype personality changers from literature—like Tolstoy (Magai & Hunziker, 1993)—quite closely. Tolstoy had a particularly traumatic childhood, losing his mother at 2, then his father, and finally an aunt who had taken over his rearing. In later adulthood, during the 2 years prior to his conversion, he experienced five more significant losses—the deaths of three of his children and of two aunts. He experienced a period of particularly intense despair and even contemplated suicide, though in later accounts of his conversion he does not attribute the despair specifically to these losses; more salient for him was his suddenly intensified experience of enchantment with the working-class peasant and his subsequent idealization and infatuation with peasant life. The thematic consistency between contextually important life events and the precipitation of conversion experience in Tolstoy's life and in the lives of individuals interviewed and tested by Ullman does much to restore one's faith (so to speak) in the credulity of biographical accounts of religious conversion.

The above provides us with an example of personality change from the genre of major enchantments. We turn now to a more extended example of another sort—that involving the terrors of heavy military combat.

Personality Change and War Experiences

A number of examples of personality change recorded in literature were given above. Here we consider the empirical literature. The clinical syndrome of posttraumatic stress disorder (PTSD), now well established in the DSM-III-R diagnostic manual, grew out of work with war veterans. Interestingly, DSM-III-R descriptions of PTSD identify five criteria for differential diagnosis. Among them is the criterion that the person has experienced an event that is outside the range of usual human experience—the surprise or shock experience we postulated as instrumental in instigating change. Another is increased arousal (i.e., emotionality); the remaining features are avoidance of stimuli associated with the trauma, a reexperience of the event including waking and dreaming states, and duration of the disturbance for at least 1 month.

The existence of the PTSD syndrome in a clinical diagnostic manual indicates the expectation that a traumatic experience such as combat will lead to numbing, emotional turmoil, and behavioral change. In fact, PTSD has become the focus of a good deal of recent research and clinical reportage (Aldwin, Levenson, & Spiro, 1994; Bradshaw, Ohlde, & Horne, 1993; Spiro, Schnurr, & Aldwin, 1994). There is apparently a whole spectrum of responses to combat trauma, ranging from no personality change, to numbing of general responsiveness and affective blunting, to grosser changes. One common PTSD pattern identified by Bradshaw et al. (1993) over the course of treating some 1,000 Vietnam War veterans—the heart of darkness syndrome—is typified by feelings of invulnerability, grandiosity, and an absence of empathy. The histories of these men failed to reveal antisocial acts before entering combat and they typically had displayed a capacity for deep and caring relationships with comrades. However, in the course of combat they became "happy killers" (Bradshaw et al., 1993), and their personality changes persisted long after they returned from combat duty. The premorbid personality character-istics and contextual determinants associated with this pattern, as distilled from hundreds of clinical interviews, include the following: individual aggressiveness, duration of danger and degree of vulnerability, number of comrades killed and the brutality of their deaths, peer group support and participation in reciprocally brutal binges of killing, and the absence of control by superior officers. The men who react to the stress of heavy combat by becoming "happy killers," in their postcombat lives—even 10 years after— typically had poor stress tolerance and tended to revert to a killer mentality quite readily.

A more systematic investigation that speaks directly to the issue of person-ality change and which is singular in its tracking of subjects longitudinally is Elder's (Elder, 1989; Elder, Shanahan, & Clipp, 1994) analysis of the data from the longitudinal samples of the Institute of Human Development. The subjects for the analysis of the effects of combat were 149 individuals born in the 1920s who had been followed longitudinally up through 1985. Elder and Clipp compared the postwar adaptations of three groups of veterans—those who had seen especially heavy combat, those who had experienced light combat, and those who had held noncombat positions. Pre- and postmeasures of personality were available from the men from earlier waves of data collection; data on self-reported symptoms of posttraumatic stress were collected in the 1985 wave. The men also described the positive and negative influences of military experience. Men who experienced heavy combat reported more negative effects of milatary service in terms of combat anxieties, misery, bad memories, thoughts of death or destruction, loss of friends, and drinking. On the more positive side, the heavy combat veterans believed that their war experiences had better equipped them to deal with adversity, had instilled in them strong self-discipline, had given them a keener valuation of human life. In terms of posttraumatic stress, the heavy combat veterans were at high risk for emotional and behavioral problems in their postwar life histories. Though the risks diminished over time, many symptoms persisted into the middle years and included nightmares, flashbacks, depressed feelings, irritability, anxiety, and hypersensitivity to startle. Fully a quarter of the heavy combat men reported one or more current symptoms of post-traumatic stress; in contrast, only three other veterans made such a report. At age 55 almost half of the heavy combat veterans had entered psychotherapy, whereas less than one third of the other veterans had sought treatment.

The above findings show that terrifying battleground experiences can produce psychic trauma that destabilizes earlier personality patterns. Similar personality dysfunction is often found in women who experienced sexual abuse as children, leading some clinicians to diagnose post-traumatic stress disorder in these women. It is obvious from in depth interviews with war veterans and sexual abuse victims that such experiences have a profound (and sometimes enduring) negative impact on personality, although some individuals appear to rise above their traumas and to use their experiences in a transformative way for personal growth. Here we pause to consider some of the post-transformation circumstances that support and maintain, and even enhance, the new adaptations and character structures in the case of positive change and that offer resistance to personality deterioration in the case of traumatic experiences.

ENDURING CHANGES AND THE PROCESSES THAT SUPPORT THEM

Great enchantments, disenchantments, and terrors do not always produce personality change of the lasting kind. Enchantments are fragile because they mostly offer utopian views of the future that are doomed to at least some disappointment. They are often originally maintained by a thickly woven structure of ideology or of life circumstance. The initiate to Communism, for example, in his or her original state of enchantment, is inspired by lofty goals and inspiring slogans extracted from densely intellectual treatises (Bruner, 1986). By donning this thickly woven mantle of ideology, the acolyte is inoculated against initial disappointment, and the well-known phenomenon of cognitive dissonance also helps initially to sustain the transformed self. In the case of romantic love the original enchantment is initially sustained in the common tendency of lovers to consolidate their rapture by bringing new life into the world; by the time the glow of enchantment has dissipated, the family structure has enlarged by virtue of a child or children and the increasingly intimate web of kith and kin.

Earlier we defined personality change as the embracing of a new ideology or lifestyle. It may also involve a change in personality of the most fundamental kind, that is, a shift from one dimension of a trait to the other. Two examples were found in biography—the introvert-extrovert and extrovert-introvert transformations of, respectively, Clive of India and Lawrence of Arabia. The heightened anxiety of those exposed to war trauma, rape, and other grave assaults can be seen as fundamentally affecting the neuroticism dimension of personality. Emotional alterations of a less severe magnitude—as in the case of Carl Rogers—are probably more common. These internal changes also require support for their maintenance. And it is to the issue of support that we now turn.

Affective, ideological, and lifestyle changes require interpersonal and other contextual scaffolding, both initially and over time, for their maintenance. Two kinds of support—interpersonal and cognitive-cultural—are intrinsic to lasting personality change.

Interpersonal Scaffolds of Personality Change

The ideological conversion to Communism for Koestler and Orwell did not occur in an interpersonal vacuum; conversion to a new religious faith, as well, does not occur in isolation from others, according to Chana Ullman's work. It is others who initiate individuals into new ideologies; human icons (Lenin, Christ, Buddha) typically serve as models to emulate; the community of "idologues" (comrades, members of the faith) provides a nurturing peer culture. Henry Murray fell in love with Christiana Morgan and with Jungian psychology. He sustained a long-term commitment to a new career in psychology for multiple reasons, but at least some of them included the continuing relationship with Morgan and her cohort of ideological fellow travelers, as well as, eventually, a cadre of students who idealized him and who spread his word. These biographical understandings receive support in empirical research. Caspi, Bem, and Elder (1989), in summarizing the research of the California longitudinal studies of life change and continuity of boys and girls reared during the Great Depression, document two types of person-environment interaction processes that serve to maintain stability. One involves *cumulative continuity*, whereby individuals select environments to match their interactional style, and which further reinforce the style and inoculate against deflecting tendencies; the other involves *interactional continuity*, in which the person behaves in ways that elicit complementary and reinforcing responses from others. Although it is only implied in Elder et al.'s work, we intuit that the power of these stabilizing influences resides in the fact that the environments are filled with people and relationships and that one's identity becomes fused with that of others. The latter aspect brings us to two other sources supporting personality change, both initially and on a continuing basis: (1) the existence of cultural models for change (both micro- and macrocultural) and (2) identity models.

Support of Culture and Cognition

In cultures that are densely homogeneous as in Japan and China, or that are highly stratified, as in India, radical change is not an idea that has very much appeal, nor are there many models for change. In contrast, America and some West European cultures see change as intrinsic to life process. America in particular has popularized and mythologized such symbols of change as the self-made man or women, the born-again Christian, and such change-oriented self-help groups as Alcoholics Anonymous. Germany is the home of the Protestant Reformation, the Protestant work ethic, and the *Wirtschaftswunder* of more recent times. In such cultures as America and Germany there is substantial economic and social mobility and, one suspects, a corresponding ethnopsychology of personality growth and change. Of course, this is not true worldwide. However, to the extent that all developed cultures now live in a "global village," with various telecommunications services bringing news of other ways of life and sparking heretofore unknown desires, accounts of change may begin to proliferate in parts of the world that had previously not been intimately acquainted with them.

At a more molecular level, identity models ("possible selves," cf. Bruner, 1986; Ryff, 1991), and the roles and scripts associated with them, also help both channel change and consolidate personality change because social identities are well scripted and thus provide a means of dealing with the instability of disequilibration and its attendant anxiety. To return to our two central biographical figures, Rogers and Watson, Rogers could assimilate his trauma to known psychological traumas and could adopt the soul-searching strategy of immersion in psychotherapy because it is a known and familiar activity for those who identify as psychologists, especially clinical psychologists. Psychotherapy in twentieth-century culture has become canonized as one of the most acceptable and recommended paths to personal transformation. Rogers did not develop a new identity, just a transformed one, and he did so by partaking of a well-scripted action plan that was congruent for someone in his profession. In an earlier time he might have consulted a pastor, or he might have joined a religious order and taken on a new identity as a monk.

In contrast to Rogers, Watson found himself in quite a different milieu in the aftermath of his traumatic ejection from academia. His identity as an academic psychologist was rudely stripped from him; as well, he had the added press of having to find a new way of making a living. As it was, Watson went almost immediately to work for the J. Walter Thompson advertising company, more by exigency than by choice. Taking a course of psychotherapy to deal with the crisis and to reinvent himself probably would not have occurred to him in the first place given his contempt for the nonobservables of introspection and feelings. Even if it had, going into psychotherapy surely would not have found much peer support with his new-found cohort of business associates.

According to British social identity theory (Tajfel & Turner, 1986), people are intrinsically motivated to look for positive identities that offer hope of absorbing the pain of negative affect associated with the old identities. Social identities, in contrast to personal identities (psychological traits, personal values) involve aspects of self-concept that derive from membership in social groups in combination with the emotional significance of membership in such groups. Attachment to a social identity—typically a positive one—is not only a way of maintaining or enhancing self-esteem but also a lifeline to coherency. Because social identities are well scripted they offer a tried and true way of being in the world; because they are limited in number most of us are acquainted with their essential outlines. The universe of new identities is constrained by culture, class, and time. Though constrained by available models, the models offer known scripts, a peer culture, and a history and future, all of which can help anchor the new identity as it recovers from the tumult of enchantment, disenchantment, and/or terror.

And here we perhaps have an answer to the seemingly genre-like, schematic, and prototypical nature of personality change described in the various literatures we reviewed above. In the midst of surprising and tumultuous junctures in our lives, perhaps it is the case that the only way we can make these dramatic changes credible—to both ourselves and others—and, perhaps more importantly, find a thread of connection so that we are not left dangling over an unknown abyss, is to make them conform to some known genre, which contains within it a known identity. Like Wiersma's midlife housewives reinventing themselves in new careers and crafting their life narratives in a way that conformed neatly with known sociological models, perhaps all persons who undergo major life change are assisted by the existence of known and well-worked identities. We seek known identities because they offer scripts and because by embracing them we reduce the uncertainty that attends novelty. This does not need to detract from the authenticity of change. As several authors have pointed out, the person providing her biography may not tell us the whole truth, but she tells us some sort of truth about herself if we have the skill and intelligence to interpret it (Dean & Whyte, 1958; Wiersma, 1988). At the same time, the existence of prototype identities does mean that there is much more to be found beneath the surface.

The Search for Confirmation

To round this volume's discussion of personality development we considered the issue of developmental change in the present chapter. We found that the developmental, personality, and clinical literatures did not have well-elaborated theories of personality change. Reflecting on the problem from a discrete emotions, functionalist analysis of personality, and using fiction, biography, and some limited empirical research as a basis of theory construction, we generated a tentative model of personality change that is grounded in discrete emotions theory and in Tomkins's affect theory. We offer this construction as a preliminary meditation. In future research we hope to validate the patterns observed in Western literature and biography in two ways. First, we seek to extend our generalizations concerning the events and mechanisms supporting life change beyond that which was distilled from accounts of eminent individuals who figured so prominently in the biographical sources cited in this chapter to more ordinary citizens. This goal can be achieved by examining archival sources, such as the diaries of nineteenth-century women archived at the Henry Murray Center at Radcliffe, or by examining the immigrant literature so copiously collected by the Chicago School anthropologists and sociologists during the 1930s and 1940s (e.g., Thomas & Znaniecki, 1918).

A second thrust involves an analysis of affective change in a large sample of individuals who participated in a study of "emotion across the lifespan" in 1986 (Malatesta-Magai et al., 1992). This follow-up study has only just been initiated. Emotion-focused personality inventories that were administered to the original subjects will be readministered in order to detect significant changes in emotion organization; as well, we will collect data on adult attachment style using the Adult Attachment Interview (AAI). It is our hunch that avoidant individuals may be less susceptible to changes because of the more limited role that interpersonal process plays in their lives versus in the lives of secure and ambivalent organizations. We will also use an adult emotions interview that we recently devised to complement the AAI and in order to extend subjects' narratives to significant events beyond the early childhood years. Participants in the study will be interviewed as to their own phenomenology of change, and verification will be sought from an intimate associate. Hopefully, these data, as well as data from the biographical analysis of diaries, immigrant records, and other archival sources, will help substantiate our initial formulations, and that they will provide even greater detail about the preconditions, emotional circumstances, and contextual factors that support change as people mature over the life course.

Summary and Future Directions

Throughout this work, especially in the last three chapters, we have taken the position that emotional experiences make things salient—emotions parse the figure from the ground of everyday life. As we grow up, emotions become linked with cognition as ideologies and coherences are elaborated. As Tomkins intuited, breaks with expectation—in the average expectable phenomenology of life—set the stage for the creation of novel emotional experiences and, potentially, for life change.

Lives are punctuated by emotional events that create change—great enchantments, disenchantments, and terrors. Of the former, romantic love and political and religious commitments are prototypical. Of the latter two, we include disappointments and disillusionments with earlier personas and ideologies, and traumatic events. Each of the above has been associated with change in the life course and, even more radically, change in personality. Thus, we have proposed that it is intense emotional experience of both a positive and negative kind that is the sine qua non of life change, but it must also include reappraisals and reevaluations and thus contain an important cognitive element. Neither emotion nor cognition alone constitutes the necessary and sufficient condition for change. Emotions to a great extent "set the stage" for the possibility of change by challenging existing structures of thought, emotion, and behavior. An individual is startled into an awareness that previous strategies of coping no longer apply, or that other strategies offer promising new alternatives. The new strategies may become assimilated into the personality provided that they afford a modicum of help in contending with the experiences at hand and provided there is mental elaboration in the form of reflection, introspection, and dialogue with others. These experiences and their integration within the personality provide the basis for still greater emotional elaboration (Haviland & Kramer, 1991), which has been associated with the production of more mature thinking processes (Haviland, in preparation) and which conforms to the picture of increasing wisdom grounded in life experience (Baltes, 1993; Baltes et al., 1992; Staudinger et al., 1993).

The next stage in the testing of our model must include a consideration of what *kind* of change can be anticipated in the context of certain kinds of events. Part of the reaction will inhere in the nature of the event itself. Is it a fundamentally joyful event such as the birth of a child? Or is it a scene that is fundamentally disgusting, horrifying, enraging, mortifying, or anguishing? The other part of it will be dictated by the person's preexisting emotional biases and attendant interpretations, as well as the larger context of the person's life. Although we cited the birth scene as being one fundamentally constituted of joy, one can easily envision other emotional reactions. In terms of specific personality dispositions, some may be more permeable to change than others. We have already mentioned our speculation that attachment styles may be differentially permeable to change. The same may apply for the basic emotion traits. In fact, we suspect that persons whose personalities are defined, to at least some extent, by interest, sadness, and shame will experience more life change (perhaps of both a positive and negative kind) than those whose personalities are defined more by contempt, disgust, and anger, since the cognitive structures associated with hostile emotion tend to be absolutistic (Haviland & Kramer, 1991) and, we suspect, characterized by more well-defended emotional perimeters. Some evidence for this is found in a study of passive-withdrawal behavior and aggression in elementary school children (Renken, Egeland, Marvinney, Mangelsdorf, & Sroufe, 1989). The former scores seem to tap shyness and the latter scores anger. Interestingly, passive-withdrawal behavior scores in this study were less stable over time (as measured when the children were in Grades 1, 2, and 3) than aggression scores.

In any case, we have no doubt that each type of emergent awareness that is prompted by the person–situation interaction will be rendered in emotional terms, and hence will alter consciousness in particular ways and make certain associations salient. The cross-products of these various interactions, theoretically, can be mapped. We have not yet undertaken this level of analysis, but it suggests a potentially fruitful direction for future research.

There are still a number of remaining problems with the issue of personality change having to do with what constitutes personality change and the duration of change. In this chapter we addressed the more dramatic form of personality change. Biographical accounts of change frequently portray certain events as having "transformed" the protagonist's life, so much so that the individual becomes a "new person." Of course, this is a metaphor rather than an iconic representation of reality. But metaphors are one of the most successful strategies for inducting others into a shared culture of meaning.

Discussions of personality development in the developmental literature often pit issues of change against continuity, as though there were but two possibilities. An alternate model, based on the principle of epigenesis, was proposed by Erikson (1963), as best exemplified by his psychosocial theory of personality development. The epigenetic model presents a stage model of personality but one in which earlier experiences interpenetrate wide domains of functioning and are absorbed into existing structure. More recent work by Campos and colleagues (Campos, Kermoian, & Zumbahlen, 1992) documents, in a sophisticated empirical manner, the way that stage-related developmental changes produce strong emotions that then ramify and permeate an array of psychological processes. Thus the issue of continuity can be viewed as involving change within continuity. To concretize this with a zoological example, although the wormlike larva of a moth transmutes into a winged insect, it is still identifiably and irrevocably a moth at both stages, and not some other creature. And so it may be with human development. We change, but the change becomes incorporated into the existing personality. It would be a bizarre world indeed, if, as in Kafka's *Metamormophis*, on awakening one day, we found ourselves encased in someone else's exoskeleton.

12

Afterword

In this volume we have sought to trace the geneology of the study of emotion as it relates to social and personality development across the lifespan, and to note its intellectual wellsprings, its luminaries, and its seminal theoretical and research contributions. We also offered an account of social and personality development based on a discrete emotions, functionalist analysis, as well as shared some reflections on the issue of personality continuity and change. Since we have spanned the research gamut from the minutia of microanalytic studies to the "big picture" of biography, it seems apropos to conclude with some reflections on the contribution of one of this century's most enterprising developmental psychologists, Charlotte Bühler.

Bühler's pioneering work (see Chapter 4) evolved from a focus on small behaviors of small individuals, to adolescents and their diaries, to adults and larger life course matters, and to a consideration of phenomena that are most quintessentially human, such as personal goals. What Bühler brought to developmental psychology—in some cases well before the world was prepared to absorb it—was a plentiful banquet of ideas and approaches that still serve the field today. She was the first to specifically take a stand on the need for both normative and individual difference approaches in the study of development (Bühler, 1933a). She gave us one of the German-speaking world's first studies of infants' reactions to facial expressions of emotion (Bühler & Hetzer, 1928). She also conducted one of the first fruitful uses of biographical technique to explore lifespan issues (Bühler, 1935) and in so doing became one of the field's first stage theorists. She was also one of the first to document secular trends in development (Bühler, 1934). Finally, she was one of the founders of humanistic psychology along with Kurt Goldstein and others (Bühler & Massarik, 1969). What we take from this for a continued examination of the role of emotions across the life course is a *contextualistic perspective*, a perspective that once again informs some of the more important developmental research being conducted today. Though emotions and emotion traits may seem impermeable to secular trends because of the biological roots of the emotion system, the constructivist approach (e.g., Averill, 1982; Harre, 1986) has illustrated that emotions and personality are also constructed over time as they absorb culture and experience. Bühler's own exploration of lives through diaries and other biographical source materials permitted her to detect secular trends in the organization of experience of three generations of young women (Bühler, 1934).

Do the personality traits subsumed by the contemporary five-factor model of personality show similar patterns across different cohorts and cross-culturally? There is not yet much in the way of explicit cross-cohort comparison of the theory, though preliminary research from the Berlin Aging Study of the Max Planck Institut für Bildungsforschung suggests that there are changes in extraversion over historical time. It is our own hunch that the five-factor traits, if we are correct about their relation to emotion dispositions, will retain their "robust status" in individual personality, but there may be growth on particular dimensions for particular individuals. We also suspect that these factors cannot help but mask the subtleties of emotional experience that perhaps can only be apprehended by more direct measures of affect, and by the use of in-depth interview methods. Hence we are drawn back once again to human biography and autobiography to teach us about the inner life of feeling, its relation to self and self-in-relation, and its connection to the cultural and temporal context of embedded lives.

In this volume we approached the issue of social and personality develop-ment from the point of view of emotions theory and research. While there is much that is now known, one senses that there is a vast subterranean continent that is still largely unexplored. In this volume we could formulate only some general ideas and some strategies to pursue in exploring the riddle of human develop-ment; these await engagement by enterprising investigators of the the next decade or so. However, we are firmly convinced that the study of social and personality development must be assisted by an understanding of how emotions work and how they organize experience. Moreover, we believe that an affect-theoretical analysis of development promises to restore some of the complexity to lives.

References

Adickman, J. D. (1993). Children's emotion biases: Their relation to internal representations of attachment security and to patterns of perceived maternal discipline. Unpublished doctoral dissertation, Long Island University, Brooklyn, NY.

Ainsworth, M. D. S. (1967). *Infancy in Uganda: Child care and the growth of love*. Baltimore: Johns Hopkins University Press.

Ainsworth, M. D. S. (1983). Autobiography. In N. O'Connell & N. F. Russo (Eds.), *Models of achievement: Reflections of eminent women in psychology* (pp. 27–38). New York: Columbia University Press.

Ainsworth, M. D. S. (1989). Attachments beyond infancy. *American Psychologist, 44*, 709–716.

Ainsworth, M. D. S. (1992). John Bowlby. *American Psychologist, 47*, 668.

Ainsworth, M. D. S. Bell, S. M., & Stayton, D. J. (1971). Individual differences in strange situation behavior of one-year olds. In H. R. Schaffer (Ed.), *The origins of human social relations* (pp. 17–57). London: Academic.

Ainsworth, M. D. S., Blehar, M. C., Waters, E., & Wall, S. (1978). *Patterns of attachment: A psychological study of the strange situation*. Hillsdale, NJ: Erlbaum.

Ainsworth, M. S., & Bowlby, J. (1991). An ethological approach to personality development. *American Psychologist, 46*, 333–341.

Alcoholics Anonymous (1976). *Alcoholics Anonymous: The story of how many thousands of men and women have recovered from alcoholism* (3rd ed.). New York: Alcoholics Anonymous World Services.

Aldwin, C. M., Levenson, M. R., & Spiro, A. (1994). Vulnerability and resilience to combat exposure: Can stress have lifelong effects? *Psychology and Aging, 9*, 34–44.

Allport, G. (1937). *Personality: A psychological interpretation*. New York: Henry Holt.

Allport, G. (1961). *Pattern and growth in personality*. New York: Holt, Rinehart & Winston.

Allport, G. (1968). *The person in psychology: Selected essays*. Boston: Beacon Press.

Allport, G., & Odbert, H. S. (1936). Trait names: A psycho- lexical study. *Psychological Monographs, 47*, 1–171.

Allport, G. W. (1954). *The nature of prejudice*. Cambridge MA: Addison-Wesley.

Allport, G. W. (1955). *Becoming: Basic considerations for a psychology of personality*. New Haven, CT: Yale University Press.

Allport, G. W. (1966). Traits revisited. *American Psychologist, 21*, 1–10.

Allport, G. W. (1967). Autobiography. In E. G. Boring & G. Lindzey (Eds.), *A history of psychology in autobiography* (Vol. 5, pp. 1–25). New York: Appleton-Century-Crofts.

Allport, G. W., & Vernon, P. E. (1931). *A study of values*. Boston: Houghton Mifflin. (Rev. ed. with P. E. Vernon & G. Lindzey, 1951).

Allport, G. W., & Vernon, P. E. (1933). *Studies in expressive movement*. New York: MacMillan.

Anderson, J. E. (1950). Changes in emotional responses with age. In M. L. Reymert (Ed.), *Feelings and emotions* (pp. 418–428). New York: McGraw-Hill.

Anderson, J. W. (1988). Henry A. Murray's early career: A psychobiographical exploration. *Journal of Personality, 56*, 139–171.

Arkin, R. M., Appelman, A. J., & Burger, J. M. (1980). Social anxiety, self-presentation, and the self-serving bias in causal attribution. *Journal of Personality and Social Psychology, 38*, 23–35.

Atwood, G. E., & Tomkins, S. (1976). On the subjectivity of personality theory. *Journal of the History of the Behavioral Sciences, 12*, 166–177.

Averill, J. R. (1982). *Anger and aggression: An essay on emotion*. New York: Springer-Verlag.

Baer, P. E., Reed, J., Bartlett, P. C., Vincent, J. P., Williams, B. J., & Bourianoff, G. G. (1983). Studies of gaze during induced conflict in families with a hypertensive father. *Psychosomatic Medicine, 45*, 233–241.

Baer, P. E., Vincent, J. P., Williams, B. J., Bourianoff, G. G., & Bartlett, P. C. (1980). Behavioral response to induced conflict in families with a hypertensive father. *Hypertension, 2*, 70–77.

Bain, A. (1868). *Mental science: A compendium of psychology and the history of philosophy*. New York: D. Appleton and Company. (Reprinted, 1973, Arno Press, New York).

Baldwin, A. L. (1967). *Theories of child development*. New York: Wiley.

Baldwin, J. M. (1894). *Mental development in the child and the race*. New York: Macmillan.

Baltes, P. B. (1993). The aging mind: Potential and limits. *The Gerontologist, 33*, 580–594.

Baltes, P. B., Smith, J., & Staudinger, U. M. (1992). Wisdom and successful aging. In T. Sonderegger (Ed.), *Nebraska Symposium on Motivation* (Vol. 39, pp. 123–167). Lincoln: University of Nebraska Press.

Bandura, A., & Walters, R. (1963). *Social learning and personality development*. New York: Holt.

Banham, K. M. (1951). Senescence and the emotions: A genetic theory. *Pedagogical Seminary and Journal of Genetic Psychology, 78*, 175–183.

Banham, K. M. (1983). Autobiography. In N. O'Connell & N. F. Russo (Eds.), *Models of achievement: Reflections of eminent women in psychology* (pp. 27–38). New York: Columbia University Press.

Barnett, M. A. (1982). Empathy and prosocial behavior in children. In T. M. Field, A. Huston, H. C. Quay, L. Troll, & G. E. Finley (Eds.), *Review of human development* (pp. 316–326). New York: Wiley.

Barnett, M. A. (1987). Empathy and related responses in children. In N. Eisenberg & J. Strayer (Eds.), *Empathy and its development* (pp. 146–162). New York: Cambridge University Press.

Barnett, M. A., Howard, J. A., King, L. M., & Dino, G. A. (1980). Antecedents of empathy: Retrospective accounts of early socialization. *Personality and Social Psychology Bulletin, 6*, 361–365.

Barrett, K. C., Zahn-Waxler, C., & Cole, P. M. (1993). Avoiders vs. amenders: Implications for the investigation of guilt and shame during toddlerhood. *Cognition and Emotion, 7*, 481–505.

Bartholomew, K., & Horowitz, L. M. (1991). Attachment styles among young adults: A test of a four-category model. *Journal of Personality and Social Psychology, 61*, 226–244.

Bates, J. E. (1987). Temperament in infancy. In J. D. Osofsky (Ed.), *Handbook of infant development* (pp. 1101–1149). New York: Wiley.

Batson, C. D. (1987). Prosocial motivation: Is it ever truly altruistic? In L. Berkowitz (Ed.), *Advances in experimental social psychology* (Vol. 20, pp. 65–122). New York: Academic Press.

Batson, C. D., Duncan, C., Ackerman, P., Buckley, T., & Birch, K. (1981). Is empathic emotion a source of altruistic motivation? *Journal of Personality and Social Psychology, 40,* 290–302.

Baumrind, D. (1971). Current patterns of parental authority. *Developmental Psychology Monographs,* 4 (1, Pt. 2).

Baumrind, D. (1978). Parental disciplinary patterns and social competence in youth. *Youth & Society, 9,* 239–76.

Bavelas, J. B., Black, A., Lemery, C. R., & Mullett, J. (1987). Motor mimicry as primitive empathy. In N. Eisenberg & J. Strayer (Eds.), *Empathy and its development* (pp. 317–338). New York: Cambridge University Press.

Beilin, H. (1983). The new functionalism and Piaget's program. In E. K. Scholnick (Ed.), *New trends in conceptual representation* (pp. 3–40). Hillsdale, NJ: Erlbaum.

Belsky, J., & Rovine, M. (1987). Temperament and attachment security in the Strange Situation: An empirical rapprochement. *Child Development, 58,* 787–795.

Belsky, J., Rovine, M. J., & Taylor, D. G. (1984). The Pennsylvania Infant and Family Development Project: III. The origins of individual differences in infant-mother attachments: Maternal and infant contributions. *Child Development, 55,* 718–728.

Berkowitz, L. (1989). Frustration-aggression hypothesis: Examination and reformation. *Psychological Bulletin, 106*(1), 59–73.

Berkowitz, L., & Heimer, K. (1989). On the construction of the anger experience: Aversive events and negative priming in the formation of feelings. In L. Berkowitz (Ed.), *Advances in experimental social psychology:* (Vol. 22, pp. 1–37). New York: Academic Press.

Berlin, L. (1993, March). Attachment and emotions in preschool children. In J. Cassidy & L. Berlin (Chairs), *Emotion and attachment.* Symposium conducted at the biennial meeting of the Society for Research in Child Development, New Orleans.

Bertalanffy, L. von (1968). *General systems theory.* New York: Braziller.

Bettes, B. A. (1988). Maternal depression and motherese: Temporal and intonational features. *Child Development, 59,* 1089–1096.

Birigin, Z. (1990). Direct observation of maternal sensitivity and dyadic interactions in the home: Relations to maternal thinking. *Development Psychology, 26,* 278–284.

Block, J. (in collaboration with N. Haan). (1971). *Lives through time.* Berkeley, CA: Bancroft Books.

Block, J. H. (1976). Issues, problems, and pitfalls in assessing sex differences: A critical review. *Merrill-Palmer-Quarterly, 22,* 283–308.

Block, J. H., & Block, J. (1980). The role of ego-control and ego-resiliency in the organization of behavior. In W. A. Collins (Ed.), *Minnesota symposia on child psychology* (Vol. 13, pp.). Hillsdale, NJ: Erlbaum.

Bloom, L., & Beckwith, R. (1989). Talking with feeling: Integrating affective and linguistic expression in early language development. *Cognition and emotion, 3,* 313–342.

Bloom, L., Beckwith, R., & Capatides, J. B. (1988). Developments in the expression of affect. *Infant Behavior and Development, 11,* 169–186.

Bloom, L., Beckwith, R., Capatides, J. B., & Hafitz, J. (1988). Expression through affect and words in the transition from infancy to language. In P. Baltes, D. Featherman, & R. Lerner (Eds.), *Life-span development and behavior* (Vol. 8, pp. 99–127). Hillsdale, NJ: Erlbaum.

Boring, E. G. (1950). *A history of experimental psychology* (2nd ed.). New York: Appleton-Century-Crofts.

Boswell, J. (1989). *The kindness of strangers: The abandonment of children in Western Europe from late antiquity to the Renaissance.* New York: Pantheon.

Bower, G. H. (1981). Mood and memory. *American Psychologist, 36,* 129–148.

Bower, G. H., & Mayer, J. D. (1989). In search of mood dependent retrieval. *Journal of Social Behavior and Personality, 4,* 121–156.

Bower, T. G. R. (1979). *Human development.* San Francisco: Freeman.

Bowlby, J. (1969). *Attachment and loss, Vol. 1: Attachment.* New York: Basic Books.

Bowlby, J. (1973). *Attachment and loss, Vol. 2: Separation.* New York: Basic Books.

Bowlby, J. (1980). *Attachment and loss, Vol. 3: Loss, sadness and depression.* New York: Basic Books.

Bradshaw, S. L., Ohlde, C. D., & Horne, J. B. (1993). Combat and personality change. *Bulletin of the Menninger Clinic, 57,* 466–478.

Bretherton, I. (1985). Attachment theory: Retrospect and prospect. In I. Bretherton & E. Waters (Eds.), Growing points of attachment theory and research (pp. 3–38). *Monographs of the Society for Research in Child Development, 50* (1–2, Serial No. 209).

Bretherton, I. (1990). Open communication and internal working models: Their role in the development of attachment relationships. In R. Thompson (Ed.), *Socioemotional development. Nebraska Symposium on Motivation* (Vol 36, pp. 58–113). Lincoln: University of Nebraska Press.

Bretherton, I., Fritz, J., Zahn-Waxler, C., & Ridgeway, D. (1986). Learning to talk about emotions: A functionalist perspective. *Child Development, 57,* 529–548.

Bretherton, I., McNew, S., & Beeghly-Smith, M. (1981). Early person knowledge as expressed in gestural and verbal communication: When do infants acquire a "Theory of mind?" In M. E. Lamb & L. R. Sherrod (Eds.), *Infant social cognition* (pp. 333–374). Hillsdale, NJ: Erlbaum.

Bretherton, I., & Waters, E. (Eds.). (1985). Growing points of attachment theory and research. *Monographs of the Society for Research in Child Development, 50* (1–2, Serial No. 209).

Bridges, K. M. (1983). Autobiography. In N. O'Connell & N. F. Russo (Eds.), *Models of achievement: Reflections of eminent women in psychology* (pp. 27–38). New York: Columbia University Press.

Bridges, K. M. B. (1930). A genetic theory of the emotions. *Journal of Genetic Psychology, 37,* 514–527.

Bridges, K. M. B. (1931). *The social and emotional development of the preschool child.* London: Kegan Paul, Trench, Trubner.

Bridges, K. M. B. (1932). Emotional development in early infancy. *Child Development, 3,* 324–341.

Brodt, S. E., & Zimbardo, P. G. (1981). Modifying shyness-related social behavior through symptom misattribution. *Journal of Personality and Social Psychology, 41,* 437–449.

Brody, L. R., & Hall, J. A. (1993). Gender and emotion. In M. Lewis & J. Haviland (Eds.), *Handbook of emotions* (pp. 447- 460). New York: Guilford.

Broverman, I. K., Broverman, D. M., Clarkson, F. E., Rosenkrantz, P. S., & Vogel, S. R. (1970). Sex-role stereotypes and clinical judgments of mental health. *Journal of Consulting and Clinical Psychology, 34,* 3.

Brown, J. M., O'Keefe, J., Sanders, S. H., & Baker, B. (1986). Developmental changes in children's cognition to stressful and painful situations. *Journal of Pediatric Psychology, 11,* 343–357.

Bruner, J. S. (1957). On perceptual readiness. *Psychological Review, 64,* 123–152.

Bruner, J. S. (1986). *Actual minds, possible worlds.* Cambridge, MA: Harvard University Press.

Bruner, J. S. (1990). Culture and human development: A new look. *Human Development, 33,* 344–355.

Buckley, K. W. (1989). *Mechanical Man: John Broadus Watson and the beginnings of Behaviorism.* New York: Guilford Press.

Bufe, C. (1991). *Alcoholics Anonymous: Cult or cure?* San Francisco: See Sharp Press.

Bugenthal, D. E., Love, L. R., & Gianetto, R. M. (1971). Perfidious feminine faces. *Journal of Personality and Social Psychology, 17,* 314–318.

Bühler, C. (1918). Das Märchen und die Phantasie des Kindes. *Zeitschrift für Angewandte Psychologie, 17*.

Bühler, C. (1933a). *Der menschliche Lebenslauf als psychologisches Problem.* Leipzig: S. Hirzel.

Bühler, C. (1933b). The social behavior of children. In C. Murchison (Ed.), *A Handbook of Child Psychology* (pp. 374–416). New York: Russell & Russell.

Bühler, C. (1934). *Drei Generationen im Jugendtagebuch.* Jena: Verlag von Gustav Fischer.

Bühler, C. (1935). The curve of life as studies in biographies. *Journal of Applied Psychology, 3*, 27–41.

Bühler, C. (1961). The goal structure of human life. *Humanistic Psychology, 1*, 8–9.

Bühler, C., & Hetzer, H. (1927). Das Inventar der Verhaltensweisen im 1. Lebensjahr. In C. Bühler (Ed.), *Soziologische und psychologische Studien ueber das erste Lebensjahr.* Jena: Fischer.

Bühler, C., & Hetzer, H. (1928). Das erste Verstehen vom Ausdruck im 1. Lebensjahr. Sammelband Wiener Arbeiten. *Zeitschrift für Psychologie, 107*, 50–61.

Bühler, C., Hetzer, H., & Mabel, F. (1928). Die Affektwirksamkeit von Fremdheitseindrücken im ersten Lebensjahr. *Zeitschrift für Psychologie, 107*, 30–49.

Bühler, C., & Massarik, F. (Eds.). (1969). *The course of human life. A study of goals in the humanistic perspective.* New York: Springer.

Bühler, K. (1927). *Die Krise der Psychologie.* Stuttgart: Fischer Verlag.

Bürmann, I., & Herwartz-Emden, L. (1993). Charlotte Bühler: Leben und Werk einer selbstbewußten Wissenschaftlerin des 20. Jahrhunderts. *Psychologische Rundschau, 44*, 205–225.

Buss, A. H. (1961). *The psychology of aggression.* New York: Wiley.

Buss, A. H. (1985). Two kinds of shyness. In R. Schwarzer (Ed.), *Anxiety and cognitions.* Hillsdale, New York: Erlbaum.

Buss, A. H., & Finn, S. E. (1987). Classification of personality traits. *Journal of Personality and Social Psychology, 52*, 432–444.

Cairns, R. B. (1983). The emergence of developmental psychology. In W. Kessen (Ed.), *Handbook of Child Psychology. Vol. 1.. History, theory and methods* (pp. 41–102). New York: Wiley.

Cairns, R. B., Cairns, B. D., Neckerman, H. G., Ferguson, L. L., & Gariepy, J. L. (1989). Growth and aggression: 1. Childhood to early adolescence. *Developmental Psychology, 25*(2), 320–330.

Cairns, R. B., & Ornstein, P. A. (1979). Developmental psychology. In E.Hearst (Ed.), *The first century of experimental psychology* (pp. 459–512). Hillsdale, NJ: Erlbaum.

Calverley, R. M., Fischer, K. W., & Ayoub, C. (in press). Complex splitting of self-representations in sexually abused adolescent girls. *Development and Psychopathology.*

Campos, J., Kermoian, R., & Zumbahlen, M. (1992). Socioemotional transformations in the family system following crawling onset. In N. Eisenberg & R. Fabes (Eds.), *New directions for child development: Emotion and its regulation in early development* (pp. 25–40). San Francisco: Jossey-Bass.

Campos, J. J., & Barrett, K. C. (1984). Toward a new understanding of emotions and their development. In C. E. Izard, J. Kagan, & R. B. Zajonc (Eds.), *Emotions, cognition, and behavior* (pp. 229–263). Cambridge: Cambridge University Press.

Campos, J. J., Barrett, K. C., Lamb, M. E., Goldsmith, H. H., & Stenberg, C. (1983). Socioemotional development. In M. M. Haith (Ed.), *Handbook of child psychology: Vol. 2. Infancy and developmental psychobiology* (pp. 783–917). New York: Wiley.

Campos, J. J., & Stenberg, C. R. (1981). Perception, appraisal and emotion: The onset of social referencing. In M. E. Lamb & L. R. Sherrod (Eds.), *Infant social cognition* (pp. 273–314). Hillsdale, NJ: Erlbaum, 1981.

Camras, L. (1991). View II: A dynamical systems perspective on expressive development. In K. Strongman (Ed.), *International review of studies on emotion* (pp. 16–28). New York: Wiley.

Camras, L., Malatesta, C. Z., & Izard, C. E. (1991). The development of facial expressions in infancy. In R. Feldman & B. Rime (Eds.), *Fundamentals of nonverbal behavior* (pp. 73–105). New York: Cambridge University Press.

Camras, L. A. (1988, April). *Darwin revisited: An infant's first emotional facial expressions.* Paper presented at the International Conference on Infant Studies, Washington, DC.

Camras, L. A. (1992). Expressive development and basic emotions. *Cognition and Emotion, 6,* 269–283.

Camras, L. A., Ribordy, S., Hill, J., Martino, S., Spaccarelli, S., & Stefani, R. (1988). Recognition and posing of emotional expressions by abused children and their mothers. *Developmental Psychology, 24,* 776–781.

Carducci, B. J., & Webber, A. W. (1979). Shyness as a determinant of interpersonal distance. *Psychological Reports, 44,* 1075–1078.

Carlson, R. (1981). Studies in script theory. I. Adult analogs of a childhood nuclear scene. *Journal of Personality and Social Psychology, 40,* 510–510.

Carmichael, L. (1970). The onset and early development of behavior. In P. H. Mussen (Ed.), *Carmichael's manual of child psychology* (pp. 447–564). New York: Wiley.

Caspi, A., Bem, D. J., & Elder, G. H., Jr. (1988). Moving away from the world. Life-course patterns of shy children. *Developmental Psychology, 24,* 824–831.

Caspi, A., Bem, D. J., & Elder, G. H., Jr. (1989). Continuities and consequences of interactional styles across the life course. *Journal of Personality, 57,* 375–406.

Caspi, A., Elder, G. H., and Bem, D. J. (1987). Moving against the world: Life-course patterns of explosive children. *Developmental Psychology, 23,* 308–313.

Caspi, A. & Moffitt, T. E. (1993). When do individual differences matter? A paradoxical theory of personality coherence. *Psychological Inquiry, 4,* 247–271.

Cassidy, J., & Berlin, L. J. (1994). The insecure/ambivalent pattern of attachment: Theory and Research. *Child Development, 65,* 971–991.

Cassidy, J., & Kobak, R. (1988). Avoidance and its relation to other defensive processes. In J. Belsky & T. Neworski (Eds.), *Clinical implications of attachment* (pp. 300–323). Hillsdale, NJ: Erlbaum.

Cattell, R. B. (1947). Confirmation and clarification of primary personality traits. *Psychological Bulletin, 72,* 402–421.

Cattell, R. B. (1957). *Personality and motivation structure and measurement.* New York: World Books.

Cattell, R. B., Eber, H. W., & Tatsuoka, M. M. (1970). *Handbook for the Sixteen Personality Factor Questionnaire.* Champaign, IL: Institute for Personality and Ability Testing.

Champneys, E. H. (1881). Notes on an infant. *Mind, 6,* 104–107.

Chandler, M. J., & Greenspan, S. (1972). Ersatz egocentrism: A reply to H. Borke. *Developmental Psychology, 7,* 104–106.

Cheek, J. M., & Buss, A. H. (1981). Shyness and sociability. *Journal of Personality and Social Psychology, 41,* 330–339.

Chittenden, G. E. (1942). An experimental study in measuring and modifying assertive behavior in young children. *Monographs of the Society for Research in Child Development, 7*(1), 1–87.

Cicchetti, D. (1990). The organization and coherence of socioemotional, cognitive, and representational development: Illustrations through a developmental psychopathology perspective on Down Syndrome and child maltreatment. In R. Thompson (Ed.), *Socioemotional development. Nebraska Symposium on Motivation* (Vol. 36, pp. 259–366). Lincoln: University of Nebraska Press.

Cicchetti, D., & Hesse, P. (1983). Affect and intellect: Piaget's contributions to the study of infant emotional development. In R. Plutchik & H. Kellerman (Eds.), *Emotion: Research and theory* (Vol. 2, pp. 115–169). New York: Academic Press.

Cicchetti, D., & Rizley, R. (1981). Developmental perspectives on the etiology, intergenerational transmission, and sequelae of child maltreatment. *New Directions for Child Development, 11,* 31–55.

Cicchetti, D., & Sroufe, L. A. (1978). An organizational view of affect: Illustration from the study of Down's Syndrome infants. In M. Lewis & L. A. Rosenblum (Eds.), *The development of affect* (pp. 309–355). New York: Plenum.

Clark, M. S., Ouellette, R., Powell, M. C., & Milberg, S. (1987). Recipient's mood, relationship type, and helping. *Journal of Personality and Social Psychology, 53,* 94–103.

Clarke-Stewart, K. A. (1989). Infant day care: Maligned or malignant? *American Psychologist, 44,* 277–273.

Clore, G. L., & Parrott, W. G. (1991). Moods and their vicissitudes: Thoughts and feelings as information. In J. P. Forgas (Ed.), *Emotions and social judgments* (pp. 107–123). Oxford: Pergamon.

Cohen, J. F., & Tronick, E. Z. (1983). Three-month-old infants' reaction to simulated maternal depression. *Child Development, 54,* 185–193.

Collins, N. L., & Read, S. J. (1990). Adult attachment, working models, and relationship quality in dating couples. *Journal of Personality and Social Psychology, 58,* 644–663.

Compayre, G. (1914). *Development of the child in later infancy* (M. E. Wilson, Trans.). New York: D. Appleton and Company.

Costa, P. T., Jr., & McCrae, R. R. (1980). Still stable after all these years: Personality as a key to some issues in adulthood and old age. In P. B. Baltes & O. G. Brim, Jr. (Eds.), *Life span development and behavior* (Vol. 3), pp. 75–102). New York: Academic.

Coyne, J. C. (1986). Depression and the response of others. *Journal of Abnormal Psychology, 85,* 186–193

Crittenden, P. M. (1981). Abusing, neglecting, problematic, and adequate dyads: Differentiating by patterns of interaction. *Merrill-Palmer Quarterly, 27,* 201–218.

Crockenberg, S. (1985). Toddlers' reactions to maternal anger. *Merrill-Palmer Quarterly, 31,* 361–373.

Crockenberg, S. B. (1981). Infant irritability, mother responsiveness and social support influences on the security to infant-mother attachment. *Child Development, 52,* 857–865.

Crozier, W. R. (1979). Shyness as a dimension of personality, *British Journal of Social and Clinical Psychology, 18,* 121–128.

Cummings, E. M. (1987). Coping with background anger in early childhood. *Child Development, 58,* 976–984.

Cummings, E. M., Ballard, M., El-Sheikh, M., & Lake, M. (1991). Resolution and children's responses to interadult anger. *Developmental Psychology, 27,* 462–470.

Cummings, E. M., Zahn-Waxler, C., & Radke-Yarrow, M. (1981). Young children's responses to expressions of anger and affection by others in the family. *Child Development, 52,* 1274–1282.

Cushman, P. (1992). Psychotherapy to 1992: A historically situated interpretation. In D. K. Freedheim, H. J. Freudenberger, J. W. Kessler, S. B. Messer, D. R. Peterson, H. H. Strugg, & P. L. Wachtel (Eds.), *History of psychotherapy* (pp. 21–64). Washington, DC: APA Press.

Darwin, C. E. (1872). *The expression of the emotions in man and animals.* London: J. Murray. (Reprinted, 1965, University of Chicago Press, Chicago).

Darwin, C. E. (1877). A biographical sketch of an infant. *Mind, 2,* 285–294.

Davitz, J. R. (1952). The effects of previous training on postfrustration behavior. *Journal of Abnormal and Social Psychology, 47,* 309–315.

Dean, J., & Whyte, W. F. (1958). How do you know the informant is telling the truth? *Human Organization, 17,* 34–38.

Dennis, W. (1936). A bibliography of baby biographies. *Child Development, 7,* 71–73.

Dennis, W. (1942). Infant reactions to restraint: An evaluation of Watson's theory. *Transactions of the New York Academy of Science, 2,* No. 7.

Diener, E., & Larsen, R. J. (1993). The experience of emotional well-being. In M. Lewis & J. Haviland (Eds.), *Handbook of emotions* (pp. 405–416). New York: Guilford.

Digman, J. M., & Inouye, J. (1986). Further specification of the five robust factors of personality. *Journal of Personality and Social Psychology, 50,* 116–123.

Digman, J. M., & Takemoto-Chock, N. K. (1981). Factors in the natural language of personality: Re-analysis and comparison of six major studies. *Multivariate Behavioral Research, 16,* 149–170.

Dodge, K. A., Pettit, G. S., McClaskey, C. L., & Brown, M. M. (1986). Social competence in children. *Monographs of the Society for Research in Child Development, 51* (2), 1–80.

Dodge, K. A., & Somberg, D. R. (1987). Hostile attributional biases among aggressive boys are exacerbated under conditions of threats to the self. *Child Development, 58,* 213–224.

Dollard, J., Doob, L., Miller, N., Mowrer, O., & Sears, R. (1939). *Frustration and aggression.* New Haven, CT: Yale University Press.

Duffy, E. (1941). An explanation of "emotional" phenomena without the use of the concept "emotion." *Journal of General Psychology, 25,* 283–293.

Duffy, E. (1962). *Activation and behavior.* New York: Wiley

Dunn, J., Bretherton, I., & Munn, P. (1987). Conversations about feeling states between mothers and their young children. *Developmental Psychology, 23,* 132–139.

Easterbrooks, M. A., and Lamb, M. E. (1979). The relationship between quality of infant-mother attachment and infant competence in initial encounters with peer. *Child Development, 50,* 380–387.

Egeland, B., & Sroufe, A. (1981). Attachment and early maltreatment. *Child Development, 52,* 44–52.

Eibl-Eibesfeldt, I. (1951). Zur fortpflanzungsbiologie und Jugendentwicklung des Eichhörnchens. *Zeitschrift für Tierpsychologie, 12,* 286–303.

Eibl-Eibesfeldt, I. (1979). Human ethology: Concepts and implications for the sciences of man. *The Behavioral and Brain Sciences, 2,* 1–57.

Eibl-Eibesfeldt, I. (1983). Patterns of parent-child interaction in a cross-cultural perspective. In A. Oliverio & M. Zappella (Eds.), *The behavior of human infants* (pp. 177–217). New York: Plenum.

Eibl-Eibesfeldt, I. (1989). *Human ethology.* New York: Hawthorne, Aldine de Gruyter.

Eisenberg, N., & Fabes, R. A. (1990). Empathy: Conceptualization, measurement, and relation to prosocial behavior. *Motivation and Emotion, 14,* 131–150.

Eisenberg, N., Fabes, R. A., Miller, P. A., Fultz, J., Shell, R., Mathy, & Reno, R. R. (1989). Relation of sympathy and personal distress to prosocial behavior: A multimethod study. *Journal of Personality and Social Psychology, 57,* 55–66.

Eisenberg, N., Fabes, R. A., Schaller, M., Miller, P., Carlo, G., Poulin, R., Shea, C., & Shell, R. (1991). Personality and socialization correlates of vicarious emotional responding. *Journal of Personality and Social Psychology, 61,* 459–470.

Eisenberg, N., McCreath, H., & Ahn, R. (1988). Vicarious emotional responsiveness and prosocial behavior: Their interrelations in young children. *Personality and Social Psychology Bulletin, 14,* 298–311.

Eisenberg, N., & Miller, P. A. (1987). The relation of empathy to prosocial and related behaviors. *Psychological Bulletin, 101,* 91–119.

Eisenberg, N., & Mussen, P. H. (1989). *The roots of prosocial behavior in children.* New York: Cambridge University Press.

Eisenberg, N., & Strayer, J. (1987a). Critical issues in the study of empathy. In N. Eisenberg & J. Strayer (Eds.), *Empathy and its development* (pp. 3–13). New York: Cambridge University Press.

Eisenberg, N., & Strayer, J. (Eds.) (1987b). *Empathy and its development.* New York: Cambridge University Press.

Ekblad, S. (1989). Stability in aggression and aggression control in a sample of primary school children in China. *Acta Psychiatrica Scandanavica, 80(2),* 160–164.

Ekman, P. (1972). Universals and cultural differences in facial expressions of emotion. In J. Cole (Ed.), *Nebraska Symposium on Motivation* (Vol. 19, pp. 207–253). Lincoln: University of Nebraska Press.

Ekman, P. (1984). Expression and the nature of emotions. In K. Scherer & P. Ekman (Eds.), *Approaches to emotion* (pp. 329–343). Hillsdale, NJ: Erlbaum.

Ekman, P. (1985). *Telling lies: Clues to deceit in the marketplace, politics, and marriage.* New York, Berkley.

Ekman, P., & Friesen, W. V. (1975). *Unmasking the face.* New York: Prentice-Hall.

Ekman, P., & Friesen, W. V. (1978). *The Facial Action Coding System: A technique for the measurement of facial movement.* Palo Alto, CA: Consulting Psychologists Press.

Ekman, P., Friesen, W. V., & Ellsworth, P. C. (1972). *Emotion in the human face.* New York: Pergamon Press.

Ekman, P., Sorenson, E. R. & Friesen, W. V. (1969). Pancultural elements in facial displays of emotions. *Science, 164,* 86–88.

Ekstein, R. (1972). Psychoanalysis and education for the facilitation of positive human qualities. *Journal of Social Issues, 28,* 71–85.

El-Sheikh, M., Cummings, E. M., & Goetsch, V. L. (1989). Coping with adults' angry behavior: Behavioral, physiological, and verbal responses in preschoolers. *Developmental Psychology, 25(4),* 490–498.

Elder, G. H., Jr. (1989). Combat experience and emotional health: Impairment and resilience in later life. *Journal of Personality, 57,* 311–341.

Elder, G. H., Shanahan, M. J., & Clipp, E. C. (1994). When war comes to men's lives: Life-course patterns in family, work, and health. *Psychology and Aging, 9,* 5–16.

Emde, R. N. (1980a). Toward a psychoanalytic theory of affect. Emerging models of emotional development in infancy. In S. I. Greenspan & G. H. Pollock (Eds.), *The course of life: Psychoanalytic contributions toward understanding personality development. Vol. I: Infancy and early childhood* (pp. 63–83). Washington, DC: National Institutes on Mental Health.

Emde, R. N. (1980b). Toward a psychoanalytic theory of affect. II. Emerging models of emotional development in infancy. In S. I. Greenspan & G. H. Pollock (Eds.), *The course of life: Psychoanalytic contributions toward understanding personality development. Vol. I: Infancy and early childhood* (pp. 85–112). Washington, DC: National Institutes on Mental Health.

Emde, R. N. (1985). An adaptive view of infant emotions: Functions for self and knowing. *Social Science Information, 24,* 337–341.

Emde, R. N., Gaensbauer, T. J., & Harmon, R. J. (1976). *Emotional expression in infancy.* New York: International Universities Press.

Emde, R. N., Plomin, R., Robinson, J., Corley, R., DeFries, J., Fulker, D. W., Reznick, J. S., Campos, J., Kagan, J., Zahn-Waxler, C. (1992). Temperament, emotion, and cognition at fourteen months: The MacArthur longitudinal twin study. *Child Development, 63,* 1437–1455.

Epstein, S. (1983). The stability of behavior across time and situations. In R. Zucker, J. Aronoff, & A. I. Rabin (Eds.), *Personality and the prediction of behavior.* San Diego, CA: Academic Press.

Epstein, S. (1993). Emotion and self-theory. In M. Lewis & J. Haviland (Eds.), *Handbook of emotions* (pp. 313–326). New York: Guilford.

Erickson, M. F., Sroufe, L. A., and Egeland, B. (1985). The relationship between quality of attachment and behavior problems in preschool in a high-risk sample. In I. Bretherton & E. Waters (Eds.), *Growing points in attachment theory and research* (pp. 211–230). *Monographs of the Society for Research in Child Development, 50* (1–2 Serial No. 209).

Erikson, E. H. (1963). *Childhood and society* (Rev. ed.). New York: W. W. Norton.

Eron, L. D. (1987). The development of aggressive behavior from the perspective of a developing behaviorism. *American Psychologist, 42,* 435–442.

Eron, L. D., Huesmann, L. R., Brice, P., Fischer, P., & Mermelstein, R. (1983). Age trends in the development of aggression, sex typing, and related television habits. *Developmental Psychology, 19,* 71–77.

Estes, D. (1981). Maternal behavior and security of attachment at 12 and 19 months. Unpublished masters thesis, University of Michigan, Ann Arbor.

Eysenck, H. J. (1947). *Dimensions of personality.* New York: Praeger.

Eysenck, H. J. (1967). *The biological basis of personality.* Springfield IL: Thomas.

Eysenck, H. J., & Eysenck, M. W. (1985). *Personality and individual differences: A natural science approach.* New York: Plenum.

Fabes, R. A., Eisenberg, N., & Miller, P. A. (1990). Maternal correlates of children's vicarious emotional responsiveness. *Developmental Psychology, 26,* 639–648.

Feeney, J. A., & Noller, P. (1990). Attachment style as a predictor of adult romantic relationships. *Journal of Personality and Social Psychology, 38,* 281–291.

Fenton, J. C. (1925). *A practical psychology of babyhood: The life.* New York: Houghton Mifflin.

Feshbach, N. D. (1979). Empathy training: A field study in affective education. In S. Feshbach & A. Fraczek (Eds.), *Aggression and behavior change: Biological and social processes* (pp. 234–249). New York: Praeger.

Feshbach, N. D. (1982). Sex differences in empathy and social behavior in children. In N. Eisenberg (Ed.), *The development of prosocial behavior* (pp. 315–337). New York: Academic.

Feshbach, N. D. (1987). Parental empathy and child adjustment/maladjustment. In N. Eisenberg & J. Strayer (Eds.), *Empathy and its development* (pp. 271–291). Cambridge: Cambridge University Press.

Feshbach, N. D., & Feshbach, S. (1969). The relationship between empathy and aggression in two age groups. *Developmental Psychology, 1,* 102–107.

Feshbach, N. D., & Roe, K. (1968). Empathy in six- and seven-year-olds. *Child Development, 39,* 133–145.

Feshbach, S. (1970). Aggression. In P. H. Mussen (Ed.), *Carmichael's manual of child psychology:* (Vol. 2, pp. 159–259). New York: Wiley.

Field, T. (1987). Affective and interactive disturbances in infants. In J. D. Osofsky (Ed.), *Handbook of infant development,* pp. 972–1005, New York: Wiley.

Field, T., Healy, B., Goldstein, S., & Guthertz, M. (1990). Behavior-state matching and synchrony in mother-infant interactions of nondepressed versus depressed dyads. *Developmental Psychology, 26,* 7–14.

Field, T. M. (1979). Visual and cardiac responses to animate and inanimate faces by young term and preterm infants. *Child Development, 50,* 188–194.

Field, T. M. (1982). Affective displays of high-risk infants during early interactions. In T. Field & A. Fogel (Eds.), *Emotion and early interaction* (pp. 101–115). Hillsdale, NJ: Erlbaum.

Field, T. M., Woodson, R., Greenberg, R., & Cohen, D. (1982). Discrimination and imitation of facial expressions by neonates. *Science, 218,* 179–181.

Fischer, K. W., & Ayoub, C. (in press). Affective splitting and dissociation in normal and maltreated children: Developmental pathways for self-in-relationships. In D. Cicchetti & S. Toth (Eds.), *Rochester Symposium on Developmental Psychopathology. Vol. 5: The self and its disorders.* Rochester, New York: University of Rochester Press.

Fischer, K. W., Shaver, P., & Carnochan, P. G. (1990). How emotions develop and how they organize development. *Cognition and Emotion, 4,* 81–127.

Fiske, D. W. (1949). Consistency of the factorial structures of personality ratings from different sources. *Journal of Abnormal and Social Psychology, 44,* 329–344.

Fogel, A. (1982). Affect dynamics in early infancy: Affective tolerance. In T. Field & A. Fogel (Eds.), *Emotion and early interaction* (pp. 25–56). Hillsdale, NJ: Erlbaum.

Forgas, J. P. (1978). Social episodes and social structure in an academic setting: The social environment of an intact group. *Journal of Experimental Social Psychology, 14,* 434–448.

Forgas, J. P. (1982). Episode cognition: Internal representations of interaction routines. *In Advances in Experimental Social Psychology* (Vol. 15). New York: Academic Press.

Forgas, J. P., & Bower, G. H. (1987). Mood effects on person-perception judgments. *Journal of Personality and Social Psychology, 53,* 53–60.

Fox, N. A. (1989). Infant response to frustrating and mildly stressful events: A positive look at anger in the first year. *New Directions for Child Development, 45,* 47–64.

Fox, N. A., & Davidson, R. J. (1984). Hemispheric substrates of affect: A developmental model. In N. A. Fox & R. J. Davidson (Eds.), *The psychobiology of affective development,* pp. 353–382. Hillsdale, NJ: Erlbaum.

Frank, L. K. (1954). Aging: Scope and perspectives. *Merrill-Palmer Quarterly, 1,* 18–22.

Freedman, D. G. (1964). Smiling in blind infants and the issue of innate vs. acquired. *Journal of Child Psychology and Psychiatry, 5,* 171–184.

Freeman, D. (1983). *On coming of age in Samoa: The nemesis of an anthropological myth.* New York: Oxford University Press.

Friedman, H., & Booth-Kewley, S. (1987). Personality, Type A Behavior, and coronary heart disease: The role of emotional expression. *Journal of Personality and Social Psychology, 53,* 783–792.

Friedman, H. S., & Riggio, R. E. (1981). Effect of individual differences in nonverbal expressiveness on transmission of emotion. *Journal of Nonverbal Behavior, 6,* 96–101.

Frodi, A., Bridges, L., & Grolnick, W. (1985). Correlates of mastery-related behavior: A short-term longitudinal study of infants in their second year. *Child Development, 56,* 1291–1298.

Frodi, A., & Thompson, R. (1985). Infants' affective responses in the Strange Situation: Effects of prematurity and quality of attachment. *Child Development, 56,* 1280–1290.

Gaensbauer, T. J., & Harmon, R. J. (1982). Attachment behavior in abused/neglected and premature infants: Implications for the concept of attachment. In R. N. Emde & R. J. Harmon (Eds.), *The development of attachment and affiliative systems* (pp. 263–280). New York: Plenum.

Gaensbauer, T. J., Harmon, R. J., Culp, A. M., Schultz, L. A., Van Doornick, W. J., & Dawson, P. (1985). Relationships between attachment behavior in the laboratory and the caretaking environment. *Infant Behavior and Development, 8,* 355–369.

Galen (1963). *On the passions and errors of the soul* (P. W. Harkins, Trans.). Columbus: Ohio State University Press.

Gardiner, H. M., Metcalf, R. C., & Beebe-Center, J. G. (1937). *Feeling and emotion: A history of theories.* Westport, CT: Greenwood Press.

George, C., Kaplan, N., & Main, M. (1984). *Attachment interview for adults.* Unpublished manuscript, University of California, Berkeley.

Geppert, U., & Heckhausen, H. (1990). Ontogenese der Emotionen. In K. R. Scherer (Ed.), *Psychologie der Emotionen.* Göttingen: C. J. Hogrefe Verlag für Psychologie.

Gesell, A. (1929). The individual in infancy. In C. Murchison (Ed.), *The foundations of experimental psychology* (pp. 628–660). Worcester, MA: Clark University Press.

Gesell, A. (1950). Emotion from the standpoint of a developmental morphology. In M. S. Reymert (Ed.), *Feelings and emotions* (pp. 393–397). New York: McGraw-Hill.

Gewirtz, J. L., & Petrovich, S. B. (1982). Early social and attachment learning in the frame of organic and cultural evolution. In T. M. Field, A. Huston, H. C. Quay, L. Troll, & G. E. Finley (Eds.), *Review of human development* (pp. 3–19). New York: Wiley.

Gianino, A., & Tronick, E. (1985). The Mutual Regulation Model: The infant's self and interactive regulation and coping defense capacities. In R. Field, P. McCabe, & N. Schneiderman (Eds.), *Stress and coping* (pp. 47–68). Hillsdale, NJ: Erlbaum.

Gibbs, J. G., & Woll, S. B. (1985). Mechanisms used by young children in the making of empathic judgments. *Journal of Personality, 53*, 575–585.

Girodo, M., Dotzenroth, S. E., & Stein, S. J. (1981). Causal attribution bias in shy males: Implications for self-esteem and self-confidence. *Cognitive Therapy and Research, 5*, 325–338.

Gladstein, G. A. (1984). The historical roots of contemporary empathy. *Journal of the History of the Behavioral Sciences, 20*, 38–59.

Glicksberg, C. I. (1976). *The literature of commitment*. London: Associated University Press.

Goldberg, L. R. (1993). The structure of phenotypic personality traits. *American Psychologist, 48*, 26–34.

Goldberg, S., Perrotta, M., Minde, K., & Corter, C. (1986). Maternal behavior and attachment in low birth weight twins and singletons. *Child Development, 57*, 34–46.

Goldsmith, H. H., & Alansky, J. A. (1987). Maternal and infant temperamental predictors of attachment: A meta-analytic review. *Journal of Consulting and Clinical Psychology, 55*, 805–816.

Goldstein, A. P., & Michaels, G. Y. (1985). *Empathy: Development, training, and consequences*. Hillsdale, NJ: Erlbaum.

Goleman, D. (1990, September, 14). John Bowlby, psychiatric pioneer on mother-child bond, dies at 83. *New York Times*.

Goodenough, F. L. (1931). *Anger in young children*. Minneapolis: University of Minnesota Press.

Gottman, J. M. (1993). Studying emotion in social interaction. In M. Lewis & J. Haviland (Eds.), *Handbook of emotions* (pp. 475–488). New York: Guilford.

Gould, J. L. (1982). *Ethology: The mechanisms and evolution of behavior*. New York: Norton.

Gould, R. L. (1978). *Transformations: Growth and change in adult life*. New York: Simon & Schuster.

Graham, S., Hudley, C., & Williams, E. (1992). Attributional and emotional determinants of aggression among African-American and Latino young adolescents. *Developmental Psychology, 28*, 731–740.

Greenberg, L. S. (1993). Emotion and change processes in psychotherapy. In M. Lewis & J. Haviland (Eds.), *Handbook of emotions* (pp. 499–508). New York: Guilford.

Griffiths, M. (1988). Feminism, feelings and philosophy. In M. Griffiths & M. Whitford (Eds.), *Feminist perspectives in philosophy* (pp. 131–151). Bloomington: Indiana University Press.

Griffiths, M., & Whitford, M. (1988). Introduction. In M. Griffiths & M. Whitford (Eds.), *Feminist perspectives in philosophy* (pp.1–28). Bloomington: Indiana University Press.

Grossmann, K., Friedl, A., & Grossmann, K.E. (1987, September). *Preverbal infant-mother vocal interaction patterns and their relationship to attachment quality*. Paper presented at the 2nd International Symposium, "Prevention and intervention in childhood and youth: Conceptual and methodological issues," Bielefeld, Germany.

Grossmann, K., Grossmann, K. E., Spangler, G., Suess, G., & Unzner, L. (1985). Maternal sensitivity and newborns' orientation responses as related to quality of attachment in northern Germany. In I. Bretherton & E. Waters (Eds.), *Growing points of attachment theory and research* (pp. 233–256). *Monographs of the Society for Research in Child Development, 50*(1–2, Serial No. 209).

Grossmann, K. E., & Grossmann, K. (1990). The wider concept of attachment in cross-cultural research. *Human Development, 33,* 31–47.

Grossmann, K. E., & Grossmann, K. (1991). Attachment quality as an organizer of emotional and behavioral responses in a longitudinal perspective. In C. M. Parkes, J. Stevenson-Hinde, P. Morris (Eds.), *Attachment across the life cycle* (pp. 93–114). London/New York: Tavistock/Routledge.

Grossmann, K. E., Grossmann, K., Huber, F., & Wartner, U. (1981). German children's behavior toward their mothers at 12 months and their fathers at 18 months in Ainsworth's Strange Situation. *International Journal of Behavioral Development, 4,* 157–181.

Guillaume, P. (1971). *Imitation in children.* Chicago: University of Chicago Press. (Original work published 1926)

Gutmann, D. (1975). Parenthood: A key to the comparative study of the life cycle. In N. Datan & L. H. Ginsberg (Eds.), *Life-span developmental psychology: Normative life crises* (pp. 167–184). New York: Academic Press.

Halford, K., & Foddy, M. (1982). Cognitive and social skills correlates of social anxiety. *British Journal of Clinical Psychology, 21,* 17–28.

Hall, G. S. (1922). *Senescence, the last half of life.* New York: Appleton.

Harburg, E., Gleiberman, L., Russell, M., & Cooper, M. L. (1991). Anger-coping styles and blood pressure in black and white males: Buffalo, New York. *Psychosomatic Medicine, 53,* 153–164.

Harre, R. (1986). An outline of the social constructionist viewpoint. In R. Harre (Ed.), *The social construction of emotions* (pp. 2–14). New York: Basil Blackwell.

Harris, P. (1993). Understanding emotion. In M. Lewis & J. Haviland (Eds.), *Handbook of emotions,* (pp. 237–246). New York: Guilford.

Harris, P., & Olthof, T. (1982). The child's concept of emotion. In G. Butterworth & P. Light (Eds.), *Social cognition: Studies of the development of understanding* (pp. 188–209). Chicago: University of Chicago Press.

Hartshorne, H., & May, M. A. (1928). *Studies in deceit.* New York: Macmillan.

Hartshorne, H., May, M. A., & Maller, J. B. (1929). *Studies in service and self-control.* New York: Macmillan.

Hartshorne, H., May, M. A., & Shuttleworth, F. K. (1930). *Studies in the organization of character.* New York: Macmillan.

Hartup, W. (1974). Aggression in childhood: Developmental perspectives. *American Psychologist, 29,* 336–341.

Hartup, W., & DeWit, J. (1974). The development of aggression: Problems and perspectives. In J. DeWit & W. Hartup (Eds.), *Determinants and origins of aggressive behavior* (pp. 595–620). The Hague: Moutin.

Hastorf, A. H., & Bender, I. E. (1952). A caution respecting the measurement of empathic ability. *Journal of Abnormal and Social Psychology, 47,* 574–576.

Hatfield, E., Cacioppo, J. T., & Rapson, R. (1992). Primitive emotional contagion. In M. S. Clark (Ed.), *Review of personality and social psychology.* (Vol. 14, pp. 151–177). Newbury Park, CA: Sage.

Hatfield, E., Cacioppo, J. T., & Rapson, R. L. (1993). Emotional contagion. *Current Directions in Psychological Science, 2,* 96–99.

Haviland, J. (April, 1975). *Individual differences in affect.* Paper presented at a meeting of the Society for Research in Child Development, Denver.

Haviland, J. (1976). Looking smart: The relationship between affect and intelligence in infancy. In M. Lewis (Ed.), *Origins of intelligence: Infancy and early childhood* (pp. 353–377). New York: Plenum.

Haviland, J. (in preparation). Passionate thought. In C. Magai & J. Haviland (Eds.), *Affect, ideology and practice*.

Haviland, J. M., & Kramer, D. A. (1991). Affect-cognition relationships in adolescent diaries: The case of Anne Frank. *Human Development, 34*, 143–159.

Haviland, J. M., & Lelwica, M. (1987). The induced affect response: 10-week-old infants' responses to three emotion expressions. *Developmental Psychology, 23*, 97–104.

Haviland, J. M., & Malatesta, C. Z. (1981). A description of the development of sex differences in nonverbal signals: Fantasies, fallacies, and facts. In C. Mayo & N. Henley (Eds.), *Gender and nonverbal behaviors* (pp. 183–208). New York: Springer-Verlag.

Hazen, C., & Shaver, P. (1987). Romantic love conceptualized as an attachment process. *Journal of Personality and Social Psychology, 52*, 511–524.

Hebb, D. O. (1946). On the nature of fear. *Psychological Review, 53*, 259–276.

Hebb, D. O. (1949). *The organization of behaviour.* New York: Wiley.

Hess, B. B. (1979). Sex roles, friendship, and the life course. *Research on Aging, 1*, 494–515.

Hiatt, S., Campos, J. J., & Emde, R. N. (1979). Facial patterning and infant emotional expression: Happiness, surprise, and fear. *Child Development, 50*, 1020–1035.

Hittleman, J. H., & Dickes, R. (1979). Sex differences in neonatal eye contact time. *Merrill-Palmer Quarterly, 25*, 171–184.

Hofer, M. A. (1987). Early social relationships: A psychobiologist's view. *Child Development, 58*, 633–647.

Hoffman, M. L. (1960). Power assertion by the parent and its impact on the child. *Child Development, 31*, 129–143.

Hoffman, M. L. (1970). Moral development. In P. H. Mussen (Ed.), *Carmichael's manual of child psychology* (Vol. 2 pp. 261–360). New York: Wiley.

Hoffman, M. L. (1975). The development of altruistic motivation. In D. J. DePalma & J. Foley (Eds.), *Moral development: Current theory and research* (pp. 137–168). Hillsdale, NJ: Erlbaum.

Hoffman, M. L. (1978). Toward a theory of empathic arousal and development. In M. Lewis & L. Rosenblum (Eds.), *The development of affect* (pp. 227–256). New York: Plenum.

Hoffman, M. L. (1982a). Development of prosocial motivation: Empathy and guilt. In N. Eisenberg (Ed.), *The development of prosocial behavior* (pp. 281–359). New York: Academic Press.

Hoffman, M. L. (1982b). The measurement of empathy. In C. E. Izard (Ed.), *Measuring emotions in infants and children* (pp. 279–296). New York: Cambridge University Press.

Hoffman, M. L. (1984). Interaction of affect and cognition in empathy. In C. E. Izard, J. Kagan, & R. B. Zajonc (Eds.), *Emotions, cognition, and behavior* (pp. 103–131). New York: Cambridge University Press.

Hoffman, M. L. (1987). The contribution of empathy to justice and moral development. In N. Eisenberg & J. Strayer (Eds.), *Empathy and its development* (pp. 47–80). Cambridge: Cambridge University Press.

Hoffman, M. L. (1990). Empathy and justice motivation. *Motivation and Emotion, 14*, 151–172.

Hofstetter, P. R. (1957). *Psychologie.* Frankfurt: Fischer Taschenbuch Verlag.

Hogan, R. T. (1983). A socioanalytic theory of personality. In M. Page (Ed.), *Nebraska Symposium on Motivation* (pp. 55–89). Lincoln: University of Nebraska Press.

Hollingsworth, H. L. (1928). *Psychology: Its facts and principles.* New York: Appleton.

Hooper, F. H. (1988). The history of child psychology as seen through Handbook analysis. *Human Development, 31*, 176–184.

Howes, C., & Farver, J. (1987). Toddlers' responses to the distress of their peers. *Journal of Applied Developmental Psychology, 8*, 441–452.

Howes, M. J., Hokanson, J. E., & Lowenstein, D. A. (1985). Induction of depressive affect after prolonged exposure to a mildly depressed individual. *Journal of Personality and Social Psychology, 49*, 1110–1113.

Hoyle, G. (1984). The scope of neuroethology. *The Behavioral and Brain Sciences, 7*, 367–412.

Huebner, R., & Izard, C. (1988). Mothers' responses to infants, facial expressions of sadness, anger, and physical distress. *Motivation and Emotion, 12*, 185–196.

Hume, D (1978). *A treatise of human nature* (2nd ed., L. A. Selby-Bigge, Ed., p. 415) Oxford: Oxford University Press.

Iannotti, R. J. (1985). Naturalistic and structured assessments of prosocial behavior in preschool children: The influence of empathy and perspective taking. *Developmental Psychology, 21*, 46–55.

IJzendoorn, M. H. van, & Kroonenberg, P. M. (1988). Cross-cultural patterns of attachment: A meta-analysis of the Strange Situation. *Child Development, 59*, 147–156.

Irwin, O. C. (1930). The amount and nature of activities of new-born infants under constant external stimulating conditions during the first ten days of life. *Genetic Psychology Monographs, 8*, 1–92.

Irwin, O. C. (1932a). Infant responses to vertical movements. *Child Development, 3*, 167–169.

Irwin, O. C. (1932b). The latent time of the body startle in infants. *Child Development, 3*, 104–107.

Isabella, R. A., & Belsky, J. (1991). Interactional synchrony and the origins of infant-mother attachment: A replication study. *Child Development, 62*, 373–384.

Isabella, R. A., Belsky, J., & von Eye, A. (1989). The origins of infant-mother attachment: An examination of interactional synchrony during the infant's first year. *Developmental Psychology. 25*, 12–21.

Isen, A. A. (1984). Toward understanding the role of affect in cognition. In R. Wyler & T. Srule (Eds.), *Handbook of social cognition* (pp. 179–235). Hillsdale, NJ: Erlbaum.

Izard, C. E. (1950). Thematic apperception reaction of crippled children. *Journal of Clinical Psychology, 6*, 243–248.

Izard, C. E. (1971). *The face of emotion*. New York: Appleton-Century-Crofts.

Izard, C. E. (1972). *Patterns of emotions: A new analysis of anxiety and depression*. New York: Academic Press.

Izard, C. E. (1977). *Human emotions*. New York: Plenum.

Izard, C. E. (1979). *The maximally discriminative facial movement coding system (Max)*. Newark: Office of Instructional Technology, University of Delaware.

Izard, C. E. (1991). *The psychology of emotions*. New York: Plenum.

Izard, C. E., & Dougherty, L. M. (1981). Two complementary systems for measuring facial expressions in infants and children. In C. E. Izard (Ed.), *Measuring emotions in infants and children* (pp. 97–126). Cambridge: Cambridge University Press.

Izard, C. E., Haynes, O. M., Chisholm, G., & Baak, K. (1991). Emotional determinants of infant-mother attachment. *Child Development, 62*, 906–917.

Izard, C. E., Haynes, O. M., Fantauzzo, C. A., Slomine, B. S., & Castle, J. M. (in press). The morphological stability and social validity of infants' facial expressions in the first nine months of life.

Izard, C. E., Hembree, E. A., & Huebner, R. R. (1987). Infants' emotion expressions to acute pain: Developmental change and stability of individual differences. *Developmental Psychology, 23*, 105–113.

Izard, C. E., Hembree, E. A., Dougherty, L. M., & Spizzirri, C. C. (1983). Changes in facial expressions of 2- to 19-month old infants following acute pain. *Developmental Psychology, 19,* 418–426.

Izard, C. E., Huebner, R. R., Risser, D., McGinnes, G., & Dougherty, L. (1980). The young infant's ability to produce discrete emotion expressions. *Developmental Psychology, 16,* 132–140.

Izard, C. E., Kagan, J., & Zajonc, R. B. (Eds). *Emotion, cognition, and behavior.* New York: Cambridge University Press.

Izard, C. E., Libero, D. Z., Putnam, P., & Haynes, O. M. (1993). Stability of emotion experiences and their relations to traits of personality. *Journal of Personality and Social Psychology, 64,* 847–860.

Izard, C. E., & Malatesta, C. Z. (1987). Emotional development in infancy. In J. Osofsky (Ed.), *Handbook of infant development* (2nd ed., pp. 494–554). New York: Wiley.

Izard, C. E., & Malatesta-Magai, C. Z. (1991). Expression-feeling relations and expressive behavior development. In K. T. Strongman (Ed.), *International review of studies on emotion* (pp. 29–32). New York: Wiley.

Jackson, D. (1990). *Unmasking masculinity.* London: Unwin Hyman.

Jacobson, J. L., & Wille, D. E. (1984, April). *The influence of attachment patterns on peer interaction at 2 and 3 years.* Paper presented to the International Conference on Infants Studies, New York.

Jacobson, J. L., Wille, D. E., Tianen, R. L., & Aytch, D. M. (1983, April). *The influence of infant-mother attachment on toddler sociability with peers.* Paper presented to the Society for Research in Child Development, Detroit.

Jaensch, W. (1926). *Grundzuege einer Physiologie und Klinik der psychophysischen Persoenlichkeit.* Berlin: Springer.

James, W. (1890). *The principles of psychology.* New York: Holt.

James, W. (1961). *The varieties of religious experience.* New York: Collier Books. (Originally published, 1902).

James, W. (1983). *The principles of psychology.* Cambridge, MA: Harvard University Press. (Originally published 1890).

Jantzen, K. A. (1992). *Patterns of emotional development and long-lasting psychological effects of adult victims of childhood physical and sexual abuse.* Unpublished doctoral dissertation, Long Island University, New York.

Jantzen, K. A., Magai, C., & Allen, R. (1993, August). *Long-term emotional/psychological effects of childhood abuse.* Paper presented at a meeting of the American Psychological Association, Toronto, Canada.

Jersild, A. T. (1933). *Child psychology.* New York: Prentice-Hall.

Jersild, A. T. (1946). Emotional development. In L. Carmichael (Ed.), *Manual of child psychology* (pp. 833–917). New York: Wiley.

Jersild, A. T., & Holmes, F. B. (1935). Children's fears. *Child Development Monographs,* No. 20, pp. 1–356.

Jones, C. (1990). *The effects of maternal emotion word use on children's emotional development.* Unpublished doctoral dissertation, New School for Social Research, New York.

Jones, H. E. (1930a). The galvanic skin reflex in infancy. *Child Development, 1,* 106–110.

Jones, H. E. (1930b). The retention of conditioned emotional reactions in infancy. *Journal of Genetic Psychology, 37,* 485–497.

Jones, H. E. (1935). The galvanic skin response as related to overt emotional expression. *American Journal of Psychology, 47,* 241–251.

Jones, H. E., & Jones, M. C. (1930). Genetic studies of emotion. *Psychological Bulletin, 27,* 40–64.

Jones, H. E., & Wechsler, D. (1928). Galvanometric technique in studies of association. *American Journal of Psychology, 40,* 607–612.

Jones, M. C. (1924). The elimination of children's fears. *Journal of Experimental Psychology, 7,* 382–390.

Jones, M. C. (1983). Harold E. Jones and Mary C. Jones, Partners in longitudinal studies. An oral history conducted 1981–1982 by Suzanne B. Riess, Regional Oral History Office, The Bancroft Library, University of California, Berkeley.

Jones, W. H., & Briggs, S. R. (1984). The self-other discrepancy in social shyness. In R. Schwarzer (Ed.). *The self in anxiety, stress and depression* (pp. 93–107). Amsterdam: North Holland.

Jones, W. H., Briggs, S. R., & Smith, T. G. (1986). Shyness: Conceptualization and measurement. *Journal of Personality and Social Psychology, 51,* 629–639.

Jones, W. H., Cavert, C. W., & Indart, M. (1983, August). *Impressions of shyness.* Paper presented at the meeting of the American Psychological Association, Anaheim, CA.

Jones, W. H., Cheek, J. M., & Briggs, S. R. (1986). *Shyness: Perspectives on research and treatment.* New York: Plenum.

Jones, W. H., & Russell, D. (1982). The social reticence scale: An objective instrument to measure shyness. *Journal of Personality Assessment, 46,* 629–631.

Kagan, J. (1971). *Personality development.* New York: Harcourt Brace Jovanovich.

Kagan, J. (1974). Developmental and methodological considerations in the study of aggression. In J. De Wit & W. Hartup (Eds.), *Determinants and origins of aggressive behavior* (pp. 107–113). The Hague: Moutin.

Kagan, J. (1978). *The growth of the child.* New York: Norton.

Kagan, J. (1982). *Psychological research on the human infant: An evaluative summary.* New York: W. T. Grant.

Kagan, J., Kearsley, R. B., & Zelazo, P. R. (1978). *Infancy: Its place in human development.* Cambridge, MA: Harvard University Press.

Kagan, J., & Lewis, M. (1965). Studies of attention in the human infant. *Merrill-Palmer Quarterly, 11,* 95–127.

Kagan, J., & Moss, H. (1962). *Birth to maturity.* New York: Wiley.

Kagan, J., Reznick, J., & Gibbons, J. (1989). Inhibited and uninhibited types of children. *Child Development, 60,* 838–845.

Kagan, J., Reznick, J., Snidman, N., Gibbons, J., & Johnson, M. (1985). Childhood derivatives of inhibition and lack of inhibition to the unfamiliar. *Child Development, 59,* 1580–1589.

Kagan, J., & Snidman, N. (1991). Infant predictors of inhibited and uninhibited profiles. *Psychological Science, 2,* 40–44.

Kagan, J., Snidman, N., & Arcus, D. M. (1992). Initial reactions to unfamiliarity. *Current Directions in Psychological Science, 1,* 171–174.

Karen, R. (1990, February). Becoming attached. *The Atlantic Monthly,* pp. 35–70.

Katz, L. F., & Gottman, J. M. (1992). *Patterns of marital conflict predict children's internalizing and externalizing behaviors.* Unpublished manuscript, University of Washington, Seattle.

Kaufman, G. (1989). *The psychology of shame: Theory and treatment of shame-based syndromes.* New York: Springer.

Kellerman, H. (1990). Emotion and the organization of primary process. In R. Plutchik & H. Kellerman (Eds.), *Emotion theory, research, and experience* (Vol. 5, pp. 9–113). San Diego, CA: Academic Press.

Kestenbaum, R., Farber, E. A., & Sroufe, L. A. (1989). Individual differences in empathy among preschoolers: Relation to attachment history. In N. Eisenberg (Ed.), *New directions in child development* (Vol. 44, pp. 51–64). San Francisco: Jossey-Bass.

Kirschenbaum, H. (1979). *On Becoming Carl Rogers.* New York: Delacourte.

Kiser, L., Bates, J., Maslin, C., & Bayles, K. (1986). Mother-infant play at six months as a predictor of attachment security at thirteen months. *Journal of the American Academy of Child Psychiatry.*

Kobak, R. R., & Sceery, A. (1988). Attachment in late adolescence: Working models, affect regulation, and perception of self and others. *Child Development, 59,* 135–146.

Koestner, R., Franz, C., & Weinberger, J. (1990). The family origins of empathic concern: A 26-year longitudinal study. *Journal of Personality and Social Psychology, 58,* 709–717.

Kogan, N. (1986). *Cognitive styles in infancy and early childhood.* New York: Wiley.

Koplow, L. (1986). Contagious sneezing and other epidemics of empathy in young children. *The Exceptional Child, 33,* 146–150.

Kopp, C. B. (1989). Regulation of distress and negative emotions: A developmental view. *Developmental Psychology, 25,* 343–354.

Kropp, J. P., & Haynes, O. M. (1987). Abusive and nonabusive mothers' ability to identify general and specific emotion signals of infants. *Child Development, 58,* 187–190.

Krystal, H. (1977). Aspects of affect theory. *Bulletin of the Menninger Clinic, 41,* 1–25.

Kuhn, T. S. (1962). *The structure of scientific revolutions.* Chicago: University of Chicago Press.

Kurtz, E. (1979). *Not-God: A history of alcoholics anonymous.* Center City, MN: Hazelden Educational Services.

Labouvie-Vief, G. (1984). Culture, language, and mature rationality. In K. A. McCluskey & H. W. Reese (Eds.), *Life-span developmental psychology: Historical and generational effects* (pp. 109–128). New York: Academic Press.

Labouvie-Vief, G., DeVoe, M., & Bulka, D. (1989). Speaking about feelings: Conceptions of emotion across the life span. *Psychology and Aging, 4,* 425–437.

Laird, J. D., & Bresler, C. (1992). The process of emotional feeling: A self-perception theory. In Margaret Clark (Ed.), *Review of Personality and Social Psychology* (pp. 213–234). Beverly Hills, CA: Sage.

Lamb, M., Gaensbauer, T., Malkin, C., & Schultz, L. (1985). The effect of child maltreatment on security of infant-adult attachment. *Infant behavior and development, 8,* 35–45.

Landis, C. (1924). Studies of emotional reactions: II. General behavior and facial expression. *Comparative Psychology, 4,* 447–509.

Landis, C. (1929). The interpretation of facial expression in emotion. *Journal of General Psychology, 2,* 59–71.

Landis, C., & Hunt, W. (1939). *The startle pattern.* New York: Farrar & Rinehart.

Langer, J. (1969). *Theories of development.* New York: Holt, Rinehart & Winston.

Langhorst, B., & Fogel, A. (1982, March) *Cross validation of microanalytic approaches to face-to-face play.* Paper presented at the International Conference on Infant Studies, Austin, TX.

Langsdorf, P., Izard, C. E., Rayias, M., & Hembree, E. A. (1983). Interest expression, visual fixation, and heart rate changes in 2- to 8-month-old infants. *Developmental Psychology, 19,* 418–426.

Lanzetta, J. T., & McHugo, G. J. (October 1986). *The history and current status of the facial feedback hypothesis.* Paper presented at the twenty-sixth annual meeting of the Society for Psychophysiological Research, Montreal, Quebec, Canada.

Larsen, R. J., & Ketelaar, T. (1991). Personality and susceptibility to positive and negative emotional states. *Journal of Personality and Social Psychology, 61,* 132–140.

Lawick-Goodall, J. van (1971). *In the shadow of man.* Boston: William Collins.

Lazarus, R. S., & Folkman, S. (1984). *Stress, appraisal, and coping.* New York: Springer.

Leary, M. R. (1983). Social anxiousness: The construct and its measurement. *Journal of Personality Assessment, 47,* 66–75.

Leary, M. R. (1984). *Understanding social anxiety: Social, personality, and clinical perspectives.* Beverly Hills, CA: Sage.

Leary, M. R. (1986). Affective and behavioral components of shyness. In W. H. Jones, J. M. Cheek, & S. R. Briggs (Eds.). *Shyness: Perspectives on research and treatment* (pp. 27–38). New York: Plenum.

Lemaire, A. (1977). *Jacques Lacan*. London: Routledge and Kegan Paul.

Lemerise, E. A., & Dodge, K. A. (1993). The development of anger and hostile interactions. In M. Lewis & J. Haviland (Eds.), *Handbook of emotions* (pp.. 537–546). New York: Guilford Press.

Lemerise, E. A., Shepard, B. A., & Malatesta, C. Z. (1986, August). *The strange situation: Differences among birth and attachment status groups*. Paper presented at the annual meeting of the American Psychological Association, Washington, DC.

Lennon, R., & Eisenberg, N. (1987). Gender and age differences in empathy and sympathy. In N. Eisenberg & J. Strayer (Eds.), *Empathy and its development* (pp. 195–217). New York: Cambridge University Press.

Lennon, R., Eisenberg, N., & Carroll, J. (1986). The relation between nonverbal indices of empathy and preschoolers' prosocial behavior. *Journal of Applied Developmental Psychology, 7*, 219–224.

Levinson, D. J., Darrow, C. M., Klein, E. B., Levinson, M. H., & McKee, B. (1978). *The seasons of a man's life*. New York: Knopf.

Levitt, M. J., Weber, R. A., & Clark, M. C. (1986). Social network relationships as sources of maternal support and well-being. *Developmental Psychology, 22*, 310–316.

Levy, R. I. (1980). *On the nature and functions of the emotions: An anthropological perspective*. Unpublished manuscript.

Lewis, H. B. (1971). *Shame and guilt in neurosis*. New York: International University Press.

Lewis, M. (1992). *Shame: The exposed self*. New York: The Free Press.

Lewis, M., Alessandri, S. M., & Sullivan, M. W. (1990). Violation of expectancy, loss of control, and anger expressions in young infants. *Developmental Psychology, 26*, 745–751.

Lewis, M., Brooks, J., & Haviland, J. (1978). Hearts and faces: A study in the measurement of emotion. In M. Lewis & L. A. Rosenblum (Eds.), *The development of affect* (pp. 77–124). New York: Plenum.

Lewis, M., & Michalson, L. (1983). *Children's emotions and moods*. New York: Plenum.

Lewis, M., & Rosenblum, L. A. (1978). *The development of affect*. New York: Plenum.

Lewis, M., & Saarni, C. (Eds.). (1985). *The socialization of emotions* (pp. 1–17). New York: Plenum.

Lieberman, A. F. (1977). Preschoolers' competence with a peer: Relations with attachment and peer experience. *Child Development, 48*, 1277–1287.

Lincoln, D. W. (1983). Physiological mechanisms governing the transfer of milk from mother to young. In L. A. Rosenblum & H. Moltz (Eds.), *Symbiosis in parent-offspring interactions* (pp. 77–112). New York: Plenum.

Lipps, T. (1906). Das Wissen von fremden Ichen. *Psychologische Untersuchnung, 1*, 694–722.

Lochman, J. E. (1987). Self- and peer perceptions and attributional biases of aggressive and nonaggressive boys in dyadic interactions. *Journal of Consulting and Clinical Psychology, 55*, 404–410.

Loeber, R. (1982). The stability of antisocial and delinquent child behavior: A review. *Child Development, 53*, 1431–1446.

Logan, D. D. (1980). Mary Cover Jones: Feminine as asset. *Psychology of Women Quarterly, 5*, 103–140.

Lore, R. K., & Schultz, L. A. (1993). Control of human aggression: A comparative perspective. *American Psychologist, 48*, 16–25.

Lorenz, K. Z. (1931). Beitrage zur Ethologie sozialer Corviden. *Journal of Ornithology, 75*, 511–619.

Lyons-Ruth, K., Connell, D., Grunebaum, H., Botein, S., & Zoll, D. (1984). Maternal family history, maternal caretaking, and infant attachment in multiproblem families. *Journal of Preventive Psychiatry, 2*, 403–425.

Lyons-Ruth, K., Connell, D. B., Zoll, D., & Stahl, J. (1987). Infants at social risk: Relations among infant maltreatment, maternal behavior, and infant attachment behavior, *Developmental Psychology, 23,* 223–232.

Maccoby, E., & Martin, J. A. (1983). Socialization in the context of the family: Parent-child interaction. In P. H. Mussen (Ed.), *Handbook of child psychology* (Vol. 4, pp. 1–102). New York: Wiley.

Maccoby, E. E., & Jacklin, C. N. (1974). *Psychology of sex differences.* Stanford, CA: Stanford University Press.

MacFarlane, A. (1975). Olfaction in the development of social preferences in the human neonate. *Ciba Foundation Symposium, 33,* 103–117.

MacLean, P. D. (1972). Cerebral evolution and emotional processes. *Annals of the New York Academy of Sciences, 193,* 137–149.

Magai, C., Distel, N., & Liker, R. (1994). Emotion socialization, attachment and adult personality traits. *Cognition and Emotions.*

Magai, C., & Hunziker, J. (1993). Tolstoy and the riddle of developmental transformation: A lifespan analysis of the role of emotions in personality development. In M. Lewis & J. Haviland (Eds.), *Handbook of emotions* (pp. 247–259). New York: Wiley.

Magai, C., & Hunziker, J. (1995). To Bedlam and part way back: The application of affect theory to clinical psychology. In W. F. Flack, Jr., & J. D. Laird (Eds.), *Emotions in psychopathology: Theory and research.* New York: Oxford University Press.

Magai, C. Z., & Haviland, J. (Eds.). (in preparation). *Affect, ideology, and practice: An ideoaffective analysis of lives.*

Mahler, M. (1975). *The psychological birth of the human infant.* New York: Basic Books.

Main, M. (1982). Avoidance in the service of attachment: A working paper. In K. Immelmann, G. W. Barlow, L. Petrinovich, & M. Main (Eds.), *Behavioral development* (pp. 651–693). New York: The Bielefeld Interdisciplinary Project.

Main, M. (1983). Exploration, play, and cognitive functioning related to infant-mother attachment. *Infant Behavior and Development, 6,* 167–174

Main, M., & Goldwyn, R. (1984). Predicting rejection of her infant from mothers's representation of her own experience: Implications for the abused-abusing intergenerational cycle. *Child Abuse and Neglect, 8,* 203–217.

Main, M., Kaplan, N., & Cassidy, J. (1985). Security in infancy, childhood, and adulthood: A move to the level of representation. In I. Bretherton & E. Waters (Eds.), *Growing points of attachment theory and research* (pp. 66–106). *Monographs of the Society for Research in Child Development 50,* (1–2, Serial No. 209).

Main, M., & Stadtman, J. (1981). Infant response to rejection of physical contact by the mother. *Journal of the American Academy of Child Psychiatry, 20,* 292–307.

Main, M., Tomasini, L., & Tolan, W. (1979). Differences among mothers of infants judged to differ in security. *Developmental Psychology, 15,* 472–473.

Main, M., & Weston, D. (1981). Security of attachment to mother and father: Related to conflict behavior and the readiness to establish new relationships. *Child Development, 52,* 932–940.

Major, D. R. (1906). *First steps in mental growth: A series of studies in the psychology of infancy.* New York: Macmillan.

Malatesta, C. Z. (1981). Infant emotion and the vocal affect lexicon. *Motivation and Emotion, 5,* 1–23.

Malatesta, C. Z. (1982). The expression and regulation of emotion: A lifespan perspective. In T.M. Field & A. Fogel (Eds.), *Emotion and early interaction.* Hillsdale, NJ: Erlbaum Associates.

Malatesta, C. Z. (1985). The developmental course of emotion expression in the human infant. In G. Zivin (Ed.), *Expressive development: Biological and environmental interactions*. New York: Academic Press.

Malatesta, C. Z. (1988). A second look at the illness/emotion specificity hypothesis: A response to Friedman and Booth-Kewley. *American Psychologist, 45,* 750–751.

Malatesta, C. Z. (1990). The role of emotion in the development and organization of personality. In R. Thompson (Ed.), *Socioemotional development* (Nebraska Symposium on Motivation, pp. 1–56). Lincoln: University of Nebraska Press.

Malatesta, C. Z., & Culver, L. C. (1984). Thematic and affective content in the lives of adult women: Patterns of change and continuity. In C. Z. Malatesta & C. E. Izard (Eds.), *Emotion in Adult Development* (pp. 175–194). Beverly Hills, CA: Sage.

Malatesta, C. Z., Culver, C., Tesman, J., & Shepard, B. (1989). The development of emotion expression during the first two years of life. *Monographs of the Society for Research in Child Development, 54*(1–2), 1–103.

Malatesta, C. Z., Fiore, M. J., Messina, J., & Culver C. (1987). Affect, personality, and facial expressive characteristics of older individuals. *Psychology and Aging, 1,* 64–69.

Malatesta, C. Z., Grigoryev, P., Lamb, C., Albin, M., & Culver, C. (1986). Emotion socialization and expressive development in preterm and fullterm infants. *Child Development, 57,* 316–330.

Malatesta, C. Z., & Haviland, J. M. (1982). Learning display rules: The socialization of emotion expression in infancy. *Child Development, 53,* 991–1003.

Malatesta, C. Z., & Izard, C. E. (1984). The ontogenesis of human social signals: From biological imperative to symbol utilization. In N. Fox & R. J. Davidson (Eds.), *Affective development: A psychobiological perspective* (pp. 161–206). Hillsdale, NJ: Erlbaum.

Malatesta, C. Z., & Lamb, C. (1987, August). *Emotion socialization during the second year*. Paper presented at the annual meeting of the American Psychological Association, New York City.

Malatesta, C. Z., & Wilson, A. (1988). Emotion/cognition interaction in personality development: A discrete emotions, functionalist analysis. *British Journal of Social Psychology, 27,* 91–112.

Malatesta-Magai, C., & Izard, C. E. (1991). Conceptualizing early infant affect: Emotions as fact fiction, or artifact? In K. T. Strongman (Ed.), *International review of studies on emotion*. pp. 1–15. New York: Wiley.

Malatesta-Magai, C. Z. (1990). Emotion socialization and developmental psychopathology. In D. Cichetti & S. Toth (Eds.). *Rochester symposium on developmental psychopathology: Internalizing and externalizing expressions of dysfunction, Vol. 2*. Hillsdale, NJ: Erlbaum.

Malatesta-Magai, C. Z., & Dorval, B. (1992). Language affect and social order. In M. Gunnar & M. Maratos (Eds.), *Modularity and constraints in language and cognition* (25th Minnesota symposium on child psychology, pp. 139–175). Hillsdale, NJ: Erlbaum.

Malatesta-Magai, C. Z., Jonas, R., Shepard, B., & Culver, C. (1992). Type A personality and emotional expressivity in younger and older adults. *Psychology and Aging, 7,* 551-561.

Malatesta-Magai, C. Z., Leak, S., Tesman, J. R., Shepard, B., Culver, C., & Smaggia, B. (1994). Emotional expressiveness and sociability of fullterm and preterm children during the second and third years of life. *International Journal of Behavioral Development, 17,* 239–269.

Malmo, R. B. (1959). Activation: A neurophsychological dimension. *Psychological Review, 66,* 367–386.

Marcus, R. F. (1986). Naturalistic observation of cooperation, helping, and sharing and their associations with empathy and affect. In C. Zahn-Waxler, E. M. Cummings, & R. Iannotti (Eds.), *Altruism and aggression* (pp. 256–279). New York: Cambridge University Press.

Marcus, R. F., Roke, E. J., & Bruner, C. (1985). Verbal and nonverbal empathy and prediction of social behavior of young children. *Perceptual and Motor Skills, 60,* 299–309.

Martin, G. B., & Clark, R. D., III (1982). Distress crying in neonates: Species and peer specificity. *Developmental Psychology, 18,* 3–9.

Maslin, C. A., & Bates, J. E. (1983, April). *Precursors of anxious and secure attachments: A multivariate model at age 6 months.* Paper presented at the biennial meeting of the Society for Research in Child Development, Detroit.

Matas, L., Arend, R., & Sroufe, L. A. (1978). Continuity of adaptation in the second year: The relationship between quality of attachment and later competence. *Child Development, 49,* 547–556.

Matthews, K. A., Manuck, S. B., & Saab, P. G. (1986). Cardiovascular responses of adolescents during a naturally occurring stressor and their behavioral and psychophysiological predictors. *Psychophysiology, 23,* 198–209.

Matthews, K. A., Rosenman, R. H., Dembroski, E.T. M., Harris, E. L., & MacDougall, J. M. (1984). Familial resemblance in components of the Type A behavior pattern: A reanalysis of the California Type A twin study. *Psychosomatic Medicine, 46,* 512–522.

Matthews, K. A., Stoney, C. M., & Rakaczky, C. J., & Jamison, W. (1986). Family characteristics and school achievements of Type A children. *Health Psychology, 5,* 453–467.

McCann, B. S., & Matthews, K. A. (1988). Influences of potential for hostility, Type A Behavior, and parental history of hypertension on adolescents' cardiovascular responses during stress. *Psychophysiology, 25,* 503–511.

McCown, W., Johnson, J., & Austin, S. (1985, June). *Inability of delinquents to recognize facial affects.* Paper presented at the British Psychological Society's International Conference on the Meaning of Faces, Cardiff, Wales.

McCrae, R. R., & Costa, P. T. (1985). Updating Norman's "Adequate Taxonomy" Intelligence and personality dimensions in natural language and in questionnaires. *Journal of Personality and Social Psychology, 49,* 710–721.

McCrae, R. R., & Costa, P. T. (1987). Validation of the five-factor model of personality across instruments and observers. *Journal of Personality and Social Psychology, 52,* 82–91.

McLeish, Mrs. Andrew (1898). Observations on the development of a child during the first year. *Transactions of the Illinois Society for Child Study, 3,* 109–124.

Mead, M. (1930). *Growing up in New Guinea.* New York: Morrow.

Meleshko, K. G. A., & Alden, L. E. (1993). Anxiety and self-disclosure: Toward a motivational model. *Journal of Personality and Social Psychology, 64,* 1000–1009.

Meltzoff, A. N. (1981). Imitation, intermodal co-ordination and representation in early infancy. In G. Butterworth (Ed.), *Infancy and Epistemology* (pp. 85–114). Brighton (England): Harvester Press, 1981.

Meltzoff, A. N., & Moore, M. K. (1977). Imitation of facial and manual gestures by human neonates. *Science, 198,* 75–78.

Meyer, M. F. (1933). That whale among the fishes: The theory of emotions. *Psychological Review, 40,* 292–300.

Middlebrook, D. (1992). *Anne Sexton: A biography.* New York: Vintage.

Mikulincer, M., Florian, V., & Tolmacz, R. (1990). Attachment styles and fear of personal death: A case study of affect regulation. *Journal of Personality and Social Psychology, 58,* 273–280.

Milgram, S. (1963). Behavioral study of obedience. *Journal of Abnormal and Social Psychology, 67,* 371–378.

Miller, G. A., Galanter, E., & Pribram, K. H. (1960). *Plans and the structure of behavior.* New York: Hold, Rinehart & Winston.

Miller, P., & Sperry, L. L. (1987). The socialization of anger and aggression. *Merrill-Palmer Quarterly, 33,* 1–31.

Miller, P. A., & Eisenberg, N. (1988). The relation of empathy to aggressive and externalizing/antisocial behavior. *Psychological Bulletin, 103*, 324–344.

Mineka, S., & Sutton, S. K. (1992). Cognitive biases and the emotional disorders. *Psychological Science, 3*, 65–69.

Mischel, W. (1968). *Personality and assessment.* New York: Wiley.

Miyake, K., Chen, S., & Campos, J. J. (1985). Infant temperament, mother's mode of interaction, and attachment in Japan: An interim report. In I. Bretherton & E. Waters (Eds.), *Growing points of attachment theory and research* (pp. 276–297). *Monographs of the Society for Research in Child Development, 50*, (1–2, Serial No. 209).

Moore, B. S. (1987). Commentary. In N. Eisenberg & J. Strayer (Eds.), *Empathy and its development* (pp. 339–348). New York: Cambridge University Press.

Moore, K. C. (1896). The mental development of a child. *Psychological Monograph Supplement, 1* (3).

Moro, E. (1918). Das erste Trimenon. *Muenchner Medische Wissenschaft, 65*, 1147–1150.

Morris, D. P., Soroker, E., & Burruss, G. (1954). Follow-up studies of shy, withdrawn children. I. Evaluation of later adjustment. *American Journal of Orthopsychiatry, 24*, 743–754.

Moss, H. A. (1967). Sex, age and state as determinants of mother-infant interaction. *Merrill-Palmer Quarterly, 13*, 19–36.

Müller-Brettel, M. (1993). *Johann Nicolaus Tetens: Die philosophischen Werke.* Unpublished manuscript.

Müller-Brettel, M., & Dixon, R. A. (1990). Johann Nicolas Tetens: A forgotten father of developmental psychology? *International Journal of Behavioral Development, 13*, 215–230.

Murchison, C., & Langer, S. (1929). Tiedemann's observations on the development of the mental faculties of children. *Pedagogical Seminary, 34*, 205–230.

Murphy, L. B. (1937). *Social behavior and child personality: An exploratory study of some roots of sympathy.* New York: Columbia University Press.

Murphy, L. B. (1983). Lois Barclay Murphy. In A. O'Connell & N. Russo (Eds.), *Models of achievement: Reflections of eminent women in psychology* (pp. 89–107). New York: Columbia University Press.

Murray, D. M., Matthews, K. A., Blake, S. M., & Prineas, R. (1986). Type A behavior in children: Demographic, behavioral, and physiological correlates. *Health Psychology, 5*, 159–169.

Nathanson, D. L. (1992). *Shame and pride: Affect, sex, and the birth of the self.* New York: Norton.

Nelson, K. (1981). Social cognition in a script framework. In J. H. Flavell & L. Ross (Eds.), *Social cognitive development* (pp. 97–118). Cambridge, MA: Cambridge University Press.

Nisbett, R. E. (1993). Violence and U.S. regional culture. *American Psychologist, 48*, 441–449.

Nolen-Hoeksema, S., & Morrow, J. (1991). A prospective study of depression and posttraumatic stress symptoms after a natural disaster: The 1989 Loma Prieta earthquake. *Journal of Personality and Social Psychology, 61*, 115–121.

Noller, P., Law, H., & Comrey, A. L. (1987). Cattell, Comrey, and Eysenck personality factors compared: More evidence for the five robust factors? *Journal of Personality and Social Psychology, 53*, 775–782.

Norman, W. T. (1963). Toward an adequate taxonomy of personality attributes. *Journal of Abnormal and Social Psychology, 66*, 74–583.

O'Connell, A., & Russo, N. (Eds.). (1983). *Models of achievement: Reflections of eminent women in psychology.* New York: Columbia University Press.

O'Donnell, J. M. (1979). The crisis of experimentalism in the 1920s: E. G. Boring and his uses of history. *American Psychologist, 34*, 289–295.

Oettinger, G., Little, T. D., Lindenberger, U., & Baltes, P. (1994). Causality, agency, and control beliefs in East versus West Berlin children: A natural experiment on the role of context. *Journal of Personality and Social Psychology, 66,* 579–595.

Olden, C. (1958). Notes on the development of empathy. *The Psychoanalytic Study of the Child, 13,* 505–518.

Oldershaw, L., & Walters, G. C. (1989). A behavioral approach to the classification of different types of physically abusive mothers. *Merrill-Palmer Quarterly, 35,* 255–279.

Olweus, D. (1979). Stability of aggressive reaction patterns in males: A review. *Psychological Bulletin, 86,* 852–875.

Olweus, D. (1980). Familial and temperamental determinants of aggressive behavior in adolescent boys: A causal analysis. *Developmental Psychology, 16*(6), 644–660.

Otis, N. B., & McCandless, B. (1955). Responses to repeated frustrations of young children differentiated according to need area. *Journal of Abnormal and Social Psychology, 50,* 349–353.

Parke, R. D., & Slaby, R. G. (1983). The development of aggression. In E. M. Hetherington (Ed.), *Handbook of child psychology: Vol. 4. Socialization, personality, and social development* (4th ed., pp. 547–641). New York: Wiley.

Passini, F. T., & Norman, W. T. (1966). A universal conception of personality structure. *Journal of Personality and Social Psychology, 4,* 44–49.

Pastor, D. L. (1981). The quality of mother-infant attachment and its relationship to toddlers' initial sociability with peers. *Developmental Psychology, 17,* 326–335.

Patterson, G. R. (1980). Mothers: The unacknowledged victims. *Monographs of the Society for Research in Child Development, 45*(5, Serial No. 186).

Pervin, L. (1988a). Affect and addiction. *Addictive Behaviors, 13,* 83–86.

Pervin, L. (1988b). *Personality and the organization of affects.* Unpublished manuscript, Rutgers University.

Pervin, L. A. (1993). Affect and personality. In M. Lewis & J. Haviland (Eds.), *Handbook of emotions* (pp. 301–312). New York: Guilford.

Piaget, J. (1952). *The origins of intelligence in children* (M. Cook, Trans.). New York: International Universities Press. (Original work published 1932).

Piaget, J. (1971). *Biology and knowledge.* Chicago: University of Chicago Press.

Pilkonis, P. A. (1977). The behavioral consequences of shyness. *Journal of Personality, 45,* 566–611.

Plunket, J. W., Meisels, S. J., Steifel, G. S., Pasick, P. L., and Roloff, D. W. (1984). Patterns of attachment among preterm infants of varying biological risk. In S. J. Meisels (Chair), *Developmental vulnerability of infants born at severely high risk.* Symposium conducted at the biennial meeting of the International Conference on Infant Studies, New York.

Plutchik, R. (1962). *The emotions: Facts, theories, and a new model.* New York: Random House.

Plutchik, R. (1980). *Emotion: A psychoevolutionary synthesis.* New York: Harper & Row.

Plutchik, R. (1987). Evolutionary bases of empathy. In N. Eisenberg & J. Strayer (Eds.), *Empathy and its development* (pp. 38–46). New York: Cambridge University Press.

Pratt, K. C. (1946). The neonate. In L. Carmichael (Ed.), *Manual of child psychology* (pp. 258–291). New York: Wiley.

Pratt, K. C., Nelson, A. K., & Sun, K. H. (1930). The behavior of the newborn infant. *Ohio State University Studies, Contributions of Psychology,* No. 10.

Preyer, W. (1882). *Die Seele des Kindes.* Leipzig: Fernau.

Radke-Yarrow, M., Cummings, E. M., Kuczynski, L., & Chapman, M. (1985). Patterns of attachment in two- and three-year-olds in normal families and families with parental depression. *Child Development, 56,* 884–893.

Radke-Yarrow, M., Zahn-Waxler, C., & Chapman, M. (1983). Children's prosocial dispositions and behavior. In P. H. Mussen (Ed.), *Handbook of child psychology: Vol. 4: Socialization, personality, and social development* (4th ed., pp. 469–549). New York: Wiley.

Rank, O. (1929). *The trauma of birth*. New York: Harcourt Brace.

Rank, O. (1932). *Modern education: A critique of its fundamental ideas*. New York: Knopf.

Rapaport, D. (1968). The psychoanalytic theory of emotions. In M. Arnold (Ed.), *The nature of emotion* (pp. 83–89). London: Penguin Books.

Rasmussen, V. (1922). *The social life of a child in its first four years*. New York: Knopf.

Rasmussen, V. (1931). *Diary of a child's life from birth to the fifteenth year* (M. Blachard, Trans.). London: Gyldendal.

Reese, H. W., & Overton, W. F. (1970). Models of development and theories of development. In L. R. Goulet & P. B. Baltes (Eds.), *Life-span developmental psychology: Research and theory* (pp. 115–145). New York: Academic Press.

Remarque, E. M. (1929). *All quiet on the western front*. Boston: Little, Brown.

Renken, B., Egeland, B., Marvinney, D., Mangelsdorf, S., & Sroufe, L. A. (1989). Early childhood antecedents of aggression and passive-withdrawal in early elementary school. *Journal of Personality, 57*, 257–281.

Retzinger, S. M. (1991). *Violent emotions: Shame and rage in marital quarrels*. Newbury Park, CA: Sage Publications.

Ribot, T. (1903). *The psychology of the emotions*. New York: Scribners.

Ricks, M. (1985). The social transmission of parental behavior: Attachment across generations. In I. Bretherton & E. Waters (Eds.), *Growing points in attachment theory and research. Monographs of the Society for Research in Child Development, 50* (Serial No. 209, pp. 211–230.)

Rieber, R. W., & Carton, A. S. (Eds.). (1987). *The collected works of L. S. Vygotsky, Volume I, Problems of general psychology*. New York: Plenum.

Roberts, W., & Strayer, J. (1987). Parents' responses to emotional distress of their children: Relations of children's competence. *Developmental Psychology, 23*, 415–422.

Rollett, B. (1984). Zum 10. Todestag Charlotte Buhlers Leben und Werk. *Psychologie in Oesterreich, 4*, 3–6.

Rosenman, R. H., Rahe, R. H., Borhani, N. O. (1974). Heritability of personality and behavior pattern. *Acta Genetica Medica Gemollol Roma, 23*, 37–42.

Rubin, K. H., & Clark, M. L. (1983). Preschool teachers' rating of behavioral problems: Observational, sociometric, and social-cognitive correlates. *Journal of Abnormal Child Psychology, 11*, 273–285.

Rubin, K. H., Moller, L., & Emptage, A. (1987). The pre-school Behaviour Questionnaire: A useful index of behavior problems in elementary school-age children? *Canadian Journal of Behavioural Sciences, 19*, 86–100.

Rubin, K. H., & Rose-Krasnor, L. (1992). Interpersonal problem solving and social competence in children. In V. B. Van Hasselt & M. Hersen (Eds.). *Handbook of social development* (pp. 283–324). New York: Plenum.

Ruckmick, C. A. (1936). *The psychology of feelings and emotions*. New York: McGraw-Hill.

Russell, B. (1926). *Education and the good life*. New York: Boni & Liveright.

Ryff, C. D. (1991). Possible selves in adulthood and old age: A tale of shifting horizons. *Psychology and Aging, 6*, 286–295.

Saarni, C. (1993). Socialization of emotion. In M. Lewis & J. Haviland (Eds.) *Handbook of Emotion* (pp. 435–446). New York: Guilford.

Sachs, R. (1893). Beobachtungen ueber das physiologische Verhalten des Gehororgans Neugeborener. *Archives Ohrenheilklinik, 35*, 28–38.

Sadger, J. (1941). Preliminary study of the psychic life of the fetus and the primary germ. *Psychoanalytic Review, 28*, 327–358.

Sagi, A., & Hoffman, M. L. (1976). Empathic distress in the newborn. *Developmental Psychology, 12*, 175–176.

Sagi, A., Lamb, M. E., Lewkowicz, K. S., Shoham, R., Dvir, R., & Estes, D. (1985). Security of infant-mother, -father, and -metapelet attachments among kibbutz-reared Israeli children. In I. Bretherton & E. Waters (Eds.), *Growing points of attachment theory and research* (pp. 257–275). *Monographs of the Society for Research in Child Development, 50*, (1–2, Serial No. 209).

Sameroff, A. J. (1983). Developmental systems: Contexts and evolution. In P. Mussen (Ed.), *Handbook of child psychology*, In W. Kessen (Ed.), *Volume I. History, Theory and Methods*, pp. 237–294. New York: Wiley.

Sameroff, A. J., & Chandler, M. J. (1975). Reproductive risk and the continuum of caretaking casualty. In F. D. Horowitz, M. Hetherington, S. Scarr-Salapatek, & G. Siegel (Eds.), *Review of child development research* (Vol. 4). Chicago: University of Chicago Press.

Sander, L. W. (1969). Regulation and organization in the early infant-caretaker system. In R. Robinson (Ed.), *Brain and early behavior*, London: Academic Press.

Santee, R. T., & Maslach, C. (1982). To agree or not to agree: Personal dissent amid social pressure to conform. *Journal of Personality and Social Psychology, 42*, 690–700.

Saxby, I. B. (1925). *The education of behavior: A psychological study*. New York: G. P. Putnam's Sons.

Schachter, S., & Singer, J. E. (1962). Cognitive, social, and physiological determinants of emotional states. *Psychological Review, 69*, 379–399.

Schaffer, H. R. (1963). Some issues for research in the study of attachment behavior. In B. M. Foss (Ed.), *Determinant of infant behavior* (Vol. 2). New York: Wiley.

Schaffer, H. R., & Emerson, P. E. (1964). *The development of social attachments in infancy. Monographs of the Society for Research in Child Development, 29* (Serial No. 94).

Schank, R. C., & Abelson, R. P. (1977). *Scripts, plans, goals and understanding*. Hillsdale, NJ: Erlbaum.

Scheff, T. J. (1984). The taboo on coarse emotions. In P. Shaver (Ed.), *Review of Personality and Social Psychology*, (Vol. 5, pp. 146–170). Beverly Hills: Sage.

Scheff, T. J. (1987). The shame-rage spiral: A case study of an interminable quarrel. In H. B. Lewis (Ed.), *The role of shame in symptom formation*. Hillsdale, NJ: Erlbaum.

Scheff, T. J. (1988). Shame and conformity: The deference-emotion system. *American Sociological Review, 53*, 395–406.

Schneider-Rosen, K., Braunwald, K. G., Carlson, V., & Cicchetti, D. (1985). Current perspectives in attachment theory: Illustration from the study of maltreated infants. In I. Bretherton & E. Waters (Eds.), *Growing points of attachment theory and research* (pp. 194–210). *Monographs of the Society for Research in Child Development, 50*, (1–2, Serial No. 209).

Schwartz, N., & Clore, G. L. (1983). Mood, misattribution, and judgments of well-being: Informative and directive functions of affective states. *Journal of Personality and Social Psychology, 45*, 53–523.

Schwartz, N., Clore, G. L. (1988). How do I feel about it? The informative function of affective states. In K. Fielder & J. Forgas (Eds.), *Affect, cognition, and social behavior* (pp. 44–62). Toronto: C.J. Hogrefe.

Sears, R. R. , Maccoby, E. E., & Levin, H. (1957). *Patterns of child rearing*. Evanston, IL: Peterson.

Seligman, M. E. P. (1975). *Helplessness*. San Francisco: Freeman.

Senn, M. J. E. (1975). *Insights on the child development movement in the United States. Monographs of the Society for Research in Child Development, 40*, (3–4, Serial No. 161).

Shand, A. F. (1914). *The foundations of character*. London: Macmillan.

Sherman, M. (1927a). The differentiation of emotional responses in infants. I. Judgments of emotional responses from motion picture views and from actual observation. *Journal of Comparative Psychology, 7*, 265–284.

Sherman, M. (1927b). The differentiation of emotional responses in infants. II. The ability of observers to judge the emotional characteristics of the crying infant and the voice of an adult. *Journal of Comparative Psychology, 7*, 335–351.

Sherman, M. (1928). The differentiation of emotional responses in infants. III. A proposed theory of the development of emotional responses in infants. *Journal of Comparative Psychology, 8*, 385–394.

Sherman, M. M., & Sherman, I. C. (1925). Sensorimotor responses in infants. *Journal of Comparative Psychology, 5*, 53–68.

Shiller, V. M., Izard, C. E., & Hembree, E. A. (1986) Patterns of emotion expression during separation in the strange-situation procedure. *Developmental Psychology, 22*, 378–382.

Shinn. M. W. (1893). *Notes of the development of a child, Part I.* Berkeley, CA: University Press.

Shinn, M. W. (1904). *Notes of the development of a child, Part II.* Berkeley, CA: University Press.

Silman, R. (1991). Melatonin and the human gonodotrophin- releasing hormone pulse generator. *Journal of Endocrinology, 128*, 7–11.

Silverstein, L. B. (1991). Transforming the debate about child care and maternal employment. *American Psychologist, 46*, 1025–1032.

Simner, M. L. (1971). Newborn's response to the cry of another infant. *Developmental Psychology, 5*, 136–150.

Simpson, J. A. (1990). Influence of attachment styles on romantic relationships. *Journal of Personality and Social Psychology, 59*, 971–980.

Singer, J. L., & Singer, D. G. (1985). Television-viewing and family communication style as predictors of children's emotional behavior. *Journal of Children in Contemporary Society, 17*(4), 75–91.

Singer, J. M., & Fagen, J. W. (1992). Negative affect, emotional expression, and forgetting in young infants. *Developmental Psychology, 28*, 48–57.

Souza e Silva, M. C. (1977). *Social and cognitive dynamics of shyness.* Unpublished master's thesis, Stanford University.

Spence, D. P. (1986). Narrative smoothing and clinical wisdom. In T. R. Sarbin (Ed.), *Narrative psychology: The storied nature of human conduct* (pp. 211–232). New York: Praeger.

Spencer, H. (1890). *The principles of psychology* (Vol. 1). New York: Appleton. (Original work published 1855)

Sperry, R. W. (1993). The impact and promise of the cognitive revolution. *American Psychologist, 48*, 878–891.

Spiro, A., Schnurr, P. P., & Aldwin, C. M. (1994). Combat-related posttraumatic stress disorder symptoms in older men. *Psychology and Aging, 9*, 17–26.

Spitz, R. (1946). Anaclitic depression. *Psychoanalytic Study of the Child, 2*, 313–342.

Spitz, R., & Wolf, K. M. (1946). The smiling response. A contribution to the ontogenesis of social relations. *Genetic Psychology Monographs, 35*, 57–125.

Spitz, R. A. (1965). *The first year of life.* New York: International Universities Press.

Spock, B. (1946). *The common sense book of baby and child care.* New York: Duell, Sloan, and Pearce.

Spranger, E. (1928). *Types of Men: The psychology and ethics of personality.* New York: Johnson Reprint.

Sroufe, L. A. (1979). Socioemotional development. In J. D. Osofsky (Ed.), *Handbook of infant development* (pp. 462–516). New York: Wiley.

Sroufe, L. A. (1983). Individual patterns of adaptation from infancy to preschool. In M. Perlmutter (Ed.), *Minnesota symposia on child psychology* (Vol. 16). Hillsdale, NJ: Erlbaum

Sroufe, L. A., Schork, E., Motti, F., Lawroski, N., LaFreniere, P. (1984). The role of affect in social competence. In C. E. Izard, J. Kagan, and R. Zajonc (Eds.), *Affect, cognition, and behavior*. New York: Plenum

Sroufe, L. A., & Wunsch, J. P. (1972) The development of laughter in the first year of life. *Child Development, 43*, 1326–1344.

Staudinger, U. M., Marsiske, M., & Baltes, P. B. (1993). Resilience and levels of reserve capacity in later adulthood. *Development and Psychopathology, 5*, 541–566.

Stein, N. L., & Jewett, J. L. (1986). A conceptual analysis of the meaning of negative emotions: Implications for a theory of development. In C. E. Izard & P. B. Read (Eds.), *Measuring emotions in infants and children* (Vol. 2, pp. 238–267). Cambridge: Cambridge University Press.

Steiner, J. E. (1973). The human gustofacial response. In J. F. Bosma (Ed.), *Fourth symposium on oral sensation and perception*. Rockville, MD: U.S. Department of Health, Education, and Welfare.

Stenberg, C. R. (1983). The development of anger expressions in infancy. *Dissertation Abstracts International, 43*(7), 2359–2360.

Stenberg, C. R., & Campos, J. J. (1990). The development of anger expressions in infancy. In N. L. Stein, B. Leventhal, & T. Trabasso, *Psychological and biological approaches to emotion* (pp. 247–282). Hillsdale, NJ: Erlbaum.

Stenberg, C. R., Campos, J. J., & Emde, R. N. (1983). The facial expression of anger in seven month old infants. *Child Development, 54*, 178–184.

Stern, D. (1974). The goal and structure of mother-infant play. *Journal of the American Academy of Child Psychiatry, 13*, 402–421.

Stern, D. (1985). *The interpersonal world of the infant*. New York: Basic Books.

Stern, D. N. (1984). Affect attunement. In J. D. Call, E. Galenson, & R. L. Tyson (Eds.), *Frontiers in infant psychiatry* (pp. 3–14). New York: Basic Books.

Stern, W. (1927). *Psychologie der Frühen Kindheit*. Leipzig: Quelle & Meyer Verlag.

Stoller, S. A., & Field, T. (1982). Alteration of mother and infant behavior and heart rate during a still-face perturbation of face-to-face interaction. In T. Field & A. Fogel (Eds.), *Emotion and early interaction* (pp. 57–82). Hillsdale, NJ: Erlbaum.

Storr, A. (1988). *Churchill's black dogs and Kafka's mice*. New York: Ballantine.

Strayer, J. (1980). A naturalistic study of empathic behaviors and their relation to affective states and perspective-taking skills in preschool children. *Child Development, 51*, 815–822.

Strayer, J. (1985). Current research in affective development: Special issue: The feeling child: Affective development reconsidered. *Journal of Children in Contemporary Society, 17*, 37–55.

Strayer, J. (1987). Affective and cognitive perspectives on empathy. In N. Eisenberg & J. Strayer (Eds.), *Empathy and its development* (pp. 218–244). New York: Cambridge University Press.

Strayer, J. (1993). Children's concordant emotions and cognitions in response to observed emotions. *Child Development, 64*, 188–201.

Strayer, J., & Eisenberg, N. (1987). Empathy viewed in context. In N. Eisenberg & J. Strayer (Eds.), *Empathy and its development* (pp. 389–398). New York: Cambridge University Press.

Strupp, H. H., & Howard, K. I. (1992). A brief history of psychotherapy research. In D. K. Freedheim, H. J. Freudenberger, J. W. Kessler, S. B. Messer, D. R. Peterson, H. H. Strugg, & P. L. Wachtel (Eds.). *History of psychotherapy* (pp. 309–334). Washington, DC: APA Press.

Suess, G. J., Grossmann, K. E., & Sroufe, L. A. (1992). Effects of infant attachment to mother and father on quality of adaptation in preschool: From dyadic to individual organisation of self. *International Journal of Behavioral Development, 15*, 43–65.

Sullivan, M. W., Lewis, M., & Alessandri, S. M. (1992). Cross-age stability in emotional expressions during learning and extinction. *Developmental Psychology, 28*, 58–63.

Sully, J. (1880). Mental development in children. *Mind, 5,* 385–386.

Sully, J. (1881). Babies and science. *Cornhill Magazine, 43,* 539–554.

Sully, J. (1903). *Studies of childhood.* New York: Appleton.

Super, C. M., & Harkness, S. (1982). The development of affect in infancy and early childhood. In D. A. Wagner & H. W. Stevenson (Eds.), *Cultural perspectives on child development* (pp. 1–19). San Francisco: Freeman.

Tajfel, H., & Turner, J. C. (1986). The social identity theory of intergroup behavior. In S. Worchel & W. G. Austin (Eds.), *Psychology of intergroup relations* (pp. 7–24). Chicago: Nelson-Hall.

Takahashi, K. (1986). Examining the strange-situation procedure with Japanese mothers and 12-month-old infants. *Developmental Psychology, 22,* 265–270.

Taylor, J. H. (1934). Innate emotional responses in infants. *Ohio State University Studies, Contributions of Psychology,* No. 12, pp. 69–81.

Taylor, L. (1992). Relationship between affect and memory: Motivation-based selective generation. *Journal of Personality and Social Psychology, 62,* 876–882.

Tennes, K. (1982). The role of hormones in mother-infant transactions. In R. N. Emde & R. J. Harmon (Eds.), *The development of attachment and affiliative systems* (pp. 75–80). New York: Plenum.

Tesman, J. R. (1992). *Affective development in five-year-olds: Consequences of early exposure to incongruent messages and maternal insensitivity.* Unpublished doctoral dissertation, New School for Social Research, New York.

Thelen, E. (1985). Expression as action: A motor perspective of the transition from spontaneous to instrumental behaviors. In G. Zivin (Ed.), *The development of expressive behavior* (pp. 221–247). New York: Academic Press.

Thelen, E., Kelso, J. A. S., & Fogel, A. (1987). Self-organizing systems and infant motor development. *Developmental Review, 7,* 39–65.

Thomas, A., & Chess, S., & Birch, H. G. (1968). *Temperament and behavior disorders in children.* New York: New York University Press.

Thomas, W. U., & Znaniecki, F. (1918). *The Polish Peasant in Europe and America.* New York: Knopf.

Thompson, R. A. (1987). Empathy and emotional understanding: the early development of empathy. In N. Eisenberg & J. Strayer (Eds.), *Empathy and its development* (pp. 119–145). New York: Cambridge University Press.

Thompson, R. A., & Lamb, M. E. (1983). Security of attachment and stranger sociability in infancy. *Developmental Psychology, 19,* 184–191.

Thompson, R. A., & Lamb, M. E. (1984). Assessing qualitative dimensions of emotional responsiveness in infants: Separation reactions in the strange situation. *Infant Behavior and Development, 7,* 423–445.

Thompson, W. R., & Grusec, J. (1970) Studies of early experience. In P. H. Mussen (Ed.), *Manual of child psychology* (pp. 565–654). New York: Wiley.

Tiedemann, D. (1787). Die Beobachtungen über die Entwicklung der Seelenfahigheiten bei Kindern. *Hessische Beitrage zur Gelehrsamkeit und Kunst, 2–3,* 313–315, 468–488.

Tinbergen, N. (1951). *The study of instinct.* Oxford University Press.

Titchener, E. B. (1910). *A textbook of psychology.* New York: Scholars' Facsimiles & Reprints.

Tomkins, S. (Ed.) (1943). *Contemporary psychopathology.* Cambridge: Harvard University Press.

Tomkins, S. S. (1962). *Affect, imagery, consciousness. Vol. 1: The positive affects.* New York: Springer.

Tomkins, S. S. (1963). *Affect, imagery, consciousness. Vol. 2: The negative affects.* New York: Springer.

Tomkins, S. S. (1965a). Affect and the psychology of knowledge. In S. S. Tomkins & C. E. Izard (Eds.), *Affect, cognition, and personality: Empirical studies* (pp. 72–97). New York: Springer.

Tomkins, S. S. (1965b). The psychology of commitment. In M. B. Duberman (Ed.), *The Antislavery vanguard: New essays on the abolitionists* (pp. 270–298). Princeton: Princeton University Press.

Tomkins, S. S. (1981). The quest for primary motives: Biography and autobiography of an idea. *Journal of Personality and Social Psychology, 41,* 306–329.

Tomkins, S. S. (1987). Script theory. In J. Aronoff, A. I. Rabin, & R. A. Zucker, (Eds.), *The emergence of personality* (pp. 147–216). New York: Springer.

Tomkins, S. S. (1991). *Affect, imagery, consciousness. Vol. 3: Anger and fear.* New York: Springer.

Tomkins, S. S. (1993). *Affect, imagery, consciousness. Vol. 4: Cognition-duplication and transformation of information.* New York: Springer.

Tomkins, S. S., & McCarter, R. (1964). What and where are the primary affects? Some evidence for a theory. *Perceptual and Motor Skills, 18,* 119–158.

Tupes, E. C., & Christal, R. E. (1961). *Recurrent personality factors based on trait ratings* (USAF ASD Tech. Rep. No. 61–97). Washington, DC: U.S. Government Printing Office.

Ullman, C. (1989). *The transformed self: The psychology of religious conversion.* New York: Plenum.

Underwood, B., & Moore, B. (1982). Perspective-taking and altruism. *Psychological Bulletin, 91,* 143–173.

Underwood, M. K., Cole, J. D., & Herbsman, C. R. (1992). Display rules for anger and aggression in school-age children. *Child Development, 63,* 366–380.

Ungerer, J. A., Dolby, R., Waters, B., Barnett, B., Kelk, N., & Lewin, V. (1990). The early development of empathy: Self-regulation and individual differences in the first year. *Motivation and Emotion, 14,* 93–106.

Vaughn, B., Waters, E., Egeland, B., & Sroufe, L. A. (1979) Individual differences in infant-mother attachment at 12 and 18 months: Stability and change in families under stress. *Child Development, 50,* 971–975.

Walker, A. (1982). *The color purple.* New York: Harcourt Brace Jovanovich.

Walters, J., & Peters, R. D. (1980, June). *Social problem solving in aggressive boys.* Paper presented at the annual meeting of the Canadian Psychological Association, Calgary.

Washburn, R. W. (1928). A study of the smiling and laughing of infants in the first year of life. *Genetic Psychology Monographs, 6,* 397–539.

Waters, E., Vaughn, B. E., & Egeland, B. R. (1980). Individual differences in infant-mother attachment relationships at age one: Antecedents in neonatal behavior in an urban and ecologically disadvantaged sample. *Child Development, 51,* 208–216.

Waters, E., Wippman, J., & Sroufe, L. A. (1979). Attachment, positive affect, and competence in the peer group: Two studies in construct validation. *Child Development, 50,* 821–829.

Watson, D., & Clark, L. A. (1991). Self- versus peer ratings of specific emotional traits: Evidence of convergent and discriminant validity. *Journal of Personality and Social Psychology, 60,* 927–940.

Watson, J. B. (1924). *Psychology from the standpoint of a behaviorist,* (2nd ed.), Philadelphia: Lippincott.

Watson, J. B. (1928). *Psychological care of the infant and child.* New York: Norton.

Watson, J. B. (1930). *Behaviorism.* New York: Norton.

Watson, J. B. (1936). Autobiography. In C. Murchison (Ed.), *A history of psychology in autobiography* (Vol. 3). Worcester, MA: Clark University Press.

Watson, J. B., & Morgan, J. J. B. (1917). Emotional reactions and psychological experimentation. *American Journal of Psychology, 28,* 163–174.

Watson, J. B., & Rayner, R. (1920). Conditioned emotional reactions. *Journal of Experimental Psychology, 3,* 1–14.

Wechsler, D., & Jones, H. E. (1928). A study of emotional specificity. *American Journal of Psychology, 40,* 600–606.

West, S. G., & Graziano, W. G. (1989). Long-term stability and change in personality: An introduction. *Journal of Personality, 57,* 175–192.

Whitbourne, S. K., Zuschlag, M. K., Elliot, L. B., & Waterman, A. S. (1992). Psychosocial development in adulthood: A 22-year sequential study. *Journal of Personality and Social Psychology, 63,* 260–271.

Wiersma, J. (1988). The press release: Symbolic communication in life history interviewing. *Journal of Personality, 56,* 205–237.

Willard, E. (1835). Observations upon an infant during its first year. By a mother. Appendix in M. N. Saussure, *Progressive Education* (M. E. Willard, and M. Phelps, Trans.).

Wilson, A. (1986). Archair transference and anaclitic depression: Psychoanalytic perspectives on the treatment of severely disturbed patients. *Psychoanalytic Psychology, 3,* 237–256.

Wispé, L. (1968). Sympathy and empathy. In D. Sills (Ed.), *International encyclopedia of the social sciences.* New York: Macmillan and Free Press.

Wispé, L. (1986). The distinction between sympathy and empathy: To call forth a concept, a word is needed. *Journal of Personality and Social Psychology, 50,* 314–321.

Wispé, L. (1987). History of the concept of empathy. In N. Eisenberg & J. Strayer (Eds.), *Empathy: A developmental perspective* (pp. 17–37). New York: Cambridge University Press.

Wispé, L. (1991). *The psychology of sympathy.* New York: Plenum.

Wispé, L. G. (1972). Positive forms of social behavior: An overview. *Journal of Social Issues, 28,* 1–19.

Wolff, P. H. (1966). The causes, controls, and organization of behavior in the neonate. *Psychological Issues, 5,* 1–99.

Woodall, K. L., & Matthews, K. A. (1993). Changes in and stability of hostile characteristics: Results from a 4-year longitudinal study of children. *Journal of Personality and Social Psychology, 64,* 491–499.

Woodworth, R. S., & Schlosberg, H. S. (1954). *Experimental psychology.* New York: Holt.

Wundt, W. (1905). *Grundriss der psychologie [Outline of psychology]* (75h rev. ed.). Leipzig, Germany: Engelman.

Young, J. Z. (1964). *A model of the brain.* London: Oxford University Press.

Zahn-Waxler, C. (1986). Conclusions: Lessons from the past and a look to the future. In C. Zahn-Waxler, E. M. Cummings, & R. Iannotti (Eds.), *Altruism and aggression* (pp. 303–324). New York: Cambridge University Press.

Zahn-Waxler, C., & Kochanska, G. (1990). The origins of guilt. In R. Dienstbier & R. A Thompson (Eds.), *The Nebraska Symposium on Motivation, Volume 36, Socioemotional development* (pp. 115–182). Lincoln: The University of Nebraska Press.

Zahn-Waxler, C., & Radke-Yarrow, M. (1990). The origins of empathic concern. *Motivation and Emotion, 14,* 107–130.

Zahn-Waxler, C., Robinson, J. L., & Emde, R. N. (1992). The development of empathy in twins. *Developmental Psychology, 28,* 1038–1047.

Zajonc, R. (1980). Feeling and thinking: Preferences need no inferences. *American Psychologist, 35,* 151–175

Zimbardo, P. G. (1977). *Shyness: What it is, what to do about it.* Reading, MA: Addison-Wesley.

Zimbardo, P. G. (1986). The Stanford shyness project. In W. H. Jones, J. M. Cheek, & S. R. Briggs (Eds.), *Shyness: Perspectives on research and treatment* (pp. 17–25). New York: Plenum.

Index